History, Memory, and the Return of Financial Crises after Bretton Woods

History, Memory, and the Return of Financial Crises after Bretton Woods

Edited by

YOUSSEF CASSIS
GIUSEPPE TELESCA

OXFORD
UNIVERSITY PRESS

OXFORD
UNIVERSITY PRESS

Great Clarendon Street, Oxford, OX2 6DP,
United Kingdom

Oxford University Press is a department of the University of Oxford.
It furthers the University's objective of excellence in research, scholarship,
and education by publishing worldwide. Oxford is a registered trade mark of
Oxford University Press in the UK and in certain other countries.

Published in the United States of America by Oxford University Press
198 Madison Avenue, New York, NY 10016, United States of America

British Library Cataloguing in Publication Data
Data available

Library of Congress Control Number: 2025948628

ISBN 9780198950127

DOI: 10.1093/9780198950158.001.0001

Printed and bound by
CPI Group (UK) Ltd., Croydon, CR0 4YY

MIX
Paper | Supporting responsible forestry
FSC® C013604

The manufacturer's authorized representative in the EU for product safety is
Oxford University Press España S.A. of Parque Empresarial San Fernando de Henares,
Avenida de Castilla, 2 – 28830 Madrid (www.oup.es/en or product.safety@oup.com).
OUP España S.A. also acts as importer into Spain of products made by the manufacturer.

Contents

List of Figures

List of Tables

List of Contributors

Carlo Edoardo Altamura is Assistant Professor, Université de Lausanne, Lausanne, Switzerland and Lecturer in Twentieth Century Latin American History, The University of Manchester, Manchester, UK.

Youssef Cassis is Professor, Robert Schuman Centre for Advanced Studies, European University Institute, Italy.

Juan Flores Zendejas is Professor of Economic History, Paul Bairoch Institute of Economic History, Université de Genève, Geneva, Switzerland.

Johanna Gautier-Morin PhD is Postdoctoral Fellow, Central European University, Vienna, Austria.

Per H. Hansen is Professor of History, Department of Business Humanities and Law, Copenhagen Business School, Denmark.

Seung Woo Kim is Assistant Professor, Department of History, Hanyang University, Seoul, South Korea.

Bruno Pacchiotti is Research Associate, European University Institute, Florence, Italy.

Alice Pearson is Leverhulme Early Career Fellow, University of Cambridge, UK.

Tobias Pforr is Postdoc, Employment Relations Research Centre, Department of Sociology, University of Copenhagen, Denmark.

Catherine R. Schenk is Professor of Economic and Social History, University of Oxford, UK.

Giuseppe Telesca is Lecturer in Economic and Social History, University of Glasgow, UK.

Niccolò Valmori is Visiting Fellow, Robert Schuman Center for Advanced Studies, European University Institute, Italy.

1

Introduction

History and memory of financial crises

Youssef Cassis and Giuseppe Telesca

In August 2007, with the first signs of the impending credit crunch, *Financial Times* columnist Gillian Tett interviewed business historian Robert Brumer who had just co-authored a book on the American Panic of 1907.[1] The book had not forecasted the arrival of the crisis but was enjoying a certain success in a sign that, after decades of indifference, a renewed interest in history was emerging in the financial world. Tett attributed this indifference towards history to the fact that new bankers and financial traders were too young to bother with the memory of economic cycles, too projected towards the future to look into the past, too convinced that the wave of financial innovation of the last decades had rewritten the rules of finance and the very way the economic cycles worked—that this time was different, to use Reinhart's and Rogoff's formula.[2] New bankers were thus feeding their models with historical data that only went a few years back, with predictable consequences for the quality of the models that provided limited historical significance.

Nevertheless, the events of the summer 2007 were stimulating a renewed desire among investors, CEOs, and regulators to look into the past for understanding the present and to foresee the future. The outbreak of the financial crisis in 2008, starting with the bailout of Bears Stearns in March, the rescue of Fannie Mae and Freddie Mac in September, and, especially, the collapse of Lehman Brothers a few days later, further stimulated a demand for history—this time in order to make sense of what was happening and ponder on the direction of things to come in the light of past experiences.[3]

[1] The project leading to this application has received funding from the European Research Council (ERC) under the European Union's Horizon 2020 research and innovation programme (grant agreement No 884910). The content of this document represents only the views of the MERCATOR team and is its sole responsibility. The European Commission does not accept any responsibility for use that may be made of the information it contains. Brumer and Carr, *The Panic of 1907*. Interview in Tett, 'Doomed to repeat it?'

[2] Reinhart and Rogoff, *This Time Is Different*.

[3] See Hansen, 'Making sense of financial crisis and scandal', for a reflection on decision-making in conditions of extreme uncertainty.

Youssef Cassis and Giuseppe Telesca, *Introduction*. In: *History, Memory, and the Return of Financial Crises After Bretton Woods*. Edited by: Youssef Cassis and Giuseppe Telesca, Oxford University Press. © Oxford University Press (2026). DOI: 10.1093/9780198950158.003.0001

The popularity of history has represented a challenge for historians. In particular, whatever the demand for history, most publications have emanated from economists, political scientists, as well as journalists, with the debate being clearly dominated by economists.[4] This is not surprising. The Global Financial Crisis of 2008 is only in the process of becoming an object of historical study, with archives still closed and the distance from the event comparatively short. Adam Tooze's book, *Crashed*, an exercise in very recent history published on the tenth anniversary of the crisis, can be seen as the exception that confirms the rule.[5]

Economists and other social scientists, as well as journalists, have made important contributions to our knowledge and understanding of the Global Financial Crisis, through the analysis of its causes and consequences, including the role of monetary authorities; through a discussion of the socio-political and geopolitical context within which it took place; and, especially as far as journalists are concerned, through a detailed account of the unfolding of often dramatic events.[6] These contributions constitute the bedrock on which any history of the Global Financial Crisis will be built.

The role of historians has been different, especially in the early post-crisis period. Historians have been mainly asked to put the Global Financial Crisis in a long-term historical perspective, by establishing parallels and making comparisons with previous financial crises. Barry Eichengreen, for example, has written a penetrating comparison between the Great Depression and the Great Recession.[7] Economists and other social scientists have also made parallels and comparisons with previous events, but that has primarily been the task of historians, whose skills lies in the in-depth study of the past, leaving no stone unturned in their emphasis on the uniqueness of past events and, thus, in their attention to both the similarities and differences between comparable events.

This book has been conceived as a contribution of history to the study of financial crises. The history of financial crises can be approached from several perspectives. We have chosen to consider the role played by memory and its relationships with history when it comes to financial crises.

There have been many debates on the relationships between memory and history since the 'memory boom' of the 1980s.[8] Recent historiographical trends have tended to play down the differences, whatever the allegedly more dynamic nature of memory, centred on the identity and perception of agents as objects of study, and the more static, codified nature of history.[9] The distinction is less clear for the

[4] Wolfers, 'How economists came to dominate the conversation'.

[5] Tooze, *Crashed*.

[6] The crisis has been deeply and extensively scrutinized and analysed, with more than 600 books in English published between 2009 and 2017 (according to a survey by the EUI library), not to mention journal articles and other periodical publications.

[7] Eichengreen, *Hall of Mirrors*.

[8] Winter, 'Notes on the memory boom'.

[9] Nora, 'Between memory and history'.

very recent past, to which the Global Financial Crisis of 2008 still belongs, where direct memory plays a major role—if only because much of the 'history' of the crisis has been written by witnesses of, and even participants to, the events.

But history can also affect memory. In the case of financial crises, especially older ones, history can become their collective memory—for instance through the direct intervention of professional historians in the media, one of the main transmitters of collective memory. Another way in which history can influence the memory of the past is through the publication of major controversial historical works that change the interpretation of past events. Milton Friedman's and Anna Schwartz's *A Monetary History of the United States*, published in 1963,[10] which framed the Great Depression as a liquidity crisis and attributed to the Fed's monetary inaction the responsibility for allowing an ordinary recession to turn into a catastrophe, is a case in point.[11]

Despite its attention to memory, the book is not primarily concerned with lesson drawing. There is of course some overlap between the two, especially in the case of financial crises—as opposed to the themes more usually discussed in memory studies, such as genocides, wars, or political violence. Yet, historians are reluctant to draw lessons from history, also because historical analogies can at times be flawed. Memory and history are better seen as providing at best guiding landmarks in the form of indirect lessons.

At the core of this book there is the question of whether or not, and how, the memory of financial crises has persisted, faded, or changed over time. The volume does not offer a new history of the Global Financial Crisis, but analyses, with the historian's tools, the financial crises that broke out since the mid-1970s, taking into account, in a long-term perspective, their singularities and commonalities and more generally the changing socio-political context within which they took place and within which they have been remembered.

The book goes beyond the Great Depression–Global Financial Crisis analogy that has been overwhelmingly suggested and analysed since 2007. Comparisons with the financial crises of the Great Depression are not avoided and can be found in most chapters of the book, though none is specifically devoted to it. The case studies gathered here are devoted to other important crises, those that have affected the international financial system since the end of Bretton Woods.

Concentrating on the post-Bretton Woods era is particularly interesting. This is a period marked by the return of financial crises, after about three decades of financial stability. The number of financial crises between 1973 and 1997 has been shown to be double that of the Bretton Woods era, though they were not necessarily more severe.[12] Major crises included the shocks of the 1970s, the International

[10] Friedman and Swchwartz, *A Monetary History*, 299–419.

[11] O'Sullivan has shown how, from the 1970s, this interpretation started to become 'the orthodoxy of the Great Depression' for practitioners and policy-makers ('History as heresy', 299).

[12] Bordo et al. 'Financial crises: Lessons from the last 120 years'.

Debt Crisis of 1982, the Stock Market Crash of 1987, the financial turbulences of the 1990s, including the Asian Financial Crisis of 1997, and the Global Financial Crisis of 2008.

However, despite the return of financial instability, somewhat paradoxically much of the period, especially the near quarter of a century extending from the mid-1980s and the Global Financial Crisis of 2008, is considered as a period of stability, also known as the 'Great Moderation'. On closer look, however, this is not surprising—from the perspective of advanced economies. Between 1970 and 2008, virtually all systemic crises took place in emerging economies, or low-income countries.[13] The only episodes of systemic crises in advanced economies are the so-called 'Big Five': Spain in 1977; Sweden, Norway, and Finland in 1991; and Japan in 1997.[14] The Savings and Loans Crisis in the United States in the 1980s has recently been added to the list, though it did not threaten the American financial system.[15] Before 2008, most rich countries only experienced 'milder' or 'borderline' crises.

Adhering to strict definitions of banking crises is essential for rigorous quantitative analysis, but it can be misleading. It does not allow for a proper differentiation between crises, in the way they have been experienced by bankers and policymakers, the impact they have had, not only on the country's GDP, but also on its various stakeholders, and the memory they have left at both individual and collective levels. These socio-cultural variables are important, especially with regard to their influence on bankers' behaviour.

Why have some crises been (selectively) remembered and others apparently forgotten? The type of financial crisis, in particular its severity, plays a crucial role: it is not without reason that 1929 is the obligatory reference in any discussion of financial crises. But there are other factors. Some events can trigger the memory of a financial crisis, for example another crisis (most recently, the Covid-19 pandemic and the return of inflation); or the political use made of a past financial crisis at a particular juncture. Anniversaries can also be moments of remembrance, especially symbolic ones such as the 10th, 25th, or 50th.[16]

The question of who remembers a crisis is also crucial. Memory is an elusive and selective process, which takes different forms depending on who evokes memory, when, and in which context. The 'who' relates to different protagonists in

[13] More than 90 per cent, on the basis of the figures provided in Laeven and Valencia, 'Systemic banking crises revisited'.

[14] Reinhart and Rogoff, *This Time Is Different*, 215–216 and 348–392, which relies on Caprio and Klingebiel, 'Episodes of systemic and borderline financial crises'. These episodes have been integrated in various ways, either together or separately, into larger databases of financial crises, mainly occurring in emerging economies, and used in a number of studies in order to empirically test various hypotheses; see Reinhart and Rogoff, *This Time Is Different*; Caprio and Klingebiel, 'Bank insolvency'; Demirgüç-Kunt and Detragiache, 'The determinants of banking crises'.

[15] Laeven and Valencia, 'Systemic banking crises revisited'.

[16] See Telesca and Cassis, 'Battles of narratives, battles of memory' for a reflection on this issue.

a financial crisis: practitioners, whether commercial and investment bankers or businesspeople engaged in other financial activities, including the shadow banking system; central bankers, regulators, and politicians; but also financial journalists, pundits, and academic experts. Every group will have a particular perspective on certain events and a particular memory of them. This memory, in turn, will change over time depending on historical but also geographical circumstances.

The memory of these various protagonists operates at both individual and collective levels, whether organizational, institutional, or even national. One of the contributions of memory studies has been to show the interconnection between the two. Maurice Halbwachs was the first to describe how individuals' memory is actually dependent on socialization. But his work has been extended by further studies, not least Jan Assmann's distinction between a 'communicative memory', consisting of fairly recent memories existing in everyday life, that can be shared with contemporaries; and a 'cultural memory', a more formalized and institutionalized type of memory.[17] The concept of cultural memory has been further elaborated in recent years, bridging the gap between individual and collective memory: while social groups or nations cannot remember in the strict sense of the word, they can construct a shared past, through media, institutions, and practices, in a process that bears some resemblance to that of individual memory.[18]

The chapters that follow consider the role played by history in the processes of remembering past financial crises. Intertwining memory and narrative representations of events, they investigate the reasons for various forms of remembrance and forgetfulness. This inquiry is motivated by one of the book's main research questions, namely the absence of experience and memory of systemic financial crises by the generation of bankers in charge at the start of the subprime crisis in 2007.

Given that the Global Financial Crisis was in many respects a 'North Atlantic' crisis, the book is primarily concerned with the crises taking place in advanced economies. However, in the absence of systemic crises affecting the leading financial centres before 2008,[19] the chapters pay particular attention to two crises originating in emerging economies, but with connections to, and repercussions on, the 'North Atlantic': the International Debt Crisis of 1982, which could have had ripple effects, leading to the collapse of the international financial system (Chapters 3 and 4); and the Asian Financial Crisis of 1997, which caused a combination of concern and complacency in Europe and America (Chapter 6).

But attention is also paid to some non-systemic crises: one good example is the failures affecting the global payments system in the 1970s, causing utter

[17] Halbwachs, *Les cadres sociaux de la mémoire*; Id., *La mémoire collective*; Assmann, 'Communicative and cultural memory'.

[18] Erll, 'Cultural memory studies: an introduction'.

[19] Those taking place in Spain in the late 1970s, in Scandinavia in the early 1990s and even in Japan in the late 1990s had little spillover on other advanced economies.

nightmares (Chapter 2); the stock market crash of 1987, far more spectacular because of the violence of the initial shock, but which proved brief and with few after-effects (Chapter 5); and, in a long-term historical perspective, 150 years, the experience of financial crises in one bank, Danske Bank (Chapter 10). In this context, one chapter is devoted to the first global and systemic financial crisis since the Great Depression: the Global Financial Crisis of 2008 (Chapter 11).

However, not all chapters are directly discussing a specific financial crisis. Three of them complement the story by considering crucial factors affecting the experience and memory that the top executives in 2008 had of financial crises: regulation (Chapter 7), education and careers (Chapter 8), and the transformation of the economics discipline, including the way it has been taught (Chapter 9).

The book starts with a chapter devoted to one of the first financial shocks of the flexible exchange rates regime that followed Bretton Wood. Catherine Schenk explores the enduring nightmare of the insolvency of Herstatt Bank, in the memory of market participants and regulators. This relatively minor bank, headquartered in Cologne and operating in cross-border payments, was a victim of the financial volatility of the 1970s and revealed, in 1974, losses for DM 470 million. The decision by the German authorities to close the bank on 26 June 1974 carried a settlement risk in foreign exchange transactions called, since then, the 'Herstatt Risk'. It prompted financial losses among the bank's creditors and, more generally, declining trust in the correspondent banking network. The chapter reflects on the persisting memory, among bankers and policy-makers, of the Herstatt crisis, which goes hand in hand with the incapacity, for many years, to reduce the 'Herstatt Risk'. In a paradoxical way, this regulatory inability—due to a mix of ideological preference for private-sector solutions, unwillingness of individual authorities to play as 'lender of last resort', inconsistencies in the legal national frameworks, and bankers' tendency to underestimate cross-border settlement risks—has contributed to rendering the memory of Herstatt as obstinate. The chapter shows that other crises/scandals—the coeval and similar episode involving the Franklin National Bank, for instance—were also easily forgotten because they proved crucial for reforming financial supervisory mechanisms. Because of the inadequate regulatory response, the recurrence of similar episodes has gained the Herstatt crisis a special place in the memory of market participants, with a central role played by the memory of individuals who had directly experienced the 1974 turmoil (the chapter refers to Gerald Corrigan, junior economist at the New York Fed and part of a task force which dealt with the fall-out of the Herstatt Bank scandal in 1974, and then president of the same institution in 1985, at the time of the crisis of the Bank of New York).

Chapters 3 and 4 are dedicated to the International Debt Crisis of 1982, which spread across the Global South during the 1980s. Since the mid-1970s international capital movements had been dominated by loans from commercial banks to Third World countries. Panic broke out in August 1982, when Mexico unilaterally declared a three-month moratorium on payment of its debt principal. The International Debt Crisis, the first global shock since the Great Depression, had the potential to bring down the international financial system. While an agreement between debtor countries and the banks avoided a generalized financial collapse, it did not prevent economic and political turmoil in many of the debtor countries.

Bruno Pacchiotti and Giuseppe Telesca's chapter, drawing on the *Financial Times* and the *Wall Street Journal* on the one hand, and the Mexican press on the other, looks at the way in which the International Debt Crisis has been told and recollected from the perspective of the 'creditors' and of a 'debtor' country. How seriously was the crisis perceived in the immediate aftermath of its outbreak? Were parallels with previous crises drawn in 1982? How intense was the level of recollection of the crisis on the occasion of its anniversaries or other financial crises? Who was blamed for the crisis? Has the narrative on the International Debt Crisis shifted since the 1980s? And how? The authors argue that significant differences can be found in the ways in which the International Debt Crisis was first narrated and then remembered. In the early 1990s, the crisis was unanimously recounted as a tale of virtuous, if painful, adaptation of Mexico to the market economy. Thereafter the Mexican press—which, during the 1980s, had developed its own narrative on the crisis, putting more weight on the exogenous shocks and the responsibilities of international financial actors—elaborated a different memory of the International Debt Crisis, where considerations on the costs of the *década perdida* occupied more space than that taken by the benefits brought about by that crisis. The *Financial Times* and the *Wall Street Journal* also developed distinct narratives and memories—with the former more inclined to remember the crisis and to recognize financial actors' responsibilities than the latter—in a confirmation that the memory of financial crises is an elusive and selective process, which depends on who evokes memory, and when.

In Chapter 4, Edoardo Altamura and Juan Flores Zendejas move from the financial press to the academic literature and provide a thorough analysis of the way in which economists, historians, and social scientists have first explained and then remembered the International Debt Crisis. While the picture which surfaces from this review is, not surprisingly, more nuanced than the one coming out from the survey on the press proposed by the previous chapter, what emerges clearly is that also the academic debate has emphasized different aspects of the International Debt Crisis depending on the economic, political, and ideological circumstances. The literature of the 1980s ascribed the origins of the crisis to three, at times interwoven, factors: macroeconomic mismanagement in borrowing countries, instability of the word economy, and/or recklessness of the banks. During the 1990s and until the beginning of the Global Financial Crisis, the liberalization of capital markets led academics to focus on topics such as the choice of exchange rate regimes, the importance of bank regulation, and the risks relative to sudden stops in capital flows or financial contagion. The post-2008 period has witnessed a return to the lines of enquiry pursued in the 1980s—including a particular attention to the role of international finance, private lenders, and the world's economic governance. The authors conclude their review by cautioning, with Eichengreen,[20] on the risks of overreacting to historical analogies or misapplying historical lessons. Taken together, Chapters 3 and 4 demonstrate that memory and historical narratives are not only linked to historical circumstances but also to ideology and power.

Johanna Gautier's chapter looks at 19 October 1987, 'Black Monday', when stock markets collapsed in 23 countries around the world, marking the biggest single-day stock markets debacle in history. By blending financial history, media analysis, and economic theory and adopting a long-term approach, this chapter considers the shadow of the 1929 Great Crash over 1987. Despite the media frenzy and the incessant references to 1929, 'Black Monday' was to some extent a 'non-event' and had certainly little in common with the Great Depression. Gautier explains that 1929 was obsessively recalled in 1987 not only as a symbol of fear, with the question 'can it happen again?' repeatedly evoked, but also as a charter to navigate unfolding uncertainty and listening to the (alleged) 'lessons of history'. The 1929 historical analogy was, in many ways, inadequate. Yet, it was the most prominent and easily available historical reference for contemporaries and ended up absolving a diagnostic and prescriptive—if ultimately confusing—function. The chapter reflects on financial crises' capacity to represent a formidable tale and put forward powerful cultural narratives that, far from being neutral, contribute to shape market response to the predicaments. But crises also provide opportunities to generate symbols and myths—as the fascinating story of the juxtaposition of Kristen Visbal's *Fearless Girl* (2017), a post-2008 symbol of defiance against financial excess and inequality, to Arturo di Modica's *Charging Bull* (1989), celebrating the determination of American people in the wake of 1987, demonstrates.

The second major financial crisis of the post-Bretton Woods era was the Asian Financial Crisis of 1997. As in 1982, it primarily affected emerging economies, with less consequences on advanced economies. One exception was neighbouring Japan, itself embroiled in its own financial crisis, though the Asian Crisis increased the pressure on distressed banks.[21] The loss of confidence caused by the Asian Crisis also played a role in the Russian Default of 1998, which contributed to the collapse later that year of the hedge fund Long Term Capital Management (LTCM), which would have had systemic effects had it not been rescued by the New York banking community under the Fed's leadership.[22] Overall, the Asian Crisis had limited impact in Europe and the United States, being neither

[20] Eichengreen, 'Economic history and economic policy'.

[21] Such major banks as Hokkaido Takushoku Bank and Yamaichi Securities (one of Japan's four largest securities houses) collapsed in 1997, and Long-Term Credit Bank of Japan in 1998. See Cassis, *Crises and Opportunities*, 42–47.

[22] Lowenstein, *When Genius Failed*.

really remembered nor entirely forgotten.[23] In addition to the geographical distance, some complacency, a feeling that such a crisis could not happen in the sophisticated financial systems of advanced economies, was clearly discernable.

The Asian Financial Crisis started on 2 July 1997 when the Thai central bank floated the national currency, the baht, whose rate had been pegged to the dollar and could no longer be sustained. The currency collapsed, leading to a very severe economic and financial crisis that soon spread to neighbouring countries, above all Indonesia and South Korea, but also Hong Kong, Malaysia, and the Philippines, requiring the International Monetary Fund's (IMF) intervention.

Seung Woo Kim's chapter concentrates on the South Korean experience, more specifically the role played by memory and history in the perception of, and the response to, the crisis by both government and public opinion. The financial crisis first changed the narrative—in other words the discourse through which the history and memory of an event are framed—of South Korea's postwar economic miracle. In particular, the model of indebted growth and the close relationships between business (the *Chaebols*) and government were criticized for respectively their unsustainability and often corrupt character. The scandal surrounding the failure of several *Chaebols* (Hanbo, Daewoo, Kia) strengthened the narrative of their responsibility for the crisis and facilitated the reform of their governance urged by the IMF. But the crisis was also reminiscent of the Japanese colonial experience. Significantly, the financial crisis has been called the 'IMF Crisis' in South Korea, underlining the perception of the IMF intervention as a humiliating foreign interference, a breach of the country's independence. One particular memory, that of the National Debt Redemption Movement in 1905, was revived to launch the highly successful nationwide Gold Collection Campaign, designed to purchase gold held by the public and hasten the country's debt repayment. This nationalist response to the crisis transcended class conflicts and enabled the government to keep control of the economic liberalization process and reestablish South Korea's financial credit.

The return of financial crises after Bretton Wood has often been linked to the wave of financial deregulation that marked the period.[24] One of the first measures was the abolition by the Securities and Exchange Commission of fixed commissions in the New York Stock Exchange from 1 May 1975. London followed with 'Big Bang' on 27 October 1986, in fact a reform of the London Stock Exchange copying what had been done in New York and abolishing fixed commissions, as well as the age-old separation between brokers and jobbers. A series of measures dubbed 'Big Bang' were implemented in all financial centres from the late 1980s to the early 2000s, abolishing, among others, the barriers separating banking activities, securities transactions, and insurance; and liberalizing foreign exchange

[23] Geithner, *Stress Test*, 2014; Roberts and Kynaston, *The Lion Wakes*, 2015.
[24] Drach and Cassis, *Financial Deregulation*.

transactions. Banking legislation was also relaxed, especially in the United States, with the phasing out of Regulation Q in 1980; the deregulation of the savings and loans association in 1982 (which ushered a crisis that devastated the industry); the lifting of the ban on setting up networks of branches throughout the country, in 1994; and the repeal of the Glass Stegall Act in 1999, which had an enormous symbolic value, including in Britain, where the commercial banks became universal banks without any legislation, and in Germany, where they never ceased to be so.

Another important feature of the deregulations of the 1980s was the non-regulation of financial innovations. This was the case of a large part of the derivatives contracts, those traded 'over the counter' rather than in an organized market. Derivatives, in all their facets, were the main innovation of the post-Bretton Woods, originating as it were as a response to the risks posed by floating exchange rates. Moreover, their unregulated development in the following decades has been closely associated with the outbreak of the Global Financial Crisis of 2008. Hence their significance from the perspective of this volume.

Tobias Pforr's chapter provides a fascinating account of the heated debates surrounding the regulation and non-regulation of over the counter (OCT) derivatives, from the appearance of the first swap contracts in 1981 to the passing of the Commodities Futures Modernization Act (CFMA) in 2000, which ensured that derivatives would remain unregulated. Interestingly, this was an unlikely outcome, which appeared even more unlikely from the perspective of the early 1980s, given the repeated attempts at regulation made over two decades against a background of scandals and failures, not least Metallgesellschaft in 1993 and Long Term Capital Management (LTCM) in 1998. This raises the question of why derivatives remained unregulated. Several factors were at play, including the innovative nature of the product, their tremendous growth, the lobbying of the industry, and the overlapping responsibilities and competition between regulatory agencies. The decisive factor, however, was the unwavering support for deregulation by leading policymakers and regulators, above all the chairman of the Federal Reserve, Alan Greenspan. Another noteworthy point concerns the collective memory of derivatives and their regulation, which was radically revised after the financial crisis of 2008—from the success story of a financial innovation to the cautionary tale of a hazardous financial experiment, as acknowledged by Greenspan himself. But as Tobias Pforr wisely warns, the narrative can rapidly change as the memory of the crisis fades.

Alongside deregulation, globalization has been one of the main transformations of the post-Bretton Woods era. Globalization has manifested itself in multiple ways, from faster communications and increased international trade to, especially, the massive growth of international capital flows: foreign assets rose from 6% of world GDP in 1960 to 20% in 1980 and 92% in 2000,[25] bringing financial

[25] Obstfeld and Taylor, *Global Capital Markets*, 53.

centres closer to one another, but also increasing the risks of financial crisis contagion. But globalization has also had cultural effects, with the world becoming 'smaller' through movements of people, ideas, fashions, more 'homogenized', and in many respects 'Americanized'. Bankers, in particular, were part of the movement, being an extremely mobile population—at once a cause and a consequence of globalization—in a highly integrated international financial system.

In his chapter, Niccolò Valmori turns his attention to these bankers, more precisely the 'elite of the elite', in other words the CEOs, CFOs, etc. of the leading American, British, and French banks. To what extent have the changes brought about by globalization affected their outlook? The question is particularly interesting in times of crisis, and the chapter considers the evolving composition of that group at three crucial moments, corresponding to each of the period's major financial crises: the international debt crisis of 1982, the Asian financial crisis of 1997, and the Global Financial Crisis of 2008. A generational change clearly took place during this quarter of a century, reflected, for example, in the decline of military veterans in the boardrooms, the rising importance of academic capital, and a global trend towards professionalization, with the proliferation of MBAs in later years. There were, however, limits to this homogenization. National educational traditions predominated, at least until the turn of the twenty-first century, as can be seen in the role of the *grandes écoles* in France, and, to a lesser extent, a humanities background in Britain and a law degree in the United States. The same applies to career patterns: horizontal integration (external recruitment) became dominant in all three countries, but executives' increased mobility did not translate into a significantly higher proportion of foreigners in the boardroom. A new banking elite emerged after Bretton Woods, but it did not quite form a 'cosmopolitan capitalist class'.

Bankers' perception of financial crises is likely to have been affected by the growing influence of a neo-liberal view of the economy and of society, symbolized by the coming to power of Margaret Thatcher in the United Kingdom in 1979 and Ronald Reagan in the United States in 1981, and characterized by a key economic dispensation: the smaller State and the strengthening of market mechanisms. This perspective was reflected in, and in many respects influenced by, developments within the economics discipline, starting with the challenge to Keynesianism by Monetarism with the stagflation of the mid-1970s. The period also saw the rise of financial economics, centred on asset pricing, corporate finance, and the efficient market hypothesis—following the works of Markowitz and Sharpe on the efficient portfolio that links risks and return; Modigliani and Miller on the conditions under which the value of a firm is independent of its leverage ratio; Fama on the efficient market where prices reflect perfectly the information available; and Black, Scholes, and Merton on calculating the value of derivatives.[26]

[26] Bernstein, *Capital Ideas*; Turner, 'Financial history and financial economics'.

From this perspective, Alice Pearson's chapter considers how the teaching of economics has apprehended financial crises from the 1950s to the early twenty-first century, taking the University of Cambridge as a case study, through a careful analysis of its economics examination papers. Of particular interest is the interaction between the shifts taking place within the economics discipline and those taking place within the students' population, against the background of changing economic challenges. Three moments are particularly significant in a development which took place, with some national specificities, in all advanced economies. The first is the Bretton Woods era, when the main concern was the declining world position of the British empire, the teaching primarily destined to a future governing elite, and economics still qualitative in its approach and integrating a historical and political dimension. The second moment is the crisis of the 1970s, when the overwhelming issues were high inflation, industrial disputes, and political governance, with economics at Cambridge somewhat resisting mathematization and students seen as future civil servants and business managers. The third phase started in the 1980s, with an economics discipline becoming increasingly abstract and modelized, concerns about crises revolving around speculation and stock market fluctuations, and students destined to be part of the financial elite.

What role do memory and history play in the long-term development of a financial institution? In Chapter 10 Per Hansen, building on insights from behavioural finance and narrative approaches, looks at the role played by history in Danske Bank's 150 years of existence, with particular attention to the postwar period and the financial crisis of 2008. Founded in 1871, Danske Bank was shaken by the 'near death' experience of the 1920s, when two of its veteran employees, who had gone through its expansion and suffered its explosion firsthand, took over the bank. The memory of the 1920s crisis—the so-called 'spirit of 1928'—shaped Danske's worldviews, practices, and cultural blueprint well into the 1980s. The crisis of the 1920s was imprinted in the personal memory (direct and indirect) of two generations of CEOs and embedded in the institutional memory of Danske, which characterized itself as having a conservative, diligent, and centralized approach to banking. History was utilized as a cautionary tale against a backdrop that—for a large part of the period considered—was one of highly regulated banking. In the 1970s–80s fast-changing context of rampant neo-liberal transformation and financial deregulation, Danske gradually adopted more aggressive and expansionary stances, while the 'spirit of 1928' was forgotten and history, in Hansen's words, was 'silenced'. If at the time of the Nordic financial crisis, in the early 1990s, Danske was still perceived as a safe harbour in a sea of financial instability, the Global Financial Crisis would catch Danske off guard (in particular because of its aggressive lending in recently acquired banks in Ireland and Northern Ireland).

The book ends with some reflections by Youssef Cassis on the Global Financial Crisis of 2008. This was a shock of unprecedented magnitude. The number of financial crises might have vastly increased after Bretton Woods, but 2008 was actually the first global and systemic financial crisis to break out since the 1930s.

Usually considered as the most severe crisis since the Great Depression, 2008 was arguably the worst financial panic in modern history. The chapter considers the memory, history, and legacy of the crisis 15 years after the collapse of Lehman Brothers, with a few incursions into the fast-moving following months.

Regarding memory, by October 2023, senior executives in the financial industry had not forgotten the Global Financial Crisis, but its precise memory was starting to fade away, and likely to disappear with the next generation. The memory of financial crises mediated by the financial press is more likely to be triggered by another crisis than by an anniversary, as witnessed during the financial turbulence of Spring 2023 when, interestingly, the Global Financial Crisis replaced the Great Depression as the obliged reference. As for history, the Global Financial Crisis could not yet be considered as an object of historical study, despite the valuable contributions of instant histories. Historical parallels, primarily provided by historians, had helped better understand the Global Financial Crisis, but had mostly run their course. However, the interest in the history of financial crises aroused by the Global Financial Crisis looked unlikely to abate. Finally, the main legacy of the Global Financial Crisis was the regulatory framework designed in its wake, a major carrier of the memory of the crisis which, however, was starting to be questioned. Unlike the Great Depression and even the financial instability of the mid-1970s, the Global Financial Crisis did not mark a turning point in economic history, though it could be clearly seen as a contributory factor to the yet unforeseen consequences of the 'crisis of the 2020s'.

In line with previous and forthcoming volumes,[27] we argue in this book that introducing the tools of memory studies into the field of economic and financial history improves our understanding of financial crises and fosters historians' contribution to the post-2008 academic debate. It is thus worth paying more attention to the impact of the knowledge, memory, and understanding of financial crises on the business behaviour of financial actors—ultimately reflecting on their awareness of the inherent instability of the financial system. Different ideas of memory are encompassed in the book, including—in addition to history—narrative, embeddedness, institutionalization, or legacy. We embrace this eclecticism, as we don't want to establish any kind of theoretical straitjacket valid for everyone and in all contexts.

References

Assmann, J. (2008). 'Communicative and cultural memory'. In A. Erll and A. Nünning (eds), *Cultural Memory Studies. An International and Interdisciplinary Handbook*. Berlin/New York: Walter de Gruyter, 109–118.

[27] Cassis and Schenk (eds.), *Remembering and Learning*; Berger and Fetzer (eds), *Collective Memory of Economic Crises.*

Berger, S. and Fetzer, T. (eds) (forthcoming 2026). *Collective Memory of Economic Crises and Transformations*. Basingstoke: Palgrave Macmillan.

Bernstein, P. (1992). *Capital Ideas: The Improbable Origins of Modern Wall Street*. New York: Free Press.

Bordo, M., Eichengreen, B., Klingebiel, D., and Martinez Peria, M.S. (2011). 'Financial crises: Lessons from the last 120 years'. *Economic Policy* 16, 32: 51–82.

Brumer, R. and Carr, S. (2007). *The Panic of 1907: Lessons from the Market's Perfect Storm*. Chichester: Wiley.

Caprio, G. and Klingebiel, D. (1997). 'Bank insolvency: bad luck, bad policy, or bad banking?'. In *Annual World Bank Conference on Development Economics*. Washington, DC: World Bank, 79–104.

Caprio, G. and Klingebiel, D. (2002). 'Episodes of systemic and borderline banking crises'. In D. Klingebiel and L. Laeven (eds), *Managing the Real and Fiscal Effects of Banking Crises*. Washington, DC: World Bank Discussion Paper no. 428, 31–49

Cassis, Y. (2011). *Crises and Opportunities. The Shaping of Modern Finance*. Oxford: Oxford University Press, 42–47.

Cassis, Y. and Schenk, C. (eds) (2021). *Remembering and Learning from Financial Crises*. Oxford: Oxford University Press.

Demirgüç-Kunt, A. and Detragiache, E. (1998). 'The determinants of banking crises'. *IMF Staff Papers* 45, 1: 81–109.

Drach, A. and Cassis, Y. (2021). *Financial Deregulation: A Historical Perspective*. Oxford: Oxford University Press.

Eichengreen, B. (2012). 'Economic history and economic policy'. *The Journal of Economic History* 72, 2: 289–307.

Eichengreen, B. (2015). *Hall of Mirrors. The Great Depression, the Great Recession, and the Uses—and Misuses—of History*. Oxford: Oxford University Press.

Erll, A. (2010). 'Cultural memory studies: An introduction'. In A. Erll and A. Nünning (eds), *A Companion to Cultural Memory Studies*. Berlin/New York: de Gruyter, 1–15.

Friedman, M. and Schwartz, A. (1963). *A Monetary History of the United States*. Princeton: Princeton University Press.

Geithner, T. (2014). *Stress Test*. London: Random House.

Halbwachs, M. (1925). *Les cadres sociaux de la mémoire*. Paris: Presses universitaires de France.

Halbwachs, M. (1950). *La mémoire collective*. Paris: Presses universitaires de France.

Hansen, P. (2012). 'Making sense of financial crisis and scandal: A Danish bank failure in the era of finance capitalism'. *Enterprise & Society* 13, 3: 672–706.

Laeven, L. and Valencia, F. (2018). 'Systemic banking crises rivisited'. *IMF Working Paper* no. 2018/206.

Lowenstein, R. (2000). *When Genius Failed: The Rise and Fall of Long-Term Capital Management*. New York: Random House.

Nora, P. (1989). 'Between memory and history. Les lieux de mémoire'. *Representations* 26: 7–24.

Obstfeld, M. and Taylor, A. (2004). *Global Capital Markets: Integration, Crisis and Growth*. Cambridge: Cambridge University Press.

O'Sullivan, M.A. (2022). 'History as heresy: Unlearning the lessons of economic orthodoxy'. *Economic History Review* 75, 2: 297–335.

Reinhart, C. and Rogoff, K. (2009). *This Time Is Different. Eight Centuries of Financial Folly*. Princeton: Princeton University Press.

Roberts, R. and Kynaston, D. (2015). *The Lion Wakes: A Modern History of HSBC*. London: Profile Books.
Schenk, C. (2021). 'The past as practice or parable? Anticipating financial crisis in the 1960s and the 1980s'. In Y. Cassis and C. Schenk (eds), *Remembering and Learning from Financial Crises*. Oxford: Oxford University Press, 82–104.
Telesca, G. and Cassis, Y. (forthcoming 2026). 'Battles of narratives, battles of memory. Making sense of the ebbs and flows of the memory of the Great Depression'. In S. Berger and T. Fetzer (eds), *Collective Memory of Economic Crises and Transformations*. Basingstoke: Palgrave Macmillan.
Tett, G. (2007). 'Doomed to repeat it?'. *Financial Times*, 27 August.
Tooze, A. (2018). *Crashed: How a Decade of Financial Crises Changed the World*. London: Allen Lane.
Turner, J. (2016). 'Financial history and financial economics'. In Y. Cassis, R.S. Grossman, and C. Schenk, *Oxford Handbook of Banking and Financial History*. Oxford: Oxford University Press, 41–61.
Winter, J. (2006). 'Notes on the memory boom. War, remembrance and the uses of the past'. In D. Bell (ed.), *Memory, Trauma and World Politics. Reflections on the Relationship between Past and Present*. Basingstoke and New York: Palgrave Macmillan, 54–73.
Wolfers, J. (2015). 'How economists came to dominate the conversation'. *New York Times*, 23 January.

2

Forgotten and remembered nightmares

Herstatt Risk in the global payments system

Catherine R. Schenk

In 1996, between the Mexican Peso Crisis of 1994 and the Asian Financial Crisis of 1997, financial journalist David Shirreff wrote, 'ask any central banker what is his worst nightmare and he is likely to say one word: Herstatt'.[1] This quotation demonstrates the enduring power of the memory of the collapse of a mid-sized German bank in the summer of 1974. Twenty years later in December 2007, in the midst of the Great Financial Crisis, the European Central Bank's Financial Stability Review also reflected that 'More than thirty years after the "Herstatt" case, foreign exchange settlement risk is still an issue'.[2] In relative terms, the impact of the insolvency of the Herstatt Bank was quite minor. There was no discernible loss of GDP among the participant countries, other banks did not suffer serious or prolonged contagion, depositors did not lose their money. Rather than the actual economic impact of this scandal, it was the potential for crisis that it exposed which created a lasting impression. The nightmare that the Herstatt Bank scandal created in central bankers' minds was the weakness that it revealed in the fundamental structure of the cross-border payments system, just as exchange controls were finally being lifted and the volume of cross-border transactions was surging. A collapse of cross-border payments threatened to lead to widespread bankruptcy and curtail international trade. It took almost 30 years to dispel the most bloodcurdling aspects of this spectre, despite the fact that it loomed large in the memory of bankers and central bankers alike. Unusually, the Herstatt Bank scandal was also memorialized for future generations of market participants via textbooks and policy-making, which makes it an interesting case study of the relationship between memory, history, and financial crisis.[3]

When thinking about *memory* of financial crises, an interesting additional perspective available to historians is to discover 'near misses' where a crisis was either

[1] Shirreff, *Euromoney*.
[2] ECB, *Financial Stability Review*, 149.
[3] Cassis and Schenk, 'Memories and uses of the past'.

Catherine R. Schenk, *Forgotten and remembered nightmares*. In: *History, Memory, and the Return of Financial Crises After Bretton Woods*. Edited by: Youssef Cassis and Giuseppe Telesca, Oxford University Press. © Oxford University Press (2026). DOI: 10.1093/9780198950158.003.0002

pre-emptively resolved through quick action by public authorities or at least its effects were mitigated and minimized by such intervention. Thus, the shudder in the international banking markets in the summer of 1974 did not prompt a major crisis—in the USA the Franklin National Bank had to be restructured and in Germany the Herstatt Bank collapsed, but other banks in Germany and the UK made less significant losses and were able to trade through their embarrassment.[4] At the same time, the collapse of a subsidiary of an Israeli bank in London (the Israel-British Bank) and a rogue trading scandal in Lloyds Bank International's Lugano office in 1974 never impressed themselves on the memory of observers. They both involved cross-border payments, but they did not implicate third parties in their downfall in the way that Herstatt Bank caused systemic effects through its correspondent contracts with other banks in Europe and the USA. Nevertheless, the forgotten collapse of Israel-British Bank and rogue trading in Lugano were the main focus of the Basel Committee's first discussions: how to allocate supervision of branches and subsidiaries between home and host authorities. In contrast, settlement risk exposed by the Herstatt Bank fraud was not a key area of the Basel Committee's deliberations. Nevertheless, *Herstatt Risk* became the recognized phrase to express foreign exchange settlement risk in payments across currencies and time zones. Despite the strong institutional memory of this episode and the way it is embedded in the training of generations of financiers, policy-makers found it extremely difficult to get banks to act to mitigate Herstatt Risk.

Figure 2.1 shows the Google Books Ngram report for Herstatt Risk as a measure of expressed memory. This shows a rapid increase in the use of the term in English language books in the 1980s, peaking in 1993 in the midst of policy discussions about eliminating the risk. The incidence then declined during the Great Moderation of the 1990s but rose again after the 2007 Great Financial Crisis and the ensuing series of financial and pandemic crises.

This chapter traces how the Herstatt nightmare evolved in the 30 years after 1974 as banking and financial markets globalized and the cross-border payments system was transformed from paper to complex ICT solutions. Along the way, we consider less well remembered episodes and demonstrate how these events were remembered by policy-makers through their own words. We then consider why it took so long to reduce Herstatt Risk despite its high visibility among bankers and policy-makers. The next section starts with a brief description of the Herstatt Bank collapse in a wider context of international monetary turmoil, and policy-makers' responses.

[4] Schenk, 'Summer in the City'.

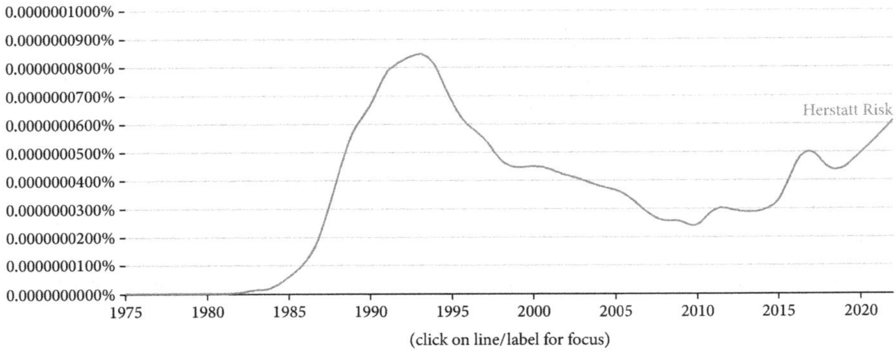

Figure 2.1 NGram for Herstatt Risk: incidence of mention in Google corpus

Source: https://books.google.com/ngrams/graph?content=Herstatt+Risk&year_start=1975&year_end=2022&corpus=en&smoothing=3 [accessed 24 November 2024] The search is not case-sensitive and covers English language books only.

Remembered and forgotten scandals

The underlying plumbing of international payments grew out of the structure of bilateral contractual arrangements between banks in different countries. These agreements set out the terms and conditions to fulfil instructions for payment from one bank's customer to another bank's customer in return for services or goods supplied. In the nineteenth century, this was achieved through telegraph instructions between banks, or through drawing and acceptance of bills of exchange.[5] The essential feature of the system was that almost all payments were made in advance of the funds being transferred between banks—this introduced foreign exchange risk (which could be covered in forward markets) and also counterparty risk. Final settlement of global payments relies on systemic interdependence—each institution might only be able to meet its obligations if its counterparties on the other side also meet theirs. In real time, the complexity of payments among correspondent banks each day meant that the failure of one counterparty to supply funds could lead to the unravelling of a series of payments across several banks. These systemic risks were abruptly exposed at the start of the most recent globalization after the collapse of the Herstatt Bank in the summer of 1974.

The story of the Herstatt Bank collapse and its systemic effects has been told elsewhere.[6] Herstatt was a middling German bank headquartered in Köln that was engaged in commercial banking and foreign exchange trading. Like other banks of the time, it expanded quickly in the wake of the opening of foreign exchange

[5] Payments are also effected via bank branches; these are internal to the bank rather than relying on arm's length contractual arrangements.

[6] Mourlon-Druol, '"Trust is good, control is better"'.

markets and was caught out by a level of volatility in the USD exchange rate that had not been experienced since the inauguration of the Bretton Woods system after 1945. The start of the last period of floating exchange rates for major currencies was from 1931/1933 to 1939, so by 1974 no foreign exchange dealer or banker under the age of about 60 years would have had direct memories of their experience in such a market. At the same time, supervisory authorities were stuck in the legacy of wartime exchange controls repurposed to support the Bretton Woods pegged exchange rate system. This framework limited central banks' supervisory space to their national borders. After 1945, the operation of exchange controls in most European states was delegated to authorized banks and, as cross-border banking and financial markets liberalized in the 1960s, central banks did not step in to enhance their supervision of the operations of foreign branches or subsidiaries.

Mourlon-Druol[7] and Schenk[8] emphasize that there were rumours about Herstatt Bank's over-trading and its large open foreign exchange positions, and the German authorities investigated the bank in the years running up to the bank's collapse in June 1974. New technology also had its role. Like other banks, Herstatt was using a computer (Nixdorf-Kleincomputeranlage) to register the foreign exchange (FX) operations of its team of seven traders thinking that this reduced operational risk, but the list of transactions was only produced on a daily basis and could be manipulated through a cancel button (Abbruchtaste) so that some transactions did not appear on the daily printout. As a result, traders could exceed daily limits on open positions and disguise them.[9] In June 1974 losses of about DM470 million were revealed.

After several days of investigation and efforts to find a rescuer, the German authorities closed the bank at 3pm German time, which was 10am in New York. The ensuing disruption led to the coining of a new phrase: Herstatt Risk, to denote the effects of time zones on settlement. US (and other international banks) had made DM payments to (or on behalf of) Herstatt but had not received the USD cover for those payments before the bank was closed by the German authorities. For example, on 26 June Morgan Guaranty delivered DM33.1835 million to Herstatt through the Frankfurt clearing in settlement of spot foreign exchange transactions entered into the previous day and had a contract to receive $13 million from Herstatt through their correspondent in New York, Chase Manhattan Bank. The second leg of the transaction through Chase Manhattan was interrupted by the withdrawal of Herstatt's banking licence in Frankfurt and Morgan Guaranty was out of pocket by the total amount.[10]

[7] Mourlon-Druol, '"Trust is good, control is better"'.
[8] Schenk, 'Summer in the city'.
[9] Mourlon-Druol, '"Trust is good, control is better"', 319.
[10] Cable from Elmore C. Patterson, Chairman of the Board of Morgan Guaranty Trust Company to Dr Klassen, President Deutsche Bundesbank, 2 July 1974. Archives of the Federal Reserve Bank of

As Herstatt's main correspondent in New York, Chase Manhattan Bank was at the centre of the scandal. On 26 June Herstatt told Chase to expect payments from a total of 13 banks to cover about $352 million of payments that it was asking Chase to make on its behalf that day.[11] In the end, Chase deleted or recalled all Herstatt's payments but also did not get the cover it was expecting except for one payment of $64 million from Commerzbank Duesseldorf. This meant that banks that were expecting dollars from Chase on behalf of Herstatt, like Morgan Guaranty, did not receive them. Some of the banks were on two sides of the payments. For example, Banco do Brasil was to pay Chase $5 million that day but was also due to receive $20 million from Chase on behalf of Herstatt. Swiss Bank Corp was to pay $500,000 and receive $3 million. This demonstrates the complex network of payments that were netted out through Chase Manhattan as Herstatt's correspondent bank.

On Thursday, 27 June, the day after Herstatt was closed, many banks around the world instructed their New York correspondents not to make any payments until they had received firm confirmation that the counter-value had been received abroad. Trust had evaporated and this led to large balances being held in accounts in New York banks pending confirmations. Since some payments were not made, this 'resulted in a chain reaction of other payments not being made'.[12] The situation was not resolved over the weekend and by Monday virtually no payments were being made and the multi-billion-dollar international dollar settlements system had ground to a halt. At this point John Lee, Executive Vice President of the New York Clearing House, consulted with member banks and told banks 'that all payment instructions they had stored in the computer would be deemed released' unilaterally, but the banks would have the right to recall individual items at 10am on Tuesday.[13] He thus wrote to all Clearing House Interbank Payments System (CHIPS) members and instructed them 'to put all of their payment orders into the System immediately, and to release them'.[14] Lee reassured Robert Crowley at the Federal Reserve Bank of New York (FRBNY) that this strategy seemed to be successful in releasing the stored up payments from Monday, 1 July to get the system moving again.[15] The ability to recall payments was extended for a further three days to the 4 July Independence Day holiday. The effect was that the volume and value of payments dropped precipitously because European banks were no longer being

New York (hereafter FRBNY) 555225 Box 1, Central Records 1. Franklin-Herstatt Failure 1963–1975 Coombs.

[11] Memo Robert J. Crowley to Coombs, 11 July 1974. FRBNY 555225 Box 1, Central Records 1. Franklin-Herstatt Failure 1963–1975 Coombs.

[12] Memo by Robert J. Crowley for Files, 2 July 1974. FRBNY 555225 Box 1, Central Records 1. Franklin-Herstatt Failure 1963–1975 Coombs.

[13] Memo by Robert J. Crowley for Files, 2 July 1974. FRBNY 555225 Box 1, Central Records 1. Franklin-Herstatt Failure 1963–1975 Coombs.

[14] Letter from John Lee to CHIPS/PEPS banks 1 July 1974. FRBNY 555225 Box 1, Central Records 1. Franklin-Herstatt Failure 1963–1975 Coombs.

[15] Memo by Robert J. Crowley for Files, 2 July 1974. FRBNY 555225 Box 1, Central Records 1. Franklin-Herstatt Failure 1963–1975 Coombs.

extended daylight overdrafts. From a daily average of about $60 billion before the collapse, daily clearings fell to about $36 billion.[16] The counterparty risk on foreign exchange business had suddenly become apparent to correspondent bankers, who had previously worried more about market risk from exchange rate movements.

A few days later, on 5 July 1974, Robert Crowley set out the risks for his Governor, Henry C. Wallich:

> In the morning when the New York banks come into work, they are faced with reams of cables instructing them to pay out large amounts for their foreign correspondents. In some cases, they are advised of from whom the cover will be received, but in the majority of cases they are not advised. In any event, they are not sure of whether it will be received since clerical errors on either side of the Atlantic, fails, mis-deliveries, a bank deliberately going into overdraft, or other reasons may result in their not receiving cover. Accordingly, when they make a payment, they are extending credit. On the other hand, they are aware that the market is highly linked and if they don't make payments, they may not get receipts. In most cases, the payments are usually made—so-called 'daylight overdrafts'—in the expectation of obtaining cover later in the day. It is a business in which trust and confidence is essential.[17]

Gerald Corrigan, later President of the FRBNY, was a junior economist at the FRBNY in 1974 and was part of a task force to deal with the fall-out of the Herstatt Bank scandal. His experience contributed to an appreciation of the importance of the plumbing of the national and international banking system. He later became Secretary to the FRBNY responsible for running Fedwire, the US national payments system. Thirty-five years after the event, Corrigan remembered that from a correspondent bank's point of view 'It was just an act of faith that you would receive the payments from Herstatt into CHIPS [Clearing House Interbank Payments System] and that your own outgoing payments could be safely made with the payments you were to receive from Herstatt and other banks. All of a sudden, that act of faith was a nightmare.'[18] It was a nightmare that continued to feature in textbooks and regulatory discussions up to the present day.

Less well remembered is the case of Franklin National Bank, which also failed spectacularly due to a mixture of over-trading and fraud in the summer of 1974. It was memorialized in a biography of the scandal published seven years later by Joan

[16] Memo by Scott E. Pardee for Files, 'Recent difficulties in payments mechanisms', 3 July 1974. FRBNY 555225 Box 1, Central Records 1. Franklin-Herstatt Failure 1963–1975 Coombs.

[17] Memo by Robert J. Crowley for Governor Wallich, 5 July 1974. FRBNY 555225 Box 1, Central Records 1. Franklin-Herstatt Failure 1963–1975 Coombs.

[18] Federal Reserve Board Oral History Project Interview with E. Gerald Corrigan, 18 November 2009, p. 36. https://www.federalreserve.gov/aboutthefed/files/e-gerald-corrigan-intervew-20090714.pdf, accessed 20 July 2024.

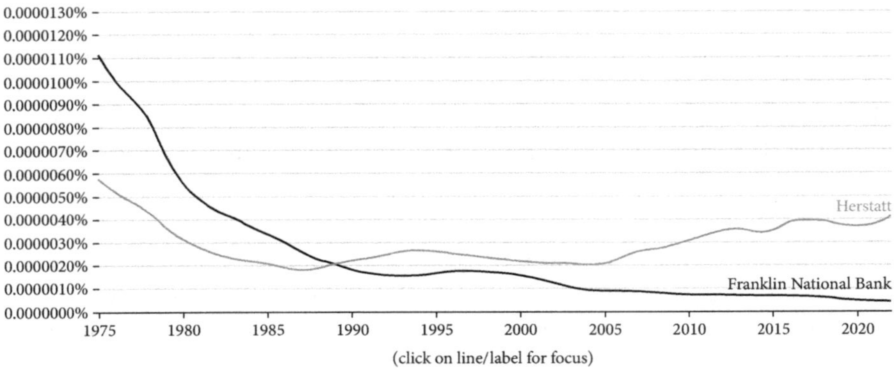

Figure 2.2 NGram for Herstatt and for Franklin National Bank: incidence of mention in Google corpus

Source: https://books.google.com/ngrams/graph?content=Herstatt%2CFranklin+National+Bank&year_start=1975&year_end=2022&corpus=en&smoothing=3 [accessed 24 November 2024].

E. Spero,[19] which was reissued on the 25th anniversary in 1999. Spero was assistant professor at Columbia University from 1973 to 1979 where she wrote this book, but she quickly gained public office; the year the book was published she became the United States Ambassador to the UN Economic and Social Council (UNESCO) from 1980 to 1981 and then was Under Secretary of State for Economic, Business, and Agricultural Affairs in Bill Clinton's administration from 1993 to 1997. As a rough indicator of the decay of memory, Figure 2.2 below shows the incidence of the mention of Franklin National Bank and Herstatt in books in the Google corpus from 1975 to 2020. Initially, Franklin National Bank loomed larger in books at the time of the events but its incidence declined and was not revived in the same way as Herstatt.

Like Herstatt, Franklin National Bank (FNB) was a mid-sized bank engaged in cross-border payments; FNB borrowed heavily in the Eurodollar market (over $1 billion) through their branch in London and speculated in the FX market leading to losses. Unlike Herstatt, the bank was not closed abruptly, leaving creditors exposed. Instead, the Fed maintained unprecedented lending (just under $2 billion) for five months (May to October) to support the winding down of Franklin's international positions and to sustain the domestic branch-based business on Long Island, NY.[20] The Fed itself took over Franklin National's huge foreign exchange position to make it a manageable target for rescue by a third party. This gave time to unwind foreign positions and to find a buyer; in October 1974 the

[19] Spero, *Failure of the Franklin National Bank*.
[20] Former Treasury Secretary Joseph W. Barr was invited to take over as CEO in May 1974 to oversee the restructuring. Barr, 'The last days of Franklin National Bank'.

New York branches were bought by European-American Bank (a consortium bank jointly owned by Midland Bank in London and its European partners).

One year after the successful resolution, former US Treasury Secretary Joseph Barr related his memories of taking over as Chairman and CEO for Franklin National during the crisis in 1974.[21] He remembered that the problems at Franklin Bank that summer captured the public imagination and there 'were front page stories and prime television time day after day'.[22] While Barr thought that he was dealing with a problem of illiquidity and that the bank could be saved through a merger, he remembered that the Chair of the Federal Reserve, Arthur Burns, told him 'I feel like I'm sitting on a volcano'; a collapse would wipe out $700 million of insured deposits and a $1 billion foreign exchange position.[23] There certainly was potential for cross-border losses. Although largely forgotten, the episode had a longer-term effect on addressing moral hazard aspects of the Fed's lender of last resort role; criticism that the Fed had supported FNB through the discount window at below market rates eventually led to an informal decision to charge 1% above Fed Funds rate after 60 days for so-called 'emergency lending'. Although the Fed was criticized for taking so long to arrange a rescue (six months), this case starkly demonstrated the different responses of German and US regulators to their responsibilities as lenders of last resort. Despite the existence of deposit insurance that reduced the public interest in a bail-out, the Fed chose to participate in restructuring the Franklin National in order to avoid the anticipated systemic effects of losses. The German authorities, in contrast, were legally obliged to cease Herstatt Bank from trading as soon as they determined that the bank was insolvent, prompting financial losses among the bank's creditors and a wider loss of trust in the correspondent banking network.

The huge size of the global USD payments that cleared and settled through New York created vulnerabilities that the FRBNY sought to contain in the wake of the Herstatt crisis. Thus, they encouraged CHIPS to bolster its resilience by requiring smaller banks to have a letter of support from their parent bank to cover their clearings and expenses in the event that they could not meet their obligations. Meanwhile, the overnight risks of cross-border USD payments were reduced gradually under pressure and guidance from the FRBNY by requiring same-day settlement from October 1981. Caps on each bank's intra-day exposure were introduced from October 1984, although the collective amount of exposure rose significantly. The Fed was able to encourage banks in the USA to enhance their resilience to settlement risk, although because CHIPS was a private-sector enterprise, they had no direct power to enforce changes and these took over a

[21] Barr's memories were part of a panel on the Franklin National Bank collapse held by Section of Administrative Law of the American Bar Association in Montreal in 1975. They were published in the section's Fall 1975 journal.

[22] Barr, 'The last days of Franklin National Bank', 309.

[23] Barr, 'The last days of Franklin National Bank', 305.

decade to be implemented. In the UK, the Bank of England focused on encouraging prudence to reduce fraud but did not address settlement risk directly. In December 1974 Governor Richardson sent out a letter to banks in London detailing how dealers and brokers should interact, sought letters of comfort from parent institutions for the liquidity of their subsidiaries in London and advised banks to use their correspondent banks in other centres to monitor the activities of their own overseas offices.[24] In Germany the Bundesbank pooled the responsibility for future bail-outs in a new Liquiditats-Konsortialbank (Liko-Bank) that was 70% owned by German banks.

While major national banking centres tightened up their procedures, reducing settlement risk required cross-border coordination. For centuries, cross-border payments business had been left to banks to manage and it was seen as a basic service that banks provided to their customers who operated beyond national borders. By the 1970s, however, the scale of the internationalization of banking meant that the market had mushroomed beyond the national supervisory mandates of central banks. At the same time, no central bank wanted to be considered the lender of last resort to the global payments system.[25]

Recognizing that the actions of one central bank had implications for jurisdictions elsewhere, at the end of 1974 the G10 Central Bank governors asked for a new committee to be hosted by the Bank for International Settlements (BIS) to survey the governance of the foreign exchange market and to enhance the scope of supervision of cross-border banking. Each central bank sent one representative from each of these functions to the initial meetings. In the end, the issue of counterparty risk, which was at the heart of the Herstatt Bank scandal, was not addressed within the Basel Committee. Instead, the Committee focused on trying to close gaps in supervision of banks operating across different jurisdictions, and enhancing individual bank resilience.

From 1975, the Basel Committee embarked on a discussion over whether host or home supervisors should be responsible for offices of banks. This related to two other scandals in 1974 that are now largely forgotten; the failure of a subsidiary of a foreign bank in London and a rogue trading scandal in a foreign branch of a British bank.[26] The Israel-British Bank (IBB) was the London subsidiary of an Israeli bank, but neither the Bank of Israel nor the Bank of England took responsibility for its supervision: each claimed to have expected the other central bank to be doing this. When the IBB collapsed in 1974, the responsibility to bail out depositors was disputed between the two central banks, ultimately resulting in a settlement later in 1975. This raised the question of who the lender of last resort

[24] Schenk, 'Summer in the city'.
[25] In the nineteenth century and in 1914 the Bank of England had discounted bills of exchange, so it had somewhat of a role as lender of last resort, but the relative scale of assets was much smaller than in the later twentieth century.
[26] Schenk, 'Summer in the city'.

was for the new generation of international banks. At the time the Bank of England did not directly supervise the overseas activities of British banks but losses from a fraud at the Lugano branch of Lloyds Bank International exposed the vulnerability of British banks to their operations in other jurisdictions and led to changes in the Bank of England's supervisory reach. Both of these episodes (IBB and Lloyds) were discussed in the early meetings of the Basel Committee as the members sought to establish principles to coordinate cross-border bank supervision. While these two cases are now largely forgotten, they had more profound (and rapid) implications for central bank cooperation than the Herstatt Bank scandal.

The Basel Concordat of 1975 set out principles for the division of responsibility between home and host authorities while establishing that effective supervision of an increasingly international system required close communication between central bankers.[27] The Basel Committee than moved on to identify common standards for capital adequacy to limit the potential for failure of individual institutions. The target of supervision was balance sheet data of stocks of assets and liabilities rather than the flows of the payments system. Meanwhile the second mandate of the original Basel Committee, which included the governance of the FX market, was de-emphasized after setting principles to minimize the corruption between brokers and traders that had underpinned the frauds perpetrated in the 1970s.

In this way, although the Herstatt Bank collapse is often credited with inspiring the G10 central bank governors to launch the Basel Committee,[28] the committee itself did not directly address the systemic issues raised by the Herstatt Bank scandal beyond agreeing that when a supervisor was going to shut a bank they should consider the wider implications. In advance of Herstatt's insolvency, the Bank of England had communicated their concerns to the Bundesbank so this was not an example of a failure of communication between supervisors to provide early warning. The Basel Committee instead focused on balance sheet supervision and credit exposure, leaving the counterparty risk element of cross-border payments aside. The following sections explore the evolution of the global payments architecture and why central bankers found it so difficult to dispel the Herstatt Risk 'nightmare'.

Building the cross-border payments system after Bretton Woods

The Herstatt Bank scandal happened just as banks were designing a multilateral computerized network for sending payments instructions across borders. From 1969, European banking groups had been thinking of ways to use their cooperative

[27] The gaps in supervision were not completely closed. The Concordat was revised in 1983 (after the failure of Banco Ambrosiano) to recommend that home authorities should supervise their banks with foreign operations on a consolidated basis.

[28] See e.g. the commissioned official history of the Basel Committee: Goodhart, *The Basel Committee on Banking Supervision.*

frameworks to streamline the cross-border payments process, which had become unwieldy under the rapid growth of international bank flows. Telegraph was expensive and labour-intensive, took time, and was constrained by cumbersome code books required to limit the length of messages (and thereby cost). Telex was an improvement that allowed more continuous bilateral communication between banks but was still labour-intensive and required time-consuming bilateral calculations for netting and clearing between institutions and therefore between customers.[29] New computer technology promised to make communications cheaper and more continuous, to allow banks to know their net international payments positions faster by processing instructions multilaterally.

In 1970, members of the New York Clearing House had introduced CHIPS as a hub and spoke computerized system for US dollar payments instructions in and out of the USA. CHIPS was designed to overcome the burden of the reconciliation of paper records among banks in New York, who operated as the correspondent banks for partner institutions around the world to settle cross-border USD payments.[30] By the 1970s, the USD was the world's dominant commercial currency, having overtaken sterling in the 1950s, and the growth in world trade and investment led to a surge in foreign exchange transactions between banks. Settlement risk was not a prominent consideration since the Clearing House banks designed CHIPS in advance of the 1974 stumble in international payments.

At the same time as New York Clearing House banks were developing CHIPS, European banks began to develop a cross-border payments system, but the coordination problems were much more challenging than for banks operating within New York. In the end it took eight years to develop the international payments messaging system, Society for Worldwide Interbank Financial Transmission (SWIFT), with a common code book and protocols.[31] Like CHIPS, it was a hub and spoke arrangement where banks connected to computers in regional centres that were consolidated to exchange messages, although (unlike CHIPS) there was no formal clearing or settlement mechanism; it was limited to standardized messaging. Nevertheless, there was an element of settlement in that the rule book set out the terms for when a message instructing payment could not be rescinded (i.e. was final). Like CHIPS, the aim was reducing operational costs by applying networked computer technology and a standardized code book, not settlement risk.

In the 1960s European banks had gathered themselves into groups of strategic partnerships, often with one or more US banks included.[32] SWIFT was spearheaded by the ABECOR group, but they quickly drew all major international banks into the planning process through country-based member groups. Such a

[29] Schenk, 'Telegraph to tether'.
[30] Schenk, 'Telegraph to tether'.
[31] Scott and Zachariadis, 'Origins and development of SWIFT, 1973–2009'; Scott and Zachariadis, *The Society for Worldwide Interbank Financial Telecommunication (SWIFT)*.
[32] Drach, 'An early form of European champions?'

system required a large user-group to exploit network externalities. Some central bankers argued that they should be involved in the planning (Banque de France, BIS) but others, especially the Bank of England in London which was the location of the world's largest foreign exchange market, resisted becoming directly involved.[33] Instead, the Bank of England and other central banks joined their national member groups and offered advice indirectly. Once it was clear that the messaging system did not include a mechanism for final settlement, central bankers were content to allow the private sector to find a market solution to their bottleneck and coordination problems. Even the Herstatt scandal in the midst of the planning did not derail this position—as noted above, regulatory energy went into central bank communication to overcome gaps in supervising international banking, rather than the Herstatt Risk per se. It is salient to recall that both Herstatt Bank and Franklin National Bank were founding members of SWIFT, paying subscription fees to support the development of the system even as their own managements were engaged in fraudulent bookkeeping and payments statements.

SWIFT was operational from 1976, but it was not all smooth sailing. In the early years, there was uncertainty about finality of messages and inconsistencies in the rule book. The computer system was unreliable at times and created outages that suspended the flow of payments for short periods.[34] High upfront costs for computer equipment and training of specialized personnel meant that telex remained the dominant mode for messaging for most banks for another decade.

Too big or too systemic to fail

In the ten years after Herstatt, there were further shocks through the cross-border payments system. Continental Illinois Bank based in Chicago had relied on short-term funding from money markets in London that was not renewed once the poor quality of the bank's asset portfolio became apparent. As in the case of Franklin National Bank, transatlantic liabilities became a source of liquidity drain once there were doubts about underlying assets. In 1978 the bank's management had taken a strategic decision to grow the balance sheet quickly by buying assets from Penn Square Bank in Oklahoma. The failure of Penn Square in July 1982 and its overcommitment to the oil sector when prices were falling led to market fears about the liquidity and then the solvency of Continental Illinois Bank. In May 1984 the large size of total assets and the bank's links through its substantial correspondent network (both domestically and internationally) led the Office of the Comptroller of the Currency and the Federal Reserve ultimately to

[33] Schenk, 'Telegraph to tether'.

[34] Scott and Zachariadis, *The Society for Worldwide Interbank Financial Telecommunication (SWIFT)*.

arrange a joint bail-out between the Federal Deposit Insurance Corporation and leading commercial banks. Chicago Illinois was a member of CHIPS and it was an important clearer for the largest US commodities market located in Chicago.

A year later, in November 1985, systemic operational risks inherent in computer-based payments systems were exposed in the USA by a software failure. When the US payments system was rocked by a major computer outage at the Bank of New York, George Corrigan was president of the FRBNY. Bank of New York (BoNY) was a major New York correspondent for national and international banks and it was also one of two clearing banks for US Treasury securities. In Corrigan's own words 'the Herstatt crisis had had a big impact on me' as he tried to deal with this problem.[35] Here was an example of the Federal Reserve having to use the discount window to provide unprecedentedly large liquidity because of operational failure affecting the payments services of a bank they considered systemically important—not because of its credit exposure but because of the bank's position in the clearing system. BoNY was making payments to customers in exchange for Treasury securities during the day but the computer failure meant it could not sell them on and recoup these funds via Fedwire. Thus, BoNY's borrowing from the Federal Reserve quickly accumulated. Corrigan arranged for BoNY to get a loan through the Federal Reserve discount window up to an unprecedented value of $22.6 billion against the bank's collateral of 'everything down to the flower pots', as well as $3 billion in overdrafts.[36] The computer problem was finally resolved the next day, the payments were unwound and the FRBNY repaid. It is clear that Corrigan's memory of the systemic impact on payments caused by the collapse of Herstatt Bank encouraged his support for nursing the bank through a severe liquidity shock.

At the time, Paul Volcker remarked that making a computer system absolutely immune to operational failure would be prohibitively costly; 'in the last analysis no mechanical system can be entirely fail-safe and also be commercially viable'.[37] The assumption behind this statement is that the incentive to make a system secure is bounded by the uncertainty of the potential costs of a collapse, and the distribution of these costs between the public and private sector. The costs to an individual bank of a payments failure are uncertain because they cannot be estimated or predicted in the way that risk associated with credit can; the network is so complex that it is almost impossible to imagine how so many transactions could be untangled or netted out in the event of a failure. The systemic importance of this complex network invites public sector intervention to sustain the flow of payments in the interests of the orderly functioning of markets. Although payments commitments

[35] Federal Reserve Board Oral History Project Interview with E. Gerald Corrigan, 18 November 2009, p. 46.

[36] Federal Reserve Board Oral History Project Interview with E. Gerald Corrigan, 18 November 2009, pp. 47–48.

[37] Quoted in Ennis and Price, 'Discount window lending', 3.

are contractual agreements between individual banks and enforceable in law, the contingent nature of the liquidity to honour these contracts creates network effects or contagion. The memory of financial crisis resolution or prevention also featured in the Fed's attitude to moral hazard arising from anticipated liquidity support or bail outs. From 2003 the Fed formalized charging a penalty rate for accessing the discount window to discourage moral hazard by bankers expecting to be bailed out.[38]

The failure to build a framework for effective cross-border supervision was critically exposed in the collapse of Bank of Credit and Commerce International (BCCI) in 1991, 25 years after the inauguration of the Basel Committee. This was an example of a transnational institution of interlinked banks so complex that it was able to obscure cross-border transfers and fraud from supervisors. BCCI was founded in 1972 by Agha Hasan Abedi with 25% of its capital from Bank of America, which added credibility to the new bank. Abedi explicitly favoured Bank of America as a partner because of its large correspondent banking business, which would give his new bank access to cross-border payments networks.[39] BCCI expanded alarmingly quickly in the UK and around the world, so that by 1981 it had 220 offices through subsidiaries in 43 countries in Europe, Africa, North America, and the Middle East.[40] After Bank of America divested from BCCI by 1980, it remained as a main correspondent, although BCC Group also secretly acquired a subsidiary, First American Bank, to act as the Group's correspondent in New York.[41] By 1991 First American Bank NA held accounts in New York for 46 BCC Group branches and subsidiaries around the world.[42] First American seemingly had an arm's length correspondent banking relationship with members of the BCC Group, but in fact was owned and controlled by the same holding company and management. The ability to use the correspondent banking system to move funds across borders on its own account and for account of their customers was an important element in the bank's money-laundering activities. The case also highlighted continuing supervisory gaps. BCCI's main holding company was in Luxembourg, but it had another holding company in the Cayman Islands and its main operational office was in London. National authorities cooperated formally in their supervision of the BCC Group for almost a decade but were unable to curtail its illegal activities or ensure its solvency.[43] Although rumours about BCCI circulated (as they had about Herstatt) for several years, the bank continued to operate until it was closed by the Bank of England in July 1991. This led to a fresh

38 The discount window rate tended to fall below the Federal Funds rate for most of the twentieth century until the policy change in 2003. Ennis and Price, 'Discount window lending', 4. Armantier et al., 'History of Discount Window Stigma'.

39 Kerry Report (1992), *The BCCI Affair*, 35.

40 BCC Information Circular 276, 19 January 1981.

41 Kerry Report (1992), *The BCCI Affair*, 46, 166.

42 Kerry Report (1992), *The BCCI Affair*, 171.

43 *Inquiry into the supervision of the BCCI*, Bingham Report (1992).

round of angst about how to effectively supervise complex international financial institutions. Although not strictly an example of Herstatt Risk, the collapse of BCCI demonstrated ongoing fragility in cross-border payments, vulnerability to fraud and the risk of systemic effects of the collapse of a large international bank. It was discussed at the BIS Committee on Payments and Settlement Systems in the 1990s and contributed to renewed momentum towards seeking a resolution to gaps in the system.

Resolving the Herstatt Risk

It is particularly striking that while the perils exposed by the Herstatt Bank collapse in 1974 were clearly understood and well remembered, they were not resolved for over 20 years despite further payments-related scandals and shocks described above. If this episode persisted as a nightmare in the minds of supervisors, why wasn't it resolved? There is a range of potential factors. The ideological position of the supervising authorities favoured a private-sector initiative to governing cross-border payments. No individual authority had any desire to be the lender of last resort to the increasingly integrated global FX market. In the 1980s central bankers focused instead on building national gross settlement systems within their mandated regulatory space but were unable to take the lead on reforming the cross-border, cross-currency architecture. During the 1980s, banks used the quickly innovating information and communications technology to build bespoke processes for their customers and to manage transactions within their bank groups, but moving beyond the boundaries of the firm and into a cross-border environment amplified harmonization and coordination problems. Inconsistency in the legal frameworks between national jurisdictions created another layer of obstacles. Given these challenges, bankers themselves tended to undervalue cross-border settlement risk; whether this was due to cognitive dissonance or to moral hazard or to a lack of appreciation of potential network effects of contagion is unclear. Cognitive dissonance may have been caused by the enormous size of potential losses on routine everyday business, which led bankers to discount this information. But unpredictable network effects also led to uncertainty over how large losses for individual institutions could be and therefore what level or term of collateral was needed. In this sense bankers were faced with uncertainty rather than measurable risk. They were better at gauging credit risk based on objective criteria than dealing with the systemic risk from inter-related but unpredictable systemic events. Since the threat of a collapse of international payments could be existential to global commerce, it was likely (especially after the regulatory forbearance shown in the sovereign debt crisis of the early 1980s) that banks would be bailed out by their central banks or by international financial institutions like the IMF. This introduced moral hazard into the market by encouraging banks to take on more risk.

After the launch of SWIFT at the end of the 1970s, the G10 Central Bank governors created a new Group of Experts on Payments Systems, which began meeting in October 1981. They were asked to write a report to Governors on the major changes in payments systems of member countries, the causes and consequences of change, and how this was likely to affect the roles of central banks. George Blunden, not a supporter of supranational regulation when chair of the Basel Committee, was the Group's first chair. Similar to the Basel Committee, a lot of the Group's time was spent on 'tours de table' sharing details of national systems, culminating in the first so-called Red Book summary of national payments systems published in 1985.

Certainly, there were profits to be made by a first mover who designed a solution, given the strong network externalities that could create monopoly for a successful scheme, but the technical, legal, and practical obstacles were daunting. The initial target was to devise a netting scheme that would reduce the amounts that ultimately needed to be settled at the end of the day and thereby reduce Herstatt settlement risk of participants. In 1984, Chemical Bank spearheaded an initiative to offer bilateral USD netting among banks in London (drawing in Lloyds Bank International as local co-chair). The initial aim was quite modest: to reduce the number of correspondent banking payments instructions received in New York, with a view to extending off-shore netting to other European centres.[44] The appetite for streamlining payments was demonstrated by the ability of Chemical Bank to quickly gather 75 attendees from 42 London institutions to a FX Netting meeting in London in July of that year; the subsequent steering board membership included banks headquartered in Canada, Switzerland, Paris, New York, London, and Tokyo. Attendees were asked to pay £6000 each for the next stage of consultancy (22 US/European/British banks in London paid up by September). The Bank of England joined the steering committee for free as a 'neutral observer'. The plan quickly expanded to more generalized FX netting via instructions sent to a centralized computer in London that would detect and match instructions during the day, making them final, as a means of bilateral netting. Only outstanding unmatched balances would need to be settled at the end of the day. Meanwhile, the FRBNY sponsored an industry-led Foreign Exchange Committee to examine similar bilateral FX netting proposals there.

The Chemical Bank proposal (FXNET) went forward in both New York and London after investigations of the legal determination of finality and liability (in case of insolvency of one party or events in another jurisdiction affecting a bank in London). By 1986, a feasibility study among 23 banks in London, each with about 600 deals per day (totalling $4.2 billion), determined that the system would reduce each bank's clean risk at settlement by about $350 million per day. They estimated that if 50 similar banks in London joined, the savings could be $23 billion each

[44] BoE C40/1431, BoE C40/1532.

day. Due to high upfront costs, only nine banks went forward to the next stage to trial the system in the summer of 1986. At this point the scheme was intra-London rather than cross-border (and cross-jurisdiction). It was fully launched in January 1987 with 10 participants by the end of the year.[45]

The initiative clearly came from the private sector but included the Bank of England (as an observer in the steering committee, making comments and suggestions) and the FRBNY in consultation. The Bank of England did not seek statutory oversight nor licensing powers, but they were asked to declare that they had 'no objections'. The FRBNY also had a steady hand on the process at the Foreign Exchange Committee that it sponsored in New York. The FRBNY gave permission to US banks to participate in FXNET in London so long as the contracts were legally binding both in London and in the country of the banks that were their counterparties, *and* that banks reduced their bilateral counterparty limits with other banks to take account of the reduced netted balances (so as not to encourage 'an increased level of trading'). The Bank of England offered 'nil obstat' or no objection to the scheme on the same basis. Table 2.1 lists the main active cross-border netting schemes by 1996.

The BIS G10 Group of Experts on Payments Systems began to compile a report on the problems of netting payments across borders in 1988. In recognition of the growing importance of these issues for central banks, the Group of Experts in Basel was reorganized into a permanent G10 Committee on Payment and Settlement Systems (CPSS) in 1990.[46] Their particular focus was liquidity and credit risk

Table 2.1 Netting schemes active in 1996

Year	Name	Location	Number of members 1996
1987	FXNET	London	57 live users; 35 signed and in process of going live
1990	SWIFT ACCORD	Belgium	420 matching; 29 netting subscribers
1992	Multinet	New York	n.a.
1995	ECHO	London	14 banks (13 currencies)
Approved but not launched	Multinet	New York	0

Source: Data from New York Foreign Exchange Committee (Jan. 1997) *Guidelines for Foreign Exchange Settlement Netting*. https://www.newyorkfed.org/medialibrary/microsites/fxc/files/guidefx.pdf

[45] FXNET in New York took longer due to technical difficulties. A FXNET scheme in Tokyo was also planned with Bank of Japan encouragement.

[46] BIS Group of Experts on Payment Systems, Angell Report on Netting Schemes, February 1989. Report of the Committee on Interbank Netting Schemes of the Central Banks of the Group of Ten countries, Lamfalussy Report, November 1990.

in cross-border payments as well as the supervisory and legal frameworks for this quickly evolving area. Their strategy was to point out the levels of Herstatt Risk among banks and to make clear what the central banks' priorities were for the design of any private-sector initiatives to resolve these risks. The 1990 Lamfalussy Report defined best practice and minimum standards for private-sector cross-border payments systems to ensure that they were robust and did not threaten the stability of the international payments system. These standards were then used as a framework for central banks (especially the Bank of England and the Federal Reserve) to vet proposals in their jurisdictions and to guide private-sector actors in their planning.

While bilateral netting of multiple currencies within a single jurisdiction (New York or London) was relatively straightforward, multilateral netting across borders raised more complex problems and risks, particularly over legal liability and redress in case of insolvency or failure of a participant, and enforcement of contracts. There was also debate over how cross-border clearing systems could be adequately collateralized. Two rival proposals emerged in the private sector; one in London (ECHO—Exchange Clearing House) and one in the USA (MultiNet).

One of the findings of the CPSS was that, although central bankers were increasingly concerned about FX risk, banks themselves were quite complacent. The CPSS surveyed 63 internationally active banks about their FX risk management in 1993 and again in 1996 and 1997. The results (presented in Table 2.2) were disappointing. Less than half had appropriate controls and only 11% were found to be measuring FX risk properly in 1993. These shares increased over time, but still, less than half the banks had proper measurement of their settlement risk at the end of 1997 despite the Asian Financial Crisis of that summer, which had caused large losses for international banks. Senior management had come to take responsibility for Herstatt Risk by 1997, but their internal measurement and controls were still weak relative to what the CPSS deemed 'proper'.

The extent of the risks the banks were supporting was evident in another survey of 77 banks in 1997, which showed the number of hours between the point where a payment outward became irrevocable and the time when funds were confirmed as received to meet those payments. This marked a period during which the bank carried counterparty risk. Table 2.3 shows that for 81% of surveyed banks, this time extended to up to 24–48 hours for Yen/USD transactions.[47] The mode across all currencies was 24–48 hours, which is a long time in financial markets during which banks were exposed to settlement risk. The CPSS's strategy of pointing out settlement risks to banks in order to encourage them to create solutions themselves was not working.

[47] A 2020 survey of SWIFT gpi found that it still took up to 23 hours to complete processing for some countries (Nilsson et al., 2022).

Table 2.2 Measures of FX settlement risk management

Percentage of banks meeting criteria			
	End 1993	**end 1996**	**end 1997**
Clear senior level responsibility	62%	84%	96%
Application of appropriate controls	47	63	73
Proper measurement of irrevocable trades	16	27	43
Proper measurement of uncertain trades	12	26	39
Proper measurement overall	11	25	39
Clear senior level responsibility. Appropriate controls and proper measurement	9	20	35

Irrevocable = payment instruction cannot be unilaterally cancelled to the time when final receipt of currency bought is due
Uncertain = following irrevocable, the time between when bought currency is due and confirmation that it has been received: e.g. after statement from correspondent bank

Source: Data from CPSS, Reducing Foreign Exchange Settlement Risk: a progress report, BIS, 1998.

After setting the minimum standards in the Lamfalussy report in 1990, the CPSS repeatedly called for a private-sector initiative to resolve Herstatt risk in FX markets. In 1996, as foreign bank credit to emerging market economies surged, the CPSS 'call[ed] upon individual banks and industry groups alike to improve current practices and devise safe mechanisms for addressing settlement risk'.[48] Two years later they noted that 'The [CPSS's] chosen strategy was founded on the belief that the private sector, with the active support of the public sector, had the power to contain the risk that first came into focus at the time of the 1974 failure of Bankhaus Herstatt' but this strategy failed to galvanize banks towards a solution.[49]

Finally, the CPSS threatened to move the responsibility to the Basel Committee, where rules for increased regulatory capital against FX risk could be devised. This threat to banks' bottom line and frustration in the Bank of England and Federal Reserve prompted a reconciliation between Multinet and ECHO. In 1997 seven banks launched an idea for a CLS Bank (continuous linked settlement) in London for foreign exchange transactions on a payment-versus-payment basis. Intra-day exposure was reduced via netting and payments were not released unless there were funds available to clear them, reducing settlement risk. Despite this promising beginning, it took a further seven years for CLS Bank to become operational for a limited group of 39 banks and across seven currencies.[50]

[48] CPSS, *Settlement Risk in Foreign Exchange Transactions*, BIS, Basel, 1996.
[49] CPSS, *Reducing Foreign Exchange Settlement Risk*.
[50] Kahn and Roberds, 'The CLS Bank'. The original currencies were USD, GBP, JPY, EUR, CHF, AUD, CAD. By 2022 CLS included 18 currencies and had more than 70 members.

Table 2.3 Banks' foreign exchange currency exposure, 1997

Outstanding currency exposure: Percentage of banks responding to a survey that have outstanding currency exposure between USD and named currency for each duration			
	>48 hours	**24–48 hours**	**<24 hours**
JPY	12%	81%	7%
BEF	9	80	11
FRF	8	81	11
DEM	5	79	16
ITL	7	77	16
NLG	9	76	15
SEK	8	73	19
CHF	5	73	21
ECU	7	72	22
GBP	4	72	24
CAD	3	59	38

Source: Data from CPSS, Reducing Foreign Exchange Settlement Risk: a progress report, BIS, 1998.

Thirty-eight years after Herstatt Bank collapsed, this private-sector solution finally reduced cross-border settlement risk, although it was not completely eliminated. In 2006, a CPSS survey of 109 leading international banks across 27 jurisdictions found that one-third of foreign exchange obligations (c.$1.2 billion) were still settled through traditional correspondent banking (subject to settlement risk) rather than through CLS or other netting schemes.[51] Of these correspondent banking transactions, almost half bore exposure to Herstatt Risk for 24 hours. By 2022, 30% of FX turnover was still vulnerable to settlement risk, and the value of that risk had increased substantially with the growth of the market. Meanwhile the limits of members and eligible currencies meant that the share of CLS declined. In 2025 CLS settled about 30% of daily total FX turnover, down from one half in 2013, although they accounted for 55% of the trades eligible for CLS in 2025.[52] Despite the revolution in the nature and structure of globalisation since 1974, on these measures Herstatt Risk lingers in the cross-border payments system.

https://www.cls-group.com/about/ [accessed 28 October 2022]. Globally the share of PvP settlement in foreign exchange markets fell since 2013, mainly because many EME currencies are not processed. CPMI (2023) Facilitating increased adoption of payment versus payment (PVP), Final Report.

[51] ECB, *Financial Stability Review*, 151.

[52] CLS settled 37% of FX turnover in 2022, Glowka and Nilsson, 'FX settlement risk: an unsettled issue'. For 2025 see CLS, BIS Triennial Survey. Not all currency pairs are eligible to be settled through CLS.

Conclusions

Why are some episodes remembered and others forgotten? The IBB, Lloyds, and Franklin National Bank scandals were important prompts for reforming supervisory structures in London and at the BIS in the 1970s and 1980s, and are now largely forgotten. In contrast, systemic cross-border settlement risk proved much more difficult to resolve and the nightmare of Herstatt Risk was resurrected repeatedly over decades. This chapter has explored how the collapse of a mid-sized German bank at the early stage of capital account liberalization came to be memorialized as a short-hand for catastrophic settlement risk. The Herstatt Bank was only one of several banks that got into difficulties in the early days of floating exchange rates and freer payments at the end of the Bretton Woods era. Gaps in supervision of foreign bank offices were exposed by the cases of IBB and Lloyds Bank International and were taken up in the Basel Committee at the BIS. However, these cases are largely forgotten while the Herstatt Bank scandal still echoes through the common use of 'Herstatt Risk' and repetition of the story in newspapers and textbooks. The differential cross-border impact of the Federal Reserve's restructuring of the Franklin National Bank in 1974 compared with the abrupt German closure of Herstatt Bank raised questions about the appropriate steps for central banks to take in the case of insolvency. The American attitude in the 1970s and 1980s leaned more to avoidance of systemic effects through forbearance and liquidity provision in a pattern that was repeated in the case of Continental Illinois Bank. Like Herstatt Risk, the appropriate level of central bank intervention to rescue failing institutions continues to linger in central bank debates.

Herstatt Bank's failure had an outsized impact through its memorialization in a specific form of settlement risk that re-emerged as cross-border payments became larger and more complex. While the Herstatt Bank scandal is often remembered as leading to the formation of the Basel Committee on Banking Supervision, this committee did not directly address Herstatt Risk in its early deliberations, so in this sense it is misremembered. Instead, Herstatt Risk emerged in the 1980s as the focus of the BIS Group of Experts on Payments Systems. Central bank cooperation over cross-border payments was hesitant; they preferred to leave this to the private sector. The Group of Experts on Payments only became a Committee at the BIS in 1989 when G10 central bankers took a more deliberate step to create minimum standards for private-sector payments schemes. However, the inability of private-sector initiatives on their own to overcome technical, operational, and jurisdictional challenges meant that they struggled to come up with robust feasible solutions. CLS Bank emerged from competing private initiatives but took many years to develop and is still not a comprehensive solution. Most emerging market currencies are still excluded and bilateral correspondent banking connections persist, leaving some Herstatt Risk in the global payments system. Nevertheless, as unmonitored crypto payments proliferate, Herstatt Risk has perhaps receded from a nightmare to a bad dream for central bankers today.

Acknowledgement

This publication arises from research funded by the European Research Council (ERC) under the European Union's Horizon 2020 research and innovation programme (Grant Agreement No. 883758).

References

Accominotti, O., Lucena-Piquero, D., and Ugolini, S. (2021). 'The origination and distribution of money market instruments: sterling bills of exchange during the first globalization'. *Economic History Review* 74, 4: 892–921.

Armantier, O., Lee, H., and Sarkar, A. 'History of discount window stigma'. *Liberty Street Economics*, 10 August 2015.

Barr, J.W. (1975). 'The last days of Franklin National Bank'. *Administrative Law Review* 27, 4: 301–315.

Cassis, Y. and Schenk, C.R. (2021). 'Memories and uses of the past'. In Cassis, Y. and C.R. Schenk (eds), *Remembering and Learning from Financial Crises*. Oxford: Oxford University Press, 1–17.

CLS (2025). *BIS Triennial Survey 2025 | CLSMarketData Insights | CLS Group* (accessed 13 December 2025).

Committee on Payments and Market Infrastructures (2023). *Facilitating increased adoption of payment versus payment (PVP), Final Report*. Basel: Bank for International Settlements.

Committee on Payment and Settlement Systems (1996). *Settlement Risk in Foreign Exchange Transactions*. Basel: Bank for International Settlements.

Committee on Payment and Settlement Systems (1998). *Reducing Foreign Exchange Settlement Risk: a progress report*, Basel: Bank for International Settlements.

Drach, A. (2024). 'An early form of European champions? Banking clubs between European integration and global banking (1960s–1990s)'. *Business History* 66, 1: 287–310.

Ennis, H.M. and Price, D.A. (2015). 'Discount window lending; policy trade-offs and the 1985 BoNY computer failure'. Richmond Federal Reserve Bank, *Economic Brief*, May.

European Central Bank (2007). *Financial Stability Review, December.*

Glowka, M., and Nilsson, T. (2022). 'FX settlement risk: an unsettled issue'. *BIS Quarterly Review*, December: 75–81

Goodhart, C. (2011). *The Basel Committee on Banking Supervision; A History of the Early Years 1974–1997*. Cambridge: Cambridge University Press.

Kahn, C. and Roberds, W. (2001). 'The CLS Bank: A solution to the risks of international payments settlement?' *Carnegie-Rochester Conference Series on Public Policy*, 54, 1: 191–226.

Mourlon-Druol, E. (2015). '"Trust is good, control is better"': The Herstatt bank crisis and its implications for international regulatory reform'. *Business History* 57, 2: 311–334.

O'Sullivan, B. (2018) *From Crisis to Crisis: The Transformation of Merchant Banks 1914–1939*. Basingstoke: Palgrave.

Schenk, C.R. (2014). 'Summer in the city: Banking scandals of 1974 and the development of international banking supervision'. *English Historical Review* 129, 540: 1129–1156.

Schenk, C.R. (2017). 'Rogue trading at Lloyds Bank International, 1974: Operational risk in volatile markets'. *Business History Review* 91, 1: 105–128.

Schenk, C.R. (2021). 'The development of international correspondent banking in the USA 1970–1989'. *Global Correspondent Banking 1870–2000 Working Papers* 1, 1: 3–32.

Schenk, C.R. (2023). 'Telegraph to tether: Challenges in the global payments system and the struggle between private and public interests'. In Aliber, R.Z., Gudmundsson, M., and G. Zoega (eds), *Fault Lines after COVID-19*. Cham: Palgrave Macmillan, 279–302.

Scott, S. and Zachariadis, M. (2012). 'Origins and development of SWIFT, 1973–2009'. *Business History* 54, 3: 462–482.

Scott, S. and Zachariadis, M. (2014). *The Society for Worldwide Interbank Financial Telecommunications (SWIFT): Cooperative Governance for Network Innovation, Standards, and Community*. Abingdon, New York: Routledge.

Shirreff, David (1996) 'The fear that dares to speak its name', *Euromoney*, 329, September, 66–72.

Spero, J.E. (1980). *Failure of the Franklin National Bank: Challenge to the international banking system*. NY: Columbia University Press.

3

Narratives and memories of the International Debt Crisis from an Anglo-American and Mexican perspective

Bruno Pacchiotti and Giuseppe Telesca

Introduction

In August 1982 Mexico unilaterally declared a three-month moratorium on payment of its debt principal: the declaration is conventionally considered the beginning of the International Debt Crisis.[1] This crisis was the first global shock since the Great Depression of the 1930s and had the potential to bring down the international financial system, as several of the world's leading banks risked failure in case of Mexico's moratorium triggering a domino effect in other heavily indebted developing countries. While an agreement between these latter and the banks avoided a generalized financial collapse, it did not prevent economic pain in many of the debtor countries.

A lot has been written about the causes, consequences, and significance of the International Debt Crisis.[2] However, little attention has been devoted to the apparent oblivion of a crisis that had such a pivotal impact on the economic and political history of developing countries. The forgotten nature of the International Debt Crisis—this chapter will focus on the Latin American (Mexican, more specifically) side of this event—became palpable during the Global Financial Crisis of 2007–2008, which stimulated policy-makers, journalists, and academics to use

[1] The project leading to this application has received funding from the European Research Council (ERC) under the European Union's Horizon 2020 research and innovation programme (grant agreement No. 884910). The content of this document represents only the views of the MERCATOR team and is its sole responsibility. The European Commission does not accept any responsibility for use that may be made of the information it contains. The conception of this chapter, as well as its writing, is the result of the common research of the authors. Nevertheless, sections 'Narratives in the Financial Times and the Wall Street Journal' and 'The Financial Times and the Wall Street Journal' have been written and researched by Giuseppe Telesca, while sections 'Narratives in the Mexican press' and 'Mexican perspectives' have been written and researched by Bruno Pacchiotti.

[2] Chapter 4, by Edoardo Altamura and Juan Florez Zendejas provides an overview of the literature produced, on this topic, in the last four decades.

Bruno Pacchiotti and Giuseppe Telesca, *Narratives and memories of the International Debt Crisis from an Anglo-American and Mexican perspective*. In: *History, Memory, and the Return of Financial Crises After Bretton Woods*. Edited by: Youssef Cassis and Giuseppe Telesca, Oxford University Press.
DOI: 10.1093/9780198950158.003.0003

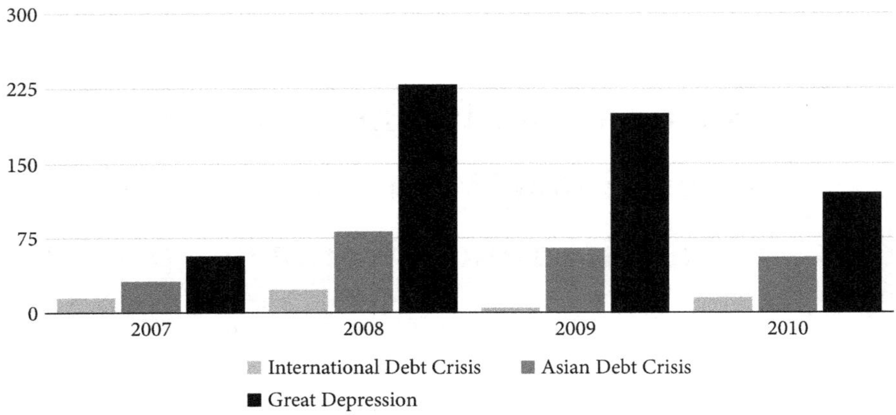

Figure 3.1 Number of FT and WSJ articles using the Great Depression, the International Debt Crisis, and the Asian crisis of the 1990s as historical analogies during the Global Financial Crisis

past crises as historical analogies.[3] If one looks at the way in which the *Financial Times* (henceforth FT) and the *Wall Street Journal* (henceforth WSJ) used past crises to draw lessons, or cautionary tales, at the height of the Global Financial Crisis, Figure 3.1 provides a measure of the International Debt Crisis oblivion.

This chapter looks at the way in which the Latin American side of the International Debt Crisis was narrated at first, and then (selectively) remembered, or even forgotten, from two different perspectives: the one of the FT and the WSJ, and the one of the Mexican press. The attention to the press, not immediately obvious when linked to the issue of memory, is motivated by the widely accepted idea that journalists write the first draft of history.[4] Journalists also utilize historical analogies to create connections, elaborate inferences, find short-hand explanations, establish a yardstick to measure the magnitude of the events they are recounting.[5] In this exercise, they become crucial 'gatekeepers of memory': they can move the memory that preserves the past as past (archive) into the actively circulated memory that keeps the past in the present (canon).[6]

As the chapter is interested in financial actors' perspectives, the focus of the analysis falls on the FT and the WSJ. The fact that these two newspapers, established in the late nineteenth century respectively in Britain and the United States, have supplied information to financial actors operating primarily in a western, particularly Anglo-American, sphere, introduces a bias in the way news—the International

[3] On the tendency of using historical analogies, and the risks this exercise involves, see Ghilani et al., 'Looking forward'.

[4] On the relation between journalism and memory see Zelizer and Tenenboim-Weinblatt, *Journalism and Memory*.

[5] Zelizer, 'Journalism's memory work'.

[6] Assmann, 'Canon and archive'.

Debt Crisis in our case—are told and remembered. The decision to look at the Mexican press represents an attempt to trace other narrative and memory perspectives on the International Debt Crisis. Two limitations affected this effort. Firstly, the availability of resources: while the FT and the WSJ have digitized their archives and made them available online, this is not the case with the Latin American press. Although some big media outlets have started to digitize their archives, online availability is limited and in person consultation of microfilms at national libraries is still required. An exception is represented by the digital database at the Mexican Centre for Economic Teaching and Research (henceforth CIDE), which offers a selection of newspaper articles concerning the 1980s debt crisis of the country. Unfortunately, the articles contained in the CIDE database don't go beyond 1993. A second limitation is linked to the Mexican political system of the period, with its authoritarian one-party system and the absence of a free press. We argue that while the Mexican government may have exerted some control over the narratives prevalent in the press, this latter represented the views and interests of Mexican elites, financial elites in particular, which were at times at odds with those in government and were published anyway.

Section 'The crisis' highlights the main causes and developments of the International Debt Crisis during the 1970s–1980s. Section 'Prevailing narratives of the debt crisis during the 1980s' reflects on how the contemporaries interpreted the crisis while it was happening and looks at the different narratives deployed to make sense of the events. Section 'The memory of the Latin America debt crisis through time' shows how the way in which the International Debt Crisis is remembered has changed over the last decades.

Two assumptions underpin this work. The first is that narratives, here defined as shared and collective stories through which people order reality, assign causality, and construct meaning, can be performative.[7] Historians need to take into serious account narrative representations as, besides giving meaning to events, they can influence their evolution.[8] The second assumption is that narratives not only help us to make sense of unfolding events but provide templates to recount the past—hence shaping both remembering and forgetting.[9] Historical narratives pick up selected events from the past and use them as historical analogies: in doing so, they create memory while creating amnesia at the same time.[10]

The crisis

The International Debt Crisis broke out in August 1982, when Mexico's Finance Minister Jesús Silva Herzog declared a debt moratorium, signalling that the country was incapable of servicing its external debt. The crisis had been years in

[7] Hansen, 'Making sense'; Hansen & Wadhwani, 'Can business history and anthropology'.
[8] MacKenzie, *An Engine*; Ho, *Liquidated*; Shiller, 'Narrative economics'.
[9] Bruner, *Acts of Meaning*, 56.
[10] Mordhorst, 'From counterfactual'.

the making. Taking the global context into account, three elements need to be highlighted: (i) the wave of financial innovations which started, already in the 1960s, with the Eurodollar and the Eurobond markets, and opened up financial markets;[11] (ii) the disruption of the international monetary system following the collapse of Bretton Woods;[12] (iii) the two oil shocks of the 1970s, which brought about a dramatic increase of the energy prices during that decade, causing a marked growth of inflation.[13] The credit boom towards the developing word accelerated as a consequence of the recycling of profits earned by oil producing countries after 1973. Middle Eastern producers, with small populations and underdeveloped financial markets, decided to overcome the little capacity to absorb earnings at home by recycling their 'petrodollars' through the big commercial banks of the industrialized world which, in turn, were looking for higher return to fend off the effects of stagflation. The increasing openness of financial markets allowed commercial banks to turn their deposits into loans to sovereign governments and foreign firms. In this context, loans from commercial banks to Third World countries went from $40 billion in 1975 to 160$ billion in 1980.[14] Many developing countries had pegged their currency to the dollar or other strong currencies after the collapse of Bretton Woods. Moreover, they could count on higher commodity prices and, in some cases (Mexico for instance), had themselves oil reserves to be utilized as collateral against default. All these factors rendered the recycling of petrodollars a theoretical risk-free game.[15]

Towards the end of the 1970s two events undermined developing countries' capacity of repaying their creditors. On the one hand, commodity prices started to collapse, thus reducing revenues for their producers. On the other hand, a policy change in the Federal Reserve (Fed), decided in 1979 by its new appointed Chairman, Paul Volcker, and aimed at containing US internal inflation, translated into higher interest rates and an increase in investor demand for dollar securities. It also produced a recession in the American economy, which further deepened the collapse of commodity prices. These factors rendered more costly for developing countries servicing their external debt.[16] After Peru's (three times) and Bolivia's defaults, between 1976 and 1980, after Poland's 1981 announcement to the creditors that it could not maintain its debt payments, the International Monetary Fund (IMF) reported, at the end of the same year, that 32 countries were in arrears on their debt. Mexican's announcement of a moratorium on its debt in 1982, followed by Brazil's and Argentina's struggles, created a crisis defined by Volcker an episode 'without precedents in the post-war world'.[17]

[11] Schenk, 'The origins of the Eurodollar market'.
[12] Schenk, *International Economic Relations*, 50–53.
[13] Thompson, *Oil and the Western Economic Crisis*.
[14] Jones, *British Multinational Banking*, 550.
[15] Gerber, *A Great Deal*, 92–98.
[16] Vargas-Machuca, 'The external debt crisis', 85–87.
[17] Palmer et al., 'The debt-bomb'.

The International Debt Crisis was initially seen as a liquidity crisis and the USA, international institutions, and commercial banks concentrated their attention on the restoration of capital flows. The commercial banks, saddled with bad loans, were spared the consequences of their reckless lending based on the conviction that—to put it with the words of the then president of Citicorp, Walter Wriston—'countries don't go bankrupt'.[18] The exposition of the nine major US commercial banks towards debtor countries in 1982, for instance, was equal to 255% of their capital.[19] To avoid a systemic banking collapse, the value of commercial banks' bad loans was not written down until sufficient reserves against losses were built. As the US banking law required banks to take losses on loans when they fell behind in interest payments, an effort was made to keep debtor countries paying the interests on their loans. In the meantime, efforts by debtor countries to cut spending often resulted in deficit increases, via the decline in tax revenues due to the recession. With borrowing unavailable and tax revenues down, annual inflation rates during the 1980s skyrocketed: 65.1% on average in Mexico; 330.2% in Brazil; 437.6% in Argentina.[20]

A first acknowledgment that things were not heading in the right direction arrived at the end of 1985, when the US Treasury secretary, James Baker, announced a plan for restructuring developing countries debt accompanied by larger loans granted for longer timeframes. The Baker Plan did not produce significant results; besides conjunctural factors—the decline of oil prices, for instance, which affected the recovery of debtor countries such as Mexico—it did nothing to address the solvency problems experienced by some of the debtor countries. In the second half of the 1980s, the awareness that economic growth in developing countries could not be restored without some form of debt relief gained ground. The 1989 Brady Plan, named after the new US Treasury secretary Nicholas Brady, combined some forms of debt relief for debtor countries with guarantees, for the creditors, to receive their remaining loans. Before qualifying for debt leniency, debtor countries had to commit to structural reforms, namely the privatization and deregulation of the public sector and measures of trade liberalization.[21]

Prevailing narratives of the debt crisis during the 1980s

The International Debt Crisis was an extended event, a complex and ongoing process which lasted for years.[22] The multifaced nature of the crisis created ideal conditions for narrating this story, while it was happening, from several perspectives. Were the main responsible of the crisis the debtor countries, for running large

[18] Cited in Cassis, *Crises and Opportunities*, 41.
[19] Cline, *International Debt Reexamined*, 73–75.
[20] Vargas-Machuca, 'The external debt crisis', 91.
[21] Gerber, *A Great Deal*, 103–108.
[22] Lee et al., 'When a historical analogy'.

fiscal deficits, perpetuating unsound domestic economic policies, and deferring structural reforms? Or were the creditor countries, or international institutions, guilty because they were forcing debt repayment to preserve the stability of the financial system? And what were the responsibilities of the United States, with the Treasury running a large twin deficit and the Fed, under Volcker, pursuing dollar stabilization without any concern for the effects of this policy on the international economy? Last but not least, there was the position of the commercial banks, which had lent recklessly to developing countries from the mid-1970s onwards. It is time to explore how these narratives took shape in the debate of the 1980s, both on the pages of the FT and the WSJ and on the Mexican press.

Narratives in the *Financial Times* and the *Wall Street Journal*

In the months preceding and following August 1982 central banks and international institutions showed a certain degree of awareness and concern about the systemic risk that an uncontrolled debt crisis posed to the international banking system. The Bank of England, for instance, embarked on an exercise—later called *Apocalypse Now*, after the film by Francis Ford Coppola—in which potential defaults by major sovereign borrowers were simulated to see how these events could affect the global financial stability.[23] Between 1981 and 1982 *Apocalypse Now* was presented to, and discussed by, central bank officials at the Bank of International Settlements. A letter accompanying one iteration of this exercise stated:

> The attached note explores how a combination of international and domestic losses could bring about the insolvency of a large US bank. *Although some quite strong assumptions are needed, they are not implausible. Although the banks are not named, the case studies are based on the balance sheets of real banks.*[24]

With the exception of the weeks following Mexico moratorium declaration, one would struggle to detect any sense of peril for the international banking system in the financial papers. Little reference was made, for instance, to previous debt defaults which had affected developing countries, Latin America in particular. The last wave of defaults went back to the 1920s–1930s and was reminiscent of the Great Depression and the connected systemic banking crises. Yet, references to this period were rare in the 1980s. This was due, according to the few journalists evoking the 1930s in relation to the International Debt Crisis, to the fact that the sovereign defaults of the interwar years were mainly seen as the consequence of political obligations—war reparations in particular. This interpretation mistakenly diverted the attention from the sovereign defaults on purely commercial debts

[23] On *Apocalypse Now* see Schenk, 'The past as practice or parable?', 94–102.

[24] Kent, P.H. 'Apocalypse now or the anatomy of a collapse of a large US bank'. Bank of England Archives, 3A143/7, 16 June 1982. Emphasis added.

which played a crucial role in the defaults of the interwar years.[25] Another reason for this lack of reference to the past was related to the lending mechanism and the ways in which defaults were settled in the 1920s–1930s. In the 1980s banks, not bondholders, were behind the inflow of capital to the developing world. This mechanism implied a concentration of risk in the balance sheets of top commercial banks, whose difficulties posed a systemic financial threat. Survival of commercial banks was thus a focal concern of creditor-countries which, not surprisingly, became more involved in the debt-settlement process than in the interwar years.[26]

Of course there were instances of criticism towards international institutions (IMF and World Bank), central banks, creditor countries, and commercial banks, but the narrative focus of the International Debt Crisis during the 1980s remained on the debtor countries. The real reason why the systemic risk that the International Debt Crisis posed to the banking system was not often evoked, may have been exposed by financier George Soros, in a paper he wrote for Morgan Stanley a year after the crisis had begun, when the worst seemed to be over:

> Discussion of the international debt problem is muted by fear that it may touch off a renewed crisis of confidence. The fear is not unfounded (…) but the attempt to sustain confidence (…) hinders proper understanding [of the crisis].[27]

The 10th anniversary of the Mexico's moratorium declaration represented a first milestone to assess lessons and legacies of the crisis. On 30 July 1992, the FT devoted a special report to the International Debt Crisis. The paper's Latin America editor, Stephen Fidler, summed up the spirit of the report writing that 'seldom have economic fortunes changed so rapidly: from being regarded as a financial disaster Latin America [was] now seen as a hot financial property', and some countries of the region were seen as potential 'tigers' (a reference to the buoyant performances of some Asian economies in the 1980s, early 1990s).[28] Among the people interviewed were José Ángel Gurría, Mexican Secretary for financial affairs and a leading negotiator for his country in the 1980s;[29] Jacques de la Rosière, then Governor of the Banque de France but IMF managing director from 1978 to 1986;[30] Paul Volcker;[31] and the vice-president of Citicorp, William Rhodes.[32]

[25] Kaletsky, 'When debtors said no'.

[26] Marsh, 'Crisis'; Kaletsky, 'A borrowers' market'; Fidler, 'History lesson'. One of the few WSJ references to the 1920s–1930s in connection with the International Debt Crisis is due to economic historian Harold James, 'The neverending tale'. See also Eichengreen and Lindert, *The International Debt Crisis*, 12–41.

[27] Soros, G. (1983). 'The International Debt problem: diagnosis and prognosis', July, 1.

[28] Fidler, 'Bouncing back'. This perspective will be later be confirmed by the World Bank's report *Global Economic Prospects and the Developing Countries*, duly commented with emphasis in an FT leader, 'Landing'.

[29] 'For us Mexicans'.

[30] Leader, 'Latin America debt'.

[31] Fidler, 'I didn't count'.

[32] Nicoll, 'Fear'.

In spite of the admission that both banks and creditor countries had committed mistakes,[33] and that 'debt relief since the onset' would have reduced the depth and length of the crisis,[34] the overall tone of the report exuded confidence. Section 'The Financial Times and the Wall Street Journal' shows that this reading of the International Debt Crisis didn't change much in the FT and the WSJ, at least until the early 2000s.

Narratives in the Mexican press

As already explained in the introduction, we decided to limit our analysis to the Mexican press, when looking at Latin America, for both methodological and practical considerations. Mexico was at the epicentre of the crisis, as it declared the moratorium in 1982 and was, at times, the country with the highest level of external debt within the developing world. In practical terms, the Mexican press was partially available in digitized form, with the already mentioned CIDE database giving access to articles concerning the external debt of the country from 1886 to 1993. The research was conducted looking at 13 of the 49 CIDE folders, which contain more than 1,000 articles published between the late 1970s and the early 1990s.

It has been already underlined that the authoritarian regime—the *one-party system* through which the Institutional Revolutionary Party (PRI) ruled the country—meant that the country lacked a truly free press for much of the twentieth century, and certainly for the 1970s–1980s. There are good reasons to contend, however, that Mexico's non-democratic regime was more open and less repressive than many other dictatorships in the region.[35] More specifically:

> the flexibility and effectiveness of [Mexico's] style of media control [...] permitted ideological pluralism and occasional criticism of the government without compromising official control of the press. As with other institutions in Mexico, control over the press was achieved mainly through co-optation [...] one of the most powerful elements of government control was the confluence of interests between media owners and PRI leaders. Media owners wanted, above all, a hospitable business environment in which they could prosper economically and protect their status as members of the country's elite.[36]

It can thus be argued that the press views on the country's external debt and its position vis-à-vis its creditors, represented not only the government's official line, but also the opinion and interests of the country's elites. Moreover, these views were often aligned with the interests of the transnational financial elites.

[33] Nicoll, 'Solution'.
[34] Leader, 'Lessons'.
[35] Wallis, 'The media and democratic change', 118.
[36] Lawson, 'Media control', 26 and 28.

Interestingly, however, the crisis itself was one of the events that gave rise to a more pluralistic debate—especially with regards to print media[37]—and, as the crisis progressed, a few but growing discordant voices, developing a more nationalist approach to it, gained space in the Mexican media.

In the period preceding the crisis—the 'formative' years—the ever-increasing size of the country's debt (as well as those of other Latin American or developing countries) stood out as the main topic of discussion in the Mexican press. It should be noticed that the analyses of Mexico's debt preceding 1982 placed their emphasis on domestic politics and on how the Mexican government was managing the debt. Critical remarks and complaints towards creditor countries, banks, and international financial institutions were rare in this phase.[38] This approach changed in the years after the moratorium declaration, when the role and responsibility of international financial actors such as the IMF and the World Bank were often highlighted.[39]

While the headlines consistently reported the growing size of the country's debt,[40] a reader of the Mexican press would be forgiven not to worry about its sustainability during the 'formative' years. In this phase, in fact, there was full confidence in Mexico's capacity to meet its obligations. Despite mounting concerns over the size of Mexico's debt and the cost of servicing it, before 1982 Mexico was portrayed as having very solid credit standings in the international capital markets. Central to this narrative was the endorsement of international bankers, who depicted Mexico as the poster boy for other developing countries. During a press conference given in June 1977, for instance, a group of British bankers which included Dennis Mitchell, the then vice-president of Lloyd's Bank, and Jasper Hollom, deputy governor of the Bank of England, argued that 'Mexico [had] managed its external debt exceptionally well', and for this reason 'it maintain[ed] an excellent reputation in the international markets'.[41] For Antonio Ortiz Mena, the then president of the Interamerican Development Bank, 'international financial organizations [had] full confidence that Mexico [would] overcome its current problems'.[42] Rolf Kübler, a Credit Suisse executive, was cited saying that 'Swiss bankers [had] full confidence in Mexico and [had] no doubt' about its imminent 'economic takeoff'.[43]

[37] For a detailed discussion on the evolution and opening of Mexican media see Lawson, 'Media control'.

[38] See, for instance: Lozano, 'Ya estuvo suave'; Colmenares Paramo, 'Algo sobre la deuda externa'; Navarrete, 'Deuda externa, Caballo de Troya'.

[39] See, for instance: Barbosa, 'Convendría diferir el pago'; Stephens García, 'Contra el débito'; Aviles 'Más allá de la deuda'.

[40] This was done by either reporting on the actual amount of the debt in US dollars in nominal terms or in relation to the country's GDP. See, for instance: Gómez Bulnes, 'La deuda externa del país es de 20.241 millones de dólares'; Serrano, 'La deuda externa de México es de 30 mil millones de dólares'; Nava, 'Duplicó en 4 años la deuda externa respecto al PIB'.

[41] Rangel, 'Sólido crédito mexicano'.

[42] De Cervantes, 'México no necesita'.

[43] Castellanos, 'Renegoció México su deuda'.

A second theme of the years preceding 1982 concerned the objectives towards which the funds received were directed. Predictably, given the state of the Mexican press at the time, international credit was said to be used wisely by competent technocrats in government to boost economic development and unleash the country's productive forces, particularly its oil sector and the iron and steel industry. *El Universal*, for instance, in February 1981 reported the following declaration by the president of Bank of Montreal:

> It is not really important how large the external debt of a country is, but rather how it is managed, and one of the most capable countries in managing its debt has been Mexico.[44]

While, given the lack of domestic savings, there was a consensus on the need for international credit, seen as the only means by which Mexico could aim at reaching a superior stage of development, a divide in the press emerged between those who were unreservedly in favour of international credit and those who accepted it as a necessary evil.[45] It must be added that a few articles criticized government policies and cast doubts on whether the resources were being used in the national interest or wasted, instead, on growing the State apparatus and other unproductive sectors.[46]

A third theme in this phase was the potential loss of sovereignty that the country's growing external debt entailed. Articles exploring this risk suggested that Mexico should have aimed at increasing domestic savings to further its development. Interestingly, this line of thought was not only supported by those critical of the government but also shared by some government officials and international financiers (although, in this case, the inevitability of having to resort to international credit in the short-term remained unquestioned).[47]

If talks about debt renegotiation and debt restructuring were rarely surfacing before the moratorium declaration, after 1982 they become a reality increasingly present in the Mexican press' headlines. It has been previously said that the Baker Plan was agreed in 1985 and, after its rather unsuccessful implementation, replaced by the Brady Plan in 1989. The debt renegotiation and restructuring process became then the salient theme of the post-1982 period, bringing about a number of different narratives: some in continuity with the 'formative' years, many in sharp contrast with them.

[44] Hewett, 'México, de los más hábiles'.

[45] For examples of articles that embrace international credit, see: Flores Zavala, 'La anarquía administrativa'; Cárdenas, 'La deuda externa solo es peligrosa' or El Heraldo 'Para reducir la deuda externa'. For articles that considers international credit as a necessary evil see: Huerta Cruz, 'Mayor control de la deuda'.

[46] See, for instance: Llamosa, 'Igual a la de todos'; Reachi, 'Doce años de deudas'.

[47] See, for instance: González, 'La deuda externa puede pagarse'; Rangel, 'México no necesita renegociar'; Castellanos, 'El endeudamiento exterior'.

The narrative in continuity with the pre-1982 period was that portraying Mexico as an example to be followed by other developing countries for the way in which it was renegotiating its debt, and the willingness it was showing to honour its commitments to international finance. In this sense *El Día*, reporting from Washington, wrote in 1986:

> The IMF and World Bank annual conference ended today with optimism, which for Latin America translates into the possibility that the agreement between Mexico and the international commercial banks could be imitated by other countries.[48]

At the same time, tensions in the negotiations emerged and a parallel narrative started surfacing, in which international organizations such as the IMF and the World Bank, creditor countries and international banks were at least partially responsible for the crisis. For instance, an editorial from *El Dia* argued, in 1985, that:

> In recent years, the country has been subjected to constant manipulation of interest rates that unilaterally increase profits for a group of bankers and obligations for the Mexican people. In this circumstance, which has its origin not only in the use of financing by Mexico, but also in the need of international banks to place their capital in order to obtain large profits, the perspective of the Cartagena Consensus effectively represents an alternative for all indebted countries as a whole.[49]

The search for radical solutions to the Mexican external debt problem was increasingly voiced in the Mexican press in the second half of the 1980s. At times it was supported, in cautious terms, by established political leaders warning that no more sacrifices in the name of the external debt could be asked of the Mexican people. This was the case of Miguel de la Madrid, President of Mexico from 1982 to 1988, who often recalled that his country was willing to 'pay only according to its capacity',[50] or of Eliseo Mendoza Barrueto, Mexico's Congress President, who addressed directly the former US President, Jimmy Carter, and highlighted that 'Mexicans [were] not willing to negotiate anything that would go beyond [their] national dignity'.[51] Even more radical calls for payment of the external debt to be suspended emerged in this phase, with *El Universal* writing, in May 1986:

[48] El Día, 'El convenio mexicano-banqueros'.
[49] El Día, '¿Todo para pagar la deuda externa?'.
[50] Sotomayor, 'Condición para pagar'.
[51] Aviles, 'Nada que esté por encima'. This line was echoed by other political figures throughout the subcontinent, such as Venezuelan ex-President Carlos Andres Pérez, who stated that Latin American governments 'were willing to pay the debt, but not at the cost of sacrificing the economic and social development of our countries' ('El pago de la deuda no debe ser a costa del bienestar general: Pérez').

> Until the government understands (…) that the only way forwards is the suspension of debt payments and to stop oil sales, we will remain tied to the northern imperial giant, and subjected to its political and economic interests.[52]

Finally, although less present in the Mexican press, the issue of international cooperation was at times underlined in connection with the so-called years of the 'Cartagena consensus', when Latin American leaders timidly attempted to organize a united response to the issue of the external debt in the subcontinent.[53] A support to these attempts was voiced in some of the articles analysed.[54] This, in spite of the fact that the cooperative approach was not welcomed in international financial circles, which lobbied for renegotiations taking place on a case-by-case basis.

The memory of the Latin America debt crisis through time

The complex nature of the International Debt Crisis created the conditions from narrating it from several perspectives. Had the International Debt Crisis been a crucial determinant in the move from state capitalism to market-led economies in developing and, particularly, Latin American economies? Or had it been an experience of loss, with restructuring programmes taking their toll on debtor countries and, as a result, provoking inflation, unemployment, and a freeze of per capita incomes? And was the International Debt Crisis destined to be remembered as an event which had the potential to bring down the international banking system and from which the banking sector had something to learn? This section provides an assessment of the ways in which the FT and the WSJ have remembered the crisis of the 1980s from its 10th anniversary onwards. It then moves to the Mexican perspective.

The Financial Times and *the Wall Street Journal*

The keyword search for the International Debt Crisis in the FT and the WSJ resulted in 503 articles for the period from 1 August 1992 to 31 December 2019.[55] 2019 was chosen as *terminus ad quem* of the research to avoid any juxtaposition with the Covid-19 pandemic, a global traumatic event which burst at the beginning of 2020 and made, at least temporarily, previous financial crises pale in comparison.

[52] Castillo, 'Los síntomas de la dependencia'.

[53] O'Connell (1988) 'La coordinación de los deudores latinoamericanos: el consenso de Cartagena y el grupo de los ocho'; Roett (1985) 'Latin America's Response to the Debt Crisis'.

[54] See, for instance, El día, '¿Todo para pagar la deuda externa?'; Gomez, 'Se insiste'; Negron, 'Pedirá México'; Stephens García, 'Contra el débito'; López, 'Se manifiesta'.

[55] The keywords utilized were International Debt Crisis; Latin America Debt Crisis; Debt Crisis and, within 10 words, 1980s; Debt Crisis and, within 10 words, Developing Countries; Debt Crisis and, within 10 words, Third World.

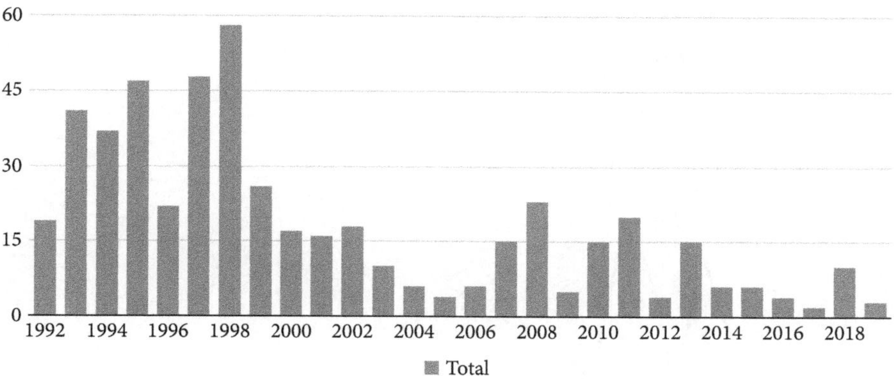

Figure 3.2 Yearly distribution of FT and WSJ articles mentioning the IDC (aggregate): August 1992–December 2019

The peak of the crisis recollection in Figure 3.2 corresponds to the second half of the 1990s: 47 articles in 1995, in the aftermath of the crisis of the Mexican peso; 48 articles in 1997 and 58 in 1998, when the Asian Debt Crisis, the Long-Term Capital Management's collapse and Russia's default renewed the interest in the International Debt Crisis. References to this event went decidedly down in the early 2000s, while slightly increasing during the Global Financial Crisis and the ensuing Eurozone crisis. This return of memory, however, did not match the levels of the 1990s, nor the levels of recollection of other crises in the same period (as shown by Figure 3.1). In other words, while the recollection of the International Debt Crisis between 1992 and 2019 goes through ebbs and flows, its overall pattern is declining. It can thus be said that this crisis has been forgotten by the FT and the WSJ: an observation even truer for all developing countries beyond Latin America, which rarely feature in the sample.

When the data are disaggregated, Figure 3.3 shows that the FT mentions the International Debt Crisis nearly twice more than the WSJ (330 versus 173 articles).

While a granular evaluation of this sample will form the object of future contributions, it appears clear that the engagement of the two papers with the memory of the International Debt Crisis is generally shallow: recalling the crisis often constitutes an afterthought of the news story.[56] The engagement with the memory of the International Debt Crisis becomes more meaningful in periods of crisis. It is time to see how, exploring the themes and historical narratives which accompanied the evocation of the International Debt Crisis.

The optimistic mood of the already mentioned 1992 FT special report on the International Debt Crisis, didn't change significantly in the following years when,

[56] Barbie Zelizer argues that this type of articles simply indulge memory. She distinguished these pieces from the ones that invite memory, where the reference to the past is used as a term of comparison with the present, and the articles that necessitate memory, which are exclusively devoted to the past ('Journalism's memory work', 83).

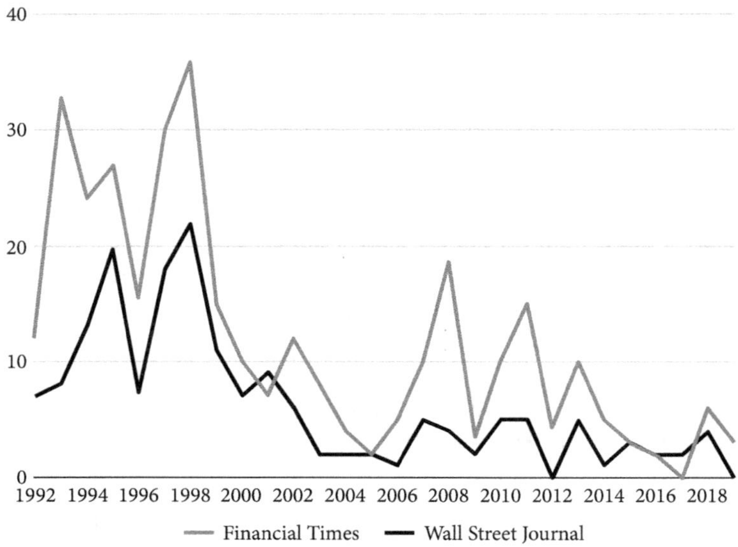

Figure 3.3 Yearly distribution of articles mentioning the IDC in the FT and the WSJ (disaggregate)

in line with the book of William Cline, endorsed by Volcker and de la Rosière,[57] the FT and the WSJ tended to identify the roots of the International Debt Crisis in dysfunctional economic systems marred by large state intervention; gave little weight to external factors (collapse of commodity prices; 'Volcker shock'); saw the drastic austerity measures implemented in many developing countries during the 1980s as a necessary evil to restore economic efficiency and get rid of corrupt and, often, dictatorial regimes.[58] The recollection of the crisis at this stage centred on a new Latin American leadership capable of erasing inflation and balancing the books,[59] creating the conditions for the return of foreign investors[60] and conjugating economic openness with democracy.[61]

The 1994 crisis of the Mexican peso intensified the references to the International Debt Crisis while slightly darkening the picture drew in the previous years.[62] What remained clear was that developing countries were in need of further 'structural reforms',[63] as there was no way back from the transformations introduced in the previous decade.[64] The paradoxical effect of the Asian Debt Crisis was that the developing countries involved in the crisis of the 1980s—particularly

[57] Cline, *International Debt Reexamined*.
[58] Kamm, 'Argentine "miracle"'; Leader, 'Latin America's success'; Rhodes, 'The Latin Tigers'.
[59] Leader, 'A return?'.
[60] Fidler, 'Boom mood'.
[61] Fidler, 'Trouble'.
[62] Leader, 'The picture darkens'; Carrington, 'Debt crisis'.
[63] Fidler, 'The patient sticks'.
[64] See, for instance, Moffett et al., 'No looking back'.

the Latin American ones, which were usually on the naughty step when it came to economic management—became, for a brief period, a virtuous example for Asian countries.[65]

A change of the mood started emerging at the turn of the century. While Moses Naim, *Foreign Affairs*' editor, underlined that the rise in democracy and multilateralism of the last two decades bode well for the future of the international economy,[66] fears of a repeat of something similar to the International Debt Crisis became more palpable,[67] and a few articles, particularly in the FT, acknowledged that the 'structural reforms' implemented to overcome the International Debt Crisis remained unpopular in the countries that had adopted, or had been obliged to adopt, them. Two episodes—Argentina's 2001 default[68] and the 2002 election of the left-leaning, Luiz Inácio Lula da Silva, in Brazil[69]—gave a contribution to this change of sentiment. The International Debt Crisis, in the early 2000s, was no longer an uncontested tale of transformation of the countries submitted to the IMF cures but became a story of painful adaptation as well. This new historical narrative, however, went hand in hand with a decline of the memory of the International Debt Crisis and was accompanied by the warning that abandonment of the 'sound' post-crisis policies would result in a rerun of the 1980s 'lost decade'.[70] If doubts about the effectiveness and fairness of the IMF's and World Bank's interventions in the crisis started to be voiced in this phase, these critical evaluations would mostly materialize after 2008.

The International Debt Crisis has been discussed so far as an event that slipped under the radar of the FT and the WSJ in the space of two decades. But beyond being forgotten, this crisis seems to be misremembered as well. To make use of the wording of an early study on the International Debt Crisis focused on Latin America, one would struggle to find in its recollection 'the supply side of the story', with its potential to bring down the international banking system.[71] Only 42 of the 503 articles in the sample make some meaningful, if superficial, reference to the potential risk of a systemic banking crisis during the International Debt Crisis. Martin Wolf, future chief economic commentator of the FT, already referred to this risk during the Asian Debt Crisis of the late 1990s.[72] In the same period, a WSJ piece hinted at the 'supply side' of the International Debt Crisis when, talking about Citigroup, explained that the relatively low exposition of this and other US banks towards the Asian countries was a consequence of the lessons learned during the 1980s crisis.[73] To be fair to the FT and the WSJ, also the academic literature, which

[65] Fidler, 'Might Asia lose?'.
[66] Naim, 'Lessons'.
[67] Luhnow, 'Argentina intensifies defense'; Leader, 'Latin America turns'.
[68] Lapper, 'Back'.
[69] Lapper, 'Piling on'.
[70] Lapper, 'Latin America recalls'.
[71] Devlin, *Debt and Crisis*.
[72] Wolf, 'Why banks are dangerous'. See also, Id. 'Frail orthodoxy'.
[73] Steinmetz et al., 'As a global behemoth'.

in the 1980s had considered the 'irrational exuberance' of banks as a cause of the crisis, ignored this aspect of the International Debt Crisis for two decades to then rediscovering it after 2008.[74]

More references to the 'supply side' of the 1980s crisis emerged at the high of the Global Financial Crisis, when the FT, generally more inclined to establish a relation between the International Debt Crisis and a potential systemic banking crisis, devoted a few articles to the issue of how to measure the financial institutions' losses. The rules existing in 2008, according to which 'companies [were] expected to report the value of their holdings in as "current" a manner as possible', risked making the crisis worse. The International Debt Crisis provided a lesson because, as we have seen above, the awareness that 'the world biggest banks would have been insolvent if their loan books had been valued realistically',[75] pushed regulatory authorities to agree on a tacit deal: 'that the auditors would not be too tough on the banks for a few years—as long as these institutions devised a strategy to deal with their bad loans'.[76]

If the difficulties of the big American and European banks in the early 1980s were acknowledged in a few articles, (western) banks' recklessness and responsibilities for the International Debt Crisis emerged even more rarely. An exception to this rule was again Martin Wolf, who during the 2008 crisis quoted a paper of Carmen Reinhard and Kenneth Rogoff which compared the recycling of petrodollars towards developing countries that preceded the International Debt Crisis to the recycling of surplus savings 'to a developing country that exist[ed] within the US: the subprime borrowers'.[77] Further references to banks responsibility in the 1980s emerged during the Euro crisis, when the European banks' exposure to Greece, Portugal, Ireland, Italy, and Spain was compared to the Western banks' exposure towards the developing countries three decades prior. Both exposures were the outcome of 'a sustained period of easy credit' and of 'debts issued in a currency over which borrowing countries had no control';[78] both posed the risk of a new 'lost decade'—this time for the peripheral countries of the Eurozone.[79] The WSJ made even more rarefied references to the responsibilities of western banks during the International Debt Crisis. A 2010 article, evoking a lesson from the 1980s, called for the Eurozone banks in difficulty to be allowed to default—hence making the banks sharing the pain of their own (bad) choices. According to the journalist, bailing out banks, an exercise which has been repeated since the 1980s, was bad economics and bad politics.[80]

[74] See Chapter 4 in this book.

[75] Plender, 'Financial crisis presents'. See also Wolf, 'Asia's revenge'; Guha, 'Two challenges'.

[76] Hughes and Tett, 'An unforgiving eye'.

[77] Reinhart, C. and K. Rogoff. 'Is the 2007 subprime financial crisis so different?', quoted in Wolf, 'Challenges ahead'.

[78] Rathbone, 'Eurozone'.

[79] Soros, 'Germany can avoid'.

[80] Davis, 'Amid Irish aid'.

Mexican perspectives

As we explained in the introduction and in section 'Narratives in the Mexican press', having to rely on a non-systematic reading of the sources,[81] we cannot say whether, as in the case of the FT and the WSJ, the International Debt Crisis has been forgotten by the Mexican press—though we would tend to exclude that a phenomenon still present in everyday life and conversation had been totally put behind.[82]

Before proceeding it would be useful to add a note on how the Mexican press evolved throughout this period. Several factors rendered the press in Mexico, particularly print media, progressively more independent in the last two decades of the twentieth century[83]. Already with the financial crisis of 1982, the government's ability to handle the economy was called into question. Ironically, some of the very reforms triggered by the crisis—such as privatization and market liberalization—had the unintended consequence of fostering a more independent press. This development played a significant role in Mexico's democratic transition in the 1990s, culminating in December 2000 with the inauguration of Vicente Fox's presidency, which marked the end of 71 years of one-party rule.

Moving back to the historical narratives, in the early 1990s there was certainly a sense of elation and optimism that both the Mexican press and the FT and the WSJ shared regarding the (fairly) successful restructuring of the external debt and Mexico's rediscovered attractiveness as a hub for international investments. The headlines of the CIDE pointed out to the reduction of the country's debt, both in nominal terms and as a proportion of GDP.[84] Mexican elites' euphoric mood was epitomized by the words of Ángel Gurría, Secretary for financial affairs, triumphally declaring that '[Mexico] success is an objective reality. It's in the numbers!'.[85]

Yet, despite this shared enthusiasm, the patterns of recollection of the International Debt Crisis are significantly dissimilar. The previous subsection has shown that the FT and the WSJ, when recollecting the International Debt Crisis during the 1990s, emphasized the governments' interference in the economic life of developing countries. The Mexican press, on the contrary, put more weight on the exogenous shocks and the international financial system responsibilities to explain the crisis. This approach was in continuity with what has been observed with reference to the immediate aftermath of the 1982 crisis, when the Mexican press

[81] We have searched for keywords 'crisis de la deuda' and '1982', which returned a total of 199 articles from January 1997 (the first year for which there are records in the database) to 31 December 2019.

[82] As recently as 2020, the movement *Promotora Nacional por la Suspensión del Pago de la Deuda Pública* was established to raise awareness about Mexico's external debt issue. In late 2024, a letter was sent from the movement to newly elected President Claudia Sheinbaum, calling for a debate on the matter. See https://nomasdeudapublica.org [last access on 16 February 2025].

[83] For a detailed discussion on the evolution and opening of Mexican media see Lawson, 'Media control'.

[84] See, for instance: Mares, 'Bajó a 2.3% del PIB', which triumphally proclaimed that the payments for the external debt 'came down to 2.3% of GDP' a year after Mexico's restructuring with the international banks.

[85] Duncan, 'Descarta José Ángel Gurría nueva crisis'. This was the same Gurría we have encountered in a FT interview for the 1992 special report on the International Debt Crisis.

called into question—more quickly and emphatically than the western financial press—the role played by international financial actors in the making of the International Debt Crisis.

Furthermore, while during the 1990s the FT and the WSJ considered the policies implemented in Mexico and elsewhere during the previous decade as a necessary evil to reanimate a dysfunctional economy, analyses of their detrimental effects on the country's economic, social, and political development could be prevalently found in the Mexican press. In the words of Ifigenia Martínez, the first woman ever to become dean of UNAM, School of Economics:

> The adjustment and structural change programs of the IMF-WB to link indebted countries to the growth of exports and the flow of private capital have led to greater dependence and vulnerability of emerging economies, a slower pace of development and a spectacular increase in poverty.[86]

And if such a radical stance was not a complete surprise, as it was coming from the pages of *El Universal*—a paper which was on the left of the political spectrum—what is striking is that similar opinions were hosted in established, market friendly newspapers like *El Financiero*.[87] This tendency would become even more evident in the aftermath of the Global Financial Crisis.[88]

Conclusion

By choosing to explore the way in which the FT and the WSJ have narrated and then remembered the International Debt Crisis, this chapter has prioritized the memory of financial actors operating primarily in a creditor/advanced economies. To balance this bias and explore a different perspective on the International Debt Crisis, we looked at the press of one of the countries most affected by the crisis.

Whereas a systematic analysis of what the Mexican press has produced since the early 1990s was not possible, through a more qualitative analysis we found significant differences in the ways in which the International Debt Crisis was first narrated and then recalled. The Mexican press developed a distinct narrative of the crisis in the 1980s and elaborated a different memory of it, later. What is more, also the FT and the WSJ diverged in their recollection of the crisis, both in quantitative and in qualitative terms. The only period in which all historical narratives on the International Debt Crisis seemed to converge was the limited window of the early 1990s, between the (fairly) successful Baker plan and the crisis of the Mexican peso. This confirms the results of research based on newspapers datasets and on methods from natural language processing, which demonstrate how periods of economic expansion are positively associated with the consolidation of narratives,

86 Martínez, 'Prosperidad y privilegios de Estados Unidos'.
87 Damián, 'Échenle la culpa al Congreso'.
88 Damián, 'Lamentable declaración'; Ramírez, 'Indicador político'.

while periods of economic contraction bring about the fragmentation of narratives into competing explanations.[89]

With some (rare) exceptions, the role played by the big (western) commercial banks in the making of the International Debt Crisis, and the systemic risk they faced in the aftermath of the 1982 moratorium declaration, went unnoticed both in the FT and the WSJ, which saw the predicaments of developing countries (nearly) exclusively through the lenses of a debt crisis, and in the Mexican press, more focused on the responsibilities of international actors such as the IMF, the World Bank, and the United States.

All in all, this work confirms that that the memory of financial crises is an elusive and selective process, which takes different forms depending on who evokes memory, and when, in which context, and against what, memory is evoked.[90]

References

Assmann, A. (2008). 'Canon and archive'. In A. Erll and A. Nünning (eds), *Cultural and Memory Studies. An International and Interdisciplinary Handbook*, Berlin-New York: Walter de Gruyter, 97–107.

Bertsch, C., Hull, I., and Zhang, X. (2021). 'Narrative fragmentation and the business cycle'. *Economic Letters* 201 (2021): art. n. 109783.

Bruner, J. (1990). *Acts of Meaning: Four Lectures on Mind and Culture.* Harvard: Harvard University Press.

Cassis, Y. (2011). *Crises and Opportunities. The Shaping of Modern Finance.* Oxford: Oxford University Press.

Cline, W.R. (1995). *International Debt Reexamined.* Washington DC: Institute for International Economics.

Devlin, R. (1989). *Debt and Crisis in Latin America. The Supply Side of the Story.* Princeton: Princeton University Press.

Eichengreen, B. and Lindert, P.H. (1989). *The International Debt Crisis in Historical Perspective.* Cambridge–London: Cambridge University Press.

Gerber, J. (2019). *A Great Deal of Ruin: Financial Crises since 1929.* Cambridge: Cambridge University Press.

Ghilani, D., Luminet, O., Erb, H.P., Flassbeck, C., Rosoux, V., Tames, I., and Klein, O. (2017). 'Looking forward to the past: an interdisciplinary discussion on the use of historical analogies and their effects'. *Memory Studies* 10, 3: 274–285.

Hansen, P.H. (2012). 'Making sense of financial crisis and scandal: A Danish Bank failure in the era of finance capitalism'. *Enterprise & Society* 13, 3: 672–706.

Hansen, P.H. and Wadhwani, R.D. (2014). 'Can business history and anthropology learn from each other?'. *Journal of Business Anthropology* 3, 1: 51–59.

Ho, K. (2009). *Liquidated: An Ethnography of Wall Street.* Durham, NC: Duke University Press.

Jones, G. (1993). *British Multinational Banking 1830–1990.* Oxford: Clarendon Press.

Lawson, C. (2013). *Building the Fourth Estate: Democratization and the Rise of a Free Press in Mexico.* Berkeley: University of California Press.

89 Bertsch et al., 'Narrative fragmentation'.

90 Zemon Davis and Starn, 'Introduction'.

Lee, F., Man Chan, J., and Leung, D. (2019). 'When a historical analogy fails: Current political events and collective memory contestation in the news'. *Memory Studies* 12, 2: 130–145.
MacKenzie, D. (2006). *An Engine, Not a Camera: How Financial Models Shape Markets.* Cambridge, MA–London: MIT.
Mordhorst, M. (2008). 'From counterfactual history to counternarrative history'. *Management and Organizational History* 3, 1: 5–26.
O'Connell, A. (1988). 'La coordinación de los deudores latinoamericanos: el consenso de Cartagena y el grupo de los ocho'. *Estudios Internacionales* 21, 83: 373–385.
Reinhart, C. and Rogoff, K. (2008). 'Is the 2007 US sub-prime financial crisis so different? An international historical comparison'. *American Economic Review* 98, 2: 339–344.
Roett, R. (1985). 'Latin America's response to the debt crisis'. *Third World Quarterly* 7, 2: 227–241.
Schenk, C.R. (1998). 'The origins of the Eurodollar market in London: 1955–1963'. *Exploration in Economic History* 35, 2: 221–238.
Schenk, C.R. (2011). *International Economic Relations Since 1945.* London, New York: Routledge.
Schenk, C.R. (2021). 'The past as practice or parable? Anticipating financial crisis in the 1960s and the 1980s'. In Cassis, Y. and C.R. Schenk (eds), *Remembering and Learning from Financial Crises*, Oxford: Oxford University Press, 82–104.
Shiller, R.J. (2017). 'Narrative economics'. *American Economic Review*, 107, 4: 967–1004.
Thompson, H. (2017). *Oil and the Western Economic Crisis.* Cham: Palgrave Macmillan.
Vargas-Machuca Salido, M.J. (2023). 'The external debt crisis and the "lost decade" in Latin America (1980–1990)'. In Matés Barco, J.M. and M. Vázquez Fariñas (eds), *The Age of Global Economic Crises (1929–2022)*, London: Routledge, 82–104.
Wallis, D. (2004). 'The media and democratic change in Mexico'. *Parliamentary Affairs*, 57, 1: 118–130.
Zelizer, B. (2008). 'Journalism's memory work'. In Erll, A. and A. Nünning (eds), *Cultural and Memory Studies. An International and Interdisciplinary Handbook*, Berlin-New York: Walter de Gruyter, 379–388.
Zelizer, B. and Tenenboim-Weinblatt, K. (eds) (2014). *Journalism and Memory.* Basingstoke: Palgrave Macmillan.
Zemon Davis, N. and Starn, R. (1989). 'Introduction'. *Representations* 26 (Special issue): 1–6.

Periodical, newspapers and web sources

FT/WSJ

Carrington, T. (1994). 'Debt crisis in the developing countries appears to be forgotten but not gone'. *Wall Street Journal*, 17 October.
Davis, B. (2010). 'Amid Irish aid, a new option'. *Wall Street Journal*, 23 November.
Fidler, S. (1988). 'History lesson for lenders and defaulters'. *Financial Times*, 20 October.
Fidler, S. (1992). 'Bouncing back from disaster in tigerish style'. *Financial Times*, 30 July.
Fidler, S. (1992). 'For us Mexicans the crisis is over'. *Financial Times*, 30 July.
Fidler, S. (1992). 'I didn't count on it taking so long'. *Financial Times*, 30 July.
Fidler, S. (1993). 'Trouble with the neighbours'. *Financial Times*, 16 February.
Fidler, S. (1993). 'Boom mood on Latin America recalls 1970s'. *Financial Times*, 31 March.
Fidler, S. (1995). 'The patient sticks with the medicine'. *Financial Times*, 27 June.
Fidler, S. (1997). 'Might Asia lose a decade?'. *Financial Times*, 27 November.

Guha, K. (2008). 'Two challenges highlight the scale of the bonanza'. *Financial Times*, 11 August.
Hughes, J. and Tett, G. (2008). 'An unforgiving eye: bankers cry foul over fair value account'. *Financial Times*, 14 March.
James, H. (1987). 'The neverending tale of debt crises', *Wall Street Journal*, 13 March.
Kaletsky, A. (1983). 'When debtors said no'. *Financial Times*, 28 December.
Kaletsky, A. (1988). 'A borrowers' market'. *Financial Times*, 15 February.
Kamm, T. (1992). 'Argentine "miracle"'. *Wall Street Journal*, 11 September.
Lapper, R. (2002). 'Back to revolution'. *Financial Times*, 21 February.
Lapper, R. (2002). 'Latin America recalls lost decade'. *Financial Times*, 6 August.
Lapper, R. (2002). 'Piling on the pressure Leftist radicals are reshaping Brazil's election'. *Financial Times*, 5 October.
Leader (1992). 'Latin America debt crisis: a great deal was at stake'. *Financial Times*, 30 July.
Leader, (1992). 'Lessons of the debt crisis'. *Financial Times*, 30 July.
Leader (1993). 'A return of the debt crisis?'. *Financial Times*, 29 March.
Leader (1993). 'Landing capital'. *Financial Times*, 19 April.
Leader (1993). 'Latin America's success story'. *Financial Times*, 28 October.
Leader (1994). 'The picture darkens'. *Financial Times*, 11 April.
Leader (2002). 'Latin America turns left'. *Financial Times*, 29 July.
Luhnow, D. (2001). 'Argentina intensifies defense of Peso-Dollar link'. *Wall Street Journal*, 3 December.
Marsh, D. (1983). 'Crisis: the call for consistency'. *Financial Times*, 27 January.
Moffett, M., Carroll, P.B., and Friedland, J. (1995). 'No looking back'. *Wall Street Journal*, 12 May.
Naim, M. (2001). 'Lessons from the recent past'. *Financial Times*, 28 December.
Nicoll, A. (1992). 'Fear brings people together'. *Financial Times*, 30 July.
Nicoll, A. (1992). 'Solution passes the test of time'. *Financial Times*, 30 July.
Palmer, J., Bolte, G., Malkin, L., and Hungeneuer, F. (1983). 'The debt-bomb threat'. *Time Magazine*, 10 January.
Plender, J. (2008). 'Financial crisis presents a test for fair value accounting'. *Financial Times*, 13 February.
Rathbone, J.P. (2010). 'Eurozone can learn grim Latin lessons'. *Financial Times*, 22 December.
Rhodes, W.R. (1993). 'The Latin Tigers are ready to roar'. *Wall Street Journal*, 31 December.
Soros, G. (2011). 'How Germany can avoid a two-speed Europe'. *Financial Times*, 21 March.
Steinmetz, G., Bray, N., and Friedland, J. (1998). 'As a global behemoth, new Citigroup won't be alone'. *Wall Street Journal*, 7 April.
Wolf, M. (1998). 'Why banks are dangerous'. *Financial Times*, 6 January.
Wolf, M. (1998). 'Frail orthodoxy'. *Financial Times*, 21 October.
Wolf, M. (2008). 'Challenges ahead for the world's divided economy'. *Financial Times*, 9 January.
Wolf, M. (2008). 'Asia's revenge'. *Financial Times*, 9 October.

MEXICAN PRESS

Avilés, J. (1985). 'Más allá de la deuda y de los empréstitos', *El Universal*, 9 October.
Avilés, J. (1986). 'Nada que esté por encima de su dignidad nacional negociará México', *El Universal*, 13 February.
Barbosa, R. (1985). 'Convendría diferir el pago de réditos de la deuda externa: Arroyo Ortiz', *El Universal*, 14 July.
Cárdenas, C. (1982). 'La deuda externa sólo es peligrosa si dificulta al gobierno el diseño de una política económica', *El Universal*, 11 May.

Castellanos, A. (1977). 'El endeudamiento exterior, peligroso', *Excélsior*, 26 January.
Castellanos, A. (1977). 'Renegoció México su deuda pública y privada con la banca Suiza', *Excélsior*, 9 February.
Castillo, H. (1986). 'Los síntomas de la dependencia', *El Universal*, 14 May.
Colmenares Páramo, D. (1979). 'Algo sobre la deuda externa', *El Día*, 27 March.
Damián (2004). 'Échenle la culpa al Congreso', *El Financiero*, 20 December.
Damián (2011). 'Lamentable declaración', *El Financiero*, 6 June.
De Cervantes, L. (1977). 'México no necesita renovar su deuda con el BID; el crédito abierto', *Excélsior*, 15 February.
Duncan, J. (1992). 'Descarta José Ángel Gurría nueva crisis por nuestra deuda', *El Nacional*, 17 March.
El Día (1986). 'El convenio mexicano-banqueros', *El Día*, 4 October.
El Día (1985). '¿Todo para pagar la deuda externa?', *El Día*, 8 February.
El Heraldo de México (1982). 'Para reducir la deuda externa debemos atraer inversiones', *El Heraldo de México*, 9 July.
Flores Zavala, E. (1982). 'La anarquía administrativa nos deja a merced de los prestamistas', *El Heraldo de México*, 30 August.
Gómez Bulnes, H. (1977). 'La deuda externa del país es de 20 mil 241,6 millones de dólares', *El Día*, 6 July.
Gómez, R. (1984). 'Se insiste por parte de otros países en un mejor trato para su deuda', *Novedades*, 10 September.
González, A. (1976). 'La deuda externa puede pagarse, afirma el subsecretario del patrimonio nacional', *Excélsior*, 13 November.
Hewett, G. (1981). 'México, de los más hábiles en el manejo de la deuda externa', *El Universal*, 25 February.
Huerta Cruz, J.L. (1977). 'Mayor control de la deuda', *El Universal*, 8 July.
Llamosa, J.A. (1982). 'Igual a la de todos los países socialistas, incluida Rusia', *El Heraldo de México*, 23 August.
López, J.M. (1985). 'Se manifiesta el MNJR por renegociar el pago de la deuda externa con Cuba', *Excélsior*, 13 September.
Lozano, S. (1976). 'Deuda externa: Ya estuvo suave', *Novedades*, 21 September.
Mares, M. (1991). 'Bajó a 2.3% del PIB el pago de deuda externa', *Uno más Uno*, 5 February.
Martínez, I. (2000). 'Propseridad y privilegios de Estados Unidos', *El Universal*, 5 April.
Nava, J.M. (1980). 'Duplicó en 4 años la deuda externa, respecto al PIB', *Excélsior*, 30 November.
Navarrete, C. (1981). 'Deuda externa, "Caballo de Troya" introductor de presiones económicas que frenan el cambio social', *El Sol de México*, 28 December.
Negrón, L. (1986). 'Pedirá México a los bancos extensión parcial de vencimientos', *Excélsior*, 20 February.
Pérez, C.A. (1984). 'El pago de la deuda no debe ser a costa del bienestar general: Pérez', *Excélsior*, 28 February.
Ramírez (2012). 'Indicador político', *El Financiero*, 21 June.
Rangel, J. (1976). 'México no necesita renegociar la deuda externa. Señala el Bank of America', *Excélsior*, 14 November.
Rangel, J. (1977). 'Sólido crédito mexicano por el buen manejo de la deuda externa', *El Sol de México*, 18 June.
Reachi, S. (1982). 'Doce años de deudas por políticas económicas erradas', *El Heraldo de México*, 17 April.
Serrano, L.A. (1978). 'La deuda externa de México es de 30 mil millones de dólares', *Novedades*, 16 March.
Sotomayor, A. (1986). 'Condición para pagar', *Excélsior*, 6 March.
Stephens García, M. (1985). 'Contra el débito', *Excélsior*, 22 August.

4

Episodic amnesia and selective memory, a literature overview of the 1982 crisis on the eve of its fortieth anniversary

Carlo Edoardo Altamura and Juan Flores Zendejas

Introduction

Certain events remain deeply ingrained in collective memory, often associated with major social, political, or economic upheavals. In Latin America—and, to some extent, in other developing regions—the 1980s undoubtedly represent one such period. The decade was marked by the collapse of a state-led industrialization model, whose final stages were frequently accompanied by brutal dictatorships and by the onset of a severe debt crisis, the return of democratic governance, and the liberalization of their economies. These profound transformations are particularly noteworthy given the region's long history of recurrent economic and financial crises.[1] Yet, even today, the debt crisis of the 1980s is widely regarded as 'the worst crisis of its entire history'.[2]

From the onset of the crisis, contemporary observers and scholars devoted extensive analysis to understanding its causes, interpreting ongoing developments, and evaluating how local policy-makers were addressing defaults and the deteriorating state of public finances.[3] These scholars also bore witness—perhaps not entirely unexpectedly, though no less strikingly—to the decisive role played by international banks, multilateral organizations, and the US government in shaping the economic policies that were ultimately implemented. From the very beginning, the structural adjustments introduced, along with their social costs, sparked intense debates and controversies.

[1] See, for instance Marichal, *Historia de la deuda externa*; Marichal, *A Century*; Marichal, *Historia mínima*.

[2] Bértola and Ocampo, *The Economic Development*, 208.

[3] On the narrative of the crisis, see Boughton, *The IMF and the Silent Revolution*, for the perspective of the IMF, Kraft, *The Mexican Rescue*, and Espinosa Yglesias 'Bancomer' for the perspective of the Mexican government.

Carlo Edoardo Altamura and Juan Flores Zendejas, *Episodic amnesia and selective memory, a literature overview of the 1982 crisis on the eve of its fortieth anniversary*. In: *History, Memory, and the Return of Financial Crises After Bretton Woods*. Edited by: Youssef Cassis and Giuseppe Telesca, Oxford University Press.
DOI: 10.1093/9780198950158.003.0004

As in any crisis, policy-makers formulated their debt-resolution strategies based on their diagnosis of its causes while also addressing the most pressing concerns of politically influential actors. In this context, the academic literature closely followed public debates, either supporting or critiquing the successive strategies implemented. With the introduction of the Brady Plan in 1989, these debates reached a standstill.

This chapter traces these debates from both Latin American and international perspectives, considering their medium-term impact on the literature and on interpretations of new debt crises, as well as the effects of economic policies imposed on crisis-hit countries. A defining feature of the 1980s debt crisis is that its perceived causes evolved over time, heavily influenced by policy-makers' primary objectives. In the early stages, the focus was on preventing unilateral defaults that could destabilize global financial markets. As these fears subsided, Latin American countries eventually received some degree of debt relief, allowing the crisis to be formally declared resolved—at least on paper.

With the resolution of the debt crisis, debates on the shortcomings of international economic governance, international lending, and unsustainable fiscal policies were largely set aside in favour of new paradigms centred on economic and financial liberalization. Discussions shifted towards the advantages of various exchange rate regimes within this new framework. As our overview of the academic literature on this crisis demonstrates, resorting to history has been largely driven by immediate needs and unresolved challenges. It is interesting that while the crisis was 'forgotten' during the decade of the 1990s, it was not until the late 2000s that scholarly interest in the 'lessons' of Latin America's debt crisis experienced a resurgence. This renewed interest was largely driven by the Great Recession and the Eurozone debt crisis, by the end of the commodity boom later in the decade, and, more recently, by the economic impact of the Covid-19 pandemic. Additionally, a growing body of literature has examined the neoliberal transformation that the crisis helped to institutionalize, something that has been increasingly criticized given the accompanying levels of inequality that it generated.

This chapter is structured as follows. Section 'An early diagnosis: the first debates on the causes of the crisis' reviews the early literature on the crisis, focusing on the initial stage of the debate. While scholars disagreed on the fundamental causes of the crisis, the IMF maintained that fiscal imbalances were the primary issue requiring corrective measures. Section 'Consequences of the crisis: from the second half of the 1980s to the early 1990s' examines the shift in focus that began in 1985, during the second phase of the crisis, when an increasing number of studies began to address supply-side factors. This period also saw a growing body of research analysing the social and economic consequences of the crisis. Section 'Amnesia and comeback after 2008' explores the renewed academic interest in the debt crisis since 2010. The final section presents the conclusions.

An early diagnosis: the first debates on the causes of the crisis

Scholars have generally divided the path to the resolution of the debt crisis into three phases. The first phase, from 1982 to 1985, was characterized by the prevailing view that the crisis was one of 'liquidity'. The dominant assumption was that fiscal and external imbalances stemmed primarily from domestic macroeconomic mismanagement. Consequently, the IMF conditioned its financial support on reductions in government expenditure and the implementation of austerity programmes to address fiscal deficits. As we will see, these policies exacerbated the economic downturn, leading to significant political and social unrest in many countries. Early academic works largely echoed this perspective, emphasizing the need for fiscal and external adjustment. However, some studies also examined the role of international financial markets, the behaviour of lending banks and the flaws in their country risk analyses.

The second phase, beginning in 1985, marked a shift in the IMF's stance as the crisis increasingly came to be recognized as one of 'insolvency'. This transition led to an expansion of conditionality, incorporating structural reforms such as privatization and trade liberalization. During this period, the Baker Plan was introduced, offering new credits to Latin American countries in exchange for economic policies aimed at fostering growth. The academic literature of this period focused on the supply of credit and the shortcomings of the initial debt-resolution efforts.

The final phase, beginning in 1989 and extending into the early 1990s, was defined by the introduction of the Brady Plan, which included provisions for debt haircuts and the securitization of bank loans to restore capital market access for formerly defaulting governments. A key development was the US government's recognition that lending banks had to accept some degree of debt reduction—something they had previously resisted in negotiations. By the early 1990s, a consensus had emerged that the resolution of the debt crisis had imposed excessive costs on Latin American economies, undermining democratic transitions and accelerating the adoption of neo-liberal policies.

In this section, we begin by reviewing the literature focusing on the initial five years of academic work. The 1982 crisis witnessed a significant clash between competing views on the key factors that led to the crisis. A useful starting point is Kahler's categorization of the main explanations for the crisis.[4] According to Kahler, these explanations can be grouped into three categories: those attributing the crisis to borrowing governments' 'failure to adjust', those emphasizing 'macroeconomic shocks', and those focusing on 'financial market imperfections'. Each perspective assigns different weight to the global economic shifts of the early 1980s,

[4] Kahler, 'Politics and international debt'.

the structural weaknesses of the international financial system, and the intrinsic macroeconomic imbalances in Latin America.

In relation to the 'failure to adjust' debates, it is worth recalling that Latin American economies had historically relied on an interventionist state as a driver of economic development. In the aftermath of the Great Depression, governments took a proactive role in economic recovery, later using state intervention to promote industrialization and strengthen domestic markets—a model that persisted until the late 1970s and early 1980s. This period, commonly referred to as state-led industrialization or import-substitution industrialization, was characterized by high levels of protectionism, rising public expenditure, and periodic inflationary surges.[5] By the 1970s, public debt levels had reached unsustainable heights, despite the fact that most countries in the region were experiencing high rates of economic growth.

As discussed later, there is significant debate regarding the long-term sustainability of these expansionary policies. Some scholars argue that the primary issue was fiscal mismanagement, which led to rising debt levels and persistent fiscal and trade deficits.[6] This perspective was notably defended by Cline, whose work provided intellectual justification for the hardline stance adopted by international creditors.[7] Sachs summarizes this position: 'Debt relief for Latin American countries was viewed as highly risky to the international financial system, no matter how realistic or desirable from the point of view of the debtor countries.'[8]

However, other scholars have challenged this interpretation. In 1984, Sachs published a comparative analysis of Latin American and East Asian economies in the years preceding the crisis. He identified the exchange rate regime as the key differentiating factor. In East Asia, governments actively promoted exports, maintaining competitive exchange rates as a key policy tool. In contrast, Latin American governments allowed their currencies to appreciate, leading to capital flight and growing current account deficits. Although both East Asian and Latin American countries experienced debt repayment difficulties and fiscal deficits, East Asia's export-oriented strategies facilitated sustained growth in global trade, setting it apart from Latin America.

Pazos also contends that the development pattern followed by Latin American countries did not inherently generate macroeconomic disequilibria.[9] On the contrary, he argues that the economic policies implemented since the post-World War II period were closely linked to the high rates of economic growth observed in the region.

[5] Bértola and Ocampo, *The Economic Development*.
[6] Wiesner, 'Latin American debt'.
[7] Cline, *International Debt*.
[8] Sachs, 'Recent studies', 173.
[9] Pazos, 'Have import substitution... ?'.

Another strand of the literature emphasizes Latin America's structural vulnerability to external shocks and its dependence on foreign capital, with particular focus on the role played by Western commercial banks in financing developing economies. In Latin America—at the time almost entirely under authoritarian rule—commercial banks increasingly replaced official lenders such as the World Bank and the Inter-American Development Bank, which had dominated development financing in the 1950s and 1960s.

Scholars have identified three key reasons for this growing reliance on commercial banks. First, geopolitical developments played a critical role. Following the 1973 oil crisis, Western commercial banks accumulated vast amounts of capital, the so-called 'petrodollars', and actively sought new markets abroad to offset the economic downturn in Europe and the United States. Second, the newly established authoritarian regimes in Latin America pursued ambitious and costly development programmes to legitimize their rule, requiring significant external financing. Third, within the Cold War context, these regimes were considered reliable borrowers; they rejected Bolshevism, welcomed foreign capital, and prioritized commercial loans over foreign direct investment. International creditors, especially international commercial banks, appeared often as the main culprits in many of the existing narratives such as Sampson[10] and Devlin.[11]

This body of literature extended previous analyses of capital flows to developing countries. Two of the earliest economists to highlight the increasing role of commercial banks in the developing world were David Beek[12] and Stephany Griffith-Jones.[13] Beek emphasized the shift in the composition of developing countries' debt, noting that while capital inflows during the 1960s primarily consisted of official assistance, direct investments, and trade credits, the 1970s saw an increasing reliance on commercial bank lending.[14] As financial intermediation between surplus and deficit countries through the international banking system appeared to function smoothly after the second oil crisis, research on commercial banks remained relatively limited until the early 1980s.

The 1980s debt crisis, however, brought renewed attention to the role of commercial banks as capital providers. Bernal analysed the interactions between commercial banks and the International Monetary Fund, arguing that bank lending to developing countries expanded after 1973 due to 'slack demand in developed countries', 'fierce competition between banks', and higher profitability compared to domestic lending.[15] Michael Moffitt took a broader perspective, attributing the crisis to a monetary system that had spun out of control, in which private financial

[10] Sampson, *The Money Lenders.*
[11] Devlin, *Debt and Crisis.*
[12] Beek, 'Commercial bank lending'.
[13] Griffith-Jones, 'El Crecimiento'.
[14] Beek, 'Commercial bank lending'.
[15] Bernal, 'Transnational banks'.

interests had supplanted official ones.[16] However, his analysis remained largely theoretical. Cline provided a more quantitative perspective, assessing the impact of external shocks on developing countries' indebtedness and identifying the transition from inflation to disinflation—particularly following the 'Volcker Shock' of October 1979—as the proximate cause of the debt crisis.[17]

Further insights into the role of commercial banks emerged from the work of international political economist Jeffry Frieden. In his seminal paper on 'indebted industrialization' in the developing world, Frieden documented how, during the 1970s, private financial institutions replaced multinational corporations and official aid as primary sources of development finance.[18] His research would later culminate in *Banking on the World*, in which he argued that authoritarian regimes relied on political repression to manage the debt-driven industrialization process, displacing millions of peasants into urban centres in search of industrial employment. Similarly, Barbara Stallings published a detailed account of American private bank lending to Latin America throughout the twentieth century, though her analysis did not fully explore the motivations behind the lending boom or its broader implications.[19]

Finally, among scholars emphasizing the problems in the international financial governance and financial markets imperfections, Kahler posited that the relaxation of International Monetary Fund (IMF) conditionality starting in 1979, coupled with increased IMF resources through quota expansions and borrowing, fostered moral hazard among both debtors and creditors.[20] He argued that lenders operated under the assumption of a de facto lender of last resort within the international banking system, despite no entity explicitly assuming this role. For Eastern European nations, this implicit guarantee was termed the 'Soviet Umbrella', humorously described as the first Communist lender of last resort. In contrast, creditor nation governments were expected to intervene on behalf of troubled borrowers due to strategic interests. This dynamic led West German banks to spearhead lending to Eastern Europe, while American banks focused on Latin America.

Folkerts-Landau and Guttentag and Herring discussed the potential for moral hazard among lenders, manifested through herd behaviour.[21] They suggest that banks were incentivized to align their country exposure with that of their peers, thereby increasing the probability of government intervention during crises, as the stability of the entire banking system would be at risk.[22] Earlier, Vaubel expressed

[16] Moffitt, *The World's Money.*
[17] Cline, *International Debt.*
[18] Frieden, 'Third World indebted industrialization'.
[19] Stallings, *Banker to the Third World.*
[20] Kahler, 'Politics and international debt'.
[21] Folkerts-Landau, *IMF Staff Papers*; Guttentag and Herring, *The Current Crisis.*
[22] Guttentag and Herring, *The Current Crisis*, 3.

concerns about moral hazard affecting both debtors and creditors due to IMF lending practices.[23] He argued that the IMF encouraged countries to rely on continuous debt rescheduling, effectively subsidizing banks' past mistakes. Vaubel concluded that IMF lending lacked economic justification and was detrimental to international finance, proposing that the institution be transformed into an 'International Monetary Information Agency'.[24]

Consequences of the crisis: from the second half of the 1980s to the early 1990s

The diagnosis of the origins of the crisis continued to be disputed but the persistence of the crisis attracted further academic interest in the second half of the 1980s. Biggs analysed several cases of debt defaults across multiple geographical regions and periods, arguing that the crisis of the 1980s was of historically unprecedented magnitude and was remarkable because of the hard stance assumed by international creditors.[25]

According to Sachs, Latin American countries—unlike East Asian borrowers—failed to use foreign capital to build resource base in tradable goods, especially export industries, for future debt servicing.[26] Sachs also highlighted the global economic events and strongly criticized the management of the crisis by creditor countries, thereby championing the idea of debt overhang and the need for debt relief.[27] Other scholars have also pointed out the international context and dynamics at play in the developing world. Griffith-Jones and Sunkel placed the Debt Crisis in the context of a broader crisis of the post-war developmental and monetary framework.[28] Consequently, they argued in favour of a complete reform of the international monetary system and of the development strategies so that developing countries would be able to provide sufficient capital in an anti-cyclical way.

The world economic situation was also central in Congdon's analysis. Congdon highlighted the detrimental effects that the mix of tight monetary policy and expansionary fiscal policy in the United States had created for debtor countries whose debts were mostly dollar-denominated at floating interest rates.[29] Summarizing, the literature maintained the idea that the origins of the debt crisis in

[23] Vaubel, 'The moral hazard'.
[24] Ivi, 301.
[25] Biggs, *La crisis de la deuda*.
[26] Sachs and Williamson, 'External debt'.
[27] Sachs and Williamson, 'Managing the LDC debt crisis'; Sachs, 'Conditionality'; Sachs, *Developing Country*. In the same vein, see Diaz-Alejandro, Krugman, and Sachs, 'Latin American Debt'; Diaz-Alejandro, 'Good-bye financial repression, hello financial crash'.
[28] Griffith-Jones and Sunkel, *Debt and Development Crises in Latin America*.
[29] Congdon, *The Debt Threat*.

three, often interrelated, forces: irrational exuberance of banks; macro-economic mismanagement in borrowing countries and instability of the world economy.

Darity and Horn argued that the lending boom of the 1920s and of the 1970s were driven by the supply of easy money rather than demand and pointed the finger directly at the commercial banks as the primary instigators of the debt crisis.[30] According to the authors the crisis of the 1980s was seen as part of a 50-year international lending cycle which had culminated in excessive and careless lending. Given the speculative nature of the book, the empirical evidence to back up these intuitions is rather slim.

A different group of academic works continued focusing on the foundations and motives behind the lending boom taking place in the years leading to the crisis. Stallings analysed US lending to Latin America between the 1920s and the 1980s.[31] Even if this author highlighted both supply and demand factors in lending cycles, Stallings claimed that supply factors, such as the irrational exuberance of foreign investors, the need to recycle huge oil surpluses after the shock of 1973 and financial innovation in the Eurodollar market, played a prominent role but that demand factors should not be forgotten. Analysing the case of Peru, she pointed out that both in the 1920s, during the presidency of Augusto B. Leguía, and in the late 1960s/early 1970s, under military rule, Peru actively sought external financing thereby nuancing the narrative of passive governments forced to accept foreign loans.

Lomax went in a similar direction when he pointed out that, despite the fact that international bankers were eagerly competing among themselves,[32] they were also actors in a much bigger game which involved supporting domestic industries, home governments' interventions and host governments' pressures to lend.[33]

Wellons underscored the significance of the relationships between banks and their respective national governments.[34] He contended that banks extended loans to developing countries with the backing of their home governments, which aimed to expand markets for their exports following the 1973 oil shock. Wellons examined the influence of governments on commercial bank lending decisions, providing a comprehensive perspective on the link between trade and finance.[35] He argued that balance of payments challenges in developed countries prompted governments to implement policies supporting exports.

Consequently, banks—the primary source of capital—were encouraged to finance potential importers, while export credit agencies enhanced their capacity to meet international competition. Commercial banks, becoming increasingly international, were well-positioned to finance trade, complementing this role

[30] Darity and Horn, *The Loan Pushers.*
[31] Stallings, *Banker to the Third World.*
[32] Lomax, *The Developing Country Debt Crisis*, 59.
[33] Lomax, 82.
[34] Wellons, 'International debt'; Wellons, *Passing the Buck.*
[35] Wellons, *Passing the Buck.*

with loans to governments and public enterprises in developing countries, which were significant borrowers in international financial markets. Additionally, export credit agencies offered direct credit to foreign buyers and provided insurance services to domestic exporters.

Other scholars support this view, including Spindler[36] and later also Devlin.[37] Devlin incorporates the structure of bank lending into his analysis, agreeing that the concentration of both lenders and borrowers increased the likelihood of governmental intervention in the event of financial difficulties.[38] Devlin insisted on the role of transnational banks in aggravating the credit cycle of Latin American countries by 'tending to overexpand on the upside and overcontract on the downside'.[39] By focusing on the 'supply side' of credit Devlin omitted the official intervention of governments on both sides of the transactions.

Contemporary observers also highlighted the IMF's role in bolstering confidence, akin to how a stable central bank strengthens a domestic monetary system.[40] The IMF's support for financially distressed countries such as Turkey, Zaire, Peru, and Jamaica during the 1970s exemplifies this function. Over time, the IMF's focus shifted from addressing balance of payments issues related to exchange rate stability to acting as a crisis manager. For instance, in 1976, Mexico sought IMF assistance to rectify its balance of payments problems and secure financial support to resolve a currency crisis. The country remained under an Extended Fund Facility programme until 1979, with regular IMF missions contributing to bankers' confidence in Mexico.

After documenting the Third World's reliance on indebted industrialization and how private financial institutions had replaced official aid during the 1970s in the financing of ambitious and costly development programmes, Jeffry Frieden published a second seminal book in 1992, titled *Debt, Development and Democracy*, in which he compared the development policies and use of foreign debt of Latin America's five largest borrowers (Argentina, Brazil, Chile, Mexico, and Venezuela).[41] Frieden argued that in all of these countries governments reacted by meeting most of the demands of the private sector while ignoring most of those coming from labour.

Frieden's work is symptomatic of a more general shift in the literature, which occurred by the end of the 1980s and in the early 1990s, concentrated on the economic and social consequences of the debt crisis. On the economic front, the crisis imposed serious adjustment costs on borrowing countries as 'neo-liberal reforms sought to subordinate political and social structures to the principles of the self-regulating free-market economy'.[42] Average GDP growth in the region was

[36] Spindler, *The Politics.*
[37] Devlin, *Debt and Crisis.*
[38] Devlin, *Debt and Crisis.*
[39] Devlin, 5.
[40] De Vries, *The IMF in a Changing World*, 180.
[41] Frieden, *Debt, Development, and Democracy.*
[42] Silva, *Challenging Neo-liberalism in Latin America*, 18.

−2% until 1986. Politically, the crisis made it impossible for authoritarian leaders to continue to satisfy all the groups that had benefited from borrowing-period policies.[43] Latin America's socio-economic indicators deteriorated dramatically ultimately provoking a dramatic 'retroceso del desarrollo'.[44] Latin America was a region of high inequality even before the crisis but during the 1980s poverty and, especially, inequality dramatically increased with tragic consequences for the poorer strata of the population.[45]

Partly as a consequence of the deterioration of living standards, violence erupted across the region notably in Caracas in 1989, in Santiago del Estero in 1993 and in Chiapas in 1994. While the literature agrees on the dramatic consequences of the crisis on the socio-economic fabric of the region, less consensus exists on the origins of the situation, that is, were international creditors at fault or were Latin American countries unprepared to protect the poor? The latter camp is represented by scholars like Lustig, who argued that, with the possible exception of Chile, Latin America's politicians did not do enough to protect its population from the effects of the structural adjustment programmes.[46] By contrast, scholars like Thorp and Whitehead, and Hinkelammert took a much more critical stance towards the IMF and its adjustment policies.[47] Gradually, the relationship between borrowers and creditors crystallized into a coherent vision, later known as 'Washington Consensus', of what policies creditors believed were appropriate for the region.[48]

Although neoliberal reforms produced some positive results in the early 1990s—in terms of inflation rates, economic growth, and infusions of foreign capital—they also had an uneven impact across and within social sectors.[49] Huber and Solt argued that more liberalized economies in Latin America had higher volatility, larger increases in income inequality, and greater poverty than less liberalized economies.[50] Other authors have pointed out that '30 years of ... neo-liberalization and structural adjustments have produced at least dubious and at worst catastrophic effects on the majority of people's lives'.[51] Sociologists[52] and political scientists[53] have conducted research on adjustment programs and the neoliberal shift in Latin America.

[43] Frieden, *Debt, Development, and Democracy*, 83; Sallum Jr. and Kugelmas, 'O Leviathan Declinante'.

[44] Escobar, *La Invención Del Desarrollo*, 149.

[45] CEPAL/ECLAC, *Equidad y Transformación Productiva*; Devlin and Ffrench-Davis, 'The Great Latin America debt crisis'; Lustig, *El desafío de la austeridad*.

[46] Lustig, *El desafío de la austeridad*.

[47] Thorp and Whitehead, *Latin American Debt*; Hinkelammert, *La deuda externa*.

[48] See, for instance, Williamson, *Latin American Adjustment*; Babb, *Behind the Development Banks*.

[49] Margheritis and Pereira, 'The neo-liberal turn in Latin America'.

[50] Huber and Solt, 'Successes and failures of neo-liberalism'.

[51] Rodríguez, 'The Politics of neo-liberalism in Latin America', 2.

[52] See, for instance, Babb, *Managing Mexico*; Babb, 'The Washington consensus'; Fourcade-Gourinchas and Babb, 'The rebirth of the liberal creed'.

[53] See, for instance, Pop-Eleches, *From Economic Crisis to Reform*; Chwieroth, *Capital Ideas*; Roos, *Why Not Default?*

A lingering question is whether the defaults could have been handled differently, and whether the crisis might have been averted altogether. Drawing on historical precedents, Eichengreen and Portes, in a set of papers published in the late 1980s and early 1990s, provided different parallels between the waves of defaults of the 1930s and those of the 1980s.[54] They referred to the Bradley and Sachs Plans, which urged banks to forgive developing countries liabilities. An alternative approach was the Dornbusch Plan, which would have allowed countries to service their debt in domestic currency. On the contrary, authors such as Feldstein and Cline criticized a global approach, and suggested rather a case-by-case solution.[55]

Previous experiences of international lending to Latin America, and other developing regions, were analysed in a collective book edited by Sachs.[56] Eichengreen (chapter 11) and Lindert and Morton (chapter 10) provided an historical analysis of international and US lending experiences in the nineteenth and early twentieth centuries that supported the view that there were elements of systemic irrationality in the booms and busts of foreign lending.

Amnesia and comeback after 2008

In the 1990s, scholarly literature on financial crises emphasized the stark contrasts between the crises of that decade and those of the 1980s. A telling example is Barry Eichengreen's description of Mexico's 1994 crisis as the 'first financial crisis of the 21st century'—a label that underscored its distinct nature in comparison to the 1982 crisis. The liberalization of capital markets during this period led academics to focus on topics such as the choice of exchange rate regimes, the significance of sudden stops in capital flows, the dangers of financial contagion, and the importance of robust banking regulatory frameworks. These issues were considered central to many emerging market crises of the 1990s.

The post-2010 literature is not entirely separate from the literature developed in the 1980s and follows three lines of enquiry. One is the role of macroeconomic mismanagement and increases in debt levels, something that was deemed to be a major factor leading to the crisis in Southern European countries. Second is the role of international finance, private lenders, and the world's economic governance. Finally, it is the theory and empirical evidence on sovereign defaults. We will now turn to each of them.

Consider first the group of works that revisit the idea that fiscal mismanagement had been at the core of the debt crisis. For instance, Ocampo and Parodi have shown that, in the years previous to the crisis, and except for the Southern

[54] Eichengreen and Portes, 'The anatomy of financial crises'; Eichengreen and Portes, 'Settling defaults'; Eichengreen and Portes, 'Dealing with debt'.

[55] Feldstein, 'International debt service and economic growth'; Cline, *Mobilizing*.

[56] Sachs, *Developing Country Debt and the World Economy*.

Cone countries, fiscal discipline was the rule rather than the exception among Latin American countries.[57] Furthermore, certain governments of the region were experiencing a transition in their economic model from the focus on state-led industrialization towards the financial liberalization model.

In this regard, Frenkel argued that sovereign external indebtedness reflects the outcome of the deregulation process of the financial sector rather than the 'populist' irresponsibility.[58]

Cavallo and Fernández-Arias propose that the Eurozone financial crisis could be managed by drawing lessons from Latin America's 1982 debt crisis.[59] They emphasize the importance of providing external liquidity to crisis-affected countries, coupled with policy reforms to address underlying structural issues. The authors caution against relying solely on fiscal contraction to resolve public debt overhangs, as this approach may lead to social unrest. Instead, they advocate for an orderly debt reduction strategy alongside the creation of an economic environment that fosters growth and attracts capital inflows. Additionally, they highlight the significant costs associated with banking crises that evolve into sovereign debt crises and recommend implementing solutions to banking problems that minimize fiscal burdens.

Recent scholarship has delved into the intricate dynamics of international lending and governance, particularly in the context of the 1982 debt crisis. Altamura and Flores Zendejas reexamined banks' risk assessment processes, revealing that political considerations significantly influenced lending behaviours.[60] Their research, grounded in newly accessible archival materials, indicates that banks' decisions were heavily swayed by the preferences of their home governments. This alignment suggests an implicit expectation that these governments, alongside international organizations, would act as lenders of last resort to support borrowing nations. The political aspects underpinning—as well as the backlash—against international lending in the 1970s have been addressed elsewhere.[61]

Further exploring the leverage exerted by creditor nations and international bodies over defaulting countries, Alvarez and Flores analysed the role of trade finance and export credit agencies during the crisis.[62] Their findings demonstrate that creditor governments strategically utilized these agencies to compel defaulting nations into agreements with the International Monetary Fund (IMF), thereby managing the crisis more effectively. Building on this discourse, Sgard employed interviews and archival research to trace the evolution of debt rescheduling efforts

57 Ocampo, 'The Latin American debt crisis'; Parodi Trece, 'La Crisis de La Deuda'.
58 Frenkel and Rapetti, 'The real exchange'.
59 Cavallo and Fernández-Arias, 'Coping with financial crises'.
60 Altamura and Flores Zendejas, 'Politics'.
61 Altamura, 'Global banks'; Altamura and Kim, 'Exclusionary regimes'.
62 Alvarez and Flores, 'Trade finance'.

throughout the 1980s.[63] His work sheds light on the perceptions of US policymakers regarding the potential global financial repercussions of the crisis, echoing longstanding debates on optimal default management strategies.

The 1982 crisis also prompted theoretical exploration into the incentives shaping sovereign debt repayment and default, leaving lasting echoes in both subsequent empirical studies and theoretical work. Eaton and Gersovitz's seminal model posited that nations choose to honour their debts to maintain access to international capital markets, as defaulting could lead to exclusion and hinder economic stability.[64]

However, subsequent research has challenged the sufficiency of reputation-based explanations, suggesting that the threat of direct sanctions or punitive measures may play a more decisive role in deterring defaults.[65] Collectively, these studies underscore the complex interplay of political, economic, and strategic factors that influence international lending practices and sovereign debt management.

Empirical studies have investigated the theoretical frameworks concerning the impact of reputational concerns versus punitive threats on a country's decision to honour its debt obligations.[66] This ongoing debate highlights the complexity of sovereign debt dynamics and the multifaceted considerations influencing a nation's choice between repayment and default.

One empirical approach involves calculating the costs associated with defaulting.[67] Another examines the long-term effects of default on access to financial capital markets. The literature presents diverse findings: as we show below, some authors suggest that financial markets have a 'memory', while others indicate that the differences between defaulting and non-defaulting countries are minimal and highly heterogeneous.

Özler posited that banks tended to 'punish' countries with prior defaults by imposing slightly higher interest rates.[68] Similarly, Lindert and Morton observed that investors often disregarded a nation's default history when making lending decisions.[69] Further studies by Bulow and Rogoff, Gelos et al., and Yeyati and Panizza, found limited evidence linking defaults to significant increases in borrowing costs or prolonged exclusion from capital markets.[70] In contrast, Cruces and Trebesch provided evidence that market penalties were present between 1970 and

[63] Sgard, *The Debt Crisis of the 1980s*.

[64] Eaton and Gersovitz, 'Debt with potential repudiation'.

[65] Bulow and Rogoff, 'A constant'.

[66] Aguiar and Gopinath, 'Defaultable debt'; Tomz, *Reputation*; Tomz and Wright, 'Do countries default'.

[67] Bulow and Rogoff, 'Sovereign debt'; Gelos, Sahay, and Sandleris, 'Sovereign borrowing'; Yeyati and Panizza, 'The elusive costs'.

[68] Özler, 'Have commercial banks ignored history?'.

[69] Lindert and Morton, 'How sovereign debt has worked'.

[70] Bulow and Rogoff, 'A constant'; Gelos, Sahay, and Sandleris, 'Sovereign borrowing'; Yeyati and Panizza, 'The elusive costs'.

2010.[71] They demonstrated that the severity of these penalties correlated with the magnitude of 'haircuts'—the reductions in debt obligations agreed upon during restructuring. Specifically, larger haircuts were associated with higher subsequent bond yield spreads and longer durations of exclusion from capital markets.

Catão and Mano found a substantial increase in the default premium of approximately 350 basis points, which gradually declined over the first five years following a settlement during the period from 1970 to 2014.[72] However, they cautioned that these results are highly dependent upon market conditions. For instance, during the mid-1970s to early 1980s, spreads were compressed due to high liquidity in syndicated bank lending, resulting in a minimal default premium.

The case of Colombia offers additional insights. Caselli et al. indicate that the Colombian government chose not to default during the 1980s, aiming to maintain a favourable reputation in international capital markets.[73] While this strategy yielded short-term economic benefits, such as comparatively better GDP growth than neighbouring countries, it did not lead to long-lasting reputational gains. These findings suggest that the consequences of sovereign default are nuanced and context-dependent, influenced by factors such as the extent of debt restructuring, prevailing market conditions, and individual country circumstances.

Finally, there is a revisionist trend since at least the beginning of the 2010s (perhaps also due to the Eurozone crisis and the criticisms against austerity measures). More and more works argue that the lack of fiscal discipline was not a major factor behind the crisis.

The pandemic has inflicted a severe blow to Latin America, inflicting incalculable human suffering and exacting a heavy economic toll.[74] In a context where governments stepped in to offset the impact of the Covid pandemic, debt levels began approaching levels seen during the international debt crisis of the 1980s, raising fears among policy-makers and business leaders of new defaults and another lost decade in development. UNCTAD reported in 2024 that global debt had reached a record high of US$97 trillion in 2023 and that developing countries' debt since 2010 increased more than twice as fast as in developed economies.[75] The World Bank reported that 'a silent debt crisis is engulfing developing economies'.[76]

Newspapers and magazines started covering the debt situation in great detail, with continuous references to the debt crisis of the 1980s. Academics also rediscovered the debt crisis as a useful prism through which analysing current events and started referring to 'The Return of Debt Crisis in Developing Countries'[77] as

[71] Cruces and Trebesch, 'Sovereign defaults'.
[72] Catão and Mano, 'Default premium'.
[73] Caselli et al., 'On the benefits of repaying'.
[74] Powell and Valencia, *Dealing with Debt*.
[75] UNCTAD, 'A world of debt 2024 report'.
[76] https://blogs.worldbank.org/en/voices/silent-debt-crisis-engulfing-developing-economies-weak-credit-ratings.
[77] Fischer and Storm, 'The return of debt crisis'.

in the aftermath of the Covid-19 pandemic 'much of the global South has been immersed in a debt crisis of a breadth and depth not seen since the early 1980s'.[78]

The financial distress experienced by numerous countries during the Covid-19 pandemic reignited scholarly interest in the 1982 debt crisis, prompting comparisons to inform current economic strategies.[79] Eichengreen contends that proposed measures to address the fiscal challenges of developing nations amid the pandemic are inadequate.[80] Drawing parallels to the Baker Plan—which presumed that economic downturns were temporary and that a brief debt standstill would enable crisis-affected countries to resume debt servicing in the medium term—Eichengreen argues that such assumptions proved ineffective in the past and are unlikely to succeed post-pandemic. He emphasizes that persistent global economic challenges and depressed commodity prices will continue beyond the pandemic, necessitating the adoption of innovative debt instruments to achieve sustainable public debt levels.

Joseph Stiglitz and Hamid Rashid highlight the severe social costs associated with global debt crises and stress the importance of prompt and decisive action.[81] They caution that a global debt crisis today could lead to widespread unemployment and instability, underscoring the need for timely interventions. Edwin M. Truman reflects on the delays in finding a permanent solution to the 1982 debt crisis.[82] He advocates for a comprehensive approach to potential debt crises arising from the Covid-19 pandemic, involving all relevant stakeholders, including foreign creditors, debtor nation governments, and international institutions. Truman warns against one-size-fits-all solutions, recommending instead a case-by-case strategy tailored to the specific circumstances of each country.

After Covid, the war between Russia and Ukraine, the rise in energy prices, growing geopolitical instability between the USA and China, also increased fears of a new debt crisis. When comparing the 1980s to the post-Covid world, many authors have insisted on the different economic and political scenario with China emerging as an important, or the most important, provider of credit to developing countries.[83] As pointed out by Chen: 'Existing analyses have interpreted China's behaviour in two ways. Some suggest China is free-riding on the international sovereign debt regime.... A second interpretation is that China is contesting the rules set up by advanced industrial economies, practising an idiosyncratic means of debt relief which differs from that practised by traditional creditors.'

[78] Fischer and Storm, 954.
[79] Altamura and Alvarez, 'Latin America in turbulent times'.
[80] Eichengreen, 'The debt dogs that didn't bark'.
[81] Stiglitz and Rashid, 'How to prevent'.
[82] Truman, 'Sovereign debt relief'.
[83] Chen, 'China's rise'.

Conclusions

Why did the literature show booms and busts in its interest on the 1980s debt crisis? In his 2012 analysis, Eichengreen delves into the reasons policy-makers often resort to historical analogies.[84] Drawing from cognitive science and organizational learning, he identifies two primary circumstances that prompt this behaviour. First, when decision-makers face time constraints and possess limited information-processing capacities, crises serve as powerful intellectual shortcuts. Second, when there's a lack of consensus on the principles required for deductive reasoning, historical analogies become a common fallback. However, Eichengreen cautions that relying on such analogies can lead to overreactions. For instance, during the 2008 financial crisis, Federal Reserve Chairman Ben Bernanke's interpretations of the Federal Reserve's actions during the Great Depression were criticized by O'Sullivan,[85] who argued that Bernanke's conclusions were fundamentally flawed, utterly based upon Milton Friedman and Anna Schwartz in *A Monetary History of the United States* (1963).

Similarly, drawing parallels with the 1980s debt crisis reveals the potential pitfalls of misapplying historical lessons.

The literature surrounding that crisis mirrors debates typical of lending booms and busts. Proponents of the 'irresponsible borrower' narrative argue that defaulting governments accumulated unsustainable debt levels while implementing policies detrimental to economic growth—parallels evident in discussions about certain Eurozone countries post-2011. Conversely, other scholars highlight issues such as flawed risk assessments and excessive lending by commercial banks, often spurred by domestic governments' geo-political considerations and international organizations.

Despite these debates, policy-makers may have overestimated the threat of a new debt crisis. Neither the 2008 financial meltdown, the European debt crisis, nor the Covid-19 pandemic precipitated a global debt catastrophe. Moreover, no sovereign default has triggered a significant banking crisis in developed nations. However, this does not imply that revisiting the 1982 crisis is without merit. Recent studies suggest that even the Brady Plan, once deemed successful, may have fallen short, despite enabling defaulting nations to re-enter capital markets. Notably, the number of countries in debt distress hasn't reached the peaks observed in the 1980s. The preparedness of the global economy for a potential surge in defaults remains uncertain. More concerning is the absence of a robust international mechanism to help defaulting nations mitigate the societal impacts of debt crises—a paradox, given the consensus over the past four decades on the necessity of such a framework.

[84] Eichengreen, 'Economic history and economic policy'.
[85] O'Sullivan, 'History as heresy'.

References

Aguiar, M. and Gopinath, G. (2006). 'Defaultable debt, interest rates and the current account', *Journal of International Economics* 69, 1: 64–83.

Altamura, C.E. (2021). 'Global banks and Latin American dictators, 1974–1982', *Business History Review* 95, 2: 301–332.

Altamura, C.E. and Kim, S.W. (2023). 'Exclusionary regimes, financial corporations, and human rights activism in the UK, 1973–92', *The International History Review* 45, 5: 787–806.

Altamura, C.E. and Flores Zendejas, J. (2020). 'Politics, international banking, and the debt crisis of 1982', *Business History Review* 94, 4: 753–778.

Alvarez, S. and Flores, J.H. (2014). 'Trade finance and Latin America's lost decade: The forgotten link', *Investigaciones de Historia Económica—Economic History Research* 10, 2: 127–139.

Altamura, C. E. and Alvarez, S. (2025). 'Latin America in turbulent times: Business, finance, and democracy during the 1970s and 1980s', *Business History*, 1–15. https://doi.org/10.1080/00076791.2025.2568535.

Babb, S. (2001). *Managing Mexico: Economists from Nationalism to Neo-liberalism*. Princeton: Princeton University Press.

Babb, S. (2009). *Behind the Development Banks: Washington Politics, World Poverty, and the Wealth of Nations*. Chicago: The University of Chicago Press.

Babb, S. (2013). 'The Washington Consensus as transnational policy paradigm: Its origins, trajectory and likely successor', *Review of International Political Economy* 20, 2: 268–297.

Beek, D.C. (1977). 'Commercial bank lending to developing countries'. *Federal Reserve Bank of New York Quarterly Review*, Summer 1977, 1–8.

Bernal, R. (1982). 'Transnational banks, the International Monetary Fund and external debt of developing countries', *Social and Economic Studies* 31, 4: 71–101.

Bértola, L. and Ocampo, J.A. (2012). *The Economic Development of Latin America since Independence*. Oxford: Oxford University Press (The initiative for policy dialogue series).

Biggs, G. (1987). *La crisis de la deuda latinoamericana frente a los precedentes históricos*. Buenos Aires: Grupo ed. latinoamericano [Programa RIAL] (Colección Estudios internacionales).

Boughton, J.M. (2000). *The IMF and the Silent Revolution: Global Finance and Development in the 1980s*. International Monetary Fund.

Bulow, J. and Rogoff, K. (1988). 'Sovereign debt: Is to forgive to forget?'. *National Bureau of Economic Research Working Paper Series*, No. 2623.

Bulow, J. and Rogoff, K. (1989). 'A constant recontracting model of sovereign debt', *Journal of Political Economy* 97, 1: 155–178.

Caselli, F. et al. (2021). 'On the benefits of repaying', *CEPR Discussion Paper* [Preprint], (No. DP16539).

Catão, L.A.V. and Mano, R.C. (2017). 'Default premium', *Journal of International Economics* 107: 91–110.

Cavallo, E.A. and Fernández-Arias, E. (2013). 'Coping with financial crises: Latin American answers to European questions', *Revue internationale de politique de développement* 4, 2: 7–28.

CEPAL/ECLAC (1992). *Equidad y transformación productiva: un enfoque integrado*. Santiago de Chile: CEPAL (Libros de la CEPAL, 32).

Chen, M. (2023). 'China's rise and the reshaping of sovereign debt relief', *International Affairs* 99, 4: 1755–1775.

Chwieroth, J.M. (2010). *Capital Ideas: The IMF and the Rise of Financial Liberalization.* Princeton, NJ: Princeton University Press.

Cline, W.R. (1984). *International Debt: Systemic Risk and Policy Response.* Washington, DC: Institute for International Economics.

Cline, W.R. (1987). *Mobilizing Bank Lending to Debtor Countries.* Washington, DC: Institute for International Economics (Policy analyses in international economics, 18).

Congdon, T. (1988). *The Debt Threat: The Dangers of High Real Interest Rates for the World Economy.* Oxford and New York: Blackwell.

Cruces, J.J. and Trebesch, C. (2013). 'Sovereign defaults: The price of haircuts', *American Economic Journal: Macroeconomics* 5, 3: 85–117.

Darity, W.A. and Horn, B.L. (1988). *The Loan Pushers: The Role of Commercial Banks In the International Debt Crisis.* Cambridge, Mass: Ballinger.

De Vries, M.G. (1986). *The IMF in a Changing World: 1945–85.* Washington, DC: International Monetary Fund.

Devlin, R. (1989). *Debt and Crisis in Latin America: The Supply Side of the Story.* Princeton: Princeton University Press.

Devlin, R. and Ffrench-Davis, R. (1995). 'The great Latin America debt crisis: A decade of asymmetric adjustment', *Brazilian Journal of Political Economy* 15, 3: 418–445.

Diaz-Alejandro, C. (1985). 'Good-bye financial repression, hello financial crash', *Journal of Development Economics* 19, 1–2: 1–24.

Diaz-Alejandro, C.F., Krugman, P.R., and Sachs, J.D. (1984). 'Latin American debt: I don't think we are in Kansas anymore', *Brookings Papers on Economic Activity* 1984, 2: 335.

Eaton, J. and Gersovitz, M. (1981). 'Debt with potential repudiation: Theoretical and empirical analysis', *The Review of Economic Studies* 48, 2: 289.

Eichengreen, B. (2012). 'Economic history and economic policy', *The Journal of Economic History* 72, 2: 289–307.

Eichengreen, B. (2020). 'The debt dogs that didn't bark', 11 December. Available at: https://www.project-syndicate.org/commentary/poor-countries-debt-challenge-will-grow-in-2021-by-barry-eichengreen-2020-12.

Eichengreen, B. and Portes, R. (1987). 'The anatomy of financial crises'. In R. Portes and A. Swoboda (eds), *Threats to International Financial Stability*, Cambridge: New York, Cambridge University Press, 10–58.

Eichengreen, B. and Portes, R. (1989a). 'Dealing with debt: The 1930s and the 1980s'. *National Bureau of Economic Research Working Paper Series*, No. 2867.

Eichengreen, B. and Portes, R. (1989b). 'Settling defaults in the era of bond finance', *The World Bank Economic Review* 3, 2: 211–239.

Escobar, A. (2014). *La Invención Del Desarrollo.* Bogota: Universidad del Cauca.

Espinosa Yglesias, M. (2008). 'Bancomer: Logro y destrucción de un ideal'. In *La Nacionalización Bancaria, 25 años después. La Historia Contada Por Sus Protagonistas*, México D.F., Centro de Estudios Espinosa Yglesias, 27–68.

Feldstein, M. (1986). 'International debt service and economic growth: Some simple analytics'. *National Bureau of Economic Research Working Paper Series*, No. 2076.

Fischer, A.M. and Storm, S. (2023). 'The return of debt crisis in developing countries: Shifting or maintaining dominant development paradigms?', *Development and Change* 54, 5: 954–993.

Folkerts-Landau, D. (1985). *The Changing Role of International Bank Lending in Development Finance.* Washington, D.C: International Monetary Fund (IMF Staff Papers).

Fourcade-Gourinchas, M. and Babb, S. (2002). 'The rebirth of the liberal creed: Paths to neo-liberalism in four countries', *American Journal of Sociology* 108, 3: 533–579.

Frenkel, R. and Rapetti, M. (2014). *The Real Exchange Rate as a Target of Macroeconomic Policy*. University Library of Munich, Germany.

Frieden, J. (1981). 'Third World indebted industrialization: International finance and state capitalism in Mexico, Brazil, Algeria, and South Korea', *International Organization* 35, 3: 407–431.

Frieden, J.A. (1987). *Banking on the World: The Politics of American International Finance*. New York: Harper & Row.

Frieden, J.A. (1992). *Debt, Development, and Democracy: Modern Political Economy and Latin America, 1965–1985*. Princeton: Princeton University Press.

Gelos, R.G., Sahay, R., and Sandleris, G. (2011). 'Sovereign borrowing by developing countries: What determines market access?', *Journal of International Economics* 83, 2: 243–254.

Griffith-Jones, S. (1978). 'El crecimiento de la banca multinacional, los mercados de euro monedas y los países de la periferia', *Estudios Internacionales* 11, 44: 71–87.

Griffith-Jones, S. and Sunkel, O. (1986). *Debt and Development Crises in Latin America: The End of an Illusion*. Oxford: Clarendon Press.

Guttentag, J.M. and Herring, R. (1985). *The Current Crisis in International Lending*. Washington, DC: Brookings Institution (Studies in international economics).

Hinkelammert, F.J. (1990). *La deuda externa de America Latina: el automatismo de la deuda*. San Jose, Costa Rica: DEI (Colección Análisis).

Huber, E. and Solt, F. (2004). 'Successes and failures of neo-liberalism', *Latin American Research Review* 39, 3: 150–164.

Kahler, M. (1985). 'Politics and international debt: Explaining the crisis', *International Organization* 39, 3: 357–382.

Kraft, J. (1984). *The Mexican Rescue*. New York: Group of Thirty.

Lindert, P.H. and Morton, P.J. (1989). 'How sovereign debt has worked'. In J. Sachs (ed.), *Developing Country Debt and the World Economy*. Chicago and London: University of Chicago Press (A National Bureau of Economic Research project report), 225–236.

Lomax, D.F. (1986). *The Developing Country Debt Crisis*. London: Palgrave Macmillan UK.

Lustig, N. (ed.) (1997). *El desafío de la austeridad: pobreza y desigualdad en la América Latina*. México: Fondo de Cultura Económica.

Margheritis, A. and Pereira, A.W. (2007). 'The neo-liberal turn in Latin America: The cycle of ideas and the search for an alternative', *Latin American Perspectives* 34, 3: 25–48.

Marichal, C. (1988). *Historia de la deuda externa de América Latina*. Madrid: Alianza.

Marichal, C. (1989). *A Century of Debt Crises in Latin America: From Independence to the Great Depression, 1820–1930*. Princeton, N.J: Princeton University Press.

Marichal, C. (2014). *Historia mínima de la deuda externa de Latinoamérica*. Ciudad de México: El Colegio de México.

Moffitt, M. (1983). *The World's Money: International Banking, from Bretton Woods to the Brink of Insolvency*. New York: Simon and Schuster.

Ocampo, J.A. (2014). 'The Latin American debt crisis in historical perspective'. In J.E. Stiglitz and D. Heymann (eds), *Life after Debt: The Origins and Resolutions of Debt Crisis*. London: Palgrave Macmillan, 87–115.

O'Sullivan, M.A. (2022). 'History as heresy: Unlearning the lessons of economic orthodoxy', *The Economic History Review* 75, 2: 297–335.

Özler, Ş. (1993). 'Have commercial banks ignored history?', *The American Economic Review* 83, 3: 608–620.

Parodi Trece, C. (2015). 'La crisis de la deuda en América Latina de la década de los ochenta'. Working Papers 15-06. Centro de Investigación, Universidad del Pacífico.

Pazos, F. (1985). 'Have import substitution policies either precipitated or aggravated the debt crisis?', *Journal of Interamerican Studies and World Affairs* 27, 4: 57–73.

Pop-Eleches, G. (2009). *From Economic Crisis to Reform: IMF programs in Latin America and Eastern Europe.* Princeton, NJ: Princeton University Press.

Powell, A. and Valencia, O. (2023). *Dealing with Debt: Less Risk for More Growth in Latin America and the Caribbean.* Inter-American Development Bank.

Rodríguez, J.P. (2021). 'The politics of neo-liberalism in Latin America: Dynamics of resilience and contestation', *Sociology Compass* 15, 3: e12854.

Roos, J. (2019). *Why Not Default? The Political Economy of Sovereign Debt.* Princeton: Princeton University Press.

Sachs, J. (1988). 'Recent studies of the Latin American debt crisis'. In B. Balassa et al. (eds) *Latin American Research Review* 23, 3: 170–179.

Sachs, J. (1989). 'Conditionality, debt relief, and the developing country debt crisis'. In J. Sachs (ed.), *Developing Country Debt and Economic Performance.* Chicago and London: University of Chicago Press (A National Bureau of Economic Research project report), 255–296.

Sachs, J. (ed.) (1989b). *Developing Country Debt and the World Economy.* Chicago and London: University of Chicago Press (A National Bureau of Economic Research project report).

Sachs, J. and Williamson, J. (1985). 'External debt and macroeconomic performance in Latin America and East Asia', *Brookings Papers on Economic Activity* 1985, 2: 523–573.

Sachs, J. and Williamson, J. (1986). 'Managing the LDC debt crisis', *Brookings Papers on Economic Activity*, 1986 2: 397–440.

Sallum Jr., B. and Kugelmas, E. (1991). 'O Leviathan declinante: a crise brasileira dos anos 80', *Estudos Avançados* 5, 13: 145–159.

Sampson, A. (1981) *The Money Lenders: Bankers in a Dangerous World.* New York: Viking Press.

Sgard, J. (2023). *The Debt Crisis of the 1980s: Law and political economy.* Cheltenham; Northampton, MA: Edward Elgar Publishing.

Silva, E. (2009). *Challenging Neo-liberalism in Latin America.* Cambridge: Cambridge University Press.

Spindler, J.A. (1984). *The Politics of International Credit: Private Finance and Foreign Policy in Germany and Japan.* Washington, DC: The Brookings Institute.

Stallings, B. (1987). *Banker to the Third World: US Portfolio Investment in Latin America, 1900–1986.* Los Angeles: University of California Press.

Stiglitz, J.E. and Rashid, H. (2020). 'How to prevent the looming sovereign-debt crisis', *Project Syndicate.* Available at: https://www.project-syndicate.org/commentary/how-to-prevent-looming-debt-crisis-developing-countries-by-joseph-e-stiglitz-and-hamid-rashid-2020-07.

Thorp, R. and Whitehead, L. (eds) (1987). *Latin American Debt and the Adjustment Crisis.* Pittsburgh, Pa: University of Pittsburgh Press (Pitt Latin American series).

Tomz, M. (2007). *Reputation and International Cooperation: Sovereign Debt across Three Centuries.* Princeton: Princeton University Press.

Tomz, M. and Wright, M. (2007). 'Do countries default in "bad times"?', *Journal of the European Economic Association* 5, 2–3: 352–360.

Truman, E.M. (2020). *Sovereign Debt Relief in the Global Pandemic: Lessons from the 1980s.* Washington, DC: Peterson Institute for International Economics.

UNCTAD (2024). *A World of Debt 2024 Report.*

Vaubel, R. (1983). 'The moral hazard of IMF lending', *The World Economy* 6, 3: 291–304.

Wellons, P.A. (1985). 'International debt: The behavior of banks in a politicized environment', *International Organization* 39, 3: 441–471.

Wellons, P.A. (1987). *Passing the Buck: Banks, Governments and Third World Debt*. Boston, Mass: Harvard Business School Press.

Wiesner, E. (1985). 'Latin American debt: Lessons and pending issues', *The American Economic Review* 75, 2: 191–195.

Williamson, J. (ed.) (1990). *Latin American Adjustment: How Much Has Happened?*. Washington, DC: Institute for International Economics.

Yeyati, E.L. and Panizza, U. (2011). 'The elusive costs of sovereign defaults', *Journal of Development Economics* 94, 1: 95–105.

5
The spectre of history
How the fear of depression haunts financial crises

Johanna Gautier-Morin

> The past is never dead. It's not even past.
> —William Faulkner, *Requiem for a Nun*, 1951.

> Good evening, everyone. The law of gravity hit Wall Street today and financial markets around the world ... as stock prices plunged even more than they did on Black Thursday of 1929.[1]
> —Dean Shepherd on *The Nightly Business Report*, 19 October 1987

Within hours on 19 October 1987, stock markets across 23 countries plummeted in a dramatic and unexpected collapse. This unforeseen crash came after months of steady praise from market commentators for the consistent rise in prices.[2] In Australia, Austria, Belgium, Canada, Denmark, France, Germany, Hong Kong, Ireland, Italy, Japan, Malaysia, Mexico, the Netherlands, New Zealand, Norway, Singapore, South Africa, Spain, Sweden, Switzerland, the United Kingdom, and the United States, traders found themselves unprepared. Many held highly leveraged positions with insufficient liquidity to absorb the cascading losses. As the day unfolded, experts and commentators quickly drew comparisons to the infamous crash of 1929, noting the striking similarities in market charts (Figure 5.1). By the close of trading, the parallel was set in stone and 19 October 1987 became 'Black Monday' after 'Black Thursday' of 24 October 1929.

The fear of history repeating itself in 1987 cast the day as a harbinger of catastrophic events. This sense of dread imbued October 1987 with a distinct historical weight, evoking both the terror and the heroism associated with past crises. Harley Bassman, a mortgage trader at Merrill Lynch, described it as an 'out-of-body experience', admitting, 'And yes, I was thinking 1929.'[3] The spectre of the Great

[1] Public Television Stations Archives, https://www.youtube.com/watch?v=5PUwr8DsYeg.
[2] Prestbo, *The Market's Measure*, 88.
[3] *Bloomberg Markets*, 16 October 2017.

Johanna Gautier-Morin, *The spectre of history*. In: *History, Memory, and the Return of Financial Crises After Bretton Woods*. Edited by: Youssef Cassis and Giuseppe Telesca, Oxford University Press. © Oxford University Press (2026).
DOI: 10.1093/9780198950158.003.0005

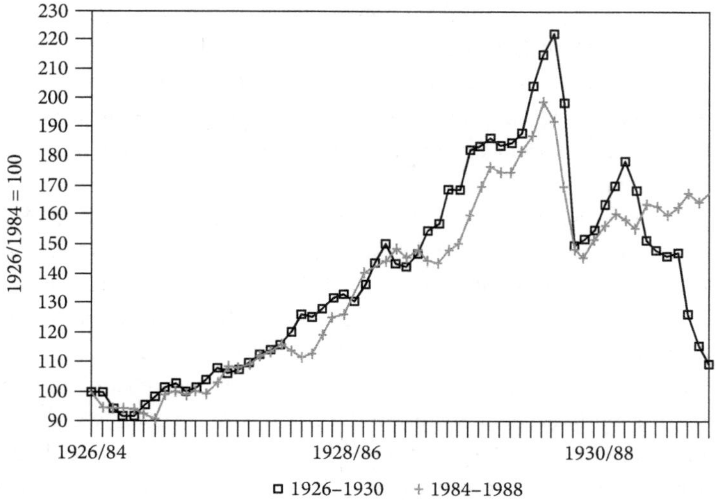

Figure 5.1 Comparative charts of 1929 and 1987 stock markets crashes
Source: Reproduced with permission from White, 'The stock market boom', 68. © American Economic Association.

Depression exacerbated the panic, and the incessant media references to 1929 fuelled overreaction.[4] Hour by hour, the crash was framed as a live historical event, with commentators using terms like 'panic', 'debacle', 'stampede', 'bloodbath', and 'massacre' to describe the unfolding chaos.[5]

This parallel was not just a matter of superimposing stock charts showing similar downturns; it reawakened the collective memory of the Great Depression's devastating consequences: widespread poverty, social upheaval, and global conflict. However, the invocation of 1929 served not only as a symbol of fear but also as a framework to navigate the unfolding uncertainty. Confronted with an event that defied immediate explanation, financial actors turned to history as a makeshift compass, using the 'lessons of history' to interpret the present and guide their actions.

Although the analogy to 1929 was far from precise, it was the most prominent and accessible historical reference point. As Harold James observed following the 2008 financial crisis, the Great Crash was 'evoked wherever and whenever financial sentiment becomes nervous' throughout the twentieth century.[6] Generations of economists had tested their theories against the Great Depression, which

[4] Shiller, 'Investor behavior'; Shiller, 'Portfolio insurance'; De Bondt and Thaler, 'Do security analysts overreact?'.

[5] Tetlock, 'Giving content to investor sentiment'. For the terminology used by traders during Black Monday and reported by the press all along the following week, see Green, 'Leçons d'octobre 1929, 1987'.

[6] James, '1929', 129.

came to be regarded as a 'natural laboratory' for economic thought.[7] Similarly, the policy frameworks, institutional regulations, and market strategies of the 1980s were deeply rooted in post-1929 economic knowledge.[8] Thus, in 1987, the October 1929 crash loomed large in collective memory. Its legacy shaped how the event was understood and acted upon, underscoring the enduring influence of past historical crises on the financial imagination.

The precise knowledge traders had about 1929 is highly uncertain. As Eugene White noted, beyond specialized debates, there had been little scholarly focus on 1929 since the publication of John Kenneth Galbraith's *The Great Crash 1929* in 1954. According to White, many of the comparisons drawn between 1929 and 1987 were superficial and revealed a lack of historical awareness among financial analysts.[9] Popular interpretations were often shaped by anachronistic ideas and trade books offering guidance on 'how to avoid the next historic crisis', which frequently presented contradictory interpretations.[10] Even respected academics like Charles Kindleberger contributed to this trend, publishing his ten lessons from 1929 in 1982.[11]

Did the proliferation of publications on this topic prepare or mislead market actors during the 1987 crash? Using Halbwachs's analytical framework on collective memory, one might argue that even unreliable traditions can act as guides to the past, irrespective of their accuracy.[12] Amin Samman expanded on this idea, observing how the 'recursive action of the past on the present' transforms abstract patterns—names, concepts, archetypes—into a historical imagination distinct from concrete historical legacies. 'The result is a quasi-historical process—a *strange history*—in which the recollected past shapes the way we apprehend and negotiate the present.'[13]

The terms 'crisis', 'panic', and 'crash' themselves illustrate the performativity of language during such events. This raises critical questions: Who had the authority to define the event? Who was socially positioned to characterize its causes and consequences? Much of the commentary on the 1987 crash was produced in real time, effectively becoming part of the event itself. Drawing on George Duby's analysis of the concept of an historical event as 'magnified by the impressions of witnesses and illusions of historians', this chapter examines how the memory of a past event takes shape through the emotions and narratives it provokes.[14] The repeated references

[7] Christiano et al., 'The Great Depression', 1120.
[8] Burgin, *The Great Persuasion*; Jones, *Masters of the Universe*; Mirowski and Plehwe, *The Road from Mont Pèlerin*.
[9] White, 'The stock market boom', 67–68.
[10] Hummel, 'Ben Bernanke versus Milton Friedman'; Bordo, 'Comment'.
[11] Kindleberger, '1929: Ten lessons for today'.
[12] Halbwachs, *La Topographie légendaire des Évangiles*; Halbwachs, *On Collective Memory*.
[13] Samman, *History in Financial Times*, 5.
[14] Duby, *Le Dimanche de Bouvines*, 8–9.

to 1929 during the 1987 crash unearthed deeper, often unacknowledged, anxieties and traces of past crises that might have otherwise remained latent.

This interplay of historical memory and market behaviour invites a dual approach. By combining the microhistory of traders' reactions with the macrohistory of global stock market interdependence, we gain insight into how historians can analyse global events through diverse and unequal sources—from institutional reports and macroeconomic data to personal memoirs and testimonies. The central hypothesis of this chapter is that the 1987 crash cannot and should not be defined by a singular narrative. Instead, its meaning emerges through the multitude of memories—divergent, inconsistent, conflicting, and layered—across different social and professional contexts. From this perspective, the very concept of a financial 'crisis' takes on a broad spectrum of interpretations. For those who lost fortunes, or feared losing them, crises represent destruction, system failure, or dysfunction. For some analysts, crashes are self-regulatory corrections that deflate speculative bubbles disconnected from underlying asset values. Advocates of free-market resilience view crises as stress tests for the system. Meanwhile, for a fortunate few, financial crashes offer opportunities for enrichment and a stage to emerge as visionary heroes.

The interpretation of each financial crash is inevitably shaped by the perspectives of those affected by the price drop. These perspectives vary depending on one's position in the financial ecosystem—whether as a trader, bank executive, hedge fund manager, central banker, regulator, or member of the general public whose pension funds are tied to the markets. Personal factors, such as age and geographical context, also play a significant role in shaping responses to such events. In the case of the 1987 crash, global financial trajectories converged briefly on Black Monday, but national experiences diverged in meaningful ways. Canada, for instance, had a remarkably stable financial history throughout the twentieth century and into the 1980s. Even the Great Crash of 1929 had minimal impact on its trading activities; none of the Toronto Stock Exchange (TSX) members defaulted. However, on 19 October 1987, the Toronto Composite 300 Index (TSE 300) experienced a historic drop of 11.3%, or 407.2 points.[15] This unprecedented plunge was particularly unsettling for Canadians, as the 1929 crash had left their markets relatively unscathed. The fact that the TSX was no longer insulated from global panic heightened fears of a widespread and irreversible financial collapse. In contrast, Argentina's response to the 1987 crash was muted. The country was already grappling with the broader market turmoil exacerbated by the ongoing Latin American sovereign debt crisis of the 1980s, making Black Monday just one element of a larger financial struggle.[16]

[15] Canadian Broadcasting Corporation (CBC) Archives, Der Hoi-Yin on The National, Live on 19 October 1987, '1987: "Black Monday" hits world's stock markets'. See online archives: https://www.cbc.ca/archives/entry/1987-black-monday-hits-worlds-stock-markets

[16] Cerro and Meloni, 'Crises and crashes'.

The uses and misuses of historical references during and after the October 1987 crash provide a lens through which we can analyse the role of memory in both amplifying and alleviating financial crises. This chapter distinguishes different types of actors and institutional 'memories' in an Halbwachsian perspective and explores how narratives of the crash occupy the intersection of shared group memories and the construction of individual self-image. Faulkner's opening quote, 'the past is never dead. It's not even past', highlights the enduring influence of historical and cultural layers—however distorted they may become through competing recollections. The echoes of past financial crises continue to resonate in the present, manifesting in words, institutions, borders, buildings, customs, knowledge, and fears.[17] The diverse social functions of crisis anniversaries and the wide range of actors who invoke historical memories reveal the complexity of interpreting financial crashes. The grammar of these questions defies simplification, requiring us to grapple with the multiplicity of memories and meanings that each event generates.

The chapter proceeds in four steps to develop this argument. I first reconstruct how Black Monday was experienced and narrated in real time, from trading floors to television studios, showing how journalists, traders, and analysts mobilized the memory of 1929 to make sense of an event that seemed to defy explanation. I then turn to the institutional arena, examining debates about halting trading, the role of central banks, and the translation of historical lessons, especially those drawn from the Great Depression, into concrete instruments of crisis management. The third section reconsiders the supposed 'non-event' status of the 1987 crash by juxtaposing its limited macroeconomic consequences with its powerful psychological and professional afterlives, and by questioning what counts as a 'real' impact in financial history. Finally, I analyse the longer-term social and cultural uses of the crash, from official inquiries and academic interpretations to films, comics, and urban symbols such as Charging Bull and Fearless Girl, to show how crisis narratives migrate across domains and acquire new meanings over time.

Mania in the Information Age: recording history in the making

By naming 19 October 1987, after a historical precedent, financiers extended the lineage of infamous market panics that influenced the interpretation of the event: Black Friday, 11 May 1866; Black Thursday, 24 October 1929; Black Monday, 28 October 1929; Black Tuesday, 29 October 1929; and once again, Black Monday, 19 October 1987. The repetition of ominous names was more than symbolic: it suggested a sense of foreboding and inevitability, as though history itself were

[17] Jablonka, *L'histoire est une littérature contemporaine*, 134.

caught in a cyclical curse. Many participants recognized that they were living through a thrilling *historical* event, one that demanded documentation.

In Hong Kong, Raymond Zepp and Rolf Cremer chronicled the crash from the office of the Bank of Credit and Commerce International (BCCI) in Macau, as the Hong Kong stock market plummeted over 1,000 points. 'We were watching the news monitor, and stories from around the world were pouring in, reporting economic disasters on many fronts', they wrote. The event, they recalled, felt like 'World War III' had erupted—a moment of cataclysmic significance. Reflecting on the media's coverage, one observer in their office lamented the lack of comparable live reports during the Great Depression, which might have preserved the raw emotion of that era's historic upheaval: 'the feeling of history in the making'.[18]

In New York, insiders also collected notes to testify to what they were witnessing in the midst of action. Michael Lewis, then a young trader at Salomon Brothers and later an acclaimed author, admitted, 'I was absolutely aware that this was literary material.' He remembered scribbling notes on scraps of paper amid the chaos of the trading room.[19] On Wall Street, crowds gathered near the New York Stock Exchange to witness the drama firsthand. Neal Cavuto, reporting for the *Nightly Business Report*, noted the onlookers' eagerness to 'see the incredible drops in the Dow, right before their eyes'.[20] Larry Wachtel, an equity analyst at Prudential Securities, described the day's absurdity as so extreme it became 'funny' by the end of the day,[21] while Paul Steiger, managing editor for the *Wall Street Journal*, recalled the tension and shock as 'awesome'.[22]

This fervor, however, was not confined to market participants and observers. The crash also generated a wave of misinformation. In Paris, Lionel Salem, an analyst at Paribas investment bank, wrote a minute-by-minute account describing widespread panic not just among traders but also the public. Salem claimed to have seen 'haggard visitors' wandering the Paris Stock Exchange, including a 70-year-old woman dressed all in green, allegedly a private investor, staring helplessly at the board. Outside, he reported banners bearing slogans such as, 'If the stock market collapses, what will we have left?'. Salem wondered if they were union members, unemployed workers, or 'bizarre characters'.[23] Yet these vivid details are riddled with inconsistencies. The Paris Stock Exchange was not open to the public,

[18] Zepp, 'The stock market crash', 28–29.

[19] Interview by Richard Dewey on account of *Bloomberg Markets* to mark Black Monday's 30th anniversary: "The Crash of '87, From the Wall Street Players Who Lived It," *Bloomberg Markets*, October 16, 2017.

[20] Live from New York on Monday, 19 October 1987, broadcast by the Nightly Business Report (NBR), available online: https://www.youtube.com/watch?v=5PUwr8DsYeg&t=200s.

[21] Interviewed by Jim Zarroli on the Morning Edition of the US National Public Radio (NPR), 19 October 2007. Broadcast online: https://www.npr.org/templates/story/story.php?storyId=15436586.

[22] Testimony collected by Weiner, *What Goes Up*, 283.

[23] Salem, *Le Krach de 1987*, 34.

and no evidence corroborates Salem's claims of demonstrators outside the Palais Brongniart. Journalists covering the area captured no images or reports of such protests, and no political organizations documented or claimed responsibility for any rallies.[24]

Why would a respected academic and financial analyst fabricate—or misremember—such implausible details? Salem's testimony may reflect the confusion and heightened emotions of the day. As Marc Bloch noted in his *Reflections of a Historian on the False News of the War*, eyewitness accounts often reveal more about the witness's state of mind than the events themselves. In moments of crisis, strained nerves and heightened imaginations can distort perceptions of reality. Bloch's analysis of false rumours among German soldiers in Belgium during World War I illustrates this dynamic, where fear and a hostile environment skewed soldiers' understanding of their surroundings.[25]

The parallel between a financial crash and warfare may seem exaggerated, and there is of course no comparison between the degrees of trauma these two different types of crises can inflict. However, both involve actors who are profoundly influenced by the narratives and fears surrounding them. In Salem's case, his description of public panic may reflect broader anxieties within elite financial circles during the 1970s and 1980s—a period marked by the fear that the 'masses' would be bluntly hostile to any form of liberal progress and financial enrichment.[26] Salem may have fantasized about the anxiety that the stock market would provoke in workers and unionists, which informs us more about his personal biases than the broader societal response to Black Monday.

Strikingly, Salem's account in Paris shares similarities with Zepp and Cremer's chronicle in Hong Kong. Both purported to offer insider perspectives but relied heavily on secondary sources and media narratives.[27] Their linear accounts, structured hour by hour, created an artificial impression of causality, linking discrete events in ways that mirrored journalistic storytelling.[28] Rather than clarifying the crash, these testimonies contributed to its mythologization by framing the event in dramatic and deterministic terms. These narratives reveal how the overproduction of discourse during a crisis can influence not only how it is remembered but

[24] According to the archives of the *Confédération Générale du Travail* (CGT), there were demonstrations elsewhere in Paris on that day in support of social workers and against university reforms. See French Communist Party Archives, Audivisual Funds: https://www.cinearchives.org/Catalogue-d-exploitation-MOBILISATION-DE-LA-JEUNESSE-CONTRE-LE-PROJET-DE-LOI-DEVAQUET-ET-GREVE-DES-CHEMINOTS-494-837-0-1.html?ref=6c8c55f53f8e4c8f6f7a545b2ac5178a.

[25] Bloch, 'Reflections of a historian', 2.

[26] This phenomenon was not limited to France as reported by future Nobel Memorial Prize-winner George J. Stigler by the end of the 1970s: see Stigler, 'Do Economists Matter?'.

[27] *International Herald Tribune, Financial Times, Frankfurter Allgemeine Zeitung, Asian Wall Street Journal, South China Morning Post, Hong Kong Standard, China Daily, Renmin Ribao, Yang Cheng Wanbao, Le Monde, Le Figaro.*

[28] By opposition to social sciences 'thick description' introduced by Clifford Geertz, these accounts are not analysing the social depth in which the events are embedded. See Geertz, 'Thick description', 3–32.

also the perception of its immediate reality. As fear spread, the panic fed on itself, necessitating intervention from external actors who were perceived as capable of maintaining composure—or at least appeared to offer a semblance of stability.

Unplug the market: stopping the course of history

As stock indices plummeted and the specter of 1929 loomed large, market participants pressed public authorities to intervene, fearing a financial collapse that could devastate the global banking system. The most dramatic intervention occurred in Hong Kong, where traders faced the aftermath of the US market crash on Black Monday, bracing for a disastrous local opening on what would become Terrible Tuesday. Ronald Li Fook-Shiu, Chairman of the Exchange Committee and Deputy Chairman of the Futures Exchange, persuaded the Exchange Committee to close the Hong Kong Stock Exchange and Futures Exchange for four trading days (20–23 October).[29]

When news of this decision broke, journalists and financial professionals worldwide debated similar measures. Many demanded the shutdown of trading systems, blaming the avalanche of sell orders on computerized trading.[30] However, no other exchanges followed Hong Kong's lead. Alan Greenspan, newly appointed Chair of the US Federal Reserve, recalled NYSE officials considering a temporary closure, a proposal the Fed firmly opposed, believing it would worsen the crisis.[31] Similarly, Robin Leigh-Pemberton, Governor of the Bank of England, argued that closing trading floors could amplify pressure on other markets and accelerate the meltdown.[32]

The reluctance to suspend operations reflected a historical aversion to such measures. In the twentieth century, Western markets only closed under extreme circumstances: the NYSE halted trading on 31 July 1914, during the lead-up to World War I, reopening gradually with price restrictions until April 1915.[33] London's financial markets closed only twice—when Britain declared war on Germany in 1939 and during the Suez Crisis in 1956.[34] Against this historical backdrop, shutting down markets in 1987 was seen as a last resort, fraught with terrible, historical risks.

[29] Fell, 'Financial market supervision'; Gunningham, 'Moving the goalposts'.

[30] As evoked earlier, John Phelan, Chairman of the NYSE, confessed he had received many pressuring calls from big securities and investment-banking firms to close the market.

[31] Greenspan, *Age of Turbulence*, 107; also reported by the SEC in Ketchum, 'The October 1987 market break', 2–20.

[32] Rt. Hon. Robin Leigh-Pemberton, Governor of the Bank of England, Speech given at the City University, 11 February 1988, 7.

[33] NYSE Trading Information, 'New York Stock Exchange special closings, 1885–date', revised through January 2011. For an analysis of the impacts and tenants of such historical closings, see Michie, 'The London and New York Stock Exchanges'.

[34] Chappell and Eldridge, 'Evidence of market inefficiency'.

When Leo Melamed, Chairman of the Chicago Mercantile Exchange (CME), heard that the NYSE might close on Tuesday, he recalled how fear spread through Chicago. The Chicago Board Options Exchange (CBOE) suspended trading in many stock-index derivatives at 11:45 a.m., followed by the Chicago Mercantile Exchange (CME) at 12:15 p.m.[35] The ensuing debates over trading halts stimulated widespread academic and policy-making discussion in the aftermaths of the crash.[36] Empirical studies soon refuted the common assumption that trading halts would give traders time to settle down and rationally get back on their feet.[37] Lee, Ready, and Seguin revealed that market volatility was higher when trading resumed after a trading halt.[38] As consensus turned against trading halts, alternative measures emerged. For instance, the Tel Aviv Stock Exchange selectively applied circuit breakers, allowing one-third of the stocks to trade while hand-picked trading halts curbed the decline of others.[39] In Japan, daily price limits mitigated wild swings but delayed price discovery and potentially triggered volatility in subsequent sessions.[40]

Hong Kong remained the sole market to halt trading entirely, a decision that carried severe long-term consequences. Analysts' warnings proved prescient: the closure damaged Hong Kong's reputation as a reliable and open financial hub. When trading resumed on 26 October, the Hang Seng Index plunged an additional 33%, triggering a wave of defaults among futures brokers.[41] The government intervened with two HK$2 billion rescue packages to save major institutions from bankruptcy, including the Hong Kong Futures Guarantee Corporation, the Hongkong and Shanghai Bank, Standard Chartered Bank, and the Bank of China.[42]

The debates over market closures during the crash underscored the complex relationship between memory, history, and crisis response. While avoiding a repetition of 1929 was paramount, the situation also drew comparisons to other historical emergencies outside the financial realm, such as the declarations of war in 1914 and 1939 or the Cold War-era Suez Crisis. These analogies highlighted a key tension: though market crashes could not be entirely prevented, responses needed to adapt in real-time to manage uncertainty effectively. The challenge lay not in halting history but in learning how to navigate it under pressure.

[35] Melamed, *Escape to the Futures*.

[36] To quote a few, see Stein, 'Informational externalities'; Grossman, 'Introduction to NBER symposium'; Gerety and Mulherin, 'Trading halts and market activity'; Corwin, 'Differences in trading behavior'.

[37] Anshuman, 'Regulatory measures'.

[38] Lee, Ready, and Seguin, 'Volume, volatility and New York Stock Exchange'.

[39] Lauterbach and Ben-Zion, 'Stock market crashes'; Kalay, Wei, and Wohl, 'Continuous trading'.

[40] This hypothesis is largely supported by Ma, Rao, and Sears, 'Volatility, price resolution'; Kim and Ghon Rhee, 'Price limit performance'.

[41] On 19 October 1987, the Hang Send index closed at 3362.4. On 26 October, it closed at 2241.7, corresponding to a loss of 33.3%. See Sornette, *Why Stock Markets Crash*, 244.

[42] Scott, *Political Change*, 259–261.

Crisis management: lessons of history

The lessons of history proved to be a confusing guide for decision-making. While the similarities to 1929 sparked widespread fear—not so much because of the crash itself, but due to its potential economic and social consequences—there was no unified understanding of how to interpret the events of 1929. Historians, economists, analysts, and financial actors debated endlessly over macroeconomic trends and the causes of subsequent bear markets. The discussions polarized around two schools of thought: one attributing large market swings to irrational 'fads and fashions', and the other viewing them as efficient market corrections responding to evolving expectations about the future.[43]

The 1987 crash, like the infamous collapse of 1929, followed a period of euphoria in the markets. While many indices had already begun to decline, trading volumes were surging, with retail investors from across the globe entering the bullish market late in the cycle.[44] The frenzy peaked in August 1987, as the Dow Jones Industrial Average rose 35% since the start of the year, hitting a record high of 2,722.42 points.

This surge reflected a broader trend of increasing retail investor participation in the stock market, particularly in the United States, despite the lingering effects of the 1970s recession.[45] However, distinguishing the behaviour of professional investment managers from that of 'noise traders' became increasingly challenging. This difficulty fuelled extensive literature on the irrationality of crowds and herd behaviour.[46] After the crash, some economists attempted to model herd behaviour as rational.[47] Regardless, critics accused global financial markets of indulging in the 'gigantomania follies' of the 1980s, characterized by excessive liquidity, volatile prices, speculative greed, and regulatory laissez-faire.[48]

Amid the chaos, commentators and officials sought to calm the general public, whose panic threatened to exacerbate the sell-off. Myron Kandel, CNN's founding financial editor, urged small investors to avoid rash decisions, stating, 'My advice is: do not panic, stay put for now. The damage has been done.'[49] Politicians echoed this sentiment. US President Ronald Reagan reassured the public, saying, 'I don't think anyone should panic because all the economic indicators are solid.... There is nothing wrong with the economy.'[50] Similarly, French Prime

[43] Barsky and De Long, 'Bull and bear markets'.
[44] Wright, *Chronology of the Stock Market*, 67–68.
[45] Seligman, 'The obsolescence of Wall Street'.
[46] Raines and Leathers, 'Veblenian stock markets'; Bloomfield et al., 'How noise trading affects markets'.
[47] Banerjee, 'A simple model'; Bikhchandani, Hirshleifer, and Welch, 'A theory of fads'.
[48] Adams and Brock, '1980s Gigantomania'.
[49] Part of CNN's launch team in 1980, Myron Kandel was considered a pioneer in the development of financial news on television, and one of the most influential business journalists of the twentieth century. See Museum of American Finance curricula of the members of the Museum's Board of Trustees. Here, Myron Kandel commenting on what happened after the closing of the market on CNN.
[50] Quoted in Robert A. Rosenblatt and Tom Redburn, 'Reagan offers southing words: Stunned US officials can't explain plunge', *Los Angeles Times*, 20 October 1987.

Minister Jacques Chirac and Finance Minister Édouard Balladur emphasized the natural and healthy fluctuations of the stock market, urging calm among small savers.[51]

These statements reflected a broader perception of retail investors as more prone to irrational behaviour than professional managers—a view frequently contradicted by empirical data. In November 1987, Robert J. Shiller, as part of Yale University's *Investor Behavior Project* and the NBER's *Financial Markets and Monetary Economics* programme, surveyed 1,000 individual and institutional investors about their actions on 19 October. The findings revealed that both groups attributed the crash to the psychology of others, and no clear distinction could be made between individual and institutional behaviour.[52] In fact, institutional accounts, as estimated by the Securities Industry Association, conducted the most volatile trades on the NYSE.[53]

Amid this volatility, central banks emerged as critical actors to save the day. Newly appointed Federal Reserve Chairman Alan Greenspan articulated the Fed's role during a market panic: to prevent financial paralysis, where businesses and banks would cease payments, potentially grinding the economy to a halt. Greenspan assembled a crisis team—including Treasury Secretary James Baker, White House Chief of Staff Howard Baker, and Treasury Undersecretary George Gould—and decided that the priority was to inject massive liquidity into the system.[54] The Fed publicly pledged unlimited support to commercial banks, provided they continued backing other financial firms, ensuring liquidity for market operations.

This approach reflected the monetarist influence of Milton Friedman and Anna Schwartz's interpretation of the Great Depression. Their analysis framed 1929 as a liquidity crisis rather than an insolvency issue. They criticized the Federal Reserve's failure to address the contraction of money supply during the banking panics of 1930–1933 and advocated for massive liquidity injections to stabilize the financial system.[55] The Fed's room for manoeuvre on that matter has long been the subject of academic debate,[56] but the Friedman–Schwartz thesis has been widely shared by the new generations of monetary experts since the 1980s.[57] Friedman himself participated extensively in the public debate and called for structural

[51] Editorial, 'MM. Chirac et Balladur cherchent à rassurer les épargnants', *Le Monde*, 18 October 1987.

[52] Shiller, 'Investor behavior'.

[53] Securities Industry Association (SIA), Investor Activity Report: October Analysis: 'The 1987 crash', 2 December 1987.

[54] In his memoirs, Alan Greenspan claimed indeed 'We don't need to wait to see what happens.... We *know* what's going to happen', in Greenspan, *Age of Turbulence*, 106.

[55] Friedman and Schwartz, *A Monetary History*, 358; Friedman and Schwartz, *The Great Contraction*; Friedman and Schwartz, 'Has government any role in money?'; Bordo and Landon-Lane, 'The banking panics'.

[56] For pros and cons studies, see among others McCallum, 'Monetary base rule'; Hsieh and Romer, 'Was the Federal Reserve constrained'.

[57] Bordo and Rockoff, 'Not just the Great Contraction'.

reforms of the central bank.[58] Greenspan's response to the 1987 crash drew heavily on these lessons. His frequent use of the term 'contraction', popularized by Friedman and Schwartz, highlighted the monetarist framework that underpinned his decision-making.[59]

Unlike targeted bailouts, the Fed's intervention during the 1987 crash focused on stabilizing liquidity without rescuing insolvent institutions. While financial firms were shaken and markets destabilized, the economy did not suffer from a collapse in financial intermediation. As *The Wall Street Journal* observed on 20 November 1987, 'The New York Stock Exchange died. But within an hour or two, it was raised from the dead.'[60] This decisive intervention prevented the crash from escalating into a systemic crisis, showcasing the critical role of central banks in managing financial panics.

Much ado about nothing? Chronicle of a non-event

In retrospect, the October 1987 global financial crash bore little resemblance to the Great Depression. Unlike 1929, it did not mark a turning point in history. The event had no dramatic economic consequences: it was not followed by a depression, most people's day-to-day lives remained unaffected, and by the end of the year, most markets had largely recovered. Since no significant new information about underlying assets had triggered the crash, it became a textbook 'counter-example' to the finance theory claim that stock price movements reflect rational expectations of future returns based on new information.[61]

Despite its limited impact, the crash left a psychological imprint on financial professionals and the media. On the 25th anniversary of the event in 2012, traders, bankers, and journalists reflected on the chaos of that day. 'People remember where they were in 1987 because the damage of that single day was so big', noted A. Michael Lipper, founder of Lipper Inc. 'What they remember is how scary it was, how they thought everything was going away. What they forget is that the market recovered in about two months.'[62] Indeed, while the immediate shock was profound, the anticipated fallout never materialized. As observers from the Bank of International Settlements aptly summarized: 'There is a widespread feeling that lessons should be drawn, but it is not easy to see what these lessons are.'[63]

[58] See Friedman's presidential address to the American Economic Association in December 1967 published in Friedman, 'The role of monetary policy'; see also, two years before the crash, Friedman, 'The case for overhauling'.

[59] Greenspan, *Age of Turbulence*, 3, 86, 103, 177, and 466.

[60] James B. Stewart and Daniel Hertzberg, *The Wall Street Journal*, 20 November 1987.

[61] MacKenzie, 'The big, bad wolf', 307.

[62] *MarketWatch* on the theme 'Investors forget pain of loss and focus on recovery', 19 October 2012.

[63] BIS, *Annual Report*, 1988, 3.

The prevailing view was that the October 1987 crash was a 'non-event' with minimal impact on the 'real' economy. Markets appeared to self-regulate, adjusting and correcting without sustained external intervention. Even major economic institutions downplayed its significance. The Organisation for Economic Cooperation and Development (OECD), meeting in the days following the crash, omitted it from its agenda entirely.[64] Similarly, Jan Toporowski, a former senior economist at Standard Chartered Bank, argued in his 1993 theoretical analysis that the crash was economically insignificant within the broader trajectory of capital market growth.[65]

In the United Kingdom, the Bank of England echoed this sentiment in its 1988/89 annual report to Parliament. The report highlighted the crash's limited impact on the economy, noting 'experience was not uniform, and securities business continued to be profitable for certain banks'.[66] Across the Atlantic, US policy-makers reached similar conclusions. The Joint Economic Committee's 1989 analysis found that the crash had barely affected the economy. Key indicators showed resilience: real output grew by an average of 2.9% in the first three quarters of 1988; inflation held at a modest 3.9%; and unemployment fell to 5.3%, its lowest level in 14 years.

Other metrics reinforced this optimistic assessment. Real personal consumption expenditures rose at an annual average of 3.8% after a slight dip in late 1987, while the personal savings rate increased compared to the previous year. Real business fixed investment grew at an annual average of 8.8%, with spending on durable equipment up nearly 15%. Real net exports surged by $32.1 billion in the first three quarters of 1988, nearly double the 1987 level. These gains demonstrated that the economy not only weathered the crash but exceeded expectations in its aftermath.[67]

The social function of the memories of financial crises

Since the October 1987 crash was an anomaly for most economic models, the premises of any *ex post* analysis were based on either rationality or irrationality. 'Overreaction or fundamentals?' was once again the question.[68] In the weeks following the crash, both the *Economist* and the *Wall Street Journal* cited Charles Mackay's 1841 classic, *Extraordinary Popular Delusions and the Madness of*

[64] OECD Archives, 'Comité de politique économique', 66th session, 28 October 1987, CPE/A(87)3.
[65] Toporowski, *The Economics of Financial Markets*.
[66] Bank of England Archives, *Banking Act Report 1988/89*, 'Report on the exercise of the Bank's functions under the *Banking Act 1987* during the year to 28 February 1989, presented to the Chancellor of Exchequer, and by him to Parliament, pursuant to section 1(3) of the Act', 1989, 7–8.
[67] Congress of the United States Archives, Joint Economic Committee, 'The Paris Economic Summit', Washington, DC, 6 July 1989.
[68] Seyhun, 'Overreaction or fundamentals'.

Crowds, which examined the irrational herd behaviour of financial markets in the nineteenth century. This critique aligned with a long-standing historical narrative: speculative bubbles and their subsequent crashes are often blamed on the irrationality of the masses.

In *Manias, Panics, and Crashes*, Charles Kindleberger observed that financial authorities and institutional investors often shield their reputations by attributing the irrationality of speculative bubbles to outsiders.[69] Anne Goldgar, in her study of the Dutch tulip mania (1634–1637), similarly noted how speculative bubbles were often portrayed as being driven by 'the wrong people'—commoners or laymen considered unfit for financial speculation.[70] Arnaud Orain showed how historical figures like John Law have long served as archetypal scapegoats, a typical example of how all intellectual, material, and political reality can be elided in favour of a myth based on a sulphurous protagonist.[71] This framing reinforces a moralistic narrative, where financial crises are explained through individual greed, rather than by interrogating broader systemic or institutional failures.

Public discourse around the 1987 crash mirrored these historical patterns. Regulatory authorities, public institutions, and institutional investors framed the crash in moral terms, focusing on the role of 'evil speculators'.[72] By 1992, the *New Palgrave Dictionary of Money and Finance* had declared that the crash defied rational explanation, as no fundamental economic factor could account for the sudden collapse.[73] This lack of clarity fuelled immediate speculation about its causes. Commentators attributed blame based on their own interests and agendas. As Alan Reynolds later summarized in *The Wall Street Journal*:

> In the wake of the crash, pundits of various stripes offered hysterical explanations to lobby for their own pet policies. Fiscalists blamed the budget deficit, monetarists blamed the Fed, supply-siders blamed the House Ways and Means Committee's tax bill, protectionists blamed the trade deficit, free traders blamed protectionists, and overeager regulators blamed options and computers. But none of these stories really captures the main event.[74]

In response to public demand for answers, institutions launched numerous investigations. The US Presidential Task Force (the Brady Commission), the General Accounting Office, the Securities and Exchange Commission, the

[69] Kindleberger, *Manias, Panics, and Crashes*.
[70] Goldgar, *Tulipmania*, 5.
[71] Orain, *La Politique du Merveilleux*.
[72] James, *The End of Globalization*, 22.
[73] Schwert, 'Stock market crash', 557.
[74] Alan Reynolds, 'The lessons of Black Monday', *The Wall Street Journal*, 17 October 1997.

New York Stock Exchange, the Chicago Mercantile Exchange, the Commodities Futures Trading Commission, the Chicago Board of Trade, the International Stock Exchange in London, and the Bank of England undertook detailed inquiries into the crash to prevent future crises and restore confidence in the market. These investigations aimed to pinpoint its causes, identify vulnerabilities in the financial system, and propose safeguards to prevent future crises. In France, Édouard Balladur appointed Daniel Deguen, president of the European Mortgage Bank, to investigate the new financial instruments and futures markets accused of exacerbating the crash.[75]

These inquiries diverged significantly in their findings and policy recommendations, reflecting broader debates among academics, regulators, and policy-makers. The key question was not whether markets were efficient—few believed that prices perfectly reflected fundamental values—but to what extent prices deviated from those values. Interpretations ranged widely. Some argued the crash exposed regulatory inadequacies, while others claimed it demonstrated the market's resilience, vindicating proponents of deregulation.[76]

However, the popular memory of the crash and the references to past financial crises diverged from the institutional narratives. Media and cultural representations often focused on the human drama and mythic dimensions of financial crises. For instance, Oliver Stone's *Wall Street: Money Never Sleeps* (2010) resurrected Gordon Gekko, the quintessential antihero of the 1987 crash. In one scene, Gekko showcases an original chart of the Dutch tulip mania, calling it 'the greatest bubble story of all time'. Yet his takeaway was not a cautionary tale about the dangers of speculation, but a celebration of the visionary genius of those who knew how to profit from it and exit before the collapse.[77] This portrayal reflects a broader archetype in popular financial culture: the thrill of the crash as an opportunity for a select few to outsmart the market. Though only a few individuals profit during financial crises, their success stories are lionized, casting them as heroes of ultimate capitalist triumph. These narratives perpetuate a seductive myth: that financial crises, while destructive for most, offer unparalleled opportunities for those clever enough to exploit them. Such stories highlight the complex social function of financial crises in collective memory. Crashes become moral lessons and aspirational myths, revealing as much about societal values and anxieties as they do about the events themselves. Whether viewed as cautionary tales of greed or celebrations of market ingenuity, these narratives continue to shape how financial crises are understood and remembered.

[75] Deguen, 'Réflexions sur les nouveaux instruments'.
[76] Cabantou and Gond, 'Rational decision making'; French, 'Crash-testing', 278.
[77] Oliver Stone, *Wall Street 2: Money Never Sleeps*, 20th Century Fox, 2010.

Narrating uncertainty: the legacy of the 1987 crash and beyond

On 16 December 1989, Wall Street awoke to an unexpected gift: a colossal statue of a charging bull. The Italian artist Arturo Di Modica had secretly placed his 3.5-ton bronze sculpture outside the New York Stock Exchange under the Christmas tree on Broad Street.[78] Intended as a symbol of resilience and strength, the *Charging Bull* celebrated the determination of the American people in weathering the 1987 stock market crash. Yet, over time, the bull's meaning evolved.[79] Today, it is recognized globally not as a tribute to resilience, but as an emblem of Wall Street's power, unpredictability, and aggressive dominance.

This evolution of meaning took another turn in 2017, when State Street Global Advisors commissioned Kristen Visbal's *Fearless Girl*, a 50-inch bronze statue embodying female empowerment in corporate America. Facing off against the *Charging Bull* on Bowling Green, *Fearless Girl* became a cultural icon, interpreted by some as a symbol of defiance against financial excess and inequality, echoing the sentiments of the 2011 Occupy Wall Street movement.[80] This reinterpretation sparked controversy. Di Modica accused State Street of altering the meaning of his work.[81] This reappropriation of urban symbols and meanings marked the beginning of a broad public debate about financial regulation and democratic control over market speculation.[82]

The juxtaposition of *Fearless Girl* and *Charging Bull* encapsulates a recurring tension in the history of financial crises: the contrast between the 'real' economy and financial speculation, and between transnational finance and local economies. These themes, rooted in debates as old as the twelfth-century European trade renaissance, reemerged with particular force following the 2008 financial crisis.[83] Popular culture amplified these tensions, often portraying financial markets as dysfunctional and driven by greed. From scandals to speculative excess, the

[78] Robert D. McFadden, 'SoHo gift to Wall St.: A 3 ½-ton bronze bull', *The New York Times*, 16 December 1989.

[79] The artist distributed flyers explaining his artwork, stating that the 1987 crash had been frightening. He wanted to salute the 'vitality, energy, and life of the American people in adversity'. See Capo and Zuckerman, *It Happened in New York City*, 107. The term 'American' is used here as a demonymic shortland for the US population.

[80] Until then, the main opposition deployed globally had focused on international financial organizations such as the IMF, the World Bank, and the World Trade Organization, during historic riots such as the 1999 Seattle protests. See on that matter Starr, *Naming the Enemy*; Kitching, *Seeking Social Justice*; Newman, 'Union and community mobilization'; Rajagopal, 'Counter-hegemonic international law'.

[81] '"Charging bull" sculptor says New York's "Fearless girl" statue violates his rights', *The Guardian*, 12 April 2017.

[82] Arup, 'The Global Financial Crisis'; Engelen et al., *After the Great Complacence*; Engelen et al., 'Misrule of experts?'; Gandrud and Hallerberg, 'Does banking union worsen'; Mattei, Mitra, and Feiler, 'The politics of "social accountability"'.

[83] Pirenne, 'The stages'; Le Goff, *Your Money or Your Life*; Weatherford, *The History of Money*.

public's fascination with the financial world fuelled a wave of creative works that shaped collective memories of financial crises.[84]

Accountability for past market panics soon became the focus of mainstream media and the entertainment industry post-2008, fuelled by the fascination with the ups and downs of shameless 'unsentimental' traders who had skirted the rules of the game.[85] The comic book *Black Monday Murders* imagines a secret financial elite trading with the devil to engineer crashes and crises.[86] Similarly, the television series *Black Monday* depicts a ragtag group of outsiders inadvertently causing Wall Street's collapse.[87] Both productions focused on individual villains who would have caused the 1987 crash—corrupt insiders or incompetent outsiders—while neglecting the structural complexities of the markets. If this wacky entertainment seems inconsistent with the social reality of the markets, it nonetheless produces representations that have an impact on collective perceptions and memories of financial crashes.

The persistent cultural fascination with crashes underscores their dual role as both economic events and powerful cultural narratives. This chapter has explored how the memory of the Great Depression shaped responses to the 1987 crash, illustrating the interplay between historical analogies and contemporary decision-making. The invocation of 1929 during Black Monday served both diagnostic and prescriptive functions, offering a framework for interpreting uncertainty while amplifying fear and driving institutional responses. These comparisons, however, were rarely neutral. They carried layers of cultural memory, institutional inertia, and ideological bias, shaping the ways crises were understood and acted upon. Ultimately, this chapter argues, the invocation of 1929 during the 1987 crash was less about historical accuracy and more about the enduring utility of crisis narratives as a way to navigate the unknown. It reveals how financial actors and institutions rely on historical imagination to cope with uncertainty, often weaving together fragmented and competing memories into coherent, though sometimes flawed, stories that guide their actions in real time.

[84] After the subprime crisis, the Enron scandal, Bernie Madoff's fraud, etc., see Roulet, 'What good is Wall Street?'.

[85] The literature on the question overflows with testimonies of disgraced traders. See, for instance, Anderson, *Cityboy*; Kerviel, *L'engrenage*. On the critic of the 'unsentimental traders' see The Walter B. Wriston Archives, Tuft University, Walter B. Wriston (1964), 'No royal road', An address given at the 48th Annual Meeting of the National Industrial Conference Board on 21 May 1964.

[86] Hickman and Cocker, *Black Monday Murders*. Mammon in Hebrew [ממון] designates money, fortune, capital, and finances. This literary *topos* first emerged in Christian Medieval literature and resurfaced during the nineteenth century. In *Money*, Zola saw the Bourse de Paris as the 'Temple of Mammon': bloody sacrifices were made to a devouring god on the trading floor, fantasized as the 'theatre of speculation'. Clerks and traders could feel like the 'chosen ones' who would see the matrix in motion. See Zola, *Money*, 15.

[87] *Black Monday* (TV series) produced by David Caspe, Jordan Cahan et al., New York City: Showtime, 2019—Present. Enlightening trailer available at https://www.youtube.com/watch?v=o2yEnwgvsts.

References

Adams, W. and Brock, J.W. (1992). '1980s gigantomania follies'. *Challenge* 35, 2: 4–8.

Anderson, G. (2008). *Cityboy: Beer and Loathing in the Square Mile.* London: Headline Book Publishing.

Anshuman, V.R. (2003). 'Regulatory measures to curb stock price volatility'. *Economic and Political Weekly* 38, 8: 677–679.

Arner, D.W. (2016). 'Hong Kong: Evolution and future as a leading international financial center'. In J. Hu, M. Vanhullebusch, and A. Harding (eds), *Finance, Rule of Law and Development in Asia: Perspectives from Singapore, Hong Kong and Mainland China.* Leyde: Brill, 49–75.

Arup, C. (2010). 'The Global Financial Crisis: Learning from regulatory and governance studies'. *Law & Policy* 32, 3: 363–381.

Baker, J.A. (2008). *Work Hard, Study ... and Keep Out of Politics! Adventures and Lessons from an Unexpected Public Life.* Evanston, IL: Northwestern University Press.

Banerjee, A.V. (1992). 'A simple model of herd behavior'. *Quarterly Journal of Economics* 107, 3: 797–817.

Barsky, R.B. and De Long, J.B. (1990). 'Bull and bear markets in the twentieth century'. *The Journal of Economic History* 50, 2: 265–281.

Bikhchandani, S., Hirshleifer. D., and Welch, I. (1992). 'A theory of fads, custom, and cultural change as informational cascades'. *Journal of Political Economy* 100, 5: 992–1026.

Bloch, M. (2013). 'Reflections of a historian on the false news of the war', trans. James P. Holoka, *Michigan War Studies Review* 051: 1–11.

Bloomfield, R., O'Hara, M., and Saar, G. (2009). 'How noise trading affects markets: An experimental analysis'. *Review of Financial Studies* 22, 6: 2275–2302.

Bordo, M.D. (2003). 'Comment on "The Great Depression and the Friedman-Schwartz Hypothesis" by Lawrence Christiano, Roberto Motto, and Massimo Rostagno'. *Journal of Money, Credit, and Banking* 35, 6: 1199–1203.

Bordo, M.D. and Landon-Lane, J. (2010). 'The banking panics in the United States in the 1930s: Some lessons for today'. *Oxford Review of Economic Policy* 26, 3: 486–509.

Bordo, M.D. and Rockoff, H. (2013). 'Not just the Great Contraction: Friedman and Schwartz's "A Monetary History of the United States 1867 to 1960"'. *The American Economic Review* 103, 3: 61–65.

Burgin, A. (2012). *The Great Persuasion: Reinventing Free Markets since the Depression.* Cambridge, MA: Harvard University Press.

Cabantou, L. and Gond, J.-P. (2011). 'Rational decision making as performative praxis: Explaining rationality's éternel retour'. *Organizational Science* 22, 3: 573–586.

Capo, F. and Zuckerman, A. (2010). *It Happened in New York City: Remarkable Events that Shaped History.* Lanham, MD: Rowman & Littlefield.

Cerro, A.M. and Meloni, O. (2013). 'Crises and crashes: Argentina, 1825–2002'. *Journal of Iberian and Latin American Economic History* 31, 2: 219–252.

Chappell, D. and Eldridge, R.M. (2000). 'Evidence of market inefficiency in a war environment'. *Applied Financial Economics* 10, 5: 489–492.

Christiano, L., Motto, R., and Rostagno, M. (2003). 'The Great Depression and the Friedman-Schwartz Hypothesis'. *Journal of Money, Credit, and Banking* 35, 6: 1119–1197.

Corwin, S.A. (1999). 'Differences in trading behavior across NYSE specialist firms'. *The Journal of Finance* 54, 2: 721–745.

De Bondt, W.F.M. and Thaler, R.H. (1990). 'Do security analysts overreact?' *The American Economic Review* 80, 2: 52–57.

Deguen, D. (1988). 'Réflexions sur les nouveaux instruments financiers et les marchés à terme'. *Revue d'économie financière* 5, 6: 238–242.
Duby, G. (1986). *Le Dimanche de Bouvines*. Paris: Folio.
Engelen, E. et al. (2011). *After the Great Complacence: Financial Crisis and the Politics of Reforms*. Oxford: Oxford University Press.
Engelen, E. et al. (2012). 'Misrule of experts? The financial crisis as elite debacle'. *Economy and Society* 41, 3: 360–382.
Fell, R. (1988). 'Financial market supervision—the Hong Kong experience'. *RSA Journal* 136, 5381: 296–307.
French, K.R. (1988). 'Crash-testing the efficient market hypothesis'. *NBER Macroeconomics Annual* 3: 277–285.
Friedman, M. (1968). 'The role of monetary policy'. *American Economic Review* 58, 1: 1–17.
Friedman, M. (1985). 'The case for overhauling the Federal Reserve'. *Challenge* 28, 3: 4–12.
Friedman, M. and Schwartz, A.J. (1963). *A Monetary History of the United States*. Princeton, NJ: Princeton University Press.
Friedman, M. and Schwartz, A.J. (1986). 'Has government any role in money?' *Journal of Monetary Economics* 17, 1: 37–63.
Friedman, M. and Schwartz, A. J. (2009). *The Great Contraction, 1929–1933*. Princeton, NJ: Princeton University Press.
Gandrud, C. and Hallerberg, M. (2015). 'Does banking union worsen the EU's democratic deficit? The need for greater supervisory data transparency'. *Journal of Common Market Studies* 53, 4: 769–785.
Geertz, C. (1973). 'Thick description: Towards an interpretative theory of culture'. In C. Geertz (ed.), *The Interpretation of Cultures. Selected Essays*. New York: Basic Books, 3–32.
Gerety, M.S. and Mulherin, J.H. (1992). 'Trading halts and market activity: An analysis of volume at the open and the close'. *The Journal of Finance* 47, 5: 1765–1784.
Goldgar, A. (2007). *Tulipmania. Money, Honor, and Knowledge in the Dutch Golden Age*. Chicago: The University of Chicago Press.
Green, N.L. (1988). 'Leçons d'octobre 1929, 1987: La presse française et américaine face aux deux crises boursières'. *Esprit* 143, 10: 91–110.
Greenspan, A. (2007). *The Age of Turbulence: Adventures in a New World*. London: Penguin Press.
Grossman, S.J. (1990). 'Introduction to NBER symposium on the October 1987 crash'. *Review of Financial Studies* 3: 1–3.
Gunningham, N. (1990). 'Moving the goalposts: Financial market regulation in Hong Kong and the crash of October 1987'. *Law & Social Inquiry* 15, 1: 1–48.
Halbwachs, M. (1914). *La Topographie légendaire des Évangiles en Terre Sainte: Étude de mémoire collective*. Paris: Presses Universitaires de France.
Halbwachs, M. (1992). *On Collective Memory*. Chicago: The University of Chicago Press.
Hickman, J. and Cocker, T. (2016 – Present). *Black Monday Murders* (monthly series). Portland: Image Comics.
Hsieh. C.-T. and Romer, C.D. (2006). 'Was the Federal Reserve constrained by the Gold Standard during the Great Depression? Evidence from the 1932 Open Market Purchase Program'. *The Journal of Economic History* 66, 1: 140–176.
Hummel, J.R. (2011). 'Ben Bernanke versus Milton Friedman: The Federal Reserve's emergence as the US economy's central planner'. *The Independent Review* 15, 4: 485–518.
Jablonka, I. (2017). *L'histoire est une littérature contemporaine. Manifeste pour les sciences sociales*. Paris: Seuil.

James, H. (2001). *The End of Globalization: Lessons from the Great Depression*. Cambridge, MA: Harvard University Press.

James, H. (2010). '1929: The New York stock market crash'. *Representations* 110, 1: 129–144.

Jones, D. S. (2012). *Masters of the Universe: Hayek, Friedman, and the Birth of Neoliberal Politics*. Princeton: Princeton University Press.

Kalay, A., Wei, L., and Wohl, A. (2002). 'Continuous Trading or Call Auctions: Revealed Preferences of Investors in Tel Aviv Stock Exchange'. *The Journal of Finance* 57, 1: 523–542.

Kerviel, J. (2010). *L'engrenage: mémoire d'un trader*. Paris: Flammarion.

Ketchum, R.G. (ed), (1988). 'The October 1987 market break: A report by the Division of Market Regulation U.S. Securities and Exchange Commission'. Washington: SEC.

Kim, K.A. and Ghon Rhee, S. (1997). 'Price limit performance: Evidence from the Tokyo Stock Exchange'. *The Journal of Finance* LII, 2: 885–901.

Kindleberger, C.P. (1983). '1929: Ten lessons for today'. *Challenge* 26, 1: 58–61.

Kindleberger, C.P. (2005). *Manias, Panics, and Crashes: A History of Financial Crises*. Hoboken, NJ: John Wiley & Sons, Inc.

Kitching, G. (2001). *Seeking Social Justice through Globalization: Escaping a Nationalist Perspective*. University Park: Pennsylvania State University Press.

Lauterbach, B. and Ben-Zion, U. (1993). 'Stock market crashes and the performance of circuit breakers: Empirical evidence'. *The Journal of Finance* 48, 5: 1909–1925.

Le Goff, J. (1988). *Your Money or Your Life: Economy and Religion in the Middle Ages*. Princeton, NJ: Zone Books.

Lee, C.M.C., Ready. M.J., and Seguin, P.J. (1994). 'Volume, volatility and New York Stock Exchange trading halts'. *Journal of Finance* XLIX, 1: 183–213.

Lewis, M. (2010). *Liar's Poker: Rising through the Wreckage on Wall Street*. London: Hodder Paperbacks.

Ma, C.K., Rao, R.P., and Sears, R.S. (1989). 'Volatility, price resolution, and the effectiveness of price limits'. *Journal of Financial Services Research* 3: 165–199.

MacKenzie, D. (2004). 'The big, bad wolf and the rational market: Portfolio insurance, the 1987 crash and the performativity of economics'. *Economy and Society* 33, 3: 303–334.

Mattei, P., Mitra, M., and Feiler, T. (2018). 'The politics of "social accountability" in England and Germany: Democratic control and moral imperatives'. *Public Organization Review* 18, 2: 399–411.

McCallum, B.T. (1990). 'Could a monetary base rule have prevented the Great Depression?' *Journal of Monetary Economics* 26, 1: 3–26.

Melamed, L. (1996). *Escape to the Futures*. New York: John Wiley & Sons.

Michie, R.C. (1986). 'The London and New York Stock Exchanges, 1850–1914'. *The Journal of Economic History* 46, 1: 171–187.

Mirowski P. and Plehwe D. (eds.) (2009). *The Road from Mont Pèlerin: The Making of the Neoliberal Thought Collective*. Cambridge, MA: Harvard University Press.

Newman, N. (2002). 'Union and community mobilization in the Information Age'. *Perspectives on Work* 6, 2: 9–11.

Orain, A. (2018). *La Politique du Merveilleux: une autre histoire du système de Law (1695–1795)*. Paris: Fayard.

Pirenne, H. (1914). 'The stages in the social history of capitalism'. *The American Historical Review* 19, 3: 494–515.

Prestbo, J.A. (1999). *The Market's Measure: An Illustrated History of America Told through the Dow Jones Industrial Average*. New York: Dow Jones & Co.

Raines, J.P. and Leathers, C.G. (1996). 'Veblenian stock markets and the efficient markets hypothesis'. *Journal of Post Keynesian Economics* 19, 1: 137–151.
Rajagopal, B. (2006). 'Counter-hegemonic international law: Rethinking human rights and development as a third world strategy'. *Third World Quarterly* 27, 5: 767–783.
Roulet, T. (2015). '"What good is Wall Street?" Institutional contradiction and the diffusion of the stigma over the finance industry'. *Journal of Business Ethics* 130, 2: 389–402.
Salem, L. (1987). *Le Krach de 1987*. Paris: Edition n°1.
Samman, A. (2019). *History in Financial Times*. Stanford: Stanford University Press.
Schwert, G.W. (1992). 'Stock market crash of October 1987'. In J. Eatwell, M. Milgate, and P. Newman (eds), *New Palgrave Dictionary of Money and Finance*. London: Palgrave Macmillan, 557.
Scott, I. (1989). *Political Change and the Crisis of Legitimacy in Hong Kong*. Honolulu: University of Hawaii Press.
Seligman, J. (1995). 'The obsolescence of Wall Street: A contextual approach to the evolving structure of federal securities regulation'. *Michigan Law Review* 93, 4: 649–702.
Seyhun, H.N. (1990). 'Overreaction or fundamentals: Some lessons from insiders' response to the market crash of 1987'. *The Journal of Finance* 45, 5: 1363–1388.
Shiller, R.J. (1987). 'Investor behavior in the October 1987 stock market crash: Survey evidence'. *NBER Working Paper Series* 2446: 1–41.
Shiller, R.J. (1988). 'Portfolio insurance and other investor fashions as factors in the 1987 stock market crash'. *NBER Macroeconomics Annual* 3: 287–297.
Sornette, D. (2003). *Why Stock Markets Crash. Critical Events in Complex Financial Systems*. Princeton, NJ: Princeton University Press.
Starr, A. (2000). *Naming the Enemy: Anti-Corporate Movements Confront Globalization*. New York: St Martin's Press.
Stein, J. (1987). 'Informational externalities and welfare-reducing speculations'. *Journal of Political Economy* 95: 1123–1145.
Stigler, G.J. (1976). 'Do economists matter?' *Southern Economic Journal* 42, 3: 347–354.
Tetlock, P. C. (2007). 'Giving content to investor sentiment: The role of media in the stock market'. *The Journal of Finance* 62, 3: 1139–1168.
Toporowski, J. (1993). *The Economics of Financial Markets and the 1987 Crash*. Cheltenham: Edward Elgar Publishing.
Weatherford, J. (2009). *The History of Money: From Sandstone to Cyberspace*. New York: Three Rivers Press.
Weiner, E.J. (2005). *What Goes Up: The Uncensored History of Modern Wall Street as Told by the Bankers, Brokers, CEOs, and Scoundrels Who Made It Happen*. Boston: Little, Brown and Company.
White, E.N. (1990). 'The stock market boom and crash 1929 revisited'. *Journal of Economic Perspectives* 4, 2: 67–83.
Wright, R.O. (2002). *Chronology of the Stock Market*. Jefferson, NC: McFarland & Co.
Zepp, R.A. (1988). 'The stock market crash and Hong Kong'. *Bulletin de Sinologie* 42: 28–29.
Zola, E. (2018). *Money* [1891]. London: The Caxton Publishing Company.

6

From a developmental to a market-oriented economy

Memory and the politics of the 'IMF' crisis in South Korea

Seung Woo Kim

Introduction

On 4 December 1997, the International Monetary Fund (IMF) approved the emergency financial mechanism to activate a stand-by credit for the South Korean government's economic and financial programme.[1] In return for the bailout fund, the recipient introduced the policies for structural adjustment. Yet, the financial crisis ensued to drive the plunge of Won, the local currency, to a record low. The *Korean Times* reported that 'The act of purchasing Christmas gifts was viewed as a luxurious indulgence for Koreans.'[2]

In the following month, in an apologetic voice, the newly elected President Kim Dae-jung warned the nation of the sufferings in the coming days; 'This year, price will rise, unemployment will increase. Income will decrease, and corporate bankruptcies will be widespread. We are all being asked to endure sweat and tears.' He added, 'If not for the political-business nexus and state-controlled finance, and if large corporations had not embraced uncompetitive companies like an octopus spreading its tentacles, I can confidently assert that such unfortunate events would not have occurred.'[3] The remark seemed to have not merely denounced the Miracle on the Han River or the post-war economic development of South Korea, but also indicated the country's lapse into a market-oriented economy. Indeed, many critics have depicted that the IMF crisis, a vernacular term in South Korea for the national financial debacle in 1997–1998, had introduced the neo-liberal turn.

[1] 'Press release' (4 December 1997), International Monetary Fund Archives (hereafter IMFA).
[2] *The Korean Herald* (13 September 2023).
[3] 'Inaugural speech by President Kim Dae-Jung' (5 February 1998), Presidential Archives.

Seung Woo Kim, *From a developmental to a market-oriented economy*. In: *History, Memory, and the Return of Financial Crises After Bretton Woods*. Edited by: Youssef Cassis and Giuseppe Telesca, Oxford University Press. © Oxford University Press (2026). DOI: 10.1093/9780198950158.003.0006

However, as this chapter argues, the implementation of financial liberalization, privatization of government-owned enterprises, and enforcement of the labour market to introduce a non-regular worker system did not eclipse the presence of the state. Instead, in contrast to developing countries with the experience of IMF bailout programmes, the South Korean government occupied the commanding height to navigate the crisis. By mobilizing the public's voluntary burden-sharing and the resultant economic sacrifice, presiding over the much-demanded restructuring of chaebols, and managing the exacerbated tension between labour and business, it successfully shepherded the country to recover its creditworthiness in the global financial market. It also pushed liberalization even after the surprisingly early redemption of IMF loans in August 2001. The experience of crisis and the swift recovery resulted in the recalibration of state's role rather than the denial. Furthermore, drawing on lessons from the previous crises, the government was able to articulate measures against the Global Financial Crisis of 2007–2008.

Beyond the scholarly engagement regarding the origins of and the social changes from the IMF crisis, this chapter examines how the politics of memory left the national government's authority unchanged during the country's shift from a developmental to a market-oriented economy.[4] It begins with the successful management of external indebtedness led by technocrats, which underpinned the government-chaebol nexus as an engine of heavy-chemical industrialization. In the age of globalization, the nexus was disenchanted by a series of chaebol failures. However, the characterization of the IMF bailout as the loss of sovereignty by foreign powers boosted nationalist sentiment to validate the centrifugal role of the government in navigating the country out of the crisis. Specifically, the Gold Collection Campaign appropriated the memory of the National Debt-Redemption Campaign during Japanese colonial rule. Owing to the proven capacity to mobilize the public at the height of the crisis, the administration's willingness to implement the IMF's bailout programme, despite the sufferings and discontent of the public, facilitated the recovery of South Korea's credit rating. The resultant symbiosis of the market economy and the strong government underpinned South Korea's strategy to safeguard its economy from external economic and financial disturbances in the following decade.

[4] For analyses of the IMF crisis within the economic development of South Korea, see, Lee, *Oehwan Wigi wa Geu Hu-ui Hanguk Gyeongje*; Ji, *Hanguk Sinjaryuijui-ui Giwongwa Hyeongseong*. Recently, economic historians have regarded the crisis within the trajectory of South Korea's economic development. See Park et al., *Financial Liberalization*; Kwon, *Changes by Competition*; Lee, *The Tortuous Path*. Sociologists pay attention to the financialization in the aftermath of the crisis and its relation to the increased level of inequality. For example, see, Eun, *IMF Wigi*. In 2019, The Center for Freedom of Information and Transparency, a civic group in South Korea, created an archive of *The IMF Collection* by acquiring historical documents from the IMF. https://97imf.kr. Regarding the social changes, see Joon et al., *Oehwan Wigi ihu 20nyeon Hanguk sahoe gujo wa saenghwal segye ui byeonhwa*.

The indebted industrialization disenchanted

Since the mid-1960s, under the authoritarian military government, South Korea exhibited a successful model of state-led industrialization in the non-Western world.[5] The government pursued the export-oriented economic development strategy against the recommendations for import substitution from advanced countries and international organizations.[6] Technocrats at the Economic Planning Board (EPB) were given tasks to set plans and coordinate policies of various governmental departments and private enterprises. While it had relied on aid and grants from the key allies of the USA and Japan, it sought to tap private capital abroad for ambitious industrialization to address the perennial lack of domestic capital formation. For the orderly inflow of capital, the government established the International Economic Consultative Organization for Korea, an inter-governmental agency between South Korea and foreign creditors.[7]

However, as in many cases of developing countries, South Korean borrowers were often marginalized in the competition for commercial loans with multinational corporations and Western governments in the Eurocurrency market, an offshore market for major Western currencies.[8] The memory of the Korean War and the potential threat from communist North Korea further deteriorated credibility. It is against parsimony of international bankers that the government was determined to provide inevitable guarantees; the Foreign Capital Inducement Deliberation Committee of EPB reviewed applications for foreign loans from ministries, public enterprises, and chaebols to manage the country's overall indebtedness. From 1962 to 1979, the military government raised more than US$9 billion of commercial loans for preferential export.[9] Chaebols exploited the funding with lower interest rates than the domestic capital market.[10] In this way, the indebted industrialization buttressed the rise of chaebols.

President Park Chung-hee's announcement in 1973 to launch heavy-chemical industrialization cemented the special relationship. EPB regulated the expansion of chaebols into new industries such as shipbuilding, petrochemicals, and the steel industry to prevent excess competition. Along with the Ministry of Finance, it exercised authority over issues of commercial loans and their distributions to chaebols. For example, the EPB closely monitored and controlled the procurement of capital from Europe and Japan to purchase machinery for the newly developed auto industry in the 1970s.[11] Galvanized by the recycling of petrodollars in the

[5] For example, see, Amsden, *Asia's Next Giant*; Cumings, *Korea's Place in the Sun*, Chapter 6.

[6] 'IBRD Consultative Group for Korea' (9 April 1969), FCO21/605, The National Archives (hereafter TNA); Park, 'W. W. Rostow and economic discourse in South Korea in the 1960s', 65.

[7] *Kyunghyang Shinmun* (13 December 1966).

[8] See, Griffith-Jones, 'The growth of multinational banking'.

[9] Cho, 'Institutions of developmental state and state capacity', 168–173.

[10] Park et al., *Financial liberalization*, 36–38.

[11] Lee, 'The automobile industry', 309–314.

aftermath of the First Oil Crisis, the internationalization of European commercial banks in the Global South facilitated South Korea's efforts to raise capital in short- or medium-term Euroloans.[12] In 1976, the South Korean government authorized the establishment of merchant bank corporations to facilitate borrowing foreign capital for chaebols' venture into the heavy-chemical industries.[13]

During the 1970s, Corporate Korea became one of the most indebted developing countries.[14] The debt-driven industrialization drew attention from the IMF. The international financial organization, which opened a Seoul office in 1965, repeatedly expressed concerns over the high level of indebtedness and inflation from the neo-mercantilist approach of the military government.[15] However, international bankers offered improved terms for the country's Euroloans, when the borrower secured US dollar income to honour debt from the export-oriented trade regime and the construction boom in the oil-producing countries in the Middle East.[16]

More importantly, international bankers trusted the capacity of technocrats to maintain the country's low debt service ratio (DSR) or the ability to generate foreign currency to service overseas loans, a key criterion for international bankers to assess the creditworthiness of sovereign borrowers.[17] Throughout the 1970s, the ratio steadily declined from 20 to 11 per cent, an acceptable level for developing countries.[18] Despite the rampant inflation of the Second Oil Crisis, EPB's target of DSR remained steadfast, as technocrats persuaded the president to announce the Price Stabilization of 1979 of anti-inflation and liberalization policies.[19] In the following decade, the South Korean government was poised to embark on liberalizing financial markets.[20]

After the assassination of President Park, technocrats at EPB assumed the commanding heights to implement austerity policies, underpinned by the oppressive rulings of the new military government.[21] Now, the IMF and the World Bank endorsed the measures with new loans. As a result, South Korea appeased international creditors to borrow more capital than other developing countries in

[12] See, Altamura, *European Banks*.

[13] For example, during the Fourth Five-Year Plan of 1997–1981, the government allocated 'nearly 80% of available resources for investment in heavy and chemical industries'. Drawing on the capital, Chaebols 'devised a plan to claim a slice of the cake'. 'Up from the depths', *Far Eastern Economic Review* (5 June 1981), pp. 44–45.

[14] *Newsweek* (26 May 1980).

[15] For example, 'Preliminary assessment of the IMF annual consultation mission' (1 February 1978), 1A00614174952214, Presidential Archives.

[16] *Euromoney* (October 1978); 'Visit to Korea—Feb.1977—JPGW', n.d., 1417/1, Barclays Banking Group Archives.

[17] 'Outlook for Korea's external debt and debt service' (24 August 1977), Box 460, Council of Economic Advisors, Jimmy Carter Presidential Library.

[18] Amsden, *Republic of Korea*, 59.

[19] Park, 'The political origin of neoliberalism in Korea'.

[20] *Far Eastern Economic Review* (22 May 1981).

[21] *Far Eastern Economic Review* (8 January 1982).

Latin America and East Asia.[22] The moratorium of the Philippines in 1983, as the South Korean embassy in Manila observed, 'will have no direct impact on the country's domestic or external debt repayment'.[23] With confidence from the record and the collusion with the government, the chaebols took advantage of the heavy-chemical industrialization to continue the octopus-like business expansion. Under the heavy-industry rationalization scheme, the government extended 'the repayment period for industrial loans' for chaebols with officially subsidized interest rates.[24] In 1982, chaebols capitalized on 'the government bank-divestiture and other reforms'; Daewoo took 'by far the largest' share in Korea First Bank.[25] Three years later, at the annual meeting of the IMF and the World Bank in Seoul, President Chun Doo-Hwan proudly boasted his country's transition from 'one of the world's most underprivileged and disadvantaged countries to one of the world's most promising and developing'.[26] In 1989, the IMF described the relations with South Korea as 'fruitful'.[27]

Marginalizing the history of the oppression of labour in the making of the Miracle on the Han River, the popular and collective memory celebrated the government–chaebol nexus as the engine of the post-war economic growth, which lifted the nation out of poverty. It also exonerated the authoritarian rule as an inevitable or necessary sacrifice to achieve compressed growth. In 1984, Kim Woo-joong, the chairman of Daewoo, recognized the role of technocrats in the planning but stressed that 'Without the sacrifice of a generation, ... no country has ever achieved prosperity'. He added, 'There have been many miracles where the impossible was achieved.'[28] Owing to the sustained high growth rate, the democratization movement in 1987 left the nexus unchanged. The state-led industrialization seemed to have refuted the free market orthodoxy.[29] The World Bank, in its 1993 report of *The East Asian Miracle*, praised that South Korea had exhibited the highest level of economic growth in the world.[30]

The 'Asian system' that preoccupied policy intellectuals of the West sparked a debate. In 1994, Paul Krugman argued that success seemed 'to be driven by extraordinary growth in inputs like labor and capital rather than by gains in efficiency'. Without a substantial increase in productivity and the continued inflow of foreign capital, the model was not sustainable. He added that 'several of the East Asian "tigers"' became 'significant exporters of capital'.[31] The Asian model

[22] *Euromoney* (August 1982).

[23] 'Philippine external debt payment deferment' (26 October 1983), DA1440280, National Archives of Korea (hereafter NAK).

[24] *Far Eastern Economic Review* (5 June 1981).

[25] *Far Eastern Economic Review* (22 October 1982).

[26] International Monetary Fund, *Summary Proceedings*, 1.

[27] IMF, 'Korea's fruitful cooperation with the Fund'.

[28] KBS, '"The world is vast, and there is much to be done"'.

[29] Amsden, *Asia's Next Giant.*

[30] World Bank, *The East Asian Miracle.*

[31] Krugman, 'The myth of Asia's miracle', 70, 77.

implied economic growth and stability could be achieved without political freedom and democracy.[32] However, one argued that South Korea invalidated such a claim. The country 'diversified into high-tech and knowledge industry products' and became 'a working democracy—accompanied by sharply rising wage levels'. A political scientist stressed the role of government to 'ensure the profitability of private investment by creating a climate of stability and subsidizing and coordinating private investment decisions'.[33] The entry of South Korea into the Organisation for Economic Cooperation and Development, a club of advanced countries, seemed to have completed the country's journey.[34]

The second wave of liberalization corresponded to the globalization strategy pursued by the civilian government of President Kim Young-sam. In 1994, the Foreign Exchange System Reform Plan envisaged 'an almost complete liberalization of current and capital account transactions and the development of an efficient foreign exchange market'. Capitalizing on regulatory freedom, banks obtained capital 'from the international wholesale funding market to lend to chaebols and large firms for their funding of long-term investments'.[35] Merchant bank corporations, which had borrowed low-interest short-term capital abroad to purchase high-interest-yielding commercial papers and bonds, went global by lending long-term investment into Southeast Asia. As a result, their maturity mismatch was severe, and the government had less capacity to manage the country's overall indebtedness.

The age of globalization encouraged chaebols' aggressive expansion abroad with mounting debts by borrowing cheaper foreign capital from merchant bank corporations. Chairman Kim of Daewoo personified the zeitgeist. His motto, 'the world is vast, and there is much to be done', emphasized the entrepreneurial spirit and international perspective.[36] In 1993, Chairman Lee Kun-hee of Samsung introduced a radical innovation in management in the Frankfurt declaration to develop the chaebol into a global corporation.[37] In 1995, the per capita income of South Koreans reached US$10,000. The public responded to the euphoria with an increased number of overseas travellers and consumption of imported goods. Some critics reminded the public of the sarcastic comment by the *Washington Times* in 1989 that South Koreans might have 'popped the champagne too early'.[38]

However, the economy was showing signs of strain. South Korea had current account deficits since 1994, which culminated in US$23 billion in 1996 owing to

[32] Lee Kuan-Yew, the former prime minister of Singapore, espoused the idea to explain his country's success. Kim Dae-jung, on the contrary, claimed that Western-style democracy was compatible with economic prosperity in East Asia. See, Zakaria, 'Culture is destiny'; Kim, 'Is culture destiny?'.

[33] Gibney, et al., 'Asia's growth',171, 175–176.

[34] 'Official gazette', no. 13490 (18 December 1996), NAK.

[35] Park et al., *Financial Liberalization*, p. 12.

[36] Kim, *Segyeneun neolgo haliranun manhda.*

[37] *Maeil Kyungje* (25 December 1993).

[38] *Dong-A Ilbo* (15 September 1996).

the fall in the price of semiconductors.[39] In the following year, galvanized by the financial difficulties of large corporations, foreign banks questioned the credibility of Corporate Korea.[40] With increased burdens on raising foreign currency and draining foreign reserves, scandals of chaebols exposed the vulnerability of the government–chaebol nexus. Now, the collusion between chaebols and politicians was characterized as irrational and greedy corruptions of the crony capitalism.

In January 1997, Hanbo Steel, a subsidiary of Hanbo Group, went bankrupt owing to over-indebtedness. The Chaebo, which made a fortune from the real estate and construction business in the 1980s, over-invested to build the fifth-largest steel factory in the world. Authorities alleged that it bribed politicians to pressure on commercial banks to lend substantial loans without due process despite the group's already excessive indebtedness. By leveraging the political connection, Chairman Chung sought to expand his reckless business into 20 sectors. The public was shocked by his evasive attitude during the parliamentary hearings. It was also reported that the chairman relied on superstitious fortune-tellers' advice to make a business decision. His appearance at the prosecutors' office, appearing to be sick in a wheelchair, showed irresponsibility and weakness; the Chung family also siphoned the group's capital offshore through a paper company.

In July, Kia, the eighth largest chaebol, failed to honour its excessive debt of 9 trillion Won. Betraying the self-portraited image of People's Corporation with no family ownership, its chairman had exercised autocratic management of reckless, over-leveraged business diversification. Later, it was revealed that the government remotely 'controlled' creditor banks favouring of Kia. During the credit crunch from the collapse of the Thai Baht, the bankruptcy of chaebols drove foreign investors to withdraw US$16 billion in the year, exacerbating the depletion of foreign reserves. In October, the Bank of Korea assessed the 'sovereign default risk' but concerned ministries denied the possibility.[41] The IMF also noted South Korea's 'sound macroeconomic fundamentals'.[42] At the end of the year, however, international banks suspended further loans, which coincided with the downgrade of the sovereign creditworthiness by major credit rating agencies. Meanwhile, the depreciation of the Won added burden to honour obligations.

The crash of Daewoo, the second largest chaebol, symbolized the collapse of the indebted industrialization and the nexus. Established in 1967 by a salaryman, it emerged into a key textile export corporation by tapping on the government subsidy of lower export financing. In the 1970s, with government-guaranteed loans, it acquired bankrupt companies in construction, shipbuilding, and car-making. In

[39] Ministry of Finance and Economy, *One Year of the People's Government*, 11

[40] Ministry of Finance and Economy, *One Year of the People's Government*, 11–12.

[41] 'Transcript of the National Assembly's Special Committee on Investigating the Causes of the IMF Financial Crisis and the Truth Behind the Economic Crisis, 200th session, 10th meeting' (25 January 1999).

[42] IMF, 'The role of the IMF in recent capital account crises'.

1975, as a general trading company (or Sogo shosha in Japanese terms), it served the government's drive for export. The success of Chairman Kim, often depicted as self-made against all odds, endorsed Daewoo's venture into the global market. The acquisition of FSO, a Polish automaker, in 1995 vindicated this vision of globalization. In the following year, Daewoo was considered the largest multinational corporation in the developing world.[43]

However, Daewoo's high-leveraged expansion was unsustainable as the poor performance in Europe left the automobile division with a massive debt. Still, Chairman Kim adhered to the leverage acquisition strategy to contend that chaebol's export would facilitate the country's efforts to manage economic difficulties. As the Asian Financial Crisis spread to Russia, international financial institutions demanded immediate repayment from Daewoo. Without governmental assistance, Daewoo had little chance of survival. Authorities' investigation uncovered fraudulent accounting, loans, and illegal foreign exchange transactions.

Such practices of chaebols, whose average debt-to-equity ratio exceeded 380% in mid-1997, were staggering enough to disenchant the public's faith in the postwar economic model of South Korea. Now, the explicit government support was seen to not merely have hampered orderly market operations but also encouraged the irresponsible expansion. Both Chairman Chung and Kim denied their wrongdoings and left the country to avoid legal responsibilities. The public accused the government's lack of leadership to preemptively prevent the catastrophic collapse.[44] Therefore, the trust in the nexus plummeted.

As an expert testified at the parliamentary hearing in early 1999, the inept response to the changing macroeconomic environment was attributable to the unprecedented failure. The financial liberalization increased the tendency of capital mobility to 'broker a fatal blow to the national economy' in times of foreign exchange instabilities. In the age of financial globalization, the government-controlled finance was considered to have distorted the market but merely encourage moral hazard. As the authorities had no systemic measures on the already over-indebted domestic financial institutions, any bankruptcy would result in 'the sharp increase in nonperforming loans'.[45]

The IMF crisis, galvanized by the unprecedented fiasco of the government-chaebol nexus, seemed to vindicate that South Korea's growth model was 'outdated' and now it was 'the time to follow the Western political-economic reform'.[46] Now, Krugman confidently contended that the family-oriented assumption was

[43] *Maeil Kyungje* (26 September 1996).

[44] 'Transcript of the National Assembly's Special Committee on Investigating the Causes of the IMF Financial Crisis and the Truth behind the Economic Crisis, 200th session, 8th meeting' (22 January 1999).

[45] 'Transcript of the National Assembly's Special Committee on Investigating the Causes of the IMF Financial Crisis and the Truth behind the Economic Crisis, 201st session, 23rd meeting' (11 February 1999).

[46] *Chosun Ilbo* (12 December 1997).

a root cause of collusion between politics and business, which had hindered the rational functioning of a capitalist society. The renowned economist blamed lax regulations and government guarantees on foreign loans.[47] Francis Fukuyama joined in by suggesting that the economic model based on the Asian values had been a politically constructed concept to legitimize dictatorships in the region.[48] Rudiger Durnbusch of MIT stressed the inefficiency of the South Korean government, which had not been determined to supervise 'drunken drivers' of private banks.[49]

The Citizens' Coalition for Economic Justice, a civic movement organization, diagnosed the bankruptcy of *Hanbo* as the culmination of 'diseases' of the South Korean economy—the unhealthy collusion and corruption between politics, business, and government, excessive government regulation and state-controlled finance, the excessive concentration of economic power in the hands of chaebols, and the inefficient management of them. 'Unless the chronic ailments of the Korean economy are addressed', it added, 'such astronomical bankruptcy crises could occur again at any time'. It called for institutional reforms to 'stabilize and modernize the Korean economy'.[50] However, the government was reluctant to embrace a democratic market economy and left chaebols untouched, if they were solvent. Only radical measures by external forces could address the national malaise.

Nationalizing the IMF crisis and the Gold Collection movement

Following the collapse of the Hong Kong stock market and the downgrading of South Korea's sovereign credit ratings in October, 'New external financing has virtually dried up, and substantial difficulties are being experienced in rolling over the relatively large amount of short-term debt'.[51] The currency depreciated 20 per cent, and the stock market reached a ten-year low. The depletion of foreign reserves, or the day of national bankruptcy, loomed large; the Bank of Korea had less than US$4 billion in the vault. Rumour had it that an internal report by an international bank recommended, 'Get out of Korea, right now!' Yet, bilateral support from the US or Japan was unavailable. On 21 November 1977, the South Korean government officially asked the IMF for assistance, which would 'serve to quickly restore market confidence'.[52] Michel Camdessus, the Managing Director

[47] *Maeil Kyungje* (12 January 1998).
[48] *Dong-a Ilbo* (26 October 1999).
[49] *Chosun Ilbo* (8 December 1997).
[50] '98-01-28 CCEJ Statement: Regarding the establishment license and loan benefits of Hanbo Steel' (28 January 1998), *The IMF Collection.*
[51] 'Republic of Korea—Letter of Intent' (3 December 1997), FO/DIS/97/101, IMFA.
[52] 'Republic of Korea—Letter of Intent' (3 December 1997).

of IMF, welcomed the request. Immediately, he sent a mission to negotiate 'a comprehensive package' for the restructuring of the country's financial system.[53]

The announcement stirred nationalist sentiment. The press referred it as 'the loss of economic sovereignty' because 'the IMF bailout requires the implementation of stringent policy recommendations', de facto interference in the government's overall macroeconomic management.[54] It also noted that austerity, liberalization, and privatization afflicted Mexicans with 'excruciating pains' in 1995 and the 1976 IMF loan for the UK collapsed 'British Empire's prestige in a single day'.[55] More recent ones in Thailand and Indonesia suffered a great cost owing to the IMF bailout's conditionality. South Koreans shared that the country was relegated to a second-tier country under economic trusteeship.[56] A journalist compared the IMF's interference with Geogsul Gukchi, the Japanese annexation of Korea.[57]

The rigid attitude of the IMF delegation further cemented the nationalist response. From the beginning, it explicitly stated that South Korea should endure 'low growth, low price level, and increased tax'.[58] Its negotiation strategy exacerbated the image of the IMF as a foreign aggressor. In the early stage, the South Korean government concluded that 'IMF's demands are acceptable'. Suddenly, the delegation demanded to 'shut down twelve insolvent merchant bank corporations'.[59] More unbearable conditions were to follow. Later, it was known that Camdessus urged the immediate dissolution of chaebols to enhance corporate governance. The public understood that the condition would merely facilitate the entry of multinational corporations into the national economy.[60] Others raised a plot that the US had 'remotely controlled' the IMF to pressure the complete opening of the domestic financial market for interests of financial capital.[61] *Default*, a 2018 movie, shows the popular perception of IMF negotiations based on such conspiracy theories. Left-wing critics condemned that the economic trusteeship would introduce neo-liberal policies to empower the transnational capital in South Korea.[62]

[53] 'Camdessus welcomes Korea's request for IMF assistance', News Brief No. 97/25 (21 November 1977), IMFA.

[54] *Maeil Kyungje* (19 November 1997).

[55] *Maeil Kyungje* (22 November 1997).

[56] *Dong-a Ilbo* (22 November 1977).

[57] *Hanguk Kyungje* (24 November 1997).

[58] *Kyunghyang Sinmun* (30 November 1997).

[59] *Chosun Ilbo* (4 December 1997).

[60] *Dong-a Ilbo* (4 December 1997).

[61] *Hangyeore* (3 December 1997). In 2009, drawing on declassified archival documents, investigative journalism found out that the US administration firmly adhered to a policy of support solely through the IMF, whose underlying premise was a strong structural reform of the Korean economy, essentially a transformation into a 'completely open market economy system'. It was also revealed that the IMF closely coordinated in advance with the USA, which demanded rapid liberalization of the capital market and labour market flexibility. KBS, 'First public release of the IMF crisis'.

[62] Labour Economic Research Institute following Jeon Tae-il, *The Economic Crisis and IMF Trusteeship*.

On the morning of 3 December, South Korea accepted most of the terms to close the negotiation. Once again, Camdessus, expressing the distrust of politicians, pressed three major presidential candidates to pledge the implementation of conditionalities. While the news humiliated South Koreans' self-esteem, there was little room for renegotiation owing to the depleting foreign exchange reserves; the IMF was poised to delay the conclusion if the requirement was not accepted.[63] In order to avoid the shameful national bankruptcy, two of them signed the memorandum from the international organization. Meanwhile, Kim Dae-jung sent a letter to President Kim pledging to carry out the terms 'in principle'.[64]

At 7:40 p.m., the South Korean government and the IMF reached an agreement on the programmes, comprised of 'strengthened fiscal and monetary policies, far-reaching financial sector reforms, and further liberalization of trade and capital flows, as well as improvements in the structure and governance of Korean corporations'. It was seen to shackle the recipient country because the provision of bailout funds was subject to the IMF's evaluation of the implementation of conditionalities. The international organization agreed to lend US$21 billion, which opened the floodgate for other assistance from the International Bank for Reconstruction and Development and the Asian Development Bank. Advanced countries, including the USA and Japan, participated in the Supplementary Financial Assistance Package for Korea.[65]

Camdessus was 'pleased to announce ... a strong economic program that provides for a decisive and welcome response to the country's present financial difficulties'.[66] The Minister of Economy and Finance, Lim Chang-yuel of South Korea, pleaded with the public to 'understand the inevitability of our pain, and kindly request your participation in the efforts to overcome the difficulties we are facing together'.[67] However, corporate bankruptcies continued, and credit rating agencies downgraded South Korea's creditworthiness close to that of junk bonds.[68] Foreign creditors tapped the bailout fund to withdraw their capital in the US dollar. Once again, the depleting foreign reserves forced further depreciation of the Won. In the first review of the stand-by arrangement, the IMF admitted that 'The initial positive market reaction ... was short-lived'.[69]

The public understood that the opening of the economy to attract foreign capital was selling off Corporate Korea to foreigners. The condition to raise the limit

[63] *Hangyeore* (3 December 1997).
[64] *Hangyeore* (4 December 1997).
[65] 'Statement by the Finance Ministers and Central Bank Governors of the Potential Participation in the Supplemental Financial Assistance Package for Korea' (24 December 1997), EBD/97/140, IMFA.
[66] 'Camdessus welcomes conclusion of talks with Korea on IMF program' (3 December 1997), IMFA.
[67] Newstapa, '1997, IMF the great lie'.
[68] *Maeil Gyeongje* (23 December 1997).
[69] 'Republic of Korea—First review under the stand-by arrangement' (17 December 1997), EBS/97/237, IMFA.

on individual foreign equity ownership of companies, combined with the depreciation of the Won, made 'productive assets, such as steel or automobile factories, cheaper in dollar terms for foreign buyers'. Substantial acquisition by foreigners could 'prompt a public backlash'.[70] The national confidence fell to its nadir when the government announced receiving de facto food assistance from the USA for the first time since 1981; the bailout fund did not address the dollar shortage problem.[71] Against the severe shortage of foreign reserves, the government proposed the 'IMF plus', additional stringent reforms to receive early capital injection from advanced countries and an extension of short-term loans. From all these episodes of unconditional surrender, loss, and the prospect of a bleak future, South Koreans felt humiliated.

It is not surprising, given the sense of loss, civic groups urged the renegotiation and trade unions warned of a general strike against the 'labour market flexibility'.[72] A new acronym for IMF was widely circulated: 'I aM Fired'. Yet, neither did such dissent voices escalate into a class movement against international capital nor challenge the authority of the national government. Instead, it historicized the structural reform of another case of foreign invasion, which shaped the identity of the Korean nation and evoked a nationalist sense of independence. For instance, a law professor stressed 'the spirit of solidarity and cooperation, which involves sharing hardships and difficulties together, ..., to demonstrate that the spirit of Korean nation is alive'.[73] At the same time, opinion leaders sought to capitalize the moment for the reform of chaebols, who were enemies within the national endeavour.[74]

Such a nationalist assumption, rather than class politics, was attributable to the collective memory of South Koreans or the way in which they historicized post-war economic growth. Under military governments, economic nationalism shaped the industrialization strategy. President Park pushed export-oriented policies in the name of 'self-reliance' and 'independence'. As Park shows, the nationalistic approach was incorporated in 'the implementation of the 1973 Long-Term Plan for the Promotion of the Automobile Industry' to manufacture the country's 'first original "people's care" model under national ownership'.[75] The public education system had been an effective means to infuse and diffuse nationalist identity and train the younger generation to be hard-working but obedient to authority. In 1976, a BBC reporter was impressed by the attitude of South Korean workers at the newly constructed Hyundai Motors factory; 'if you work

[70] CIA Director of Intelligence, 'Economic Intelligence Weekly' (20 December 1997), The IMF Collection.

[71] *Dong-a Ilbo* (11 December 1997).

[72] *Hangyeore* (5 December 1997).

[73] *Hangyeore* (15 December 1997).

[74] Lee, *Foreign Exchange Crisis and the Korean Economy Thereafter*, 153–162.

[75] Park, 'Economic nationalism and the Korean developmental state', 163. Also, see Rhyu, 'Park Chung Hee's monetary reform in 1962 and Korean nationalism'.

hard and the company makes money, the [working] environment will improve'.[76] The loyalty could be easily extended to the national government.

At the same time, South Koreans were determined to remain open to the global economy. Its strong commitment to the export-oriented economy did not allow it to introduce insular economic policies; the heavy-chemical industrialization, as President Chun stressed in his 1985 IMF Annual Meeting speech, hinged upon 'a global community of interdependent nations'.[77] Disobeying international rules would disconnect the country from natural resources and foreign capital—key sources of its economic success. The globalization was inevitable.

Under the political culture, the public prioritized independence from the IMF. The secretary of the Citizens' Coalition for Economic Justice urged, 'Everyone in the nation must share the burden of hardship to overcome the crisis'.[78] The solution was to address indebtedness; the IMF leveraged the bailout fund to seize economic sovereignty. Various civic groups called for a national salvation movement. South Koreans had the precedent of a government-led national campaign to discourage the purchase of imported goods in the 1980s.[79] The movement kindled the nationalist sentiment by characterizing the redemption of external debt an act of independence.[80]

Once again, civic groups awakened patriotism to launch campaigns to reduce unnecessary expenditures and increase exports to generate revenue in foreign currency. Yet, the severe recession caused by the bailout conditions of high interest rates exceeding 20 per cent to attract foreign capital limited its effectiveness. The expenditure on overseas travel, falsely demonized to have driven the country into bankruptcy, had already decreased. A domestic campaign to collect the US currency was not feasible because household holdings of foreign currency were not common. It is interesting that South Korea's current account returned to surplus in December 1997.

Instead, the press, civic groups, and politicians recalled the National Debt Redemption Movement (NDRM) to mobilize the public into a nationwide campaign. In 1905, after the Russo-Japanese War, Japan coerced the Korean Empire to sign the Protectorate Treaty. It compelled the de facto colony to take loans to subordinate the economy. Two years later, when the national debt amounted to the fiscal capacity of Korea, independence leaders in Daegu, a commercial centre, proposed a campaign to repay it by quitting smoking for three months, depicting indebtedness 'as a life-and-death problem for the nation'. Securing economic sovereignty with financial relief received widespread support and spread

[76] BBC, 'The car makers'.

[77] International Monetary Fund, *Summary Proceedings*, 1.

[78] *Dong-a Ilbo* (21 November 1997).

[79] *Joong-Ang Ilbo* (7 September 1985); Park, 'Economic nationalism and the Korean developmental state', 133–136.

[80] Youn, 'An issue of Korean nationalism'; *Chosun Ilbo* (21 March 1985).

throughout the peninsula. When Gojong, the first emperor, joined, it escalated into a donation campaign against the foreign aggressor. While the intervention by the Japanese colonial government frustrated the movement, the spirit was repeatedly rekindled in times of economic distress.[81] As Park shows, NDRM, as a shared public memory, emerged as a benchmark to organize national efforts.[82]

In February 1997, the Centennial Anniversary Commemoration Committee of the National Debt Redemption Movement, led by the Chamber of Commerce in Daegu, called for the revival. It mainly campaigned for more savings by the public to repay foreign loans. A local commercial bank resonated with the NDRM passbook with preferential interest rates. When the IMF bailout rekindled the collective memory of independence by financial means, the Korean Housewives' Club Federation proposed to collect 'patriotic rings'.[83] During presidential debates, a candidate stressed 'a new NDRM and Economic Righteous Army Movement'.[84] Kim Dae-jung, as the president-elect, suggested the second NDRM—the nationwide Gold Collection Campaign (GCC) to purchase gold stored in people's houses at market prices for export. The rationale was that the initiative would advance the full resumption of national sovereignty from the IMF, as NDRM aimed to do so from Japan, by repaying the bailout fund with the revenue in the US dollar.[85]

From 5 January to 14 March 1998, a state-run broadcasting station aired the 'KBS Gold Collection Campaign' programme. Politicians and religious leaders, as well as celebrities, encouraged the public's participation. For instance, Cardinal Kim Sou-hwan donated his gold cross to the nation. His promise not to reveal the identity of sellers enticed the upper class, who held large amounts of gold bars. The press used moral suasion and repeatedly linked GCC with NDRM.[86] The campaign was a great success. The collection point was bustling with people who had kept gold in the wardrobe. An old woman brought 'a gold ring that my son-in-law gave us for my husband's 60th birthday' and said, 'The individual is wealthy, but the country is poor, so I must diligently give everything I have to repay.'[87] The press relentlessly reported stories of ordinary people to inspire the public. By the end of the first phase, foreign press highlighted GCC as 'a united display showcasing Korea's strength and resilience'.[88] South Koreans were determined to demonstrate the willingness to sacrifice to weather the national crisis.

[81] The Commemorative Association of the National Debt Redemption Movement, 'Significance of the National Debt Redemption Movement', http://www.gukchae-archive.org/ge/about/movement (accessed on 3 January 2025).

[82] Park, 'A study on the social construction of collective memory', 136.

[83] Park, 'A study on the social construction of collective memory', 141.

[84] Park, 'A study on the social construction of collective memory', 142.

[85] A dissenting view dismissed the implication of NDRM and GCC for such nationalist responses merely masked the culprit of the crisis. Lee, 'The National Debt Redemption Movement'.

[86] Cheon, 'Social memory of IMF's bailout in 1997', 373.

[87] KBS, 'Miracle through unity'.

[88] *Chosun Ilbo* (2 February 1998); Associated Press, 'South Korea'.

From January to April of 1998, more than three million South Koreans raised more than US$2.1 billion with 225 tons of gold, which was 20 times bigger than the Bank of Korea's holdings.[89] An international banker remembered, 'when I saw what they were doing to avoid the default, a Korean woman were [sic] lined up around the central bank, the Bank of Korea to melt their jewellery, the gold jewellery so that Korea would not go into default.... I've negotiated debt arrangements throughout the world and I've never seen like that.' A former South Korean minister also recalled that GCC 'gave the trust that the country would never fail.'[90]

Whereas the practical contribution of GCC is in question, the campaign certainly impressed the IMF and relieved foreign creditors; the assurance that South Korea would honour its obligations helped to restore the country's creditworthiness.[91] Its political success in mobilizing the public instilled confidence in government-led reforms. The public lost faith in chaebols, the other leg of the nexus, whose failure was considered 'a root cause of the financial crisis.'[92]

State-led reform and the introduction of a market economy

On 18 December 1997, Kim Dae-jung won the presidential election, the first government change after the democratization, with a promise to overcome the national crisis. As a president-elect, he vowed to 'fully comply with the agreement between the IMF and the current government' to address concerns of foreign creditors regarding the new government; as a candidate, he suggested renegotiations with the international organization. Now, he expressed commitment to 'implement a market economy and boldly open the market.' He added, 'We will completely free all businesses from the shackles of power and the protection of power.' In return, he asked for the 'essential' cooperation of South Koreans with the intention of discussing the problem of mass unemployment with the IMF.[93]

On 19 January 1998, during the transition of power, the government faced the imminent task of negotiating the roll-over of short-term loans with international commercial banks on behalf of its private banks in New York City. Without maturity transformation, national bankruptcy was unavoidable. A South Korean delegate remembers that 'private banks were in de facto technical default. Debt restructuring was impossible because the counterparty did not trust.'[94] The

[89] Cheon, 'Social memory of IMF's bailout in 1997,' 371–372.
[90] KBS, 'Miracle through unity.'
[91] In 2008, the Prosecutor's Office found that large corporations running trading companies colluded with gold wholesalers and exploited the exemption system to evade taxes. *Hankookilbo* (27 November 2018).
[92] 'Republic of Korea—Selected issues' (15 May 1998), SM/98/99, IMFA.
[93] *MBC* (19 December 1997).
[94] KBS, 'Miracle through unity.'

amount of foreign debt due for repayment in January amounted to US$22.5 billion when the Bank of Korea held US$45 billion of foreign reserves.

In Seoul, South Korean officials demonstrated a commitment to implement structural reforms. They leveraged the national sentiment of the GCC to persuade the business community and trade unions to ensure losses and suffering. On 13 January, a week prior to the negotiation in New York City, the president-elect convened a meeting with the four largest chaebols for stringent corporate restructuring to strengthen transparency, improve the debt–equity ratio, and improve finance structure with strategic elimination of unnecessary business operations. The government persuaded trade unions to participate in the Labour–Management–Civilian Council, a tripartite social dialogue body, to consult on employment and labour policies and related economic and social issues. Under the pretext of a national crisis, the government was able to persuade the layoff of workers and the introduction of labour flexibility for non-regular employees.

The news of the agreement to establish the council empowered the South Korean delegation in New York City. One American banker remembered, 'The main selling point was that Korea want to live up to its obligation and we should help it to do so.'[95] On 28 January, the South Korean government agreed with a group of international creditors on a proposal to restructure the short-term external debt, which would be exchanged for 'new instruments with bullet maturities of 1–3 years'. It also offered 'a sovereign guarantee'.[96] A Japanese banker mentioned it was a 'really successful completion of negotiations, in which all international banks and Korean governments are very satisfied'. Immediately, the Won appreciated against the US dollar and the domestic stock market rallied. When the liquidity problem was under control, the credit rating agency of Moody's upgraded the country's credit ratings. By mid-March, South Korea continued to make 'substantial progress toward restructuring the short-term external debt' of US$21.8 billion out of US$22.6 billion of eligible debt with 134 global creditor banks. Foreign exchange reserves rose by US$6 billion.[97] The maturity extension agreement is suggested to have been more effective than the IMF bailout fund, whose immediate impact worsened the economy.

In March, President Kim further pushed the drive for corporate restructuring and introduced reforms in the financial and labour market by leveraging the guarantee on external loans of domestic banks, therefore, chaebols. Legislations to enhance corporate governance and accounting practices were followed. Some chaebols began to restructure their operations by freezing investment projects, laying off workers, selling off real estate and affiliated companies and seeking 'foreign partners for mergers and acquisitions'.[98] Three months later, chaebols began to

[95] KBS, 'Miracle through unity.'
[96] 'Republic of Korea—Bank debt exchange offer- Status report' (17 March 1998), SM/98/73, IMFA.
[97] KBS, 'Miracle through unity.'
[98] 'Republic of Korea—selected issues'.

coordinate 'big deals' to exchange businesses in the name of specialization. While the scheme did not follow the market principle, it was underpinned by political considerations that the crisis provided an opportunity for reform that could not be missed.[99] The recession in the first quarter of 1998, with the contraction of GDP and 6.7% of unemployment, rendered the scheme inevitable.[100]

In May 1998, the Executive Board of IMF assessed that 'the authorities' commitment to reforms had been a key factor' contributing to 'a rapid rebuilding of usable reserves, the strengthening and stabilization of the Won, and Korea's successful re-entry into international capital markets'. It admitted 'steadfast implementation' of a 'wide-ranging stabilization and reform program' by the authorities. It also recognized 'the need for an adequate social safety net to protect vulnerable groups in the economy'.[101] In the year, the new government allocated funds for unemployment measures to provide temporary jobs through public works projects and support vocational training for the unemployed.[102] Camdessus expressed satisfaction that the government, 'in several areas, exceeded' the commitments under the reform programme.[103] South Korean government, owing to the strengthening of the external position, shifted 'the focus of macroeconomic policies toward supporting an early recovery of domestic demand'. President Kim reiterated his commitment to 'the ongoing reform process'.[104]

It is against the confidence that the South Korean government held the initiative to lead the reform. From the notion that the crisis was attributable to 'the accumulated drawbacks of the authoritarian state-led economy and directionless globalization' in the previous regimes, it was determined to 'strongly push forward economic structural reforms to strengthen the competitiveness of our economy by enhancing flexibility in finance, corporate restructuring, and the labour market'. Yet, it expressed willingness to assume the commanding heights to introduce the market-oriented economy by coordinating agreements between labour, management, and government. In doing so, it intended to 'declare both domestically and internationally that economic reforms and opening measures would not be reversed' and planned to implement the IMF measures ahead of schedule.[105]

The government joined the reform to privatize public enterprises. Recognizing 'the lack of ownership mentality leading to lax management and inefficiency', it benchmarked the Office of Public Service of the UK government in the aftermath of the 1976 IMF crisis to establish the Public Enterprise Privatization Promotion Committee to oversee the process. Against the accusation of allowing foreign

[99] Jang, 'How to reform the Chaebols?', 206.
[100] IMF, 'IMF concludes Article IV consultation with Korea' (19 June 1998), IMFA.
[101] IMF, 'IMF concludes Article IV consultation with Korea'.
[102] Ministry of Finance and Economy, *Byeonhwahaneun Hanguk*, 16.
[103] *International Herald Tribune* (7 April 1998).
[104] Untitled draft letter (July 1998), IMFA.
[105] 'Comprehensive plan for the restructuring of the Korean economy' (20 May 1998), DA1042275, NAK.

acquisition of South Korea's valuable assets, it listed key national industries, such as the Pohang Iron and Steel Company, a symbol of state-led industrialization, for sale.[106] Such a decisive action leveraged the restructuring of Daewoo, which 'demonstrated that the large conglomerates are not "too big to fail"'.[107] With the cause of saving the nation and sharing the burden, it was able to marginalize the dissenting voices from the continued recessions in the real economy. On New Year's Day of 1999, Camdessus praised it 'the tremendous solidarity of Korean society that has helped to propel the country out of the crisis'. He added that 'the labor movement has shown a high sense of responsibility in working with the government and business under the tripartite arrangement'.[108]

With the progress of domestic reforms, the South Korean government began to devise measures against financial crises in the future; in the age of capital mobility, the potential dangers would always lurk.[109] A set of principles regarding exchange rates and foreign reserves was needed to prevent excessive capital flows or speculative movements. In February 1999, the International Finance Department of the Ministry of Finance and Economy formulated the basic strategy for foreign exchange management, drawing on 'lessons of financial crises' in the past. Amid the voices to postpone the foreign exchange market liberalization and doubts about the claimed notion that capital liberalization increased welfare, plus the ongoing debate regarding the origin of the Asian financial crisis, it reviewed three cases of 'foreign speculative cases' in the 1990s—the UK, Thailand, and Hong Kong. It analysed those past crises commonly relevant to the level of foreign reserves that each national authority held and showed the importance of cooperation with other countries.[110] Accordingly, the government decided to actively build up the available foreign exchange reserves and establish an institution to monitor the global financial market. Such a response was partially attributable to the notion that South Korea was not 'well represented in the IMF's governance structure'.[111]

From 1998 to 2000, with a current account surplus of US$75.9 billion plus a foreign direct investment of US$40.1 billion, South Korea became a country with the fifth largest foreign reserves.[112] In April 1999, the government and the Bank of Korea sponsored the foundation of the Korea Center for International Finance

[106] 'Public enterprise management innovation and privatization plan' (24 June 1998), 1A00614174944947, Presidential Archives.

[107] 'IMF concludes Article IV consultation with Korea' (29 December 1999), IMFA.

[108] *The Korea Times* (1 January 1999).

[109] On 1 April 1999, the South Korean government allowed the first flotation of *Arirang bond*, Won-denominated international loans by foreign entities, signalling the currency's internationalization. Korean Center for International Finance, *KCIF Report* (10 June 1999).

[110] 'Foreign exchange trading stage 1 liberalization supplementary measures' (10 February 1999), DA1039342, NAK.

[111] Allen and Hong, 'Why are there large foreign exchange reserves?', 1.

[112] Ministry of Finance and Economy, *Byeonhwahaneun Hanguk*, 12–13.

to operate an early warning system and strengthen pre-emptive responses to foreign exchange instabilities. The Center also emphasized the need to accumulate reserves more than deemed appropriate.[113] In 2004, South Korea maintained the ratio of foreign reserves over short-term debt at around 300% (see Figure 6.1).[114] These policies proved to have attained the desired outcome. During the 2007–2008 Global Financial Crisis, the IMF acknowledged that 'Korea's large reserve buffers had helped provide liquidity and confidence to markets in times of crisis.'[115]

In August 2001, the IMF congratulated South Korea's 'early repayment of the full amount of loans from the IMF', three years ahead of schedule.[116] Its final review of the programme noted 'a wide range of structural reforms that ... increased market orientation ... an improvement in confidence resulting from both the implementation of strong economic policies and the recovery and buildup in foreign exchange reserves', as factors behind 'the rebound' from the financial crisis and deep recession.[117] President Kim, before the celebration banquet, visited Kia Motors to praise the corporation's re-emergence as an export leader from bankruptcy. The corporation indicated the success of South Korea's reform since the crisis. He attributed it to the burden sharing by corporations and workers. The press heralded 'the

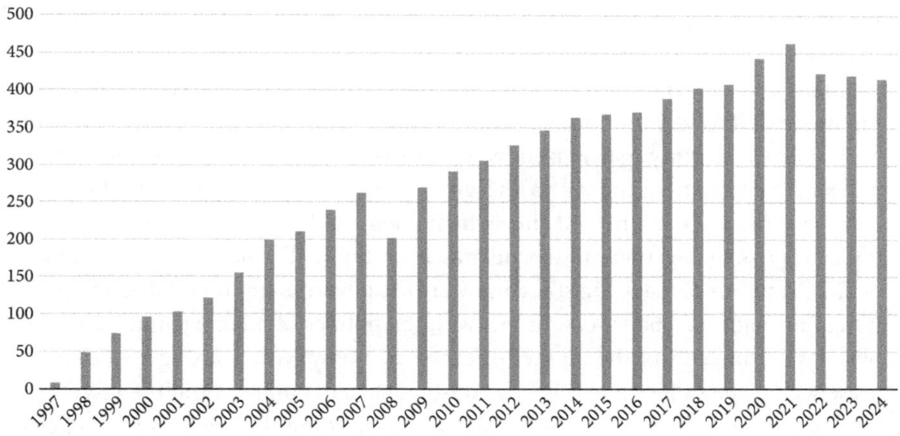

Figure 6.1 South Korea's foreign exchange reserves, 1997–2024 (in US$ billion)
Source: Data from Statistics Korea (index.go.kr).

[113] *KCIF Report* (21 June 1999).
[114] Hwang, 'The analyse of international reserve in Korea after financial crisis', 1. After the Asian Financial Crisis, the policy to maintain large foreign reserves as a self-insurance against future crises was widespread in East Asian countries.
[115] 'The Acting Chair's summing up, Republic of Korea—2009 Article IV consultation' (7 August 2009), SUR/09/93, IMFA.
[116] News Brief No. 01/81 (22 August 2001), IMFA.
[117] News brief No. 00/72 (23 August 2001), IMFA.

graduation from the IMF' as 'the recovery of economic sovereignty'.[118] After the IMF programme, South Korea was transforming into a market-oriented society. Yet, it was led by the government whose leadership remained after the failure of indebted industrialization.

Conclusion

South Koreans still vividly remember the IMF crisis, which they repeatedly recall in times of economic misfortune. The characterization of it as a national disaster arouses ~~stirs~~ a collectivist response to prioritize the nation rather than individuals. The cold winter of 1997–1998 is, therefore, remembered as a story of overcoming crisis rather than pains and suffering from corruptions and policy mistakes of chaebols and the government. In this regard, the official memory tends to marginalize the pains and sufferings, which transformed the structure of South Korean society.

This chapter examines the way in which the IMF crisis leveraged the transformation of South Korea from a developmental to a market-oriented economy. The indebted industrialization, which had underpinned the Miracle on the Han River, was inept in the age of liberalization but merely cemented the collusion of business and politics, which failed to foresee the vulnerability of the national economy from external forces. The IMF crisis indicated the failure of the existing model. However, the characterization of the IMF programme as 'the loss of economic sovereignty', galvanized by South Korea's experience of Japanese colonialism, conferred legitimacy to the government as the leader to weather the national crisis, which enabled the swift implementation of national restructuring as well as the eventual independence from the IMF. The recurring memory of GCC and burden-sharing still empowers the government to mobilize the public against national challenges. In this way, the politics of memory underpins the post-IMF symbiosis of the market-oriented economy with a strong government presence. At the same time, it is in a constant state of contestation; the increased level of inequality in the post-IMF crisis society questions the validity of the official memory.

References

Archives

Barclays Banking Group Archives, Manchester, United Kingdom
IMF Collection, On-line

[118] *Yonhap News* (22 August 2001).

International Monetary Fund Archives, Online
Jimmy Carter Presidential Library, Georgia, United States
National Archives, Kew Gardens, United Kingdom
National Archives of Korea, Seongnam, South Korea
Presidential Archives, Sejong, South Korea

Periodicals

Chosun Ilbo
Dong-A Ilbo
Euromoney
Far Eastern Economic Review
Hangyeore
Hankookilbo
International Harold Tribune
Joong-Ang Ilbo
KCIF Report
Korean Herald
Kyunghyang Shinmun
Newsweek
Maeil Kyungje
Yonhap News

Allen, F. and Hong, J.Y. (2011). 'Why are there large foreign exchange reserves? The case of South Korea'. *Korean Social Science Journal* 38, 2: 1–33.

Altamura, C.E. (2016). *European Banks and the Rise of International Finance: The Post-Bretton Woods Era*. Abingdon: Routledge.

Amsden, A.H. (1987). *Republic of Korea*. Helsinki: World Institute for Development Economic Research.

Amsden, A.H. (1989). *Asia's Next Giant: South Korea and Late Industrialization*. Oxford: Oxford University Press.

Associated Press (10 January 1998). 'South Korea: Gold collection scheme proving successful'.

BBC (1976). *The Car Makers: George goes East*, Panorama, narrated by T. Mangold, BBC, 5 April.

Cheon, H.J. (2017). 'Social memory of IMF's bailout in 1997: Recollection of "gold-collection campaign"'. *Ehwa Journal of Social* Science 33, 2: 359–395.

Cho, S.H. (2009). 'Institutions of developmental state and state capacity: Industrialization strategy and foreign capital policy of Park Chung-Hee government'. *The Journal of Korean Policy Studies* 9, 2: 161–188.

Cumings, B. (1997). *Korea's Place in the Sun*. New York: W.W. Norton.

Eun, S.M. (2009). *IMF Wigi [The IMF Crisis]*. Seoul: Chaeksesang.

Gibney, F. et al. (March–April 1995). 'Asia's growth: Miracle or myth?'. *Foreign Affairs* 74, 2: 170–176.

Griffith-Jones, S. (1980). 'The growth of multinational banking, the Eurocurrency market and their effects on developing countries'. *The Journal of Development Studies* 16, 2: 204–230.

Hwang, S.I. (2005). 'The analysis of international reserve in Korea after financial crisis'. *Journal of Korean Economic Development* 11, 2: 1–22.

International Monetary Fund (1985). *Summary Proceedings of the Fortieth Annual Meeting of the Board of Governors*. Washington DC: International Monetary Fund.
International Monetary Fund, External Relations Department (1989). 'Korea's fruitful cooperation with the Fund'. *Finance & Development*, 26, 1: 18–19.
Jang, H.S. (1998). 'How to reform the chaebols?'. *Dangdae Bi-pyeong [Contemporary Criticism]* 3: 202–223.
Ji, J.H. (2011). *Hanguk Sinjaryuijui-ui Giwongwa Hyeongseong [The Origins and Formation of Korean Neo-liberalism]*. Seoul: Chaeksesang.
Joon, H. et al. (2018). *Oehwan Wigi ihu 20nyeon Hanguk sahoe gujo wa saenghwal segye ui byeonhwa [The Changes in Korean Social Structure and the World of Life 20 Years after the Financial Crisis]*. Seoul: National Museum of Korean Contemporary History.
KBS (1 September 2009). 'First public release of the IMF crisis: US secret documents—the IMF and the "Trojan horse"'.
KBS (19 October 2013). 'Miracle through unity: Overcoming the IMF crisis'.
KBS (7 November 2019). '"The world is vast, and there is much to be done". How did Daewoo disappear in an instant? Modern Korea—Grand aspiration'.
Kim, D.J. (November–December 1994). 'Is culture destiny? The myth of Asia's anti-democratic values'. *Foreign Affairs* 73, 6: 189–194.
Kim, W.J. (2018[1989]). *Segyeneun neolgo haliranun manhda [The World Is Vast, and There Is Much to Be Done]*. Paju: Akanet.
Krugman, P. (November–December 1994). 'The myth of Asia's miracle'. *Foreign Affairs* 73, 6: 62–78.
Kwon, H.K. (2021). *Changes by Competition: The Evolution of the South Korean Developmental State*. Oxford: Oxford University Press.
Labour Economic Research Institute following Jeon Tae-il (1998). *The Economic Crisis and IMF Trusteeship*. Seoul: Labour Economic Research Institute following Jeon Tae-il.
Lee, J. (2011). *Oehwan Wigi wa Geu Hu-ui Hanguk Gyeongje [Foreign Exchange Crisis and the Korean Economy Thereafter]*. Paju, Hanul Academy.
Lee, J. (2023). *The Tortuous Path of South Korean Economic Development*. Cambridge: Cambridge University Press.
Lee, N.Y. (2011). 'The automobile industry'. In B.K. Kim and E.F. Vogel (eds), *The Park Chung Hee era: The Transformation of South Korea*. Cambridge, MA: Harvard University Press, 295–321.
Lee, S.C. (1998). 'The National Debt Redemption Movement and the falseness of the IMF "Gold Collection Campaign"'. *Critical Review of History* 43: 15–23.
Mangold, T. (1976) 'The car makers: George goes East'. *BBC Panorama*.
Ministry of Finance and Economy (February 1999). *One Year of the People's Government: Achievements and Challenges for Economic Policy*. Seoul: Ministry of Finance and Economy.
Ministry of Finance and Economy (2001). *Byeonhwahaneun Hanguk, Doyakhaneun Gyeojgje [Changing Korea, Rising Economy]*. Seoul: Ministry of Finance and Economy.
Newstapa (29 January 2025). '1997, IMF the great lie'.
Park, C.J. (2018). 'The political origin of neoliberalism in Korea: Economic policy shift after the Busan-Masan and the Gwangju protest movements'. *Society and History* 117: 133–154.
Park, G. (2007). 'A study on the social construction of collective memory: Focusing on NRC and GCC'. *The Korean Journal of Cultural Sociology* 2, 1: 117–164.

Park, S.Y. (2020). 'Economic nationalism and the Korean developmental state: The development of Korea's automobile industry under the Park Chung Hee regime'. *Journal of Asia-Pacific Studies* 27, 4: 163–193.

Park, T.G. (2001). 'W. W. Rostow and economic discourse in South Korea in the 1960s'. *Journal of International and Area Studies* 8, 2: 55–66.

Park, Y.C. et al. (2021). *Financial Liberalization and Economic Development in Korea, 1980–2020*. Cambridge, MA: Harvard University Press.

Rhyu, S.Y. (2020). 'Park Chung Hee's monetary reform in 1962 and Korean nationalism'. *Journal of Contemporary Politics* 13, 2: 119–153.

World Bank (1993). *The East Asian miracle: Economic Growth and Public Policy*. Washington DC: World Bank.

Youn, D.S. (2013). 'An issue of Korean nationalism: The apology of self-respect on ambivalent recognition'. *Korean Studies Quarterly* 36, 2: 330–360.

Zakaria, F. (March–April 1994). 'Culture is destiny: A conversation with Lee Kuan Yew'. *Foreign Affairs* 73, 2: 109–126.

7

The end of Bretton Woods and the rise of over-the-counter derivatives

The mostly forgotten regulatory debates

Tobias Pforr

Introduction

The end of the Bretton Woods system and the world of over-the-counter (OTC) derivatives may at first appear as two entirely unrelated phenomena. After all, OTC derivatives tend to be associated with high-speed global electronic trading and the Global Financial Crisis which at first sight has little to do with the quaint financial world of the 1970s.[1] Yet a closer historical analysis reveals that they are much more intimately intertwined than first appears. In some ways this should not be surprising. After all, a system of flexible exchange rates has much greater requirements for private actors to hedge their currency exposures as well as much greater room to engage in speculation, as also noted by the Bank of International Settlements (BIS): 'The collapse of the Bretton Woods system of fixed exchange rates in 1971 increased the demand for hedging against exchange rate risk.'[2] As a consequence, the Chicago Mercantile Exchange opened a currency futures exchange in 1972, the Chicago Board of Trade allowed interest rate futures to trade in 1975, and the first OTC derivative transaction occurred in 1976.[3]

[1] I purposefully restrict the discussion here to post-Bretton Woods. For scholarship on derivative products in ancient Mesopotamia or medieval Venice, see: Swan, *4,000 Year History of Derivatives.* In addition, there was a lively regulatory discussion in the USA from the 1880s onwards on the legality of futures. See: Stassen, 'The Commodity Exchange Act'.

[2] Chui, Derivative markets, p. 4.

[3] As the name suggests, a derivate is any instrument that derives its value from another asset. Traditionally, these have been futures, forwards, swaps, and options. Any derivatives can in principle be traded on an exchange or over-the-counter, that is, intermediated by a by a dealer. Some derivatives have predominantly been traded on exchanges, like futures, whereas others have predominantly been traded over the counter, like forwards and swaps. Newer derivative products, like credit default swaps, have been over the counter products. Over time, some exchange traded products were also increasingly offered over the counter, with the result that the distinction became much less important in a material sense, even if it remains of legal importance.

Tobias Pforr, *The end of Bretton Woods and the rise of over-the-counter derivatives*. In: *History, Memory, and the Return of Financial Crises After Bretton Woods*. Edited by: Youssef Cassis and Giuseppe Telesca, Oxford University Press.
 DOI: 10.1093/9780198950158.003.0007

But it is not only the historical development of OTC derivatives that is frequently neglected. Equally overlooked is the fact that the expansion of OTC derivatives was accompanied by ongoing, intense, and highly controversial regulatory debates over two decades. When awareness of these debates does exist, it is typically confined to discussions from the late 1990s.[4] These debates were decisive for the passage of what became the Commodities Futures Modernization Act (CFMA) in December 2000 which ensured not only that OTC derivatives would remain unregulated but also because this was subsequently singled out as a crucial element that made the Global Financial Crisis possible.

This chapter attempts to resurrect a rough outline of entire regulatory debate, for four main reasons. First, seen from the perspective of the 1980s, it makes the eventual non-regulation of derivatives an even more unlikely event than if we just consider the discussions of the 1990s. Their lack of regulation was not just the outcome of a single bad decision or a single lost regulatory struggle. Rather, regulatory attempts by a variety of actors were continuously thwarted over a period of two decades. In each case, the anti-regulation voices within a single regulator or between regulators somehow won out. One especially important voice in this regard was Fed chairman Alan Greenspan as well as various other professional economists, mostly from, or influenced by, the Chicago School.

Second, the non-regulation of OTC derivatives proved particularly fateful. The Financial Crisis Inquiry Commission (FCIC) interviewed over 700 expert witnesses on the causes of the Global Financial Crisis and unequivocally concluded that 'over-the-counter derivatives contributed significantly to the crisis'.[5] In fact, it found that 'the enactment of legislation in 2000 [CFMA]... was a key turning point in the march toward the financial crisis'.[6] This sentiment is also widely shared within the academic community. Cassis states that 'no financial innovation has been more closely associated [with] the 2007–8 Financial Debacle than "derivatives"'.[7] Stout is even more specific in her assessment: 'Put simply, the credit crisis was not primarily due to changes in the markets; it was due to changes in the law. In particular, the crisis was the direct and foreseeable (and in fact foreseen by the author and others) consequence of the CFMA's sudden and wholesale removal of centuries-old legal constraints on speculative trading in OTC (OTC) derivatives.'[8]

Third, the regulatory evolution of OTC derivatives stands in contrast to how one imagines the regulatory process to proceed. When financial innovation occurs, it is generally unclear whether new regulation is required. Different regulators and practitioners may have intuitions about likely scenarios and the extent to which a

[4] Funk and Hirschman, 'Derivatives and Deregulation' is one prominent exception to this tendency.
[5] FDIC, *Report*, xxiv.
[6] FDIC, *Report*, xv.
[7] Cassis, *Crises and Opportunities*, 101.
[8] Stout, 'Legal origin', 1.

new innovation will take hold in the market but there is little empirical evidence by which to substantiate claims. Over time, however, an innovation may emerge as the 'new normal' within market activity and it may also start to be implicated in actual financial problems. This should clarify the need for regulatory reform. Depending on the relative power of those who favour regulation over those who do not, regulatory attempts will either succeed or lead nowhere. If problems continue to mount, however, one expects those in favour of regulation eventually to succeed.

Yet, this is not what happened. OTC derivatives grew from a niche product to one of the most widely traded instruments. Even before they became implicated in an increasing number of financial scandals, there were lively discussions within the public sphere and amongst regulators.[9] The Securities Exchange Commission (SEC), Commodity Futures Trading Commission (CFTC), and Financial Accounting Standards Board (FASB) made regulatory suggestions as early as the mid-1980s. Charles Schwab, founder of the eponymous Charles Schwab Corporation, wrote an open letter to the *New York Times* in March 1990, arguing that 'every investor should urge his or her Congressional representative to expand the jurisdiction of the Securities and Exchange Commission to include power over both the securities markets and all derivative contracts....'[10] Yet, industry push-back and regulations sceptics prevailed, which culminated in the 'Futures Trading Practices Act (FTPA)' in January 1992, giving congressional approval to the CFTC to continue to exempt OTC derivatives from all regulation. After the failure of Metallgesellschaft, some regulators made another stab at regulation. The Comptroller of the Currency published a damming report and some leaders of the House of Representatives were eager to pass new legislation. This led to the proposed 'Derivatives Safety and Soundness Supervision Act' of 1994, first sponsored by Henry Gonzales and James Leach but subsequently developed by Donald Riegle.[11] However, these attempts did not succeed either. Rising problems and scandals soon lead to a third major attempt at regulation, this time strongly driven by Brooksley Born of the CFTC. However, rather than being able to muster more support in favour of regulation (as more failures and problems with OTC derivatives had occurred), there was even stronger pushback from industry and other regulators. Instead of passing a law that would regulate OTC derivatives, the anti-regulation camp was able to prohibit any future regulation of OTC derivatives.

Fourth and last, the forgotten length and breadth of regulatory struggle make the eventual non-regulation of OTC derivatives seem more inevitable in hindsight

[9] The list of even the most high-profile scandals is scandalously long: Tateho Chemical Company in 1988, State of West Virgina in 1989, Allied Lyons in 1991, Shell Showa and Metallgesellschaft in 1993, Bank Negara and Proctor and Gamble in 1994, Gibson Greeting Cards, Orange County, Sumitomo, and Barings Bank in 1995; and finally Long-Term Capital Management (LTCM) in 1998.

[10] Schwab, 'More power'.

[11] Culp and Mackay, 'Regulating derivatives'.

then it really was. There is frequently a lively contemporaneous debate over the extent to which different negative financial events should be seen as connected to a single underlying cause or the extent to which they can serve as indicators of a looming larger systemic crisis.[12] Such judgements matter greatly, for they influence the urgency and importance which regulators attach to these events. A number of seemingly unconnected negative financial events may be regarded as unfortunate but usually do not prompt an impetus for regulatory intervention. If they are seen to be linked to a single root cause, however, the impetus for regulatory action is much higher.

Such interpretations also influence the way these events enter into collective memory: Seen as unconnected events, they attain little importance. Seen as connected by a single cause, they are often considered harbingers of a larger crisis to come and will enter collective memory as such. This means that contestations over differing interpretations of what happened and ultimately caused a financial crisis at the same time are controversies over how such events will be remembered collectively. Consequently, it matters greatly whose interpretation of events eventually becomes the orthodox view on the matter. In addition, the original contestation of any one interpretation tends to be forgotten over time, allowing the orthodox interpretations to attain near hegemonic status. However, the case also demonstrates that a renewed crisis of sufficient proportion can end up calling into question orthodox interpretations. Put differently, subsequent financial crises can rewrite the collective memory of earlier crises. As such, although the collective memory of financial crises matters greatly for financial regulation, it is itself subject to repeated historical revisions.

From the birth of the OTC derivative to the Futures Trading Practices Act of 1992

The most frequently encountered story about the birth of OTC derivatives involves Solomon Brothers, IBM, and the World Bank in 1981.[13] IBM had issued bonds in Swiss Francs and Deutsche Mark but preferred to receive US dollars. The World Bank, by contrast, had issued US dollar bonds but needed European currencies. After two years of work, Solomon Brothers brokered a deal for these two entities to swap payment streams and hence the currency swap was born.

[12] The loose terminology of the term 'financial crisis' does not help in this regard. For some commentators, any single negative financial event may constitute a financial crisis while other commentators reserve the term for only the largest systemic crises, that is, the Great Depression and Global Financial Crises.

[13] Tett, *Fools Gold*, 63; Funk and Hirschman, 'Derivatives and deregulation'. However, Funk and Hirschman are also aware of earlier derivatives trading.

However, although this Solomon deal received widespread attention, modern day derivatives had been in existence since the early 1970s.[14] Currency futures began trading on the Chicago Mercantile Exchange in 1972 and interest rate futures began trading on the Chicago Board of Trade in 1975. These, however, were still exchange-traded derivatives. The move to OTC derivatives did not have to wait much longer as Goldman Sachs, ICI, and Monsanto attempted to structure a currency swap in early 1976.[15] However, due to legal difficulties, this deal never materialized. A few months later, ICI completed the first successful currency swap (£5 million into Dutch guilders) with Bos Kalis Westminster Group in August 1976.[16] By 1980, the *Wall Street Journal* was regularly reporting on the new market for swaps.[17]

Swaps offer a whole array of benefits. They are nearly infinitely customizable, off-balance sheet, and offer preferential tax treatments. An academic paper of the time put it this way: 'with the introduction of swaps, a U.S. firm could issue a yen-denominated issue in the Eurobond market, structure the issue so as to receive a favourable tax treatment under the Japanese tax code, avoid much of the U.S. securities regulation, and yet still manage its currency exposure by swapping the transaction back into dollars'.[18]

A crucial issue with swaps in the USA and UK, however, was that they were potentially illegal. Their legality depended on whether a swap (and an OTC derivative by extension) should be classed as a security and/or a futures contract. The 1936 Commodities Exchange Act required that all futures be sold on organized and regulated exchanges. As late as 1980, the CFTC successfully sued companies for offering futures contracts outside of a regulated market, for example in CFTC v. Co Petro Marketing Group, Inc.[19] In the UK, this strict (but clearly selective) stance lasted even longer. In 1991, the House of Lords voided swaps contracts between British municipalities and over 75 banks over the fact that it considered swaps to be speculation, causing derivatives dealers to lose an estimated $179 million.[20]

Subsequently, various regulators thought to not only clarify the status of OTC derivatives but also to regulate them more directly. In 1985, the SEC called for

[14] This discussion also ignores a very close relative to derivatives—central banks swap arrangements. The Federal Reserve first initiated a standing OTC currency swap agreement with the Bank of England in 1917. This was soon followed by further agreements with the Banque de France, Bank of Italy, and Bank of Japan. The period of the 1960s subsequently marked another high mark for these so-called central bank swap lines. Central bank swap lines are analogous to currency swaps, except that there is no dealer involved. It is worth bearing this in mind when private actors claim to have invented the currency swap. See also: Potter, 'The Federal Reserve'; McCauley and Schenk, 'Central bank swaps then and now'.

[15] Hodgson, 'The birth'.

[16] Hodgson, 'The birth'.

[17] See, for example: The Wall Street Journal, 'More direct currency swaps'; The Wall Street Journal, 'Jal gets yen-for-mark swap'.

[18] Smith et al., 'The evolving market'.

[19] See: https://law.justia.com/cases/federal/district-courts/FSupp/502/806/1512318/.

[20] Hirschman and Funk, 'Derivatives and deregulation', p. 689; Lynn, 'Enforceability', pp. 308–309.

public comments on stricter accounting requirements of interest-rate swaps and other derivative products.[21] In 1986, the Financial Accounting Standards Board proposed that swaps should no longer be carried off balance sheet.[22] In 1987, the CFTC issued an advance notice of proposed rulemaking. Noting that 'uncertainty has been expressed concerning the legal status', the CTFC suggested that OTC derivatives may be akin to regular futures and thus illegal.[23]

In January 1988, the report of Presidential Task Force on Market Mechanisms, today better known as the 'Brady report', added to the case for regulatory intervention. The aim of this task force had been to analyse and understand the events that unfolded between 13 and 19 October 1987 (also known as Black Friday and/or Black Monday), during which time the Dow Jones Industrial Average lost 769 points or 31%. The report prominently found two new and growing phenomena, the rise of derivatives and the rise of over-the-counter markets. It found that 'OTC trading has also gained in relative importance in recent years'[24] and the 'prominence during this period of new derivative instruments'.[25] Although the report still treated these two developments under separate headings, there was already some sense that derivative trading might also be taking place OTC, that is, via a dealer. In fact, the central finding of the report was that all these different markets were highly interdependent. As the report notes: 'The stock market and the derivative instrument market (options and futures) are, in reality, segments of a single equity market, rather than separate markets'.[26] The report noted that this interdependence could increase volatility and that derivatives were used in all manner of arbitrage operations. One of the recommendations of the report was 'to assign the SEC the responsibility for stocks and all derivative instruments'.[27] Even more so, this report found that 40% of the recommendations seen as beneficial by private market actors had to do with better regulation of OTC derivative.[28]

However, each of these attempts at regulation was met with significant pushback from the financial industry. In 1988, the *Wall Street Journal* noted that 'many major commercial banks are expected to fight a proposed federal regulation [on swaps]'.[29] In 1989, McKinsey strongly supported commercial banks in their fights, saying that 'regulation should focus much more on the institutions that have problems, not on the entire industry'.[30]

[21] Ingersoll, 'SEC proposes'.
[22] Berton, 'FASB begins project'.
[23] Federal Register, 'CFTC regulation'.
[24] Brady, 'Report', II-12.
[25] Brady, 'Report', III-1.
[26] Brady, 'Report', IV-3.
[27] Brady, 'Report', p. 61.
[28] Those recommendations were: Improve market making of OTC; Limit/ban financial derivatives; Higher margins on futures/options; Price limits on futures.
[29] Guenther, 'Banks expected to fight proposal'.
[30] Bryan, 'Capital guidelines'.

The financial industry also had one particularly powerful supporter in the regulatory community: Alan Greenspan, who had been made Chairman of the Board of the Federal Reserve in 1987. Greenspan continuously sought to protect what he saw as efficient and innovative financial markets from what he regarded as the overreach of the government. In response to the findings of the Brady report, he noted that 'it also is encouraging that so much can and is being done within the existing legislative and regulatory framework'.[31] In this speech, Greenspan even singled out OTC derivatives for more effectively distributing risk thereby making financial markets safer: 'Exchange rate and interest rate swaps together with financial futures and options have become important means by which currency and interest rate risks get shifted to those most willing to take it on.'[32] Later that year, he defended higher and rising leverage in financial sectors, saying 'moreover, innovations in capital markets have made the increased propensity to leverage feasible'.[33] In 1990, he highlighted that 'markets are more dynamic than regulations and regulators' and he went so far as to suggest that there was already too much regulation, saying: 'We should be as open to the possibility that some regulation should be relaxed as we are to the possibility for additional regulation.'[34] In addition, he noted that 'we cannot realistically expect to eliminate all risks to these [financial market] systems',[35] suggesting existing regulation was more than sufficient in dealing with any present or future challenge.

The CFTC in particular was unable to follow through on its regulatory proposal. In 1989, it gave updated guidance that abandoned its earlier regulatory efforts from 1987, saying that it 'will take no action to preclude the effectuation of or to regulate such transactions'.[36] This, however, prompted some unease within public discussions. For example, the *Wall Street Journal* noted in 1990 that 'U.S. regulators worry that light, and uneven, regulation of derivative markets could lead to major financial losses for investors'.[37] Yet, many members of congress were in favour of continued non-regulation. Consequently, the CTFC exemption was greatly strengthened by a proposed bill in the US house in January 1991 which granted the CFTC congressional approval to permanently exempt OTC derivatives from regulation. After first being indefinitely delayed in the Senate, a modified bill was signed into law in October 1992 by President George H.W. Bush as the Futures Trading Practices Act (FTPA) of 1992. President Bush was very clear that the aim was to allow the expanding OTC derivative markets to grow further: 'The bill also gives the Commodity Futures Trading Commission (CFTC) exemptive authority to remove the cloud of legal uncertainty over the financial instruments

[31] Greenspan, 'Testimony June 14, 1989'.
[32] Greenspan, 'Testimony June 14, 1989'.
[33] Greenspan, 'Statement January 26, 1989'.
[34] Greenspan, 'Remarks May 2, 1990'.
[35] Greenspan, 'Testimony June 14, 1989'.
[36] Federal Register, 'Policy statement concerning swap transactions'.
[37] Torres, 'Bull market'.

known as swap agreements. This uncertainty has threatened to disrupt the huge, global market for these transactions.'[38]

The next attempt at regulation: the fight for the Derivatives Safety and Soundness Supervision Act of 1994

Concurrently to regulatory discussions on the FTPA, some regulators continued to express concern about the developments in derivative markets. One such person was Senator Riegle, who launched a series of regulatory requests about the dangers of derivatives to the American public. One such request was made in September 1992 to the Board of Governors of the Federal Reserve System, the Federal Deposit Insurance Corporation, and the Office of Comptroller of the Currency and answered in January 1993. Another request was made in December 1992 to the Office of Thrift and Supervision (OTS) and answered in March 1993.[39]

These two reports anticipated a recurring dynamic throughout the 1990s: some regulators consistently downplayed the risks posed by derivatives, while others pushed for decisive action. Alan Greenspan continued to heavily support the non-regulation of derivatives. In this vein, the first report merely noted that 'the risks associated with derivative instruments are the same types of risks banking institutions face daily in their lending, treasury and trading functions'.[40] This assessment was very much based on a vision of financial markets as perfectly competitive. For example, the first report argued that 'Since most derivatives involving firm commitments are entered into at no cost (other than possibly a nominal fee) to either party, they have zero value and therefore, no credit exposure at inception.'[41] The fact that no party would ever enter into a contract that has no value to them is somehow not taken into account in such a model. In any case, the report strongly cautioned against further regulation as 'regulation cannot substitute for effective management' and that 'to date, those management processes have been generally successful'.[42] The possibility that systemic risk might be of relevance was not even addressed in this report. Its findings were supported on the international stage by a widely circulated report on derivatives by the Global Derivatives Study Group of the Group of Thirty, an informal working group of major financial institutions and various national and international financial regulators. They unequivocally rejected any need for further regulation: 'The general attitude of the Study towards regulation is plain: derivatives by their nature do not introduce risks

[38] Bush, 'Statement'.

[39] The OTS at the time was a relatively new regulator, only founded in 1989, in response to the failures of the Savings & Loan crisis, thereby superseding the previous regulator of Savings & Loan institutions, the Federal Home Loan Bank Board (FHLBB). The OTS, in turn, would be abandoned in response to some perceived failings during the financial crisis in 2008.

[40] US Congress, Serial 103–188, p. 774.

[41] US. Congress, Serial 103–188, p. 775.

[42] U.S. Congress, Serial 103–188, p. 795.

of a fundamentally different kind or of a greater scale than those already present in the financial markets. Hence, systemic risks are not appreciably aggravated, and supervisory concerns can be addressed within present regulatory structures and approaches.'[43]

The OTS report, by contrast, strongly favoured regulation. It noted that 'derivatives can be a source of risk if they are used for speculative purposes or if they are used improperly'.[44] It added that 'some participants have voiced concern that disruptions in one market, such as might be triggered by the default of a major counterparty, could spread to other markets, and in a worst-case scenario cause a collapse of the global financial system'.[45] As a result, 'OTS as a regulator of savings associations, exercises its authority in an effort to ensure that savings associations that use derivatives do not become a source of systemic risk.'[46]

The SEC was internally divided over the dangers posed by derivatives, as noted by previous scholarship such as Lockwood who writes that 'the early 1990s were marked by strong differences between individual SEC commissioners regarding OTC derivatives'.[47] For example, SEC Commissioners Mary Schapiro and J. Carter Beese favoured greater regulation. Schapiro said in 1993: 'Regulators do not need to fear the brave new financial world of the 1990s but they do need to keep pace with it and anticipate problems before they occur ... nothing will interrupt the progress of the derivatives markets more abruptly than a financial crisis that is perceived to be caused or exacerbated by unregulated activity in those markets'.[48] Beese similarly noted the danger in 1993: 'More than anything else has in years, the OTC derivatives market has increased the probability that a meltdown in one financial sector will spread to others.'[49] Chairman Richard Breeden, by contrast, was not convinced and regarded the dangers as exaggerated: 'There is too much alarmist rhetoric involving these products.... We've seen 2,500 banks fail because of credit risk. We have a long way to go before the swaps market is as threatening.'[50]

The early 1990s was also the period when the first derivative scandals started to make popular headlines. One case that proved to be particularly prominent and far reaching was that of Metallgesellschaft. *The New York Times* and *International Herald Tribune*[51] wrote dozens of articles each on Metallgesselschaft, writing that 'the story of Metallgesellschaft's near insolvency has grown into an ugly corporate

[43] Group of Thirty, 'Derivatives'.
[44] US Congress, Serial 103–188, p. 159.
[45] US Congress, Serial 103–188, p. 162.
[46] US Congress, Serial 103–188, p. 167.
[47] Lockwood, 'From bombs to boons', p. 220.
[48] Schapiro, 'The derivatives revolution'.
[49] Beese, 'Remarks'.
[50] Quoted in Muehring and Hansell, 1992.
[51] In 2002, The New York Times acquired the *International Herald Tribune* and named it the *International Edition of The New York Times.*

melodrama'.[52] It also referred to the story as the 'Oil-futures bloodbath'.[53] Another article in 1994 stated: 'Depending on whom you speak to, derivatives are either the latest saviours or the threatening destroyers of the financial world.'[54] Even in 2007, the memories of the Metallgesselschaft case still were present in the public debate, as *The New York Times* ran a story which read that 'some here view the Metallgesellschaft debacle as a forerunner to the risky trading schemes that sunk Enron'.[55]

The case of Metallgesellschaft (MG) has been described as the 'first case of "derivatives malpractice"'.[56] At the time, Metallgesellschaft was Germany's 14th largest industrial company, employing 58,000 people. Deutsche Bank served as both MG's primary creditor and controlling shareholder, with a Deutsche Bank executive acting as chairman of MG's board of supervisors. One of MG's American subsidiaries, Metallgesellschaft Refining and Marketing (MGRM), had implemented an aggressive marketing strategy offering customers a guaranteed supply of gasoline and heating oil at fixed prices for the next 10 years. By September 1993, MGRM had committed to supply 160 million barrels at prices ranging from $24 to $27 per barrel. To manage its exposure to rising prices, MGRM attempted to hedge some of this risk. However, because 10-year oil hedges did not exist, it relied on shorter-term hedges that needed to be rolled over as they matured. When spot prices for oil products fell, MGRM faced escalating cash flow issues and significant hedging losses. By December 1993, these losses had reached $1.3 billion, prompting MG to liquidate all remaining hedges. The upfront costs of liquidation were so high that it required a $1.9 billion rescue package from 150 German and international banks to accomplish.

After the failure of Metallgesellschaft, regulatory discussions reached a completely new sense of urgency. But stark divisions remained. For example, the Federal Reserve Bank of Atlanta sponsored a workshop in February 1994 of about 100 government officials, academics, and professionals to discuss the risks posed by OTC derivatives. In this workshop, Susan Phillips, a Federal Reserve Governor, is reported to have criticized 'the persistence of what appears to be exaggerated fears of the risk of derivatives activities'.[57] This was reported by *The New York Times* as a reduction of regulatory concern, saying that 'the nation's top regulators are having fewer nightmares about a potential crisis from the explosive growth of a new category of financial transactions known as derivatives'. The story goes on to note that 'gone, though, were the concerns that have plagued some

[52] Friedman, 'Pointing the finger'.
[53] Nasar, 'The oil-futures bloodbath'.
[54] Nezter, 'Are derivatives a blessing'.
[55] Landler, 'Spotlight'.
[56] Jacque, *Derivatives Debacles*, p. 73.
[57] Hansell, 'Regulators mute their fears'.

regulators—that derivatives were making the financial system more vulnerable to a financial market meltdown'. A paper in the *Economic Review of the Federal Reserve Bank of Atlanta* in March 1994, however, came to a different conclusion. It noted that 'because of their perceived riskiness and their relatively unregulated status, the OTC derivatives markets have been under increasing scrutiny' and also argued that 'few observers of derivatives markets would deny that systemic risk is potentially a concern; the controversy is over measures to minimize that risk'.[58]

In May 1994, a major report by United States General Accounting Office (GAO) found that 'no comprehensive industry or federal regulatory requirements existed to ensure that US OTC derivatives dealers followed good risk-management practices'.[59] As a result it strongly recommended that Congress 'bring the currently unregulated OTC derivatives activities of securities firm and insurance company affiliates under the purview of one or more of the existing federal financial regulators'.[60] The House immediately acted upon this recommendation and proposed the Derivatives Safety and Soundness Supervision Act in May 1994, with congressional discussions taking place in July. *The New York Times* reported on this development as 'G.A.O. Seeks Sweeping Rules for Derivatives'.[61] Further hearings were scheduled and held in December 1994.[62]

Anti-regulatory groups mobilized en masse in anticipation of these hearings. One group that was particularly active in defending the use of derivatives and which urged regulators that derivatives pose no serious risk to the financial system was a group of orthodox financial economists surrounding five Nobel Laureates in economics—Robert C. Merton, Merton Miller, Franco Modigliani, Myron Scholes, and William F. Sharpe.[63] Together with 27 other senior economists, they launched a campaign in autumn 1994 to urge regulators not to intervene in OTC derivative markets, despite 'the huge derivatives loss suffered recently by Metallgesellschaft'.[64] In a statement, they acknowledged that 'both the Congress and regulators remain uneasy about the misuse of derivative instruments and the potential consequences that might flow from a major default in derivatives markets'.[65] However, they thought this fear was completely unfounded: 'the use of OTC derivatives does not justify the current fear that they might cause a systemic meltdown'.[66] Even more, they thought that any attempt at regulation would threaten

[58] Abken, 'Over-the-counter financial derivatives', p. 11.

[59] US Congress, Serial 103–188, p. 7.

[60] US Congress, Serial 103–188, p. 127.

[61] Hansell, 'G.A.O. seeks'.

[62] Unfortunately, the bill did not make it to a vote before the dissolution of the 103rd Congress and it was subsequently not taken up in later sessions.

[63] Merton and Scholes would only receive their award in 1997 though. Both were also directly involved in the LTCM derivative debacle.

[64] Abdel-Khalik, 'Statement', 7.

[65] Abdel-Khalik, 'Statement', 4.

[66] Abdel-Khalik, 'Statement', 5.

the efficiency of financial markets. In other words, rather than derivatives being a potential danger, it was government regulation that threatened the stability of financial markets: 'precipitous and unnecessary government intervention directed at preventing such a possibility [systemic meltdown] may create rigidities that impede the responsiveness of markets in times of stress'.[67] They were joined in their attempt by another anti-regulatory economist, Alan Greenspan, who in a congressional testimony rejected the finding by GAO. *The New York Times* reported his position as 'strongly disagreeing with a new Congressional study, the chairman of the Federal Reserve Board, Alan Greenspan, said today there was "negligible" risk that the rapidly growing market for financial derivatives might someday require a taxpayer bailout. In testimony before a House subcommittee, Mr. Greenspan and other senior financial regulators said there was no need for new legislation to supervise derivatives.'[68]

This mobilization once again had the desired effect. Bowing to the pressure, the OCC in September 1994 for the first time gave a formal permission to a major commercial bank, in this case Citibank, to sell stock-index derivatives, a practice which it had been doing for years.[69] The CFTC authorized the operators of the large exchanges in Chicago to operate a quasi-OTC derivative club 'to help the futures exchanges better compete with off-exchange derivatives trading'.[70] The Chairman of the Chicago Board of Trade took this as a positive sign of the 'recognized the need for loosened regulation of exchange products'.[71] Some regulators also felt increased pressure from Congress, especially a bill that threatened to merge the SEC and CFTC. By January 1995, the situation had evolved to a point where *The New York Times* noted a 'broad hostility to regulating the derivatives market'.[72] By December 1995, a fine by the CFTC for Metallgesellschaft prompted a stark rebuke by US lawmakers, saying that this may be seen as a threat to the existing derivatives market.[73] Given the overall climate, it was thus not surprising that the Derivatives Safety And Soundness Supervision Act was abandoned in 1995 and was never put up for a vote. In fact, writing in 1996, the *Wall Street Journal* noted that six different regulatory attempts that were started in 1994 had been abandoned by 1996: 'At the end of 1994, the U.S. Congress alone had no fewer than six bills pending that would have banned or restricted the use of derivatives by a range of investors. Those have since been dropped....'[74]

[67] Abdel-Khalik, 'Statement', 5.
[68] Hansell, 'Derivatives get a key supporter'.
[69] Special to the New York Times, 'U.S. allows'.
[70] The Wall Street Journal, 'CFTC votes'.
[71] The Wall Street Journal, 'CFTC votes'.
[72] Bradsher, 'Regulators see no need for tougher rules on derivatives'.
[73] Bloomberg Business News, 'Derivatives are center of protest'.
[74] McGee and Hayes, 'Derivatives are a tempting option again'.

The mid-1990s and the last attempts at regulation

Despite the growing number of highly publicized issues with OTC derivatives, the regulatory sentiment in the mid-1990s remained strongly opposed to regulating derivatives. SEC Chairman Arthur Levitt is a case in point. He strongly defended them in 1995: 'We must avoid the temptation to demonize derivatives, which are a vital tool in modern financial markets. They are so useful in managing risk that if they didn't exist, we would surely have to invent them.'[75] Levitt was aware that derivatives had been involved in recent crises: 'Over the past two years, the headlines have been filled with significant derivatives losses by corporate and municipal end-users and dealers alike. The collapse of Britain's Barings Bank; the problems at Metallgesellschaft, and, in the United States, the "Bankers Trust" enforcement action are all still fresh in our minds.'[76] Yet, for Levitt, derivatives were not to blame in these crises because 'like any financial instrument, derivatives require certain ground rules, and regulators can provide that. But we must resist the siren call for stringent regulation that occurs in the wake of every new loss—especially since the typical derivatives loss is less a failure of regulation, than a failure of oversight by the parties involved.'[77]

This change in regulatory approach was very much recognized within financial markets. For example, in March 1996, the chairman of the International Swaps & Derivatives Association happily noted that 'For the first time in years, [the derivatives industry] is beginning a new year not under the shadow of pending regulation.'[78] This development led the *Wall Street Journal* to conclude that derivatives were losing their bad reputation, or as a piece put it: 'The "D" word is losing some of its bad connotation, at least according to the dealers who flog the complex products known as derivatives.'[79]

However, this period of regulatory calm only lasted for a short period. Starting in the middle of 1996, each regulator began proposing new attempts at regulation. The SEC and FASB made a start by 'proposing sweeping changes to the way derivatives are accounted for and disclosed in financial statements.'[80] Unsurprisingly, these attempts proved hugely unpopular with the financial industry, with the *Wall Street Journal* reporting that 'dealers who sell the financial instruments known as derivatives and the companies and agencies that use them blasted proposed regulatory changes.'[81] In 1997, the new CFTC Chairwoman Booksley Born immediately clashed with industry representatives over the further regulation, as

[75] Levitt, 'Derivatives use.'
[76] Levitt, 'Derivatives use.'
[77] Levitt, 'Derivatives use.'
[78] McGee and Hayes, 'Derivatives are a tempting option again.'
[79] McGee and Hayes, 'Derivatives are a tempting option again.'
[80] McGee, 'Derivative dealers blast rule proposals.'
[81] McGee, 'Derivative dealers blast rule proposals.'

reported by the *Wall Street Journal*: 'the top regulator of U.S. futures markets clashed with the industry's trade group yesterday over deregulatory legislation before Congress.'[82]

Each of these attempts was once again opposed by Greenspan. In August 1997, Greenspan intervened by fighting to discredit the FASB proposal.[83] Under existing regulations, companies were allowed to keep exposures from derivatives off balance sheet. Greenspan was supported by the majority of the financial industry, which successfully lobbied congress to force a delay of the implementation to the year 2000. He noted that 'in the case of the institutional off-exchange derivatives markets, it seems abundantly clear that private market regulation is quite effectively and efficiently achieving what have been identified as the public policy objectives of government regulation.... Thus, there appears to be no need for government regulation of off-exchange derivative transactions between institutional counterparties.'[84]

The regulatory fight, however, only properly started when the CFTC issued a new concept release concerning the OTC derivatives market which was issued 'as part of a comprehensive regulatory reform effort designed to update the agency's oversight of both exchange and off-exchange markets' in May 1998.[85] This new attempt led to an unprecedented backlash by the finance industry and other regulators. The very same day, Robert E. Rubin, Secretary of the Treasury and former co-chairman of Goldman Sachs, joined Alan Greenspan, and Arthur Levitt to issue a statement which unequivocally condemned this release. They noted that the CFTC 'issued a concept release on OTC derivatives. We have grave concerns about this action and its possible consequences. The OTC derivatives market is a large and important global market. We seriously question the scope of the CFTC's jurisdiction in this area, and we are very concerned about reports that the CFTC's action may increase the legal uncertainty concerning certain types of OTC derivatives.'[86] Not even a month later, they went further and submitted a legislative proposal to Newt Gingrich, Speaker of the US House of Representatives that asked Congress to enact a law to temporarily ban the CFTC from enacting any legislation.[87]

In further Congressional hearings, the financial industry wholeheartedly supported Greenspan, Rubin, and Levitt. Joseph Bauman, a Managing Director at Bank of America who represented the International Swaps and Derivatives Association (ISDA), for example, said the following: 'the CFTC has sent a chill through

[82] Lucchetti, 'CFTC Chief, Futures Industry Group clash over Exchange-Deregulation Bill.'
[83] Noris, 'Greenspan opposes accounting change.'
[84] Greenspan, 'Government regulation and derivative contracts.'
[85] Federal Register, 'Over-the-counter derivatives.'
[86] US Department of the Treasury, 'Joint statement.'
[87] US Department of the Treasury, 'CFTC letter'; House Republican James Leach obliged and submitted the Financial Derivatives Supervisory Improvement Act of 1998.

this business by raising the spectre that it may seek to impose new restrictions on privately negotiated swap transactions. For these reasons ISDA wholeheartedly supports the proposal of the Treasury, Federal Reserve, and SEC.'[88] Congress also reissued the threat to merge the CFTC with the SEC. A member of the congressional hearing was reported in the *Wall Street Journal* as saying, 'As part of the arm twisting, lawmakers will raise the spectre of merging the CFTC into the SEC.'[89]

Even at the time, the animosity between Born and Greenspan, Rubin, and Levit was a topic of much discussion. The *Wall Street Journal* went so far as to say that 'Brooksley Born has been bullied by no less than Alan Greenspan, Arthur Levitt and Robert Rubin, but she's not backing off.'[90] Another piece wrote that 'no less than Federal Reserve Chairman Alan Greenspan, Treasury Secretary Robert Rubin and Securities and Exchange Commission Chairman Arthur Levitt have tried to muzzle her, claiming threats of new oversight could unsettle markets and trigger lawsuits'.[91] Over time, this conflict has become somewhat legendary. Alan Binder, a former Federal Reserve board member, put it this way: 'Proposals to bring even minimalist regulation were basically rebuffed by Greenspan and various people in the Treasury ... I think of him as consistently cheerleading on derivatives.' In fact, Michael Greenberger, who was a senior director at the CFTC said in a documentary that 'each of the principals in turn, that is to say, Rubin, Greenspan and Levitt take their shot at telling Brooksley that she shouldn't do what she's doing'.[92]

Yet, again, this popular interpretation of events may overstate the amount of agreement among the group that opposed Born. For example, Rubin in his memoirs written in 2002–2003, writes that the problem of derivatives 'was a frequent topic of discussions among Larry, Alan and me'.[93] He maintains that he was strongly in favour of regulating derivatives but eventually relented and went along with Larry Summers and Alan Greenspan. He writes that 'I thought both derivatives and leverage could pose problems'.[94] He goes on to note that 'I had been involved with derivatives from the pioneering days of the founding of the Chicago Board Options Exchange ... they can create additional problems when the system is stressed'.[95] However, Larry Summers belittled Rubin's concerns as antiquated. At one point, Summers apparently compared Rubin's concern about derivative to a preference 'for playing tennis with wooden racquets—as opposed to the more powerful graphite and titanium ones used today'.[96] According to Rubin,

[88] Bauman, 'Regulation'.
[89] Schroeder, 'House Committee'.
[90] Schroeder, 'CFTC Chairwoman'.
[91] Schroeder, 'Born, again'.
[92] Kirk, 'The warning'.
[93] Rubin, 'In an uncertain world', p. 287.
[94] Rubin, 'In an uncertain world', p. 287.
[95] Rubin, 'In an uncertain world', p. 287.
[96] Rubin, 'In an uncertain world', p. 198.

Summer thought Rubin just 'wanted to keep the market the way they were when he had learned the arbitrage business', whereas Greenspan and Summers regarded derivatives as a useful and efficient innovation.

The collapse of Long-Term Capital Management (LTCM) complicated the situation further. Born once again strongly held that the failure of LTCM showed the need for regulation: 'The LTCM episode also highlights a pressing need to address the appropriate role of regulation in the OTC derivatives market and whether there are unacceptable regulatory gaps relating to trading by hedge funds and other large OTC derivatives market participants.'[97] For Born, it was clear that 'the LTCM episode demonstrates the potential risks that use of OTC derivatives may pose to financial stability in our global markets'.[98] In a rebuke to those who believed in a non-regulation approach she said: 'This effort [regulation of derivatives] is required to realize the goal of a stable international financial system which fosters market integrity and the protection of market participants. That goal cannot be reached simply through reliance on measures to enhance market discipline, admirable as those efforts may be. Market discipline failed to restrain LTCM.'[99]

Born, Rubin, Greenspan, and Levitt were jointly appointed to head a new presidential working group on Financial Markets to study the failure of LTCM. Although Born would initially not back down, her position became severely weakened once it became clear in January 1999 that she would not seek to be reappointed when her term ended in June. As a result, although she was a signatory to the eventual report, her recommendations were essentially disregarded. This was especially true because the initial report by the working group was quickly overshadowed by another report, requested by Richard G. Lugar, Chairman of the Senate Committee on Agriculture, in September 1998. This report largely reflected the perspective of William Rainer, who President Clinton had nominated to succeed Born as Chairperson of the CFTC. Rainer made it clear that he was in favour of further deregulation of the derivatives market.[100] The complete reversal of the CFTC position was well noted at the time: 'The chairman's approach is an about-face from that of Ms. Born, who, before she left in June, alienated lawmakers, some fellow commissioners and other federal financial regulators by arguing the CFTC should consider tightening regulation of the $70 trillion OTC derivatives market.'[101]

As a result of this change in position of the CFTC, the overall dynamics now very much favoured either continued non-regulation or even further deregulation. As a result, a *Wall Street Journal* piece in November 1999 noted that 'top financial regulators asked Congress to bar regulation of the multitrillion-dollar

[97] Born, 'Remarks'.
[98] Born, 'Remarks'.
[99] Born, 'Remarks'.
[100] Schroeder, 'CFTC Chairman'.
[101] Schroeder, 'CFTC Chairman'.

over-the-counter financial derivatives market, ending a long-running regulatory spat'. It noted that 'in contrast to his combative predecessor [Born], William Rainer supports the Working Group's recommendations and advocates further deregulation of the futures exchanges'.[102] This was now also reflected in the new report of the Working Group which 'presses for deregulation of the derivatives market, both OTC and exchange-traded'.[103] However, there were still some select holdouts who were incensed by the abandoned attempt at regulation. For example, Congressmen John Dingell, chairmen of the Commerce Committee, responded to the report with a press release which read: 'Derivatives Report Eunuchs CFTC and Slashes Market-Integrity Protections.'[104]

A few months later, Greenspan went on the offensive again. He argued that 'over-the-counter derivatives have come to play an exceptionally important role in our financial system and our economy', and that 'these instruments allow users to unbundle risks and allocate them to the investors most willing and able to assume them'.[105] As reported by *The New York Times*, Greenspan urged 'Congress today to encourage the growth of complex financial contracts known as derivatives before the United States share of that market and associated benefits are lost to other countries.'[106] Before long, this urging found backers in Congress which introduced what would become the Commodity Futures Modernization Act in May 2000. However, before it eventually passed in December, there were a few more issues that needed to be overcome.

One of the primary challenges remained the same as it had been for two decades: the question of the relative authority of different agencies. In particular, the SEC and CFTC were unable to agree on which agency should have control. In hearings before the Senate, many congressmen expressed frustration. Robert F. Bennett commented that 'this situation is fraught with turf battles between the CFTC and the SEC';[107] Senator Schumer commented that it 'is always a turf war ... and neither side wants to give us their turf'.[108] Larry Summers attempted to assuage those concerns, saying that these turf battles reflected very real concerns: 'I think it is tempting for those looking on to these issues to see only concerns of turf, but in that issue there were real concerns on both sides.'[109] He received support from Arthur Levitt who stated that 'some may dismiss this concern as a guise for protection of turf. I assure you, the questions ... are profoundly serious and substantive to me'.[110] By September, Summers and the Treasury had managed to broker a deal

[102] Schroeder, 'New derivatives regulation'.
[103] Schroeder, 'New derivatives regulation'.
[104] The Wall Street Journal, 'Swaps still free'.
[105] Greenspan, 'Testimony February 10, 2000'.
[106] Bloomberg News, 'Greenspan urges'.
[107] US Congress, 'S. 2697', p. 26.
[108] US Congress, 'S. 2697', p. 27.
[109] US Congress, 'S. 2697', p. 28.
[110] US Congress, 'S. 2697', p. 33.

between SEC and CFTC. A press release read: 'I salute the leadership of Chairman Rainer and Chairman Levitt in reaching this agreement.'[111] As part of this deal, SEC and CFTC would be jointly responsible for regulating traditional futures markets but this regulation would exclude all privately negotiated derivatives from government oversight and single-stock futures.[112] The *Wall Street Journal* hailed this development as 'a boost to popular legislation to deregulate U.S. derivatives markets.'[113] In October, the Commodity Futures Modernization Act of 2000 was passed in the House.

However, confirmation in the Senate was far from guaranteed. In fact, as reported in the *American Banker*, the bill was seen as having a slim chance of passing in the Senate as 'observers have predicted that Sen. Gramm will attempt to block Senate passage.'[114] One of the reasons given for Gramm's refusal was that he supported stricter regulation which was espoused by some commercial banks, such as J.P. Morgan. As a consequence, a spokeswoman for Gramm was quoted as saying that 'there is a lot of work to do .... I don't want to downplay how difficult this is.'[115] A senator even suggested that a deal may not be found: 'Unfortunately, negotiations have appeared to stall.'[116] However, it was once more Summers at the Treasury who managed to broker a deal. A press release read: 'We are pleased with the agreement reached last night on over-the-counter derivatives. We hope that Congress will now pass this important legislation that will allow the United States to maintain its competitive position in this rapidly growing sector by providing legal certainty and promoting innovation, transparency and efficiency in our financial markets.'[117] After some further changes to language of the Act, it was passed into law on 21 December 2000, marking the end of two decades of more or less continuous debates over whether and how to regulate OTC derivatives.

Conclusion

The history of OTC derivatives offers a valuable case study for understanding both the significance of collective memory in the regulatory process and the evolution of financial regulation, as well as the challenges in achieving a shared consensus on the lessons to be learned from specific events and how they should be incorporated into new legislation.

[111] US Treasury, 'Statement', 14 September 2000.
[112] Schroeder, 'New derivatives regulation'.
[113] Schroeder, 'New derivatives regulation'.
[114] Anason, 'Swaps bill'.
[115] American Banker, 'House backs swaps bill'.
[116] Anason, 'Bottleneck'.
[117] US Treasury, Statement, 14 December 2000.

For example, it is probably true to say that even Born did not imagine the kind of crises which OTC derivatives would eventually cause. Writing in 2001, Born identified a 'lack of transparency, excessive leverage, insufficient prudential controls, and a need for greater international cooperation and coordination' as some of the persistent problems which beleaguer the OTC derivative market.[118] Her lesson from the LTCM rescue was 'these concerns had not been adequately addressed in the domestic and international responses to the Barings and Sumitomo crises'.[119] However, Born's reservations still stemmed from a concern that the Federal Reserve may be unwilling to intervene in future problems, rather than a recognition that these problems may be of a magnitude which the US Federal Reserve would no longer be able to control. As she wrote, 'The LTCM incident did not cause a global financial melt-down because ... the Federal Reserve Bank acted promptly and decisively.... Next time we may not be as fortunate.'[120] So even for Born, the lessons to be drawn from 1990s were not as clear at the time as they have become in hindsight of the Global Financial Crises.

It is therefore unsurprising that OTC derivatives have been the source of prolonged and ongoing conflicts between those who viewed them as a vital financial innovation and those who saw them as hazardous tools for unregulated risk-taking. Key regulatory bodies, including the SEC, CFTC, FASB, OTS, the US Treasury, the Federal Reserve, the US House of Representatives, and the US Senate, were often not only in disagreement with each other but also internally divided on whether and how to regulate these instruments. The resistance to regulation was not uniform but rather evolved alongside the markets themselves. Early efforts in the 1980s and 1990s reflected a nascent understanding of OTC derivatives and their implications, with proposals often dismissed as premature or overly burdensome. As the markets expanded and various crises underscored their vulnerabilities, calls for regulation intensified. Yet even in the face of mounting evidence, anti-regulation forces successfully reframed the narrative, portraying derivatives as essential tools of financial innovation and casting regulation as a threat to market efficiency.

It is also correct that regulatory divisions were successfully exploited by the substantial parts of financial industry, for whom new derivative markets proved immensely profitable and which wanted to avoid oversight at all costs. In this attempt, however, they were also always supported by those who favoured minimal regulation and government, most notably the representatives of the Chicago School and policymakers like Alan Greenspan and Larry Summers. In other words, any regulatory attempt takes place within the context of an overall ethos or approach to regulation. If this overall ethos consistently denies the need for

[118] Born, 'International regulatory responses', p. 636.
[119] Born, 'International regulatory responses', p. 636.
[120] Born, 'International regulatory responses', p. 639.

regulatory intervention, any smaller scale crises are unlikely to be taken as a serious need for change. Michael Hirsh put this in the following way: 'the people in charge of our economy, otherwise intelligent and capable men like Greenspan, Rubin, and Summers—and later Hank Paulson and Tim Geithner—permitted themselves to believe, in the face of a rising tide of contrary evidence, that markets are for the most part efficient and work well on their own'.[121]

The financial crisis of 2007–2008 exposed the fragility of this approach. In its aftermath, the collective memory of OTC derivatives underwent a dramatic revision. In the face of a crisis of such a magnitude, even Alan Greenspan was no longer able to maintain that derivatives were the innovation-driven success story he had promoted for over three decades. So, the history of OTC derivatives became reinterpreted as a cautionary tale of unchecked financial experimentation that subsequently also prompted a significant surge in academic interest on the subject. It even led to the birth of a new scholarly literature, called critical macro-finance, which aimed to better understand the role and importance of wholesale funding markets for the economy.[122] The relation of derivatives to other financial instruments and whether they constitute a special form of money called 'shadow money' that are essential to financial stability became a topic of particular debate.[123] Economists at the BIS even went so far as to claim that the off-balance sheet nature of currency swaps obscures the fact that they should be treated like any other debt, meaning that global debt levels would increase by about $58 trillion (or about 75% of global GDP).[124] The debate on derivatives thus remains ongoing, lively, and unlikely to abate any time soon. Indeed, it resurfaced in 2025 amid growing concerns that the Trump administration's assault on the global economic order was eroding the global primacy of the US dollar—an order whose stability is underpinned in no small part by the functioning of derivatives markets.[125]

This further complicates the notion, place, and permanence of collective memory in relation to financial crises. In the regulatory community, as the immediacy of a crisis fades, so too can the lessons it imparts, leaving the door open for new cycles of under-regulation. In the academic community, by contrast, it may take substantial periods of time until the evolution of financial markets and financial regulation is captured by new scholarship. This temporal asymmetry between academia and the regulatory community is one reason why we are unlikely to ever

[121] Hirsh, 'Capital offense', p. 27.
[122] Dutta et al., 'Critical macro-finance'.
[123] See: Gabor, 'Shadow interconnectedness' and Gabor and Vestergaard 'Towards a theory of shadow money'; Mitchell, 'Do shadow banks create money?' and 'Theorising non-bank financial intermediation'; Murau and Pforr, 'Private debt as shadow money?', 'What is money'; and 'Shadow money'; Ingrao et al. 'Are shadow moneys money proper?'.
[124] Borio et al., 'Missing global debt'.
[125] Pforr et al., 'Dollar Diminished'.

reach a uniform consensus on the exact nature of the collective memory of a particular crisis. But even if we did, it would only take a new crisis for this consensus to be disrupted again.

References

Abdel-Khalik, R. et al. (1994) 'The financial economists' statement on derivatives markets and financial risk'. *Journal of Applied Corporate Finance* 7(3): 4–8.

Abken, P. (1993) 'Over-the-counter financial derivatives: risky business?'. *Federal Reserve Bank of Atlanta Economic Review* 79, 2: 1–22.

American Banker (2000) 'House backs swaps bill; Senate in doubt'. *American Banker*, 23 October 2000.Pf

Anason, D. (2000) 'Swaps bill getting slim odds in Senate'. *American Banker*, 19 October 2000.

Anason, D. (2000) 'Bottleneck seen on swaps exemption bill'. *American Banker*, 16 October 2000.

Bauman, J. (1998) 'Regulation of the over-the-counter derivatives market'. Testimony before the Subcommittee on Risk Management and Specialty Crops, Committee on Agriculture, House of Representatives, Washington, DC, 10 June 1998. http://commdocs.house.gov/committees/ag/hagOTC.000/hagOTC_0f.htm.

BIS (2002) 'Press Release: Rapid expansion of OTC derivatives market in the second half of 2001'. Basel: Bank of International Settlements.

Beese, J.C. (1993) 'OTC derivatives: Taking risk management to new heights'. Speech in London, England 20 April. https://www.sec.gov/news/speech/1993/042093beese.pdf.

Berton, L. (1986) 'FASB begins project that could alter accounting rules on some borrowings'. *The Wall Street Journal*, 16 May 1986.

Bloomberg Business News (1995), 'Derivatives are center of protest'. *The New York Times*, 22 December 1995.

Bloomberg News (2000) 'Greenspan urges Congress to fuel growth of derivatives'. *The New York Times*, 11 February 2000.

Board of Governors of the Federal Reserve System (1998). 'Application of the Commodity Exchange Act to transactions in over-the-counter derivatives'. Statement submitted before the Subcommittee on Risk Management and Specialty Crops of the Committee on Agriculture, US House of Representatives. 10 June. https://www.federalreserve.gov/boarddocs/testimony/1998/199806102.htm.

Borio, C., McCauley, R., and McGuire, P. (2017) 'FX swaps and forwards. Missing global debt?'. *BIS Quarterly Review*, September 2017: 37–54. https://www.bis.org/publ/qtrpdf/r_qt1709e.htm

Born, B. (1999) 'Remarks' at round table on securities markets reform—Organization for Economic Cooperation and Development and the Asian Development Bank Institute'. Tokyo, Japan. https://www.cftc.gov/sites/default/files/opa/speeches/opaborn-47.htm.

Born, B (2001) 'International regulatory responses to derivative crises: The role of the U.S. Commodity Futures Trading Commission'. *Northwestern Journal of International Law & Business* 21, 3: 607–640.

Bowsher, C.A. (1994) *Financial Derivatives: Actions Needed to Protect the Financial System* GAO/T–GGD–94–170. General Accounting Office: Washington, DC. https://www.gao.gov/assets/ggd-94-133.pdf.

Bush, G.H.W. (1992) 'Statement on signing the Futures Trading Practices Act of 1992'. Available at http://www.presidency.ucsb.edu/ws/index.php?pid=21696.

Bradsher, K. (1995) 'Regulators see no need for tougher rules on derivatives'. *The New York Times*, 6 January 1995.

Brady, N.F. (1988) 'Report of the Presidential Task Force on market mechanisms'. January 1988.

Bryan, L. (1987) 'Capital guidelines could weaken banks'. *The Wall Street Journal*, 23 April 1987.

Carruthers, B. (2013) 'Diverging derivatives: Law, governance, and modern financial markets'. *Journal of Comparative Economics* 41, 2: 386–388.

Cassis, Y. (2011) *Crises and Opportunities: The Shaping of Modern Finance*. Oxford: Oxford University Press.

Chui, M. (2012) 'Derivatives markets, products and participants: An overview'. *Bank of International Settlements ICF Bulletin* 35: 3–12.

Culp, C.L and Mackay, R.J. (1994) 'Regulating derivatives: The current system and proposed changes'. *Regulation* 17, 4: 38–51.

Dutta, S.J. et al. (2020) 'Critical macro-finance: An introduction'. *Finance and Society* 6, 1: 34–44.

Federal Register (1987) 'CFTC regulation of hybrid and related exchange instruments', 52: 47022–47029.

Federal Register (1989) 'CFTC policy statement concerning swap transactions', 54: 30694–30699.

Federal Register (1998) 'Over the counter derivatives', 63: 26114–26126.

Financial Crisis Inquiry Commission (2010) *The Financial Crisis Inquiry Report: Final Report of the National Commission on the Causes of the Financial and Economic Crisis in the United States*. Washington, DC: Financial Crisis Inquiry Commission. https://www.govinfo.gov/content/pkg/GPO-FCIC/pdf/GPO-FCIC.pdf.

Friedman, A. (1994) 'Pointing the finger in Germany's ugly corporate melodrama. International'. *The New York Times*, 25 February 1994.

Funk, R.J. and Hirschman, D. (2014) 'Derivatives and deregulation: Financial innovation and the demise of Glass–Steagall'. *Administrative Science Quarterly* 59, 4: 669–704.

Gabor, D. (2013) 'Shadow interconnectedness: The political economy of (European) shadow banking'. 16 September 2013. Available at SSRN: https://ssrn.com/abstract=2326645.

Gabor, D. and Vestergaard, J. (2016) 'Towards a theory of shadow money'. *INET Research Paper*.

Global Derivatives Study Group [GDSG] (1993) *Derivatives: Practice and Principles*. Washington, DC: Group of Thirty.

Goodman, P.S. (2008) 'The reckoning—taking hard new look at a Greenspan legacy. *The New York Times*, 9 October 2008.

Greenspan, A. (1989) 'Testimony by Alan Greenspan Chairman, Board of Governors of the Federal Reserve System before the Subcommittee on Securities of the Committee on Banking, Housing and Urban Affairs United States Senate', 14 June 1989.

Greenspan, A. (1989) 'Statement by Alan Greenspan, Chairman, Board of Governors of the Federal Reserve System, before the Committee on Finance, U.S. Senate', 26 January 1989.

Greenspan, A. (1997) 'Government regulation and derivative contracts'. Remarks at the Financial Markets Conference of the Federal Reserve Bank of Atlanta. Coral Gables, Florida. 21 February. https://www.federalreserve.gov/boarddocs/speeches/1997/19970221.htm.

Greenspan, A. (1990) 'Remarks by Alan Greenspan Chairman, Board of Governors of the Federal Reserve System before the Joint Conference of the Commodity Futures Trading Commission and the Futures Industry Institute Washington, D.C', 2 May 1990.

Guenther, R. (1988) 'Banks expected to fight proposal on swaps income', *The Wall Street Journal*, 9 November 1988.

Hansell, S. (1994) 'Regulators mute their fears over derivatives'. *The New York Times*, 29 February 1994.

Hansell, S. (1994) 'G.A.O. seeks sweeping rules for derivatives'. *The New York Times*, 19 May 1994.

Hansell, S. (1994) 'Derivatives get a key supporter'. *The New York Times*, 26 May 1994.

Hodgson, R. (2009). 'The birth of the swap'. *Financial Analysts Journal* 65, 3: 32–35.

Hirsh, M. (2010) *Capital Offense: How Washington's Wise Men Turned America's Future Over to Wall Street*. Hoboken: Wiley & Sons.

Ingersoll, B. (1985) 'SEC Proposes Disclosure Requirements for Certain Repurchase Agreements'. *The Wall Street Journal*, 28 June 1985.

Ingrao, B., Ruggeri, F., and Sardoni, C. (2022) 'Are shadow moneys money proper? A critical discussion from the perspective of the history of monetary theory'. *Review of Political Economy* 34, 4: 647–664.

Jacque, L.L. (2010) *Global Derivative Debacles: From Theory to Malpractice*. Singapore: World Scientific.

Kirk, M (2009). 'The warning'. *PBS Productions*. Transcript available at: https://www.pbs.org/wgbh/pages/frontline/warning/etc/script.html.

Landler, M. (2007) 'Spotlight: Heinz Schimmelbusch's comeback'. *The New York Times*, 10 August 2007.

Levitt, A. (1995) 'Derivatives use in the 1990s'. Speech before the IBD/ISDA Conference. Washington, DC. 9 November. https://www.sec.gov/news/speech/speecharchive/1995/spch066.txt.

Lockwood, E. (2020) 'From bombs to boons: Changing views of risk and regulation in the pre-crisis OTC derivatives market'. *Theory and Society* 49: 215–244.

Lucchetti, A. (1997) 'CFTC chief, futures industry group clash over Exchange-Deregulation Bill'. *The Wall Street Journal*. 14 March 1997.

Lynn, D.M. (1994) 'Enforceability of over-the-counter financial derivatives'. *Business Lawyer* 50: 291–337.

McCauley, R.N. and Schenk, C.R. (2000) 'Central bank swaps then and now: Swaps and dollar liquidity in the 1960s'. *BIS Working Paper No 851*.

McGee, S. (1996) 'Derivative dealers blast rule proposals'. *The Wall Street Journal*, 26 September 1996.

McGee, S. and Hayes L. (1996), 'Derivatives are a tempting option again—trading is up and regulatory fears are subsiding'. *The Wall Street Journal*, 8 March 1996.

Michell, J. (2017). 'Do shadow banks create money? 'Financialisation' and the monetary circuit'. *Metroeconomica* 68, 2: 354–377.

Michell, J. (2024) 'Theorising non-bank financial intermediation'. *Review of Keynesian Economics* 12, 2: 181–196.

Muehring, K. and Hansell, S. (1992) 'Why derivatives rattle the regulators'. *Institutional investor* 26 (10). https://www.institutionalinvestor.com/article/b14zplyt0c5ql2/from-the-archive-why-derivatives-rattle-the-regulators-september-1992.

Murau, S. and Pforr, T. (2020) '*Private debt as shadow money? Conceptual criteria, empirical evaluation and implications for financial stability*'. Philadelphia, PA: Private Debt Project.

Murau, S. and Pforr, T. (2020) 'What is money in a critical macro-finance framework?'. *Finance and Society* 6 (1): 56–66.

Murau, S., and Pforr, T. (2025). 'Shadow Money in the History of Monetary Thought'. *Review of Political Economy*, 37(4), 1664–1680.

Nasar, S. (1994) "The oil-futures bloodbath: Is the bank the culprit?" *The New York Times*, 16 October 1994.

Nazareth, A.L. (2000). Testimony before the Senate Committee on Agriculture, Nutrition, and Forestry, re: The Report to Congress on over-the-counter derivatives markets and the Commodity Exchange Act by the President's Working Group on Financial Markets. 10 February 2000. https://www.sec.gov/news/testimony/tsty2999.htm.

Nezter, B. (1994) 'Are derivatives a blessing or a burden? Regulators want to know more'. *International Herald Tribune/The New York Times*, 4 October 1994.

Noris, F. (1997), 'Greenspan opposes accounting change on derivatives'. *The New York Times*, 7 August 1997.

Pforr, T., Pape, F. and Petry, J. (2025) 'Dollar Diminished: The Unmaking of US Financial Hegemony Under Trump'. *International Organization*, 79 (S1): S117–S133.

Potter, S. (2018) 'The Federal Reserve and central bank cooperation over the past 100 years'. Remarks for the Commemoration of the Centennial of the Federal Reserve's US Dollar Account Services to the Global Official Sector, New York City, 20 December 2017.

Protzman, F (1994) 'When German safeguards fail'. *The New York Times*, 28 February 1994.

Remolona, E.M. (1992) 'The recent growth of financial derivative markets'. *Federal Reserve Bank of New York Quarterly Review*, Winter 1992–1993: 28–43.

Schapiro, M.L. (1993) 'The derivatives revolution and the world financial system'. Speech at the Eighth Annual Symposium for the Foundation for Research in International Banking and Insurance. Lugano, Switzerland. 14 October. https://www.sec.gov/news/speech/1993/101493schapiro.pdf.

Schroeder, M. (1998) 'CFTC chairwoman won't halt study of OTC derivatives rules'. *The Wall Street Journal*, 11 June 1998.

Schroeder, M. (1998) 'House Committee to hold hearings on CFTC review'. *The Wall Street Journal*, 6 July 1998.

Schroeder, M. (1998) 'Born, again: CFTC chief refuses to take back seat in derivatives debate—combative regulator seeks to leverage a big role for her little agency—an "I told you so" moment'. *The Wall Street Journal*, 3 November 1998.

Schroeder, M. (1999) 'CFTC chairman seeks to deregulate trading', *The Wall Street Journal*, 29 October 1999.

Schroeder, M. (1999) 'New derivatives regulation is opposed—OTC-sector rules termed unneeded'. *The Wall Street Journal*, 10 November 1999.

Schwab, C. (1990) 'More power to the regulators', *The New York Times*, 18 March 1990.

Smith, C.W., Smith Son, C.W. and L.M. Wakeman (1986) 'The evolving market for swaps'. *Midland Corporate Finance Journal* 3: 20–32.

Stassen, J.H. (1982) 'The Commodity Exchange Act in perspective: A short and not-so-reverent history of futures trading legislation in the United States', *Washington and Lee Law Review* 39, 3: 825–843.

Stout, L.A. (2011) 'Derivatives and the legal origin of the 2008 credit crisis'. *Harvard Business Law Review* 1: 1–38.

Special to The New York Times (1994) 'U.S. Allows Citibank to Sell Derivatives', *The New York Times*, 15 September 1994.

Swan, E. (2000) *Building the Global Market: A 4000 Year History of Derivatives*, Alphen aan den Rijn: Kluwer Law International.

Tett, G. (2009) *Fool's Gold: The Inside Story of J.P. Morgan and How Wall St. Greed Corrupted Its Bold Dream and Created a Financial Catastrophe*. New York: Free Press.
Torres C. (1991) 'Bull market for derivatives outruns rules'. *The Wall Street Journal*, 24 July 1991.
United States Congress (1994) 'Serial No. 103-88: Safety and soundness issues related to bank derivatives activities: hearing before the Committee on Banking, Finance, and Urban Affairs, House of Representatives, One Hundred Third Congress, first session', 28 October 1993.
United States Congress (2000) 'S. 2697—The Commodity Futures Modernization Act of 2000', Joint Hearing before the Committee on Agriculture, Nutrition, and Forestry United States Senate and the Committee on Banking, Housing, and Urban Affairs, 21 June 2000.
US Department of the Treasury (1998) 'Joint Statement by Treasury Secretary Robert E. Rubin, Federal Reserve Board Chairman Alan Greenspan and Securities and Exchange Commission Chairman Arthur Levitt', 7 May 1998.
US Department of the Treasury (1998) 'CFTC letter', 5 June 1998.
US Department of the Treasury (2000) 'Statement by Treasury Secretary Lawrence H. Summers Chairman of the President's Working Group on Financial Markets'. 14 September 2000.
US Department of the Treasury (2000) 'Statement by Treasury Secretary Lawrence H. Summers', 14 December 2000.
The Wall Street Journal (1980) 'More direct currency swaps by companies are expected'. *The Wall Street Journal*, 1 December 1980.
The Wall Street Journal (1981) 'Jal gets yen-for-mark swap facility via Citibank unit'. *The Wall Street Journal*, 5 May 1981.
The Wall Street Journal (1995), 'CFTC votes to allow derivative exchanges with little oversight'. *The Wall Street Journal*, 22 September 1995.
The Wall Street Journal (1999) 'Swaps still free'. *The Wall Street Journal*, 12 November 1999.

8

Bankers in times of crisis

A prosopographic study of global financial elites, 1982–2008

Niccolò Valmori

In 2022 we marked a series of anniversaries of past financial crises: it was the 40th anniversary of the International Debt Crisis, the 25th anniversary of the Asian crisis, and the 15th anniversary of the beginning of the 2007–2008 Global Financial Crisis.[1] This chapter aims to look back at those different financial crises by considering the composition of the banking elites active in those turbulent times. In doing so we follow the French philosopher Bruno Latour's invitation to 'follow the actors themselves rather than focusing on capitalism'.[2] Paying heed to this suggestion we present a prosopographic study of banking elites with a specific focus on their educational background and career patterns. Studying the academic and career capital of bank elites adds an analytic layer that allows a better understanding of financial markets and the memory of past financial crises.

Our analysis of financial elites is based on a sample of international commercial banks based in France, United Kingdom, and the United States of America. I choose three banks for each country: Paribas, Crédit Lyonnais, and Société Générale for France; Barclays, HSBC, and Lloyds for the United Kingdom; Bank of America, Citibank, and J.P. Morgan for the United States. The choice of the banks is based on two ratios: on the one hand all selected banks were both national banking champions as well as first-rank global players; on the other hand the crises taken as benchmark years—the 1982 International Debt Crisis, the 1997 Asian Crisis, and the 2007–2008 Global Financial Crisis—affected in different ways the banking population.[3]

[1] The project leading to this application has received funding from the European Research Council (ERC) under the European Union's Horizon 2020 research and innovation programme (grant agreement No. 884910). The content of this document represents only the views of the MERCATOR team and is its sole responsibility. The European Commission does not accept any responsibility for use that may be made of the information it contains.

[2] Latour, *Reassembling the Social.*

[3] During the period studied here some of the banks changed their name as consequence of mergers or stopped their activities due to internal crisis. In 1998 Citicorp and Travelers Group merged to become the first bank in the world for assets with the new name of Citigroup. In 2000 J.P. Morgan merged with Chase Manhattan Company to constitute J.P. Morgan & Chase. In the same year in France

Niccolò Valmori, *Bankers in times of crisis*. In: *History, Memory, and the Return of Financial Crises After Bretton Woods*. Edited by: Youssef Cassis and Giuseppe Telesca, Oxford University Press. © Oxford University Press (2026).
DOI: 10.1093/9780198950158.003.0008

The chapter is divided in three parts: first, I briefly introduce the prosopographic method and the main features of the three different financial crises; second, I examine the educational background of the executives of the different banks, highlighting national features and commonalities; in the third section I analyse the career patterns of my transnational sample. I conclude with some observations on the evolution of financial elites through the three financial crises.

A composite sample: international commercial bank through the prosopographic lens

The analysis of banking executives in this chapter follows a prosopographic approach. The prosopographic method involves collecting and analysing a series of features of a population group that has something in common (geographical origins, professions, club membership, etc.).[4] Using this approach, historians conduct collective studies of the lives of such groups.[5] For the purpose of this chapter the analysis highlights two crucial aspects of the global banking elite: their education and career patterns. By exploring these distinguishing elements, we can assess whether, during the period under consideration, a new generation of senior banking directors took the lead of some of the most powerful banking firms. A growing homogenization of the educational background across different countries would suggest the decline of national traditions, paving the way for the rise of a cosmopolitan executive—a figure who moves across nations and increases their educational capital with an international higher education.[6]

Similarly, career patterns reveal important trends within the banking world: increasing executive mobility often results in shorter tenures within the same bank, thus making more complex the development of an institutional memory of past crises. Though it remains difficult to correlate bank results with the board composition, the study of the cultural and economic capital of banking elites highlights the key attributes of those who were called to navigate through financial crises.

Before introducing the sample of bankers examined here, the main characteristics of the three crises taken as benchmark years are briefly outlined. The international debt crisis broke out in 1982, but its roots were in the 1970s excessive lending of international banks to developing countries. This phenomenon was part of the larger financial landscape shaped by the oil crisis of the early 1970s.

Paribas merged with Banque Nationale de Paris, giving birth to BNP Paribas. After a series of scandals in the 1990s, Crédit Lyonnais was acquired by Crédit Agricole in 2003.

[4] Verboven et al., *A Short Manual*; Düppe and Weintraub, *A Contemporary Historiography*.

[5] Stone, 'Prosopography'.

[6] Sklair, *The Transnational Capitalist Class*; Carroll, *The Making of a Transnationalist Capitalist Class*; Carroll and Fennema, 'Is there a transnational business community?'; Kentor and Jang, 'Yes, there is a (growing) transnational business community'; Pijl, *Transnational Classes and International Relations*.

Oil producing countries invested their oil-generated money in the Eurodollar market and international commercial banks recycled these funds by lending to Third World governments and local corporations. Historically US and British banks were particularly active in lending to South American governments. The international debt crisis was the dramatic outcome of three concurrent factors that severely affected developing countries: the rise of interest rates in the USA, thus making heavier the debt service; the fall of commodities price on which emerging countries largely relied to balance their payments; the over-lending of Western and Japanese banks eager to invest funds of the oil producing countries.[7] This situation came to a head when the Mexican government announced its inability to meet its debt obligations and sought to reschedule payments. US banks were the most affected. However, Mexico was just the tip of the iceberg: at the end of 1983 27 countries needed to reschedule their debt. International commercial banks did not worry about the outlook of the borrower countries and often adopted a herd behaviour where they simply followed into the footsteps of bigger banks who were already lending money to a developing country.[8]

Citicorp and Bank of America were by far the most affected: the former had over $5 billion exposure towards Brazil and $3.2 billion towards Mexico. Bank of America followed with $2.3 billion towards Brazil and $2.5 towards Mexico.[9] J.P. Morgan figured in the leader group of banks who most actively lent to developing countries having $1.6 billion exposure towards Brazil and $1 billion towards Mexico.[10] A significant part of this lending was allocated to specific infrastructures projects or to refinance long-term debt with short-term loans. However commercial banks did not monitor how the borrower countries utilized these funds, lacking a comprehensive view of the soundness of the project financed with borrowed capitals. Coming immediately behind the US banks Lloyds had to put up important provisions to match the exposure towards the South American market. Lloyds had acquired the full control of Bank of London South America (BOLSA) and created a vehicle Lloyds Bank International (LBI) devoted to international investment.[11] On the French side Crédit Lyonnais had increased its exposure towards South American countries in the last years of 1970s.

It took all the 1980s to find a solution to the international debt crisis: a series of new credits and international plans, such as the Baker plan and the Brady plan, contributed to a slow resolution of the intricated problem of international debt payment. However, only the activism of the IMF under the lead of Jacques De Larosière and the several bridging loans opened by the BIS paved the way

[7] Stallings and Kaufman, *Debt and Democracy in Latin America.*

[8] See Chapter 3, by Bruno Pacchiotti and Giuseppe Telesca, and Chapter 4, by Edoardo Altamura and Juan Florez Zendejas. Devlin, *Debt and Crisis in Latin America.*

[9] Makin, *The Global Debt Crisis.*

[10] Slager, *Banking across Borders.*

[11] Altamura, 'Global banks and Latin American dictators'.

for a solution acceptable to debtor countries and international creditor banks.[12] However the IMF bridging loans did not come without costs. Latin American governments found themselves forced to impose strict fiscal and monetary policies and orienting production towards exports. This gravely affected the growth of South American countries who spent the following decade, ominously known as 'the lost decade', to recover the lost ground. Moreover, the reduction of public investment led to a growing inequality across Latin American societies.[13]

The 1997–1998 Asian crisis showed the fragility of the Asian miracle and sent shockwaves that reached Russia as well as Brazil.[14] The crisis badly hit countries like Thailand, Malaysia, Indonesia, South Korea, and the Philippines that have been previously heralded as emerging countries with rosy economic perspectives on the basis of presumed high private savings, strong economic performances of real estate sector as well as for manufacturer performance. The 1995 'Tequila crisis' led many investors to look for safer alternatives for their capitals. Rapidly the Asian tigers became the preferred market for short-term capital investments that boosted confidence towards but also contributed to the creation of a bubble that later revealed its limits. On 2 July 1997 Thailand authorities devalued the baht, pegged on the US dollar, due to the increasing pressures on the reserves of the Thai central bank as a result of capital outflow. By the end of summer 1997 all East Asian countries had devalued their currencies and Thailand and Philippines were on an IMF support programme. European and American banks had been particularly active as arrangers and managers of syndicated loans to East Asian countries. As a 'twin crisis', financial and currency crisis, the Asian crisis was fuelled by the excessive lending of foreign investors who relied on the assumption that governments would intervene to defend the national currencies and bailout national firms.[15] The IMF recipe of imposing major structural reform and asking for a restriction of monetary supply to bring back confidence in the local currencies had a dramatic social and economic costs on the Asian countries.[16]

While French and German banks were directly hit by the losses in South-east Asia (Thailand, Malaysia, Indonesia, the Philippines, and South Korea) the United States banks were less exposed, though the US trade deficit towards East Asia was larger than Europe one.[17] US banks' exposure towards Asian emerging markets amounted to 30% of their capital while for French banks this reached 45% and for German banks peaked at 60%.[18] The picture was more nuanced for the British banks: Lloyds did not have to put up provisions for its exposure in Asia, while

[12] Boughton, *The IMF and the Silent Revolution*.
[13] Dietz, 'The debt cycle'; Capraro and Perrotini, 'Revisiting Latin America's debt crisis'.
[14] See Chapter 5 by Seung Woo Kim.
[15] Corsetti et al., 'Paper tigers?'; Furman and Stiglitz, 'Economic crises'.
[16] Krugman et al., 'Analytical afterthoughts'.
[17] Yellen, *Lessons from the Asian Crisis*.
[18] Kho and Stulz, 'Banks, the IMF, and the Asian crisis'.

Barclays and HSBC were more heavily affected. Barclays had £1.2 billion exposure in Asia but only £10 million were non-performing loans.[19] HSBC had £5.3 billion operating exposure towards Thailand, Indonesia, and South Korea, but this sum represented only 2% of all its assets.[20] Overall the Asian crisis reached the Western financial banks and the core financial markets only as a remote and limited crisis affecting emerging economies and not the leading economies.[21]

Differently from the two previous crises, where financial distress originated in peripherical areas of the global economy, the 2007–2008 global financial crises sparked at its core: the US financial markets. The crisis was the result of the excessive circulation of subprime mortgages and the mortgage-backed securities that bank sold to each others. The circulation of these toxic assets weakened not only banks but also insurance companies (AIG) as well as government-sponsored institutions like Freddie Mac and Fannie Mae. The crisis rapidly spread to Europe and the rest of the world and the Fed not only played the role of lender of last resort for the US banks but also opened providential lines of credit to foreign banks who had bought US derivatives.[22] The collapse of Lehman Brothers and the following liquidity freeze led the US federal government to intervene with the Troubled Asset Relief Program (TARP). All the main US banks accessing this programme aimed to recapitalize the main financial institutions. Bank of America, Citigroup, and J.P. Morgan received $25 billion each.[23] By the end of 2009 all these banks had repaid the Treasury and were then free to operate again with fewer restrictions especially regarding managers' compensations and bonuses.[24] On the other side of the Atlantic HSBC and Barclays managed to raise private capital to strengthen their balance sheet while Lloyds—who had merged with the ailing HBOS—received a capital injection from the government. French banks were less exposed to the global crisis but they received a government capital injection following a scheme similar to the British one. Thanks to the government capital BNP-Paribas posted a profit of €3 billion in 2008 when all their competitors were suffering the effects of the collapsing US real estate and financial markets.[25]

Throughout these different crises the banking executive population did not stop evolving and changing. What follows it is an analysis of this specific sample of

[19] Ascarelli, 'Barclays share drops as profit declines 26%'.

[20] Graham, 'Results calm investors' Asia fear'.

[21] Noble and Ravenhill, *The Asian Financial Crisis.*

[22] Cassis, *Crises and Opportunities*; Sorkin, *Too Big to Fail*; Tooze, *Crashed.*

[23] Although the three banks received support through the TARP programme, their exposure to the financial crisis was not equal. While J.P. Morgan Chase rapidly 'freed' itself from Federal support, through the repurchase of preferred stocks, Citigroup and Bank of America were helped with further $20 billion provided through the Targeted Investment Program. In total they received more than 18 per cent of the TARP: no other financial institutions received the same financial support from government programmes. For an evaluation of TARP and the other federal assistance programmes, see Gaby and Walker. 'Impacts of TARP on financial institutions'.

[24] Calomiris and Khan, 'An assessment of TARP assistance'.

[25] Clift, 'Comparative capitalisms'.

the 'elite of the elite'[26] thus taking only the executive members of the board and narrowing my choice to strategic figures like the CEO, CFO, COO, CRO, chairman and deputy CEO or chairman, excluding positions related to the back-office business and non-executive directors. Therefore while the results of this study cannot be generalized to the entire banking executive population, they do provide an overview of the very highest echelons of the banking elite between the end of the last century and the first decade of the twenty-first century.[27] Moreover the study of the evolution of banking executives across three decades highlights certain common features as well as divergences that characterized the different generations of bankers.[28]

Towards standardization? The educational background of financial elites across crises, 1982–2008

The most persistent characteristic of the banking elites across different countries and periods is their composition: the bank executive population has remained largely composed of white, middle-aged men in their late 40s and early 50s. The representation of women and minorities remained minimal: no women held strategic posts in the French banks, only one, Dame Lydia Dunn, non-executive director (1981–1992) sat on the HSBC board, and the only US bank where women figured in crucial roles (CRO Amy Woods, 2002–2009, and COO Barbara Desoer, 2004–2008) was Bank of America in 2007. In 2021, Jane Fraser's appointment as chair made Citigroup the first major US bank to have a woman at its helm, while Alison Rose became the first woman to lead a major commercial bank in the UK becoming CEO of NatWest in 2019. Minority representation was equally scarce. In the United Kingdom, no minority members were identified in strategic posts. Among French banks, there was only one notable case: the Paribas chair André Levy-Lang (1990–1999), a French Jewish banker born in Egypt who moved to Turkey before becoming a French citizen after attending the prestigious École Polytechnique. In the United States, the most prominent example was Roberto Mendoza, Vice Chair at J.P. Morgan (1990–2000), the son of a wealthy Cuban exile. Mendoza was raised in England, where he attended the prestigious Downside public school.

[26] Stanworth and Giddens, *Elites and Power in British Society*.

[27] The bankers included in the sample are 115. The small size of the banking population here considered provides an opportunity for a more detailed analysis of certain elements that otherwise would be lost in the survey of a larger sample.

[28] The collection of prosopographic data relied on bank almanacs, *Who's Who*, business press, annual reports, and a database like *BoardEx* that offers a rich array of information concerning education and career of banking executives. Besides these classic sources internet websites starting from Wikipedia and Prabook offered rich biographical details of bank executives. Moreover, an extensive secondary literature provides further information on many bankers studied here.

The absence of women in the strategic seats of the board as well as the very slow increase of minorities align with the existing literature on diversity within power elite.[29] While women were not entirely excluded from high-ranking positions, they often held non-executive directorship or led diversity committees. These roles have often been perceived as window dressing, a response to the mounting pressure for greater equality within the managerial banking elite and the broader corporate world.

Let us now focus on the educational capital of banking elites starting with British executives. The existence of an 'old boy club'—a system characterized by passage through certain public schools and graduating from an Oxbridge institution—has long been central to studies of British elites.[30] The first notable trait of British bank executives is the high proportion of individuals holding only high school diplomas. In 1983 only 38,4% of the executives held a university degree. All the British executives with a university degree had studied at either Oxford or Cambridge. The two exceptions were the Hong Kong national Lynn Dunn who had studied at Berkeley and the HSBC American executive (former Midland Marine CEO), John Petty who had studied at New York University. By the time of the 2007–2008 global financial crisis, the educational landscape had undergone a complete transformation: all British executives held university degrees. However, this shift was gradual, as reflected in the data for the 1997 Asian crisis. At that time, only 46% of bankers held a university degree and half of these graduates were Oxbridge alumni. Among executives who attended only secondary schools, the Clarendon schools—a group of prestigious institutions that includes Eton, Harrow, Rugby, Westminster, Winchester, Charterhouse, Shrewsbury, St Paul's, and Merchant Taylors'—were notably present, but not as dominant as suggested in earlier studies of British economic elites.[31] In 1983 only 25% came from a Clarendon school with Eton and Harrow equally represented; the proportion did not increase in 1997; and none of the 2007 bankers attended a Clarendon school, with only one coming from a public school. This shift reflects the end of the paradigm of the 'old boy network', where attendance of a Clarendon school was a crucial step towards a successful career in banking.[32]

The evolution of the educational background of British banking executives between 1982 and 2007 can be effectively illustrated through the careers of two Lloyds Bank chairs: Sir Jeremy Morse (1977–1992) and Lord Peter Levene (2002–2011). Morse attended Winchester College, one of the prestigious Clarendon schools, before earning a degree in Classics at New College, Oxford.

[29] Singh and Vinnicombe, 'Why so few women directors in top UK boardrooms?'; Zweigenhaft and Domhoff, *Diversity in the Power Elite.*

[30] Scott, *The Upper Classes*; Reeves et al., 'The decline and persistence of the old boy'.

[31] Stanworth and Giddens, *Elites and Power in British Society*; Windolf, *Corporate Networks in Europe and the United States.*

[32] Rubinstein, *Capitalism, Culture and Decline in Britain.*

By contrast, Lord Peter Levene, who attended the private City of London School, opted for a degree in Economics at the University of Manchester.

This comparison highlights a key change: the declining centrality of Oxbridge institutions in shaping the educational capital of British banking elites. By 2007, only 38.4% of the British banking cohort had studied at Oxford or Cambridge. The remaining directors earned degrees from institutions such as London, Glasgow, Exeter, Reading, and Manchester, or from universities abroad.[33] This shift underscores a significant feature of the British banking elite that distinguishes it from its French counterpart: the dispersed nature of higher education institutions. In France the Paris region with its *grandes écoles* and business schools holds a lion's share in the formation of financial elites. In the UK Cambridge and Oxford remained the most prestigious higher education institutions, but the United Kingdom offered many other university venues providing an excellent formation for a banking career.[34]

After analysing the evolution of the higher education and secondary school attendance, it is worth examining the fields of study pursued by British banking executives. In 1983 the only executives who studied economics were foreigners while the British nationals studied humanities (classics, history) or pursued degrees in engineering and sciences programmes. The 1997 cohort presented an equally variegated picture: over one-third studied economics, less than one-third pursued humanities, and others majored in sciences and engineering and business administration. By 2007 the importance of an economics background became increasingly prominent: 30.7% held a degree in economics, 23% in sciences and/or engineering, while a smaller proportion pursued degrees in Law (6%) or Humanities (16%). Another remarkable evolution that emerged in the educational formation of British financial elites is the growing importance of obtaining an MBA as a source of symbolic and educational capital. 30% of the 2007 cohort held an MBA, of which three out four were granted by an American higher education institution. In contrast to German executives—where advanced academic qualifications are more common—only one British executive in this sample held a PhD.[35]

In few countries around the world are academic titles as crucial to have access to the C-suite as in France. Business elites, including banking executive directors, are largely selected through the system of *grandes écoles* such as Polytechnique and École Nationale de l'administration (ENA), École Normale supérieure, Haute École de Commerce (HEC). However as much as this selection is based on meritocracy, the homogeneity of French leading class is higher than in many other countries.[36] The centrality of cultural capital in the shaping of French elites has

[33] Hannah, 'Cultural determinants of economic performance'.
[34] Maclean et al., *Business Elites*.
[35] Windolf, *Corporate Networks*.
[36] Bauer, *Des élites légitimes?*; Bourdieu, *La noblesse d'etat*.

also led to define the French system as based on 'the tyranny of degree'.[37] Before passing the exam to enter a *grande école*, the future banking executives often opted for training at the Institut d'études politiques (IEP, commonly known as Sciences Po) instead of going through a university degree. Within this prestigious institution economics was thought both in the course to prepare for passing the exam to join the *grandes écoles* and a specific training in economics.[38] Sciences-Po was the preparatory step towards integrating a *grande école* for many of the bankers studied here: 36.3% in 1983 and almost half (42,8%) in 1997 were Sciences Po alumni. Considering the two main *grandes écoles*, Polytechnique and ENA, a noticeable trend seems to take place: while ENA dominated in 1983 (54% of executives attended the prestigious institution) and Polytechnique trailed with less than 10%, in 2007 the ENA dominance fell to one-third of the French executives and Polytechnique raised to one-fourth of the French executives here considered. Unlike British executives, French executives with no higher education were infrequent: in 1983 only executive director Jacques Roche, of Crédit Lyonnais (1974–1987) had no university degrees while in 2007 the Crédit Agricole president René Carron had started working in his family farming activity straight after high school.[39] Certainly French banking executives tended to build their educational capital through an exclusive French (mostly Paris-based) higher education and the centrality of the capital city is an inescapable set to join the ranks of French elites.[40] Yet it should not go unnoticed that several French banking executives spent some time abroad to widen their educational capital attending prestigious foreign institutions, with a specific preference for US universities. The supposed insularity of the French elites should thus be nuanced: a not insignificant proportion of banking executives (around a quarter) attended a prestigious US business school (Harvard, Stanford, Chicago) and this trend was surprisingly stronger for bankers in the 1980s and 1990s than for those active at the time of the global financial crisis.

As a matter of fact, none of the 2007 French senior executives had in their educational background a period of study abroad. If we consider the entire sample of French executives across the period almost all executives (five out of six) who had international educational background were board members of Paribas thus showing the added value of international background for highflying investment bankers. The attendance of the *grandes écoles* with the possible passage through

[37] Bauer and Mourot, 'La tyrannie du diplôme initial et la circulation des éLites; la stabilité du modèle français'

[38] Dreyfus, *L'enseignement de l'économie à Sciences Po.*

[39] Crédit Agricole figured as one of the French banks in the sample after its takeover of Crédit Lyonnais in 2003. The presence of Crédit Agricole can explain also the decline of ENA and other *grandes écoles* in the educational capital of French executives. The presence of Crédit Agricole bankers in the 2007 sample contributes to this decline: Crédit Agricole, a decentralized, regional, and cooperative bank, tended to promote internal managers whose educational background was not so centred on the attendance of a *grande école*.

[40] Maclean et al., *Business Elites.*

Sciences Po also defined the main subjects studied by the future banking executives. Almost none of the French executives majored in humanities (18% in 1983, none in the following years), the majority opted for political sciences and law degrees (27% in 1983, while in 2007 only 8% specialized in law). There is a clear preference for sciences and engineering (only 18% in 1983 rising to 36% in 1997 and 50% by 2007). However, the lack of humanities in the educational background of French financial elites should not be overstated. The most attended higher education institution, IEP, always provided some classes on history thus partially filling this gap in the managers' formation. Business schools like HEC, ESSEC, EDHEC also played an important role in the executives' training. However, they never matched the importance and prestige of such *grandes écoles* as ENA and Polytechnique. Tellingly, attending HEC was often only a stepping stone towards entering the ENA, as happened for two-thirds of bankers in 1983, and 100% in 1997 and 2007.

Like their French peers, US banking executives largely attended academic institutions before starting their business career. Significantly, the few executives who had no academic background were foreigners: the chair of the executive committee of J.P. Morgan, the British Dennis Weatherstone (1991–1995), had only an accounting diploma earned from the Northwestern Polytechnic London, while Morgan vice chair, the German Kurt Viermetz (1990–2000), started working for the US bank immediately after having completed his high-school. When it comes to the choice of university, attending a private institution emerges as the most common choice: in 1983 only 20% US executives had attended a public university reaching one-third in 2007. Within the private universities the most attended were those of the Ivy League: they made up one-third of the sample in 1983 and more than half (53%) at the time of the Global Financial Crisis. This increasing importance of recruiting from the Ivy League seems to reflect similar conclusions reached by Hamori and Capelli who observed that in 2001 US executives in the service sector were more likely to be Ivy League graduates than their peers in the manufacturing sector.[41]

As in other countries sciences and engineering came to the forefront of the educational background of banking executives without completely dismissing other disciplines such as humanities and law. The 1983 banking cohort saw half bankers majoring in humanities and almost one-third (30%) holding a law degree, with only 20% with a background in any economics programme. The proportion of humanities declined in the two other periods (33% in 1997, 18.7% in 2007) but still remained larger than in the UK or France.

One of the distinctive features of the US banking executive sample is the substantive presence of MBA holders. The creation of business schools started at the end of the nineteenth century (Wharton Business School was the first to open in

[41] Hamori and Cappelli, *The Path to the Top.*

1881) with the specific aim to provide not only a professionalization path for those who wanted to start a business career, but also the same degree of respectability that other professions like lawyers, clerics, and doctors enjoyed. In the 1950s MBA programs received an important support from private foundations like the Ford and Carnegie. At the end of the decade highly critical reports from the two foundations led to a new turn in the evolution of US business schools. MBA programmes gave more emphasis to quantitative analysis and increased the proportion of research-oriented faculty.[42] In the variegated world of business schools a main split emerged in the approach to the discipline of management: on one hand Stanford opted for a more theorical research-led approach to the various issues emerging in the different business sectors; on the other hand, Harvard privilege a more practical case-based approach asking students to consider how they would deal with specific business challenges if they were managing a business firm. Overall, in the 1970s and 1980s MBA students looked at business schools as the stepping stones towards a brilliant career in finance and consulting rather than pursuing careers as corporate managers.

Within the field of management studies there is an ongoing heated debate on whether the increasing importance of MBA's programmes in the career of managing directors has led to a worrying rise of self-interest policies shaping the strategies of big corporations.[43] Self-serving behaviours involve efforts to make the firm grow at any costs, undeserved increases in compensation, and long-term declining returns.[44] This is not the place to test this assumption but tracing the weight of MBAs in the educational capital of US bankers can be a contribution to the ongoing debate on MBAs and their impact on moulding the profile of banking executives.

Two aspects are distinctive of the US banking world: the presence of MBA holders in the bank boardrooms back in the 1980s and their unexpected decline in the 2007 sample. MBAs were already a crucial part of the educational path for executives active in 1983 (30%). They peaked for the 1997 cohort (50%) and then declined for 2007 cohort (27%).[45] While MBA holders were absent in the French case, unless we consider HEC as a business school and its degrees similar to MBAs titles, in the case of British banks we note an opposite trend: while no executive banker held a MBA in the 1980s, at the time of the 2007 crisis 23% of them had attended a MBA programme before starting their career.

The different relevance of MBAs in the educational capital of banking executive is significant for two reasons: one is the importance of MBA changes through

[42] Khurana, *From Higher Aims to Hired Hands.*
[43] Ghoshal, 'Bad management theories'; Giacalone and Thompson, 'Business ethics'.
[44] Miller and Xu, 'A fleeting glory'.
[45] The decline of MBA holders in the key positions within the boardroom of main US commercial banks seems to contrast with the higher presence of MBA holders in private equity and venture capital firms. See, Khurana, *From Higher Aims to Hired Hands*, 349.

different generations of banking executives, the second is the lack of convergence between different national traditions when it came to the educational background of executives. As we will observe in the next section, MBAs were not the only feature distinguishing banking elites across countries. The analysis of career patterns shows that both convergence and divergence marked the evolution of banking elites in the period here considered.

The road to success: career patterns and national traditions

In this section I examine the different career patterns of banking executives across the three national samples. Through this analysis it will emerge how different national traditions remain active even in an extensively globalized financial world. In particular, I focus on how executives integrated into the financial firm.

The integration of banking executives can happen in two ways: horizontally or vertically. The horizontal integration means that an executive joins the bank either from a public institution or another firm (financial or in another sector). The vertical integration happens when someone is promoted to an executive position within the same company.

In the UK banking environment, there is a clear tendency towards the dismissal of the vertical integration. In 1983 almost half of the executives had an internal career: their first job was in the company that they later led from the board room. This percentage drastically collapse to 31% in 1997, and in 2007 only 15% of the executives had spent all their career within the same firm. The internal career trajectory usually follows this pattern: after a series of stints in different departments of the bank, the rising banker was ready to join the board. This trajectory lasted between 20 and over 30 years. This long internal trajectory made it harder to become CEO before 50. Yet, the decline of the vertical career pattern did not significantly alter the average CEOs' age: from 51.6 in 1983 to 50.6 in 2007. On the other hand, the tenure of CEOs and chairmen tended to become shorter in the more recent years. The CEOs and chairman active in 1983 spent on average more than ten years at the helm of the bank (10.5 years) while those heading the banks during the financial crises had a span of less than six years (5.8 years). Long careers like those of Sir Jeremy Morse (chairman of Lloyds for 14 years) or the long tenure of William Purves as CEO of HSBC (12 years) had become monuments of a past epoch in the evolution of banking elites.

With the declining importance of vertical integration, horizontal integration gained more relevance. The horizontal integration largely happened between firms operating in the same sector. The few exceptions to this model were of two kinds: those joining the bank board as executives of an important firm active in another sector; and former high-ranking public officers taking up the challenge of a post in a commercial bank. Lloyds traditionally had on its board executives of companies relying heavily on insurance (shipping, car and airplane industry, oil). However horizontal integration did not always work smoothly, as illustrated by Barclays CEO Martin Taylor. Taylor, an Oxford graduate in Asian languages, had been working as a journalist for the *Financial Times* and *Reuters* before joining the textile firm Courtauld. In 1994, aged 42, Taylor was chosen as the youngest CEO in the Barclays's history. However, the attempt to sell BZW (Barclays de Zoete Wede), followed by heavy losses due to the 1998 collapse of the Russian market and the fall of LTCM, led him to resign after only four years.[46]

Executives with a former career in the civil service were rare in the British banking context. For the period considered here two profiles perfectly embody the exceptionality of this pattern. The first is Sir Peter Middleton, who, after a long career in Her Majesty Treasury, joined the board of Barclays in 1991. The passage from Whitehall to the Barclays boardroom was termed a 'cultural shock'.[47] Incidentally, Middleton found as non-executive director his former boss, the former Chancellor, Nigel Lawson. The former civil servant was called to a difficult mission: to steer the market and investment banking division, which included BZW, into solid growth. Middleton did not remain a marginal figure in the history of Barclays: when in 1998 the CEO Martin Taylor resigned, it was Sir Peter who jointly held the position of CEO and deputy chairman before becoming chairman of Barclays in 1999. Reflecting on how his past experience in the civil service helped him to lead Barclays in challenging times, Middleton highlighted how his 30-year career at the Treasury taught him to work with different governments and chancellors, dealing with strong personalities such as Thatcher and Lawson.[48] With this expertise Middleton adapted to the different internal dynamics of a complex bank like Barclays and he did not refrain from taking unpopular steps like axing 6,000 jobs in 1998.[49] The other figure of former civil servants who emerged as one of the most eminent members of the British banking elites is Sir Stephen Green, CEO and Chairman of HSBC from 2003 to 2010. Green started his career in the civil service working in the Department of Overseas Development and later joined McKinsey before entering HSBC. Interestingly, Green not only reached the highest role within the bank, but he also went back to the public service becoming Minister of Trade and Investment within the Cameron cabinet between 2011 and 2013.[50]

[46] Vander Weyer, *Falling Eagle*. BZW was the investment branch of Barclays from 1985 to 1997. It was the result of Barclays' acquisition and merger of two London firms: the stokbrokerage firm de Zoete & Bevan and the jobbing firm Wedd Durlacher Mordaunt & Co. However, the lack of strong returns and a series of underperforming deals led to the sale of most equity and advisory business to Credit Suisse First Boston.

[47] Leonard, *The Times*, 8.11.1991.

[48] Fildes, *The Spectator*, 23.9.2004.

[49] Hamilton, *The Sunday Times*, 23.05.1999.

[50] Green's profile is particularly peculiar not only for his personal career but also for his status of being an Anglican priest and author of several books on the efforts to conjugate Christian values with working in the financial world. See, Green, *Serving God?*

Horizontal integration plays an essential role in the career patterns of French banking executives. In particular, to reach the most prestigious positions within the bank boardroom, French executives typically started their careers in the civil service, preferably in either the Ministry of Economy or the Treasury; alternatively, becoming part of a ministry cabinet or an economic advisor to the government were equally prestigious. By far the most looked after position in the civil service was to become *inspecteur des finances*. Working as *inspecteurs* offered the opportunity to monitor and becoming familiar with specific economic sectors in which the French State had relevant interest at stake. Moreover, the experience as *inspecteurs* guaranteed the creation of lasting bonds with political stakeholders as well as financial actors. The pervasive presence of the state in the French economy made the *inspecteurs* the strategic linkers between the political stakeholders and the economic interests. This specific setting did not change when different political parties controlled the government: in 1981 the Socialists under François Mitterand promoted trusted *inspecteurs des finances* to lead the main French nationalized banks, as did their opponents when Jacques Chirac won the legislative elections in 1986 and privatized the bank.[51] The transition from the civil service to the most strategic posts within the bank boardroom is called *pantouflage* and it conveys how smoothly former high-ranking civil servant moved directly from the public administration to the bank boardroom.[52]

Scholars considered the prominence of the *inspection des finances* in the career of French banking executives as the clear sign of two aspects which constitute core features of the French banking world: first, state interventionism, a heritage of the Napoleonic state; second, the higher value given to engagement with public policy that French bankers learn through years of training in the *grandes écoles*.[53] If we consider the career of many *inspecteurs des finances* what made their career pattern particularly fit to lead them to an executive banking role was their engagement with international institutions. In 1983 60% of the *inspecteurs des finances* who worked for the three French banks considered here had had a spell in international organizations such as the IMF, the World Bank, the European Commission or had been placed as advisor in the French embassy in the United States. In some cases, these were short spells, in others the international vocation of the banker was not just a peripheral episode. Pascal Lamy, for example, head of capital markets and member of the executive committee of Crédit Lyonnais (1994–1999), held important political offices under the president of the European Commission, Jacques Delors, and after his spell as bank executive was appointed European Trade Commissioner, then becoming president of the World Trade Organization from 2005 until 2013.

[51] Maclean, *Economic Management*; Quenouëlle-Corre, 'French bankers'.
[52] Rouban, 'L'inspection générale des Finances'.
[53] Maclean et al., *Business Elites*.

A specific form of *pantouflage* sees high-ranking civil servants being parachuted (from which this process takes the name of *parachutage*) directly in some of the strategic positions within the board. These executives reached the highest echelons of the bank without having spent any period before in the institution that they lead. This is certainly due to the infiltration of political power in the economic sphere but also to the high symbolic and cultural capital that these high-ranking public officers had acquired. For example, the *inspecteur des finances* Jacques Mayeux was CEO of Crédit Agricole before becoming president of Société Générale. The reviled *inspecteur des finances* Yves Haberer, whose faulty leadership contributed to the collapse of the Crédit Lyonnais, held the chair of Paribas and Crédit Lyonnais between 1982 and 1993. The collapse of the Crédit Lyonnais had a restraining effect on the appointment of parachuted managers with no previous banking experience.

Another specific feature of French banking elites is the trend that sees the average tenure of CEOs and chairmen becoming longer rather than shorter. The average tenure of CEOs and chairmen active in 1983 was 5.8 years while those active during the Global Financial Crisis had an average tenure of 8.8 years. Particularly representative of this trend are the chairman and CEO of BNP-Paribas, Michel Pébereau and Baudouin Prot. Both had attended ENA and started their career as *inspecteurs des finances.* Péberau spent 12 years in the civil service working for different ministers of the Economy, including Valéry Giscard d'Estaing and René Monory, and the Treasury before joining the Crédit Commercial de France in 1982. Here he was called to lead the privatization of the bank before becoming the CEO of BNP in 1993. For 10 years he held the reins of the bank, which in 2000 became BNP-Paribas, as CEO before becoming chairman in 2003; it was in this position that he experienced the 2007 crisis. Baudoin Prot spent seven years in the civil service before joining BNP and beçoming CEO in 1996. In 2003 Pébereau decided to split the position of chairman and CEO, and Prot became CEO of BNP-Paribas. Overall, the average age of French banking executives holding strategic positions within the board did not vary significantly between 1983 and 2007, oscillating: between 50 years in 1983 and 52.5 in 2007.

The analysis of the evolution of US banks between 1983 and 2007 shows a clear trend towards horizontal integration replacing vertical integration of the 1980s. In 1983 70% of executives had never worked in another firm before reaching the bank's executive board. Bankers honed their skills through a series of appointments within different areas of the bank (investment banking, retail banking, international banking) and spending time in different outposts of the bank, within the USA or elsewhere in the world. A few executives joined the banking world after a career in a law firm. While the 1997 sample did not show any relevant change from 1983, the vertical integration almost disappeared in the 2007 sample (only 12% of US banking executives had spent their entire career in the same bank). The horizontal integration of US banking executives shows certain features that were not present in other countries: first, the importance of stints in law firms, second, the crucial relevance of period in investment banking as a credential to reach strategic positions within the boardroom. Twenty-five per cent of US banking executives active in 2007 had a previous experience in a law firm. This legal background was profoundly related to the financial world: working in the 1980s in a law firm offered plentiful opportunities to become active protagonist in the wave of mergers that marked that decade. The knowledge of the legal framework shaping the financial markets and the variety of financial products constituted an important asset once former attorneys and partners left the law firm to join the bank.

The high number of US executives who had spent part of their career in investment banking (44%) is indicative of the weight of this specific banking sector in the US banking environment. The higher percentage of investment bankers on the boards of US commercial banks can explain the ascendancy of short-termism and the incentives to expand the use of high-risk products that were common in investment banking to other banking areas. The horizontal integration happened largely between banking firms or law firms. Unlike the French case, the US sample does not include many bankers who had previously served the public administration and then switched to the banking sector. The only case is Robert Rubin, a long-time Goldman Sachs partner, who became Secretary of the Treasury under the Clinton presidency before becoming vice chairman at Citigroup between 1999 and 2009. The issue of 'revolving doors' between investment banks and government seems to be an issue of the last 20 years rather than a long-established American feature.[54]

Conclusions

The comparative study of banking elites during three distinct financial crises reveals a complex picture where convergence and national traits intertwine. This combination sheds light on how different generations of bankers navigated crises by leveraging distinct forms of cultural and career-based capital. Overall, the sample analysed shows the persistent underrepresentation of women and minority members in strategic positions within the global banking elites. Besides this common feature the sample of bankers analysed showed a clear generational evolution within the banking population. A clear generational element was the high presence of former military veterans in the banking boardrooms in the 1980s and even in the 1990s. Service in the armed forces was often valued as a formative experience, equipping individuals with the discipline and hierarchical awareness necessary for success in large, rank-based institutions like banks. Another generational change lies in the rising importance of academic capital. While banking executives in the

[54] Bazin, 'Problematizing Goldman Sachs'.

1980s—particularly in Britain—often lacked university degrees, this became an exception in later decades. By the 1990s and 2000s, the attainment of an MBA became a defining feature of executive education, reflecting a global trend towards professionalization. Interestingly, however, US banks witnessed a slight decline in the percentage of MBA holders in 2007.

Yet this trend towards a higher standardization should not overshadow the persistent national tradition in the field of higher education. In Britain the percentage of executives with a humanities background decreased but did not disappear as had happened in France. US executives largely specialized in business administration, but a significant number of law alumni remained active in the highest echelons of banks. French financial elites did not dismiss their *grandes écoles* that remained the stepping stone for a successful career in the highest financial spheres. The different features of national banking elites confirm how much elites are socially embedded in national traditions while evolving on global level.[55]

Similarly, the career patterns tended towards a higher grade of standardization: horizontal integration became more largely diffused in all the three countries. Lifers, executive who spent their entire career within the same bank, became rarer and spells in other banks became crucial to demonstrate essential skills required for reaching the highest echelons in the bank administration. Nonetheless even in this field national peculiarities permeated the career patterns: British and American executives had spells in different financial firms and more rarely in non-financial firms. French executives followed two distinctive patterns when it came to career development: either they moved from being part to the civil service to the banking sector or they reached the highest seats of the board through vertical integration remained more than in the other countries.[56] The increasing mobility of bank executives to reach the highest echelons of banks did not bring a more noticeable presence of foreigners in the boardroom. The number of foreigners occupying strategic seats increased but slowly and not for all countries: in 2007 only 15% of British executives within the three banks here considered were foreigners; in France no foreigners had a seat in the board room while in the USA only 13% were not US citizens. Figures of cosmopolitan executives or globetrotter banker working in different countries for different banks largely remain the exception and for this reason they were the target of press campaigns.[57]

To conclude, this study of academic background and career patterns has shown that generational changes took place within the banking elites active in the

[55] Morgan, 'Elites, varieties of capitalism'.

[56] How entrenched was the horizontal integration, through the *pantouflage*, in the French banking system is evident from this article of the *Wall Street Journal* that saluted the appointment of the Saint-Gobain executive Thierry Marraud to the board of Crédit Lyonnais as part of 'France's board revolution' because Marraud came from a non-financial firm and had not attended any *grande écoles*. See *Wall Street Journal*, 6 October 1995.

[57] Malmendier and Tate, 'Superstar CEOs'.

different financial crises considered here. However, the national diversities remain stronger in the formation of educational capital than in the career paths taken by executives. Moreover, it is important to acknowledge that even common phenomena, such as the rise of MBA programmes in the formation of banking executives, did not take place everywhere at the same time. The diachronic nature of these changes affects also the different memories of past crises, as differing generational and cultural perspectives influence how crises are understood and addressed within financial institutions.

References

Altamura, C.E. (2021). 'Global banks and Latin America Dictators, 1974–1982'. *Business History Review* 95, 2: 301–332.

Ascarelli (1998). 'Barclays share drops as profit declines 26%'. *WSJ*, 18 February.

Bauer, M. (2000). *Des élites légitimes?* Paris: La Documentation Française.

Bauer, M. and Bertin-Mourot, B. (1995). 'La tyrannie du diplôme initial et la circulation des élites; la stabilité du modèle français'. In E. Suleiman and H. Mendras (eds), *Le recrutement des élites en Europe*, Paris: La Découverte, 48–63.

Bazin, Y. (2014). 'Problematizing Goldman Sachs: Indoctrination, paradigm shift and revolving doors'. *Society and Business Review* 9, 1: 98–105.

Boughton, J. (2000). *The IMF and the Silent Revolution: Global Finance and Development in the 1980s*. Washington: IMF.

Bourdieu, P. (1989). *La Noblesse d'Etat: grandes écoles et esprit de corps*. Paris: Les Èditions de minuit.

Carroll, W. and Fennema, M. (2002). 'Is there a transnational business community?'. *International Sociology* 17, 3: 393–419.

Calomiris, C.W. and Khan, U. (2015). 'An assessment of TARP assistance to financial institutions'. *Journal of Economic Perspectives* 29, 2: 53–80.

Cassis, Y. (2013). *Crises and Opportunities: The Shaping of Modern Finance*. Oxford: Oxford University Press.

Corsetti, G., Pesenti, P., and Roubini, N. (1999). 'Paper tigers? A model of the Asian crisis'. *European Economic Review* 43, 7: 1211–1236.

Courtney, C. (1993). 'Interview to Sir Timothy Bevan'. In *National Lives Stories. City Lives*.

Clift, B. (2012). 'Comparative capitalisms, ideational political economy and French post-dirigiste responses to the Global Financial Crisis'. *New Political Economy* 17, 5: 565–590.

Devlin, R. (1989). *Debt and Crisis in Latin America: The Supply Side of the Story*. Princeton: Princeton University Press.

Dietz, J. (1989). 'The debt cycle and the restructuring in Latin America'. *Latin American Perspectives* 16, 1: 13–30.

Dreyfus, E. (2011). *L'enseignement de l'économie à Sciences Po de 1945 à 1989. Idées économiques et formation des élites*, Paris: thèse de doctorat.

Düppe, T. and Roy Weintraub, E. (2018). *A Contemporary Historiography of Economics*. London: Routledge.

Fildes, C. (2004). 'However bad things may be, says Sir Peter, governments can always make it worse'. *The Spectator*, 23 September.

Furman, J. and Stiglitz, J. (1998). 'Economic crises: Evidence and insights from East Asia'. *Brookings Papers on Economic Activity* 2: 1–135.

Ghoshal, S. (2005). 'Bad management theories are destroying good management practices'. *Academy of Management, Learning and Education* 4, 1: 75–91.

Giacalone, R.A. and Thompson, K.R. (2006). 'Business ethics and social responsibility education: Shifting the worldview'. *Academy of Management Learning & Education* 5, 3: 266–277.

Graham, (1998). 'Results calm investors' Asia fear'. *Financial Times*, 14 February.

Green, S. (1996). *Serving God? Serving Mammon?*. London: Marshall Pickering.

Green, S. (2009). *Good Value. Choosing a Better Life in Business.* London: Penguin Books.

Hamori, M. and Cappelli, P. (2004). *The Path to the Top: Changes in the Attributes and Careers of Corporate Executives, 1980–2001.* Cambridge, Mass.: National Bureau of Economic Research.

Hannah, L. (1993). 'Cultural determinants of economic performance: An experiment in measuring human capital flows'. In G. Snooks, *Historical Analysis in Economics*, London: Routledge, 158–171.

Kentor, J. and Jang, Y. (2004). 'Yes, there is a (growing) transnational business community: A study of global interlocking directorates 1983–98'. *International Sociology* 19, 3: 355–368.

Kho, B-C. and Stulz, R. (2000). 'Banks, the IMF, and the Asian crisis'. *Pacific-Basin Finance Journal* 8, 2: 177–216.

Khurana, R. (2007). *From Higher Aims to Hired Hands: The Social Transformation of American Business Schools and the Unfulfilled Promise of Management as a Profession.* Princeton: Princeton University Press.

Krugman, P., Negishi, T., Ramachandran. R., and Mino, K. (2001). 'Analytical afterthoughts on the Asian crisis'. In T. Negishi and K. Mino (eds), *Economic Theory, Dynamics and Markets: Essays in Honor of Ryuzo Sato.* New York: Springer, 243–255.

Latour, B. (2005). *Reassembling the Social: An Introduction to Actor-Network-Theory.* Oxford: Oxford University Press.

Leonard, C. (1991). 'Ministering to Middleton—new deputy chairman of Barclays Bank'. *The Times*, 8 November.

Maclean, M., Harvey, C., and Press, J. (2006). *Business Elites and Corporate Governance in France and the UK.* Basingstoke, Palgrave Macmillan.

Maclean, M. (2002). *Economic Management and French Business: From de Gaulle to Chirac.* Basingstoke, Palgrave Macmillan.

Makin, J. (1984). *The Global Debt Crisis: America's Growing Involvement.* New York: Basic Books.

Miller, D. and Xu, X. (2016). 'A fleeting glory: Self-serving behavior among celebrated MBA CEOs'. *Journal of Management Inquiry* 25, 3: 286–300.

Morgan, G. (2015). 'Elites, varietis of capitalism and the crisis of neo-liberalism'. In G. Morgan, P. Hirsch, and S. Quak, *Elites on Trial.* Bingley: Emerald Publishing Limited, 55–80.

Noble, G. and Ravenhill, J. (eds) (2000). *The Asian Financial Crisis and the Architecture of Global Finance.* Cambridge: Cambridge University Press.

Pijl, van der, K. (1998), *Transnational Classes and International Relations.* London: Routledge.

Quenouëlle-Corre, L. (2018). 'French bankers and the transformation of the financial system in the second half of the twentieth century'. In Y. Cassis and G. Telesca (eds), *Financial Elites and European Banking: Historical Perspectives*, Oxford: Oxford University Press, 117–133.

Reeeves, A. et al. (2017). 'The decline and persistence of the old boy: Private schools and elite recruitment 1897 to 2016'. *American Sociological Review* 82, 6: 1139–1166.

Rouban, L. (2010). 'L'inspection générale des Finances, 1958–2008: pantouflage et renouveau des stratégies élitaires'. *Sociologies pratiques* 21, 2: 19–34.

Rubinstein, W.D. (2002). *Capitalism, Culture and Decline in Britain: 1750–1990*. London: Routledge.

Scott, J. (1982), *The Upper Classes: Property and Privilege in Britain*. London: Macmillan.

Singh, V. and Vinnicombe, S. (2004). 'Why so few women directors in top UK boardrooms? Evidence and theoretical explanations'. *Corporate Governance: An International Review* 12 (4): 479–488.

Sklair, L. (2001), *The Transnational Capitalist Class*. Oxford: Blackwell.

Slager, A. (2004), *Banking across Borders*. Rotterdam: ERIM.

Sorkin, A. (2010). *Too Big to Fail: Inside the Battle to Save Wall Street*. London: Penguin.

Stallings, B. and Kaufman, R. (eds) (2019). *Debt and Democracy in Latin America*. London: Routledge.

Stanworth, P. and Giddens, A. (1974). *Elites and Power in British Society*. Cambridge: Cambridge University Press.

Stone, L. (1971). 'Prosopography'. *Daedalus* 100, 1: 46–79.

Tooze, A. (2018). *Crashed: How a Decade of Financial Crises Changed the World*. New York: Viking.

Vander Weyer, M. (2000). *Falling Eagle: The Decline of Barclays Bank*. London: Weidenfeld & Nicholson.

Verboven, K., Carlier, M., and Dumolyn, J. (2007). 'A short manual to the art of prosopography'. In K.S.B. Keats-Rohan (ed.), *Prosopography: Approaches and Applications. A Handbook*. Oxford: Prosopographica and Genealogica, 35–70.

Windolf, P. (2002). *Corporate Networks in Europe and the United States*. Oxford: Oxford University Press.

Yellen, J. (1998). 'Lessons from the Asian crisis'. *Council on Foreign Relations*, 15 April.

Zweigenhaft, R. and Domhoff, G.W. (2006), *Diversity in the Power Elite: How It Happened, Why It Matters*. Lanham: Rowman & Littlefield.

9

The problems of economics

Shifting crises in economics education after Bretton Woods

Alice Pearson

The context of crises

Since the financial crisis of 2008, economics education has been scrutinized for its role in training financial elites.[1] Historians and sociologists have unpacked tenets of economics textbooks[2] and suggested training with such materials shapes students' beliefs and behaviours, including as they enter finance.[3] This has contributed to wider discussions on the performativity of economics in financial markets,[4] while the 2008 financial crisis was in turn a catalyst for critiques of economics. However, these approaches have largely overlooked how financial crises themselves are understood in economics education, and how this in turn shapes financial instabilities.

This chapter charts how financial events were conceived in undergraduate economics education after Bretton Woods. Drawing on archival materials at the University of Cambridge, it interrogates the problematization of 'economy' and conceptualization of 'crisis' in economics education. I ask what constitutes a problem in economics, which dynamics were deemed worthy of problematization, and

[1] The project leading to this application has received funding from the European Research Council (ERC) under the European Union's Horizon 2020 research and innovation programme (grant agreement No. 884910). The content of this document represents only the views of the MERCATOR team and is its sole responsibility. The European Commission does not accept any responsibility for use that may be made of the information it contains.

[2] e.g. Graupe, 'The power of ideas; Graupe and Steffestun, '"The market deals out profits and losses"'; Heath, 'Value judgments'; Hill and Myatt, 'Overemphasis on perfectly competitive markets'; Klamer, 'The textbook presentation of economic discourse'; Watts, 'Ideology, textbooks, and the teaching of economics'; Zuidhof, 'Thinking like an economist'.

[3] e.g. Colander and Klamer, 'The making of an economist'; Colander, 'The making of an economist redux'; Muniesa. 'The live act of business'; Ortiz and Muniesa, 'Business schools'; Pearson, *The Discipline of Economics*; Pforr, *Meaning Construction*.

[4] e.g. Boldyrev and Svetlova, *Enacting Dismal Science*; Callon, *The Laws of the Markets*; Callon and Muniesa 'Economic markets'; MacKenzie, *An Engine Not a Camera*; MacKenzie et al., *Do Economists Make Markets?*.

Alice Pearson, *The problems of economics*. In: *History, Memory, and the Return of Financial Crises After Bretton Woods*. Edited by: Youssef Cassis and Giuseppe Telesca, Oxford University Press. © Oxford University Press (2026).
DOI: 10.1093/9780198950158.003.0009

the perspectives from which problems were to be solved. This elucidates how course materials in economics education situate the elites that they train, in order to decipher how shifts in the subject of economics corresponded to shifts in the subjectivities they cultivate. In particular, I focus on the iterations or erasures of 'crises', and the tensions these foregrounded to be resolved, therefore revealing shifting objects of economic concerns in the latter half of the twentieth century. Unpacking the problematization of money, inflation, and finance through designated social and economic crises, I trace concerns with stagnation, speculation, and the uncertainties of increasingly deregulated markets in the (post-)Bretton Woods era.

This history of economics education reveals intertwined crises both within and for the discipline: as crises featured in economics courses, they mirror the contours of challenges posed for the profession itself. Crises expose faultlines in the discipline, with both the form and content of analysis contested. Considering 'crises' within economics thus shows the shifting scope of the problems the discipline sought to address. Economics education over the latter half of the twentieth century changed from foregrounding qualitative questions to calculative mathematical problems, which increasingly erased historical and social context of economic life. Changes in the visibility and substance of 'crises' on economics papers render visible these wider shifts. The consolidation of modelling increasingly elided substantial discussion of financial crises. As financial, trade, and fiscal crises were progressively erased from economics education, economics became increasingly formalised in a mathematical approach. Moving from broad reflective prompts to calculative questions with exact answers significantly shifted the scope of tension, deliberation, and reflection in economics.

The chapter centres on examination questions posed to economics undergraduates. The correct response to these prompts in examination papers was not necessarily anticipated to be affirmation: indeed, the pedagogical device may provoke destabilization, and answers may have been valued for challenging the quotes, questions, and provocations offered. However, I suggest that these questions are underpinned by a dialectic of invoked relations (of states internationally; conflicting classes; detached speculators on financial markets), and dynamics that they seek to resolve. These relations reveal the changing foundations and focus of the discipline. They represent different disciplinary constellations of economics, and their arc over the (post-)Bretton Woods era reveals a shift to increasing formalization and mathematization, abstracting away from specific historical contexts. These problematizations set the terms for what constitutes proper economic concerns, and how they may be concerning for the students being trained.

Scholars have interrogated crisis as a category that reveals conceptions of order and its destabilization.[5] Koselleck traced the emergence of crisis through medicine,

[5] e.g. Koselleck, *Critique and Crisis*; Roitman, *Anti-Crisis*; Samman, *History in Financial Times*.

law, and religion, with different strands foregrounding distinct temporalities of recurring events, thresholds, and existential states.[6] The category of crisis came to mark a moment that provokes a decision as well as an era characterized by its lack of resolution.[7] Janet Roitman has argued that the use of 'crisis' reveals conceptions of normality, while divergences from it are designated as situations to be resolved.[8] While 'crisis' as category reveals notions of normality, the erasure of crisis as category is also revealing. The invisibility of crises can render them beyond reflection. In economics, an explicit focus on financial crises has been progressively eroded, supplemented by categories such as 'cycles'.[9] When financial instabilities feature on economics courses, it is usually not in the guise of categories of 'crisis', but rather as cycles, market correctives, (dis)equilibriums, and speculative opportunities. Financial events are conspicuous in their disappearance from papers in the late twentieth century and not recalled in examinations: historicity is eroded as analyses are increasingly formalized in abstract mathematical models. Therefore, I chart how economic instabilities are transfigured, enrolled, or erased as concerns.

The chapter focuses on conceptions of financial, monetary, and fiscal crises, as the (post-)Bretton Woods era witnessed the problematization of money as a mediator of social and economic relations. With the dissolution of Bretton Woods, economic concerns centred on the management, circulation and (de)regulation of money. Fluctuations in inflation, interest, and exchange rates were scrutinized, as deregulation dislocated attempts at state control of money. A focus shifted from seeking stability to trading on volatility, as money moved from an object that was keenly managed by national policy-makers towards being speculated upon in financial markets. Rather than a conduit to substantive investment in industries, the productivity of money increasingly came from the ability to arbitrage across space and time in financial markets. Money became an object of economic activity, rather than merely the medium.

I analyse how economic and social challenges of inflation, speculation, and deregulation at the end of Bretton Woods emerge or are eclipsed as problems and problematizations within economics education in the UK. At stake in these concerns are conceptions of the proper orders of relations. This includes national class relations and their relationship with inflation, to international trade relations and their relationship with exchange rates, to relationships between states and markets. Anxieties with these relations were animated by the shifting role of Britain in the global order at the end of empire, and the emergence and later demise of Bretton Woods. Economic and financial crises were challenges to relations between persons, classes, and states.

6 Koselleck and Richter, 'Crisis', 358.
7 Samman, *History in Financial Times*, 27.
8 Koselleck, *Critique and Crisis*; Roitman, *Anti-Crisis*.
9 Samman, *History in Financial Times*.

Economics education at Cambridge

The chapter centres on the teaching of economics at Cambridge, which was selected for both analytical and methodological reasons. Firstly, Cambridge was a preeminent university in economics in the UK in the mid-twentieth century, and influential in the development not only of economic theory but also of the pedagogical practices through which this was imparted to students, reproducing a discipline.[10] In particular, Cambridge provides a unique site to chart shifts in the (post-)Bretton Woods era, as the foremost British architect of Bretton Woods, Keynes, was based at King's College Cambridge. Later, the disparate heterodox tendencies of the Faculty in the 1970s render visible debates in the discipline. Finally, the purging of the Economics Faculty in the 1980s and 1990s reveals the consolidation of an economics mainstream based on formalist axiomatic mathematical modelling in the post-Bretton Woods era.

Secondly, Cambridge, along with LSE and Oxford, was prominent in training elites, including those entering finance, particularly with the ascendency of the City of London as a site of international financial markets in the second half of the twentieth century. Finally, Cambridge is unique in conserving records of examinations questions across papers, while UK universities outside of LSE and Cambridge have less archival records documenting the Faculty and teaching in economics departments from the 1940s to the early 2000s.[11] While Oxford was also notable for its role in reproducing elites in the UK, teaching in Oxford was predominantly housed in colleges rather than at university level, and thus the material was less centralized, standardized, or archived. For these historical and archival reasons, Cambridge has been central to prior histories of economics education in the UK.[12]

While Cambridge was prominent in UK economics, it had notable differences to economics in other universities over the latter half of the twentieth century, and distinct relations to the Bretton Woods world order. In the 1930s, debates between Robbins and Hayek at LSE and Keynes, Pigou, and colleagues at Cambridge laid foundations for disputes in the discipline that would recur over the course of the century, although these figures engaged in sympathetic exchanges while LSE decamped to Cambridge during the Second World War. Keynes had not worked in isolation at Cambridge, and his theoretical contributions to policy-making were fostered in a collective of economists known as the Cambridge Circus in the 1930s. By the post-war period, Cambridge was an internationally recognized department engaged in key disciplinary debates, having housed significant figures such

[10] Backhouse, *The Changing Character of British Economics*; Tribe, *Constructing Economic Science*.

[11] Tribe, *Constructing Economic Science*, 10.

[12] e.g. Backhouse, *The Changing Character of British Economics*; Tribe, *Constructing Economic Science*.

as Keynes, Marshall, and Pigou. While Marshall and Pigou had engaged in neoclassical marginalist modelling at the start of the century, in the Bretton Woods era and its immediate aftermath, Cambridge was home to a resistance to the ascending dominance of this neoclassical mathematical mainstream.[13]

During Bretton Woods, Keynes' influence was core to the economics practised in universities, administrations, and international organizations across Europe and the USA. Keynesianism elsewhere increasingly rested on axiomatic mathematical principles, with Paul Samuelson coining a 'neoclassical synthesis' in his influential textbook *Economics*. This neoclassical synthesis inscribed ostensibly Keynesian precepts in mathematical models. Samuelson's mass-produced textbook was used in schools and universities and exported across the US-influenced Cold War world. As Bretton Woods collapsed, the rational expectations revolution aimed critique at Keynesian models by focusing on axiomatic atomized individuals anticipating markets, giving traction to the precepts of the neoclassical revival pressed by the Chicago School. These rational expectations approaches facilitated the deregulation of finance, by suggesting that the foresight of rational agents populating markets protected economies from financial crises and rendered government interventions futile. Such logics animated macroeconomics following the Lucas critique, and financial economics with the rise of Capital Asset Pricing Models. This included in the UK, where economics education became increasingly centred on a standardized and streamlined 'mainstream' that proliferated certain forms of rational expectations equilibrium models.

However, departments followed this move in different moments and trajectories. While LSE was relatively international in Faculty and students, and more readily shaped by American influences, Cambridge had a staggered trajectory. The Faculty continued to engage in substantive debates over tenets of equilibrium modelling that were increasingly standardized elsewhere and thus became increasingly estranged from the mainstream of the discipline. Cambridge was the site of a series of intellectual and political disputes that split economists, particularly according to their support for modelling.[14] The Faculty contained 'a loose heterodox formation, with its many constituents loyal to their own chosen version of the testament; there were Ricardians and neo-Ricardians, Marxists and marxists, Sraffians, post-Keynesian lineages, socially committed Cambridge empiricists or philosophers, economic historians'.[15] This diversity of perspectives reflects the debates, stakes, and contentions of political economy, yet stands counter to the consensus that increasingly characterized standardization of economics after Bretton Woods.

[13] Hodgson, 'Is there a future for heterodox economics?'; Saith, *Cambridge Economics in the Post-Keynesian Era*.
[14] Saith, *Cambridge Economics in the Post-Keynesian Era*.
[15] Saith, *Cambridge Economics in the Post-Keynesian Era*, 101.

In the 1970s and 1980s the Cambridge Faculty continued a Keynesian legacy by being defined by a left-leaning politics, occupied partly by heterodox economists who challenged the increasingly narrow orthodox mainstream. Figures such as Joan Robinson and Piero Sraffa contested core precepts of modelling, including in debates with their US colleagues in the Cambridge capital controversy. Alternative perspectives to the emerging mainstream were espoused in the *Cambridge Journal of Economics*, launched in 1977. Meanwhile, the Department of Applied Economics housed economists concerned with empirical and applied questions concerning the UK economy. However, economics at Cambridge also retained a focus on equilibrium modelling through the work of figures such as Kaldor and Kahn, although still articulating a left-liberal politics. The debates among the department in the 1960s and 1970s concerned appropriate economic relations at the end of Bretton Woods. However, the Economics Faculty was ultimately purged of heterodox figures in the 1980s and 1990s, converging on the increasingly standardized discipline that had taken root after the fall of Bretton Woods. This was reflected in an economics education that increasingly encouraged students to enact calculations within financial capitalism, rather than reflect on the terms and desirability of this ordering of economic relations.

The chapter proceeds in four parts, tracking stages of the (post-)Bretton Woods era. Each section centres on different dynamics of concern in these transitions, while triangulating between changes in: objects of economic concern; the anticipated subject position of the elites trained; and the subject of economics as discipline. In doing so, I ask how students were cultivated as elites with shifting subjectivities vis-à-vis recollected dynamics in 'the economy'. These positions shape which events are remembered and how dynamics are evoked, and the approach taken to addressing them. How students are situated in relation to these events reveals the type of elites that they are anticipated to enter in their future careers, with students shifting from adopting the perspective of national policymaker managing a variety of potential monetary and fiscal levers to cultivating the rationalities of speculators on financial markets.

In the first section I highlight anxieties animating social science education at the end of the British empire and establishment of Bretton Woods, with shifting configurations of political and economic power in a changing global order. This international constellation was initially largely conceived in examination papers as a political order shaping economic exchanges, through the role of Britain vis-à-vis former colonies, the reconfiguration of post-war European relations, and shifting power relations between the UK and US. In the 1960's, the emphasis foregrounded economic relations, such as balances of trade. Students were situated as a discerning elite set to occupy positions of colonial and national rule and were trained to cultivate an authoritative affect through qualitative prompts on a wide variety of topics, including crises. This differs from the formalized abstract mathematical models that would come to dominate economics education in later decades.

Secondly, I show how the breakdown of Bretton Woods in the 1970s provoked reflection on appropriate systems of national and international relations that money mediated. Uncertainties with the collapsing of Bretton Woods brought contemplation on inflation, trade balances, and stagnation. These were situated in comparative economic and social systems, reflecting vigorous debates amidst Cambridge Faculty during the Cold War, and concerns of the Department of Applied Economics with empirical questions amidst the turbulent 1970s. Examinations entailed explicit consideration of the functioning, desirability and volatility of capitalist systems, and the manifold crises they provoked.

Thirdly, I unpack preoccupations with industrial relations and class conflict, articulated through issues of inflation and wage rises as Bretton Woods was collapsing. Inflation crises consumed attention, with unions and wages the spectre of concerns over the value of money and the structure of economic relations that it circulates within. National class relations absorb syllabi in the 1960s–1980s, with questions on how to negotiate, manage, or mitigate collective action by trade unions. However, in doing so, there was a move from comparative analysis to formal rational choice theory, and from states managing markets to rational economic actors anticipating states. The demise of unions in the 1980s coincided with the rise of models of efficiency wages and Laffer curve, which acted through incentives to financial and managerial workers, often operating through logics of abundance rather than constraint. This also anticipated the future incentives of students themselves, as elites who may enter finance.

Finally, I elucidate how the growth of finance after Bretton Woods in the 1980s provided an arena for situating students as speculators trained in formalized mathematical economics. Transitions in the City of London following the Big Bang, and the rise of Euro-dollars and futures markets, became a site of both possibility and anxiety. Financial speculation was set as calculative questions, while its moral, economic, and political consequences were intermittently concerns. This engendered a post-Bretton Woods move from money as an object to be carefully calibrated and managed by policy-makers to being speculated upon on financial markets. Whereas in the mid-twentieth century students were tasked with reflecting on the desirability, implications, and functioning of comparative systems, by the end of the twentieth century they were positioned as individual maximizers calculating risk and return within narrow parameters of financial capitalism.

International order at the end of empire: 1950s and 1960s

Economics education at the University of Cambridge in the mid-twentieth century entailed a degree structure of 'Tripos', enacted across the institution. The Tripos is the form of undergraduate degrees across the university and consisted of two 'parts': Part I, studied in the first year; and Part II, examined at the end of third year. The Economics Tripos was formed with the leadership of Alfred Marshall in 1903, despite opposition, in an attempt to separate economics from the study of history.[16] Marshall's development of an economics degree at Cambridge at the start of the twentieth century was influential in the model of economics education adopted at other institutions.[17] The structure of teaching allowed students to complete a degree whilst potentially, although not necessarily, transitioning between subjects between stages. A 1966 pamphlet detailing the Economics Tripos to potential candidates highlighted the possibility in particular of taking Part I in Mathematics and Part II in Economics, or Part I in Economics and Part II in an alternate humanity or social science, such as History, Politics, Archaeology or Anthropology.

Up to 1965, the Economics Tripos contained a paper simply titled 'Essay', in which students were to write for three hours on one topic from a list of circa 6–9 prompts. These comprised short phrases or sentences, often nouns of only one to two words. Their breadth provides a lens through which to grasp the concerns that were cultivated. As the 1950s progressed and into the 1960s, at least one question would appear each year inflected by anxieties around the dissolution of empire and Britain's orientation to a changing international order, in which its power vis-à-vis other states was diminished. These triangulated between: relations with newly independent former colonies, shifting from colonial administration towards immigration to the UK; the changing institutional formations of Europe; to the post-war balance in power with the United States. These questions thus reflected the role of Britain in the post-1945 Bretton Woods world order.

The style of questions was grand in scope and commanding in tone. They were animated by anxieties about the loss of empire and postcolonial governance. Prompts to 'discuss' on the Part II 'Essay' paper included: '"England is finished" (a U.S. Congressman)' (1952); 'Immigration from the West Indies' (1955); 'Free Trade in Europe' (1957); 'Parliamentary Democracy is not designed for export' (1959); 'The Awakening of Africa' (1960); 'Europe is well lost if we gain a Commonwealth thereby' (1960); 'Immigration of Coloured Peoples' (1961). The didactic enterprise sought to cultivate an assertive and authoritative disposition towards an informal and expansive array of topics, in contrast to the formalized exercises that dominated economics education in later decades. Solutions were sought to contemporary problems, including decolonization, as opposed to mathematical abstractions that students would later be confronted with across all courses. The concerns evoked in UK economics education in the era of Bretton Woods thus mirrored the crises for Britain amid the reconfiguration of the global world order.

[16] Saith, *Cambridge Economics in the Post-Keynesian Era*, 93; Tribe, *Constructing Economic Science*.
[17] Tribe, *Constructing Economic Science*.

Both the content and form of the questions are distinct from the economics that would dominate later syllabi. The style of questions was qualitative, rather than the mathematical modelling that came to dominate 'mainstream' economics during the latter twentieth century. Similarly, the breadth of the questions belies a particular form of polymath governance, parallel to the Oxford PPE degree. These genres gesture towards their production of colonial administrators and politicians who were not necessarily honed experts in a particular field of technocratic management but rather cultivated an authoratitive affect by articulating on broad subjects.

Meanwhile, other papers during this period featured concerns with the proper balance of power between Britain and the USA. The paper *The Political Institutions and Ideas of Great Britain and the United States* in the 1960s focused on the emerging order of Anglo-American institutions through post-war debt relations, destabilizing the UK's status as expansive economic and political force. In the *Money* paper that would prefigure papers on finance and banking at the end of the decade, a 1956 paper asked '"The burden on this country of meeting the annual charges on the United States and Canadian loans is not properly indicated by the actual sums of money transferred between governments." Elucidate.' These concerns about international order included reflections on the functioning of the Bretton Woods system, with the same paper also asking: 'Why is it that there appears to have been such a small part for the International Monetary Fund to play in connection with adjustments of exchange rates? Discuss whether this means that the world economic system has been working well or badly.' The concerns of UK economics education reflected the crises of British authority in the reconfigured Bretton Woods world order.

This problem of the balance of power also articulates with analysis of balance of payments, with questions such as 'Explain what is meant by the phrase "an adverse balance of payments". Illustrate your answer by reference to recent United Kingdom experience' (Elementary Economic Theory II, Part I, 1960). In doing so, international relations during the 1960s increasingly took an explicitly economic tack, compared to previous grand political visions of the imperial nation, giving space for trade theory that would crystallize macroeconomic expertise in later separate papers. This increasing delineation and prioritization of an 'economic' sphere in economics education coincided with situating students as imagined future technocrats tasked with governing 'the economy' in institutions whose horizons were more formally and nationally constrained. The end of Bretton Woods presented a reconfiguration of global relations coinciding with the loss of empire and a corresponding crisis of British authority. In contrast to economics education at the end of the century, the late Bretton Woods era entailed explicit reflection on the economic systems that ordered relations, and the threats and crises experienced within these.

Crises of capitalism at the end of Bretton Woods: 1970s

As Bretton Woods was collapsing, concerns with the management of money, exchange rates, and inflation consumed economics courses. The calibration of money and the social and economic relations it mediates were a central focus, both in terms of national inflation rates and international exchange rates. The end of Bretton Woods provoked Cold War ideological rifts to become increasingly visible in the academy, which was also populated by students and staff protesting atrocities of the conflict such as the Vietnam War. The proper relations populating economies was contested, including between persons, classes, and nations. The political stances of economists and departments was reflected in the content of their degrees, which at the University of Cambridge continued to require explicit reflections on the crises of the 1970s.

The demise of Bretton Woods heralded explicit existential deliberation on appropriate modes of organizing economic relations both within the UK and with the wider world. Keynes' role as an architect of Bretton Woods was reflected in discussions among Cambridge Faculty, where there was ongoing debate between socialist supporters such as Joan Robinson, and more centre-left reformers of the Labour Party such as Nicholas Kaldor, who was advisor to the newly elected Labour Government under Harold Wilson in 1964.[18] Animating disputes between Faculty was an assertion that neoclassical equilibrium economics implied support for capitalist market systems while those contesting these mathematical precepts had socialist credentials.[19] This was despite a variety of the Faculty at Cambridge involved in both equilibrium modelling and its critiques articulating left-leaning sentiments.[20]

Economics Faculty at Cambridge were therefore engaged in debates to determine the direction of the economics discipline and the economic systems it supported. Disputes such as the Cambridge Capital Controversy between the University of Cambridge and MIT in Cambridge Massachusetts concerned the definitions of capital deployed in marginalist analyses and the production functions they assumed. By critiquing relations between capital and labour inscribed in neoclassical production functions, which undergirded models with a capitalist realism,[21] figures such as Joan Robinson and Piero Sraffa sought to critique wider capitalist systems.[22] The debates that animated Economics departments directly related to the imagined systems that Faculty sought to support during the antagonisms of the Cold War.

[18] Hodgson, 'Is there a future for heterodox economics?', 42.

[19] Hodgson, 'Is there a future for heterodox economics?'; Saith, *Cambridge Economics in the Post-Keynesian Era.*

[20] Hodgson, 'Is there a future for heterodox economics?', 42; Sen 1998.

[21] Mann, *In the Long Run We Are All Dead.*

[22] Hodgson, 'Is there a future for heterodox economics?'; Saith, *Cambridge Economics in the Post-Keynesian Era.*

Meanwhile, some members of the Department of Applied Economics also foregrounded interest in empirical concerns in the UK economy and its shifting international relations with the USA. In the focus on applied and empirical methods, they shared an opposition to the increasingly abstract formulations of neoclassical economics.[23] The department's research on the deindustrializing UK economy during the turbulent 1970s, with the end of Bretton Woods and the uncertainties of systems that would supplant it, refracted in the prompts offered to students. For example, in May 1974, the core *Macro-Economic Theory I* paper required undergraduates to answer four questions from a selection of 11, which included:

> Q3. **Either** 'Exchange rates should be left to be determined entirely by the market; Central Banks should be completely passive so that monetary reserves and the I.M.F. could be dispensed with.' Do you agree with this view?
>
> **Or** An important lesson of recent economic experience in this country is that it is impossible to control inflation without controlling the exchange rate. Elucidate and discuss.
>
> Q7. **Either** Outline the classical theory of the Gold Standard. How relevant is it to present attempts to reform the international monetary system?
>
> **Or** In what circumstances and under what conditions should the United Kingdom seek to accelerate (or retard) progress towards monetary unification in the E.E.C.?

Unlike at the end of the twentieth century, in the 1970s economics education at Cambridge still required reflection on the reconfiguration of economic relations and the comparative systems through which they are organized. The end of the Bretton Woods world order provoked discussion of the appropriate reorganization of national and international relations.

In the 1970s, questions of money, unemployment and inflation were situated by some within a potential 'crisis' of capitalism. In 1973, Question 1 of the *Economic Principle and Problems* paper asked:

> **'Salient facts:**
>
> 1972: number of unemployed averages 885,000—highest figure since 1940
>
> 1972: working days lost in strikes reach 24m—highest figure since 1926

[23] Saith, *Cambridge Economics in the Post-Keynesian Era*, 101.

> 1972: basic weekly wage rates increase by 14% over 1971—highest figure this century
> 1971: share of profits in G. D. P falls to 15% - lowest figure since the slump of the 1930s.
> Those who do not believe that British capitalism is in crisis have a lot of explaining to do. Those who believe that it is have yet to get their analysis of the situation widely accepted'. (J. Gardiner et al.). Discuss.

Such questions of a 'crisis' of capitalism continued throughout the decade. The explicit focus in Cambridge on crises in the 1970s reflected economic instabilities and also facilitated their reordering through the future bureaucratic and corporate elites that the degree educated. In 1979, the *Economic Principles and Problems* paper required students to spend four hours addressing a single question, selected from a dozen. The options included:

> Question 1: 'Belief in the permanence of rapid growth and full employment within the "mixed economy" has proved a myth; the long post-war wave of rapid growth in the international capitalist economy has given way to another long-wave of increasing social and economic crisis for world capitalism, characterised by a far lower rate of overall growth.'
>
> 'The mixed economy is fundamentally sound; all that is required for the resumption of world economic expansion are sensible and suitably coordinated monetary and fiscal policies in the industrial countries.'
>
> Comment on these alternative interpretations of the present and the prospective state of the world economy.
>
> Question 8: 'One important way to pull the international economy out of its present trade and financial crisis is for the advanced countries to accede to the demands of the Third World countries for the establishment of a New International Economic Order.' Discuss, paying careful attention to the effects of specific proposals on the international trade and financial systems.

These questions interlinked economic and social crises of capitalism, trade, and finance, taking a comparative historical and geographical perspective. They placed financial crises within the workings of capitalist systems, and the tensions in shifting world orders these were situated within. Crisis and disorder constituted potential threats either to or from specific systemic dynamics. In considering economic life, students were tasked with deliberating principles, policies and institutions through which it should be organized.

Within these, inflation remained a central concern. In the same year, a question on the *Banking, Credit and Public Finance* paper asked, 'Is the notion of a "fiscal crisis of the state" of any assistance in analysing current inflationary problems in the UK?' Inflation was thus cast amidst financial, fiscal, and trade crises that posed challenges for capitalist systems.

Class conflict, inflation, and the management of industrial relations: 1960s–1980s

The focus on inflation was also set amidst industrial and class relations that preoccupied in the era. It is hard to overstate the fixation with inflation, trade unions and associated industrial relations from 1950 to a climax in the early 1980s, peaking during the industrial disputes of the 1970s. These reflected concerns about the production, circulation and valuation of money and labour. While the Bretton Woods system had carefully calibrated the management of money and the balances in trade it mediated, its unwinding against a backdrop of rising inflation and industrial dispute animated anxiety as to the proper order of class and global relations that would emerge.

In the latter phase, it became possible to answer final papers through selecting questions almost exclusively on intersecting topics of unions, collective action, class conflict, wages, and inflation. On the *Social Problems* paper, 5 out of 10 questions in 1956 and 7 out of 10 in 1957 implicitly or explicitly addressed trade unions and associated industrial disputes; this emphasis would continue to the 1980s, when in 1981 9 out of 14 questions on the *Labour* paper contained references to 'unions', 'strikes', or 'collective bargaining'. In addressing this nexus, unions were problematized as threats to price stability, foregrounding associated concerns with decreasing inflation and increasing wages.

In the early 1970s, this focus on trade unions was still often situated in a comparative analysis of differing economic structures across national, historical, and organizational contexts. Despite the left-leaning Faculty at Cambridge, unions could still be imbued with characteristics of unruly yet predictable actors, addressed through an economic science that sought to anticipate, moderate, and mitigate collective action and the agency of workers. Question 1 on a 1960 paper on *Social Problems* posited '"The responsibility for preventing unofficial strikes rests on the Trade Unions, not on management". Comment', presenting strikes as events to be contained and pressing students to locate the onus for doing so. However, trade unions were still situated as a potential benefit to living standards. The first four questions of the Part II *Labour* paper the following year, in 1974, asked:

1. '"The organisation of the British trade union movement has been a major institutional obstacle to the United Kingdom's economic progress since Word War I [sic]". How far do you accept this comment? Would a

reorganisation of the unions as a unified national movement, with strongly centralised control, have improved the living standards of their members?'

2. 'Contrast the distinctive features of trade unionism in an industrial capitalist and an underdeveloped economy, citing specific national examples.'
3. 'Consider the view that the Donovan Report's central recommendations for plant-and-company based collective agreements, incorporating productivity bargaining, were mistaken from the standpoint of industrial relations and, in their actual contemporary context, economically disastrous.'
4. 'In the 1960s, the policy pronouncements of both the major British political parties emphasised unofficial strikes as the main problem of industrial relations, consider this view in the light of the following figures. Explain the trends these figures show.' [Table denoting increases in: 'official strikes'; stoppages; 'working days lost'; and 'percentage of all working days lost' between 1960 and 1972.]

In answering these questions, students inhabited the perspective of potential civil servants tasked with organizing an economy. Industrial relations were echoed in pamphlets for aspiring Economics students detailing their potential careers, which suggested that students would be well positioned to enter industry or the civil service, and a 'large proportion of graduates in economics go into business, public administration, and professions such as accounting' (1966: 5). The management of industrial and bureaucratic relations was thus foremost in the careers considered appropriate to economics graduates, in contrast to later decades, when significant proportions of economics students were segwaying into finance.

During the mid 1980s there was a distinct decrease in the concern with the efficacy of trade unions. This shift was in explicit response to the erosion of trade union power, which was variously linked to Thatcherite policy, economic recession, and an associated decrease in public concern, as evoked in the following questions in the period: 'Examine the view that the Thatcher government has made more effective use of legislative intervention in industrial relations than any other government in the post-war period'; '"The single most important consequence of the recession of the 1980s for British industrial relations has been the undermining of the power of the shop steward." Discuss'; 'In 1979 a survey showed that 73% of respondents believed trade union power to be the chief issue facing the country. In 1987 only 1% of respondents thought so. Is this an accurate measure of the effectiveness of the present Government's trade union legislation?' (1988, *Selected Aspects of Political Economy*). Each of these examples situate the declining power of trade unions within a specific historical and social milieu.

Meanwhile, questions increasingly took the form of formalized mathematical models and theories that were cohering in a mainstream economics. Analysis of trade unions was increasingly subsumed in the emerging approaches of rational choice theory, which foregrounded strategic interactions between self-interested rational actors and their aggregation in collectives. Concern with trade unions declined, and the state itself emerged as a site conceived of through these relations between self-interested strategic agents of rational choice theory. Following the end of Bretton Woods, there was a shift in emphasis from how the state should manage markets to how markets and rational actors could mitigate, moderate, or contain the role of the state.

These arenas of the same forms of rational choice theory used to analyse unions and the state sometimes collided. For example, in 1981, a question asked:

> 'A major difficulty in government-union relations since 1965 has been a failure of successive administrations to perceive that the trade unions see politics mainly as a continuation of collective bargaining by other means.' Discuss."

At the same time, relations that had previously been approached through the explicit class categories of worker and capitalist increasingly took more latent classed dynamics. On the same paper, a question asked:

> 'The shop steward system can best be interpreted as an instrument of the "effort bargain" (and associated aspect of "job control"), which neither the broader labour market nor employer/union negotiations above the workplace level can effectively regulate.' Discuss.

This framing invoked the terms of the emerging analyses of 'asymmetric information' economics, which conceived of work in terms of workers' 'effort'. These models focus on the relationship between incentives and information through notions of 'moral hazard' and 'adverse selection', including 'efficiency wages', which suggested that increases in wages above labour market-clearing supply and demand equilibriums could serve as a mechanism to increasing effort. Meanwhile, the Laffer curve implied that decreases in tax rates could lead to increases in the tax base, similarly by incentivizing workers to increase their labour. For example, the following questions posit the possibility of governing fiscal balances through anticipating the incentives of a managerial class to the benefit of the broader public: '"A reduction in the progressiveness of the income tax system would benefit almost everyone." Discuss' (1987, Public Economics); '"The case for reducing higher rates of income tax in the U.K., towards the levels prevailing in the U.S., rests on the need to provide appropriate incentives for British managers." Discuss' (1988, Economic Problems and Principles). Whereas analysis of trade unions had previously concerned mitigating and subverting incentives, these economic theories increasingly operated through incentivising particular types of workers.

'Incentives' ceased to be a substance to be resisted, but rather the incentives of a substrate of managerial and professional classes became a matter to be divined, anticipated, and deployed. The mid-1980s thus heralded the end of an era of fixation with the constraint of wages through class conflicts, yielding instead to regimes of abundance through anticipating 'incentives'. This shift in emphasis from constraint to abundance coincided with a change in the representative agents being evoked, from the class conflict of trade unions to an emerging managerial and financial class. The labour that economists analysed after Bretton Woods increasingly moved from factory workers to financial and managerial elites, in line with the shift in the UK economy from manufacturing to finance. As economists moved from analysing shop floor and factory workers to managers and financiers, they increasingly focused on 'incentivizing' these agents with higher pay. Meanwhile, students themselves were increasingly placed as inhabiting the perspective of these elites, tasked with undertaking the calculative exercises of financial markets.

By the 1980s, a contextual and comparative approach had been eroded in favour of an abstract and universalized rational expectations analysis, although these were often critically evaluated. These fields elided specificities of economic structures, centring on assumptions of rational actors with homogenous incentives. Questions of the broader significance of financial and trade instabilities for capitalist systems faded.

The rise of speculation and financial futures as future: 1980s and 1990s

The formalization of economics crystallized a mathematical and model-based analysis in examination papers. These equipped students with the speculative rationalities that animated financial markets. After the end of Bretton Woods, the focus on economics papers shifted from national policy-makers managing markets and their monetary, fiscal, and industrial levers, towards individuals operating through markets. The rise of financial speculation coincided with a decline of concern with specific historical events or their social contexts. In economics education, speculative activities were cultivated that would foster financial volatilities, while eclipsing their historical occurrence.

At the University of Cambridge, the 1980s heralded three interrelated dynamics: the rise of financial markets as objects of economic analysis; increasing mathematization in the examined subject; and the shift to situating students as financial speculators in encountering finance. These moves were related, as the decade saw the reorganization of Cambridge economists. While Faculty had previously housed figures who contested tenets of general equilibrium modelling, several of these figures reached retirement, while remaining heterodox figures were explicitly purged from economics at Cambridge in a series of moves during the decade.[24] Some Faculty were moved to parallel departments, such as History, Sociology, or Development, allowing Economics to align with standardized forms of equilibrium mathematical modelling that had come to dominate the discipline in Western Europe and the United States.[25]

This coalescence of shifts in economics is visible in economics papers. On 2 June 1987, four months before Black Monday, the core *Economic Theory and Analysis* paper contained two consecutive questions on emerging futures markets: (a) 'How would you calculate the benefits of risk reduction and the value of information procured by the opening of a previously absent futures market?', and (b) 'Suppose that news arrives of a severe frost in Brazil that has killed a significant fraction of coffee trees that would normally be harvested in nine months from now. Explain how production, investment (planting), storage and hedging activities are likely to respond to this news, and how you would predict the likely impact on the spot market for coffee now.' This provocation invokes the future as a calculative concern of the present, situating students as speculators through a temporal arc between anticipated supply and current prices. By instructing students to explain multiple factors influencing this relation—'production, investment (planting), storage and hedging activities'—they encounter manifold elements of 'economic' life as filtering into and crystallizing within trading on futures markets, serving as training for speculative sites they are increasingly expected to enter.

This positioning of students as speculating subjects occurred concomitantly with moves to the mathematization of the economics subject. Calculating risks and returns of financial products on recently deregulated markets became the arena for testing the ability of students to enact the increasing mathematical techniques of economics. In 1989, the *Banking and Credit* paper asked:

1. Let R1 and R2 be the returns from two securities with E(R1) = .03, E(R2) = .08VAR(R1) = .02, VAR(R2) = .05, and COV(R1, R2) = −.01

    (a) Plot the set of feasible mean-variance combinations of return, assuming that the two securities above are the only investments available.
    (b) If we wish to minimise risk, how much of our portfolio will we invest in security 1?
    (c) Find the mean and standard deviation of a portfolio which is 50% in security 1?
    (d) Comment on the usefulness of this approach to financial decision-making.

Yet, the emergence of complex financial products, and the speculative activities they enabled, also animated anxieties. The above question was immediately

[24] Saith, *Cambridge Economics in the Post-Keynesian Era.*
[25] Saith, *Cambridge Economics in the Post-Keynesian Era.*

preceded by others approaching financial markets from different angles, the first alluding to the recent instabilities of the 1987 stock market crash:

10. '......options...... are themselves subject to sharp fluctuations... (due to) the flimsiness of the basis of knowledge on which they depend'. (KEYNES). Discuss in the contexts of the stock market crash of October 1987.
12. 'Distinguish carefully between forward and futures contracts'.

'Financial crises', crashes and cycles were relatively rare on examination papers in the 1980s until the end of the decade, with specific events only very occasionally explicitly evoked. 1987 temporarily altered this. Stock market crashes recurred several times across papers in the following years, reigniting fears regarding the stability of financial markets and the moral integrity of the speculative practices they facilitated. In 1988, the first question of the core *Economic Principles and Problems* paper asked:

Either (a) How does a stock market crash affect the level of economic activity?
Or (b) Compare the causes and likely consequences of the recent stock exchange crash with those of either 1929 or 1974.

In doing so, Black Monday catalysed the reemergence of specific events in examinations, with recollections of historical moments temporarily re-occupying syllabi. However, during the 1990s this historical context was again progressively lost to abstract exercises of calculating risk and return on financial markets, with the language of 'likely consequences' later becoming quantified probabilities and averages. This formalization of the future coincided with the formation of futures markets, which cultivated speculation as a set of calculations that could be deployed in an emerging economic science.

By the mid-1990s, the Part II *Banking and Credit* paper had spilt into two sections. In the second, students addressed qualitative questions, which occasionally invoked specific financial events. Students were called to reflect upon the consequences of financial turbulence following the Big Bang, for example: '"The stock market boom of late 1993 demonstrates once again that the stock market is a casino with no link to the real economy." "The stock market provides the mechanisms by which fluctuations in confidence are translated into booms and slumps." With which of these do you agree and why?' (1994); 'Assess the lessons of the United States' Savings and Loans debacle for prudential regulation' (1994). Such questions inhabit genres of identifying underlying dynamics and lesson-learning that situated students in role of potential policy-maker or economic analyst, reflecting on the desirability and functioning of economic systems.

By contrast, the first section increasingly placed students in the perspective of speculator, crystallizing the mathematical endeavours of the emergent economic orthodoxy: 'The portfolio manager of life insurance company is considering a duration-based immunization strategy for a portfolio involving a long position in Bond A and a short portion in Bond B. The following information is available for the two bonds: [contains numerical percentages and values for: coupons (paid annually); yield to maturity; maturity (years)]. (a) Using modified duration for each bond, calculate the hedge ratio, (b) Discuss the risks associated with the immunization strategy in (a)' (1996); 'Consider a world in which there are two assets, a stock and a bond. The stock goes up or down by 10% once a year, the bond returns 0% a year with certainty. Given the stock is currently priced at £100, find the price for: (a) a two year European put with exercise price £100; (ii) a two year American put with exercise price £100; (iii) use (i) and (ii) to price two year European and American calls with exercise price £100. (b) in the above model explain carefully why the bond's rate of return must lie between +-10%.' (1997). In doing so, students were increasingly situated as financial elites trading novel products populating growing financial markets. While the second part of the paper required students to reflect on financial markets, the first part placed students within them, seeing through their lens to optimize individual gain. This endeavour of calculation over reflection increasingly absorbed economics education, and the historical, ethical and political implications of markets were occluded.

In the latter decades of the twentieth century, analyses shifted from managing inflation to enacting speculation. There was a corresponding move from situating students as policy-maker to trader. While immediately after Bretton Woods students were tasked with designing appropriate economic systems, by the 1990s they came to operate within narrow confines of financial capitalism. Financial, fiscal, and trade crises ceased to mark thresholds that may provoke existential reflection on appropriate organization of economic relations, and these reflections were supplemented by speculation on the fluctuations of financial markets. Rather than considering the social import of crises, students increasingly inhabited the perspective of atomized self-interested agents calculating the risks and rewards of volatility for individual gain. This demise of reflecting on financial crises created the conditions for such crises proliferating, as deregulated financial markets became normalized as the singular possibility for ordering economic worlds, and students ceased to be trained in deciphering their limits, faultlines, and failures.

Conclusion

The shifting concerns animating economics education and modes of resolving them reflect broader changes in political economy in the latter half of the twentieth century. This chapter has examined relations between shifts in how crises are conceived in economics and the elites that it trains at the University of Cambridge. Cambridge's pedagogical materials are significant in two major senses: they reflect debates in economics, and they were instrumental in producing governmental and corporate elites who in turn shaped the economic systems they populated. The Cambridge trajectory gives a vantage point to track shifting concerns in economics since 1945. While the legacy of early twentieth century figures such as Marshall, Pigou, and Keynes temporarily placed Cambridge central to debates in the discipline, their heterodox economists increasingly diverged from the mainstream.

In the post-war period, examinations at Cambridge were animated by anxieties concerning the role of Britain within a shifting global order, while students were situated as potential governing elites trained in eclectic qualitative forms of analysis that cultivated an assertive disposition of authority with discernment on broad topics. As Bretton Woods disintegrated in the 1970s, examinations entailed explicit reflection on functioning, desirability, and calibration of comparative economic systems, with crises of capitalism set against the spectre of fiscal, trade, and monetary issues amidst the Cold War. The bureaucratic and corporate governance of relations between workers and firms in a national economy was a primary object of concern, yet the approach to states, markets, and workers shifted from contextual and comparative historical analysis to abstract formalizations of rational choice. Explicit reflection on merits of different economic systems gave way to enacting narrow calculations of agents within financial capitalism. As the 1980s heralded the unleashing of speculation on the movements of markets and exchange rates that Bretton Woods had sought to control, the increasing dominance of equilibrium analysis positioned students in calculative assessments of risk and return, set to become a financial elite speculating on international markets. Money moved from an object to be managed towards an object to be speculated upon. Economics education increasingly normalized speculation within financial capitalism, rather than requiring explicit reflection on the crises that it provoked.

References

Backhouse, R. (1996). 'The changing character of British economics'. *History of Political Economy* 28: 33–60.

Boldyrev, I. and Svetlova, E. (eds) (2016). *Enacting Dismal Science*. London: Palgrave Macmillan.

Callon, M. (eds) (1998). *The Laws of the Markets*. London: Blackwell.

Callon, M. and Muniesa, F. (2005). 'Economic markets as calculative collective devices'. *Organization Studies* 26, 8: 1229–1250.

Colander, D. (2005). 'The making of an economist redux'. *Journal of Economic Perspectives* 19, 1: 175–198.

Colander, D, and Klamer, A. (1987). 'The making of an economist'. *Journal of Economic Perspectives* 1, 2: 95–111.

Earle, J., Moran, C., and Ward-Perkins, Z. (2017). *The Econocracy*. Manchester: Manchester University Press.

Frank, R., Gilovich, T., and Regan, D. (1993). 'Does studying economics inhibit cooperation?'. *Journal of Economic Perspectives* 7, 2: 159–171.

Graupe, S. (2012). 'The power of ideas: The teaching of economics and its image of man'. *Journal of Social Science Education* 11, 2: 60–84.

Graupe, S. and Steffestun, T. (2018). '"The market deals out profits and losses"—how standard economic textbooks promote uncritical thinking in metaphors'. *Journal of Social Science Education* 17, 3: 5–8.

Heath, W.C. (1994). 'Value judgments and the principles of economics textbooks'. *Southern Economic Journal* 60, 4: 1060–1064.

Hill, R. and Myatt, A. (2007). 'Overemphasis on perfectly competitive markets in microeconomics principles textbooks'. *Journal of Economic Education* 38, 1: 58–76.

Hodgson, G. (2019). *Is There a Future for Heterodox Economics?: Institutions, Ideology and a Scientific Community*. Cheltenham: Edward Elgar Publishing.

Klamer, A. (1990) 'The textbook presentation of economic discourse'. In W.J. Samuels (ed.), *Economics as Discourse: An Analysis of the Language of Economists*. London/Dordrecht: Kluwer Academic, 129–154.

Koselleck, R. (2000). *Critique and Crisis: Enlightenment and the Pathogenesis of Modern Society*. Cambridge, MA: MIT University Press.

Koselleck, R. and Richter, M.W. (2006). 'Crisis'. *Journal of the History of Ideas* 67, 2: 357–400.

MacKenzie, D. (2008). *An Engine Not a Camera: How Financial Models Make Markets*. Cambridge, MA: MIT Press.

MacKenzie, D., Munieasa, F., and Siu, L. (2007). *Do Economists Make Markets? On the Performativity of Economics*. Princeton: Princeton University Press.

Mann, G. (2017). *In the Long Run We Are All Dead: Keynesianism, Political Economy, and Revolution*. London: Verso.

Muniesa, F. (2017). 'The live act of business and the culture of realization'. *HAU: Journal of Ethnographic Theory* 7, 3: 347–362.

Muniesa, F. (2024). 'Finance: cultural or political?'. *Journal of Cultural Economy* 17, 5: 716–719.

Ortiz, H. (2021). 'A political anthropology of finance: Studying the distribution of money in the financial industry as a political process'. *Anthropological Theory* 21, 1: 3–27

Ortiz, H. and Muniesa, F. (2018) 'Business schools, the anxiety of finance, and the order of the "middle tier"', *Journal of Cultural Economy* 11, 1: 1–19.

Pearson, A. (2020). *The Discipline of Economics: Performativity and Personhood in Undergraduate Economics Education*. PhD Thesis, University of Cambridge.

Pforr, T. (2015). *Meaning Construction and the Socialisation of Economic Ideas*. PhD Thesis, University of Warwick.

Roitman, J. (2013). *Anti-Crisis*. Durham, NC: Duke University Press.

Saith, A. (2022). *Cambridge Economics in the Post-Keynesian Era: The Eclipse of Heterodox Traditions*. London: Palgrave Macmillan.

Samman, A. (2019). *History in Financial Times*. Redwood City, CA: Stanford University Press.

Sen, A. (1998). Biographical, The Nobel Prize.

Tribe, K. (2022). *Constructing Economic Science: The Invention of a Discipline 1850–1950*. Oxford: Oxford University Press.

Watts, M. (1987). 'Ideology, textbooks, and the teaching of economics'. *Theory into Practice* 26, 3: 190–197.

Zuidhof, P. (2014). 'Thinking like an economist: The neoliberal politics of the economics textbook'. *Review of Social Economy* 72, 2: 157–185.

10

Banking under the influence of history?

Remembering and forgetting at Danske Bank

Per H. Hansen

Introduction

Since its establishment as Landmandsbanken in 1871 Danske Bank has seen great victories and devastating defeats.[1] From 1871 to 1920, the bank only knew progress and growth, but that ended abruptly in the 1920s when it failed miserably. In 1928 it was taken over by the state and was gradually privatized again between 1936 and 1952.

From the 1930s, the bank worked hard to get back on its feet and regain its position. In the 1980s and 1990s it finally returned to the top with a reputation to die for and an image as 'infallible' according to the head of the Financial Supervision Authority. From the late 1990s, the bank embarked on a strategy of growth and expansion, but that came to a stop with the financial crisis in 2008 when the bank needed state support once again. How was it possible when the bank already had gone through one near-death experience in the 1920s? Had memories faded or was the interwar crisis never remembered and used in the first place by the bank's management?

In this chapter, I discuss if and how history, remembering and forgetting, or silencing played a role in Danske Bank's approach to banking between the post-war period and the financial crisis of 2008.[2] Did internal and external remembering of the fatal crash in the 1920s contribute to shape the worldview, practices, and cultural blueprint of Danske's shifting top managers, and how was history used and embedded in the organization? The analysis seeks to consider the shifts in context, from the period of so-called financial repression (also known as the

[1] This research is supported by the Carlsberg Foundation, grant CF21-0090. Landmandsbanken was established in 1871 and went into business in 1872. The bank was called Landmandsbanken between 1871 and 1976 when it changed its name to Den Danske Bank. Since 2000 its name has been Danske Bank.

[2] Though relevant in any discussion of Danske Bank's decisions, actions and practices, I do not consider the money laundering case against Danske Bank, see US Department of Justice, 'United States v. Danske Bank A/S. plea agreement'; Bruun & Hjejle, 'Report'; Hansen, *Danske Bank*, 204–205.

Per H. Hansen, *Banking under the influence of history?* In: *History, Memory, and the Return of Financial Crises After Bretton Woods*. Edited by: Youssef Cassis and Giuseppe Telesca, Oxford University Press.
 DOI: 10.1093/9780198950158.003.0010

golden age of economic growth) to the neo-liberal great transformation that followed the failure of Bretton Woods and the stagflation crisis of the 1970s.[3]

Below, I introduce my conceptual framework and analytical strategy. Following that, I briefly describe Danske Bank's descent into crisis and its gradual rise from the ashes of the 1920s failure and socialization in 1928. I then discuss the role of history, remembering, forgetting, and silencing in the bank from the 1940s to the financial crisis of 2008. In the final section, I discuss my results.

Framework and analytical strategy

In rational expectations theory, decisions are made by utility optimizing individuals on the basis of calculable risk, stable preferences, and full information. History and memory enter into rational decision-making only as information but are otherwise considered irrelevant.[4] In a world populated by humans, things are more complicated.

Most decision-making takes place under uncertainty and is shaped by history, analogies, and narratives, including imagined futures and fictional (as opposed to rational) expectations.[5] Decision-makers navigate uncertainty through prospective sensemaking, and narratives shaped by and reshaping their worldview and cultural blueprint.[6] Historical narratives can be a resource or a constraint to decision-makers who navigate an uncertain and unshaped future.[7]

For instance, Bouwman and Malmendier argue that 'a bank's history affects its risk-taking'. Experience of macroeconomic and bank-specific shocks 'propagate into the future and generate some form of institutional memory' leading some bankers to become risk averse. In contrast, 'bankers who see other banks fail but their own bank survive build on this (relatively) good experience to take on more risk and hold less capital'.[8]

There is a generational and contextual angle to this as generations' worldviews are partly shaped by significant events. In 'Depression babies' Malmendier and Nagel argue that memories of extreme events 'such as the Great Depression (or

[3] See Hansen, 'From finance'.

[4] Malmendier and Wachter, 'Memory'.

[5] For radical uncertainty and decision-making, see Beckert and Bronk, *Uncertain Futures*; Beckert and Bronk, 'Uncertain futures'; Kay and King, *Radical Uncertainty*; Popp, 'Making choices', 471. More generally for historical perspectives on decision-making in banking, see Schönhärl, *Decision Taking*. For historical analogies and decision making, see Eichengreen, 'Economic history'. For a discussion of uses of history and narratives, see Eichengreen, *Hall of Mirrors*. On narratives, see Hansen, 'Business history'; Mordhorst and Schwarzkopf, 'Theorising'; Plough, 'The power of shifting narratives'.

[6] For instance, Reinhart Koselleck refers to space of experience and horizon of expectations, see Koselleck, *Futures Past*. For sensemaking, see Weick, *Sensemaking*.

[7] Suddaby et al., 'Rhetorical history'; Hansen, 'Business history'; Hansen, 'Organizational culture'.

[8] Bouwman and Malmendier, 'Does a bank's history?', 1 and 5. For similar conclusions, see Yu, 'Do bank CEOs?'.

maybe the 2008 downturn) can last for a long time', and influence risk taking in stock markets.[9]

At the societal level new era narratives foster (over)optimism that may lead to forgetting or silencing of history. Keynes referred to 'spontaneous optimism' and 'animal spirits' and Hyman Minsky argued that 'success breeds a disregard for the possibility of failure; ... and the absence of serious financial difficulties over a substantial period led to the development of a "euphoric" economy'.[10] Competition in banking may itself lead to financial instability, since aggressive banks' results will be superior until the downturn hits. As a result, 'established banks will be drawn into bad banking in order to rescue their profitability'.[11]

Remembering and using history may provide a guardrail against animal spirits and competitive pressure, but conservative bankers who remember previous crises will have to accept lower profits and stock prices in the short or medium term in order to survive in the long term. That can be a challenge in periods when 'masters of the universe' are out to play and in a context of a strong shareholder value focus and institutional frameworks that encourage strong competition such as was the case before the 1930s and again from the 1980s.

For historical experience to work, it must be turned into narratives that remember important events such as great crises and spell out what exactly the perceived lessons are. To preserve such lessons and turn them into a long-term cultural blueprint for the organization's decisions, actions, and practices, narratives about the past must be used actively and embedded in the organization's culture. Otherwise, remembering will fade over time and lose its significance or be silenced by other interests and counternarratives inside or outside of the organization.[12]

I consider the concepts of remembering and uses of history better suited than the concept of memory to empirically trace if and how an organization and its decision-makers were banking under the influence of history.[13] Therefore, I do not relate directly to the abundant literature on memory and organizational memory.[14] Remembering can be carried on and embedded in an organization through uses of history practices that include narratives, rituals, and material 'lieux de memoire' as well as by key persons in the organization, not least top management.

[9] Malmendier and Nagel, 'Depression babies', 379. See also Malmendier et al., 'Overconfidence', 1730. See also Lemieux, 'Bank strategies', 10–11; Donaldson, 'voluntary restructuring', 125.

[10] Keynes, *The General Theory of Employment*, 161. Minsky, 'A theory of systemic fragility', 146. See also Fisher, 'The debt-deflation theory of Great Depressions', 349; Kindleberger and Aliber, *Manias, Panics and Crashes*.

[11] Revell and Heremans, 'The complementary', 170.

[12] For example, it is often claimed that fading memories of the Great Depression led to the Global Financial Crisis of 2008. See Krugman, 'How did economists get it so wrong?'; Cassis, 'Banking and finance'; James, *The Creation and Destruction of Value*; Straumann, 'The UBS crisis'; Moss, 'Reversing the null'; Minsky, 'A theory of systemic fragility', 146. For work on institutionalizing memory, see also Eichengreen, 'Economic history'.

[13] On uses of history, see Wadhwani et al., 'History as organizing'; Lubinski, 'From "History as told"'.

[14] For an overview of memory, see Cassis and Schenk, *Remembering*; Rowlinson et al., 'Social remembering'; Rowlinson et al., 'Narratives'; Linde, *Working the Past*.

External perceptions and publicly circulating narratives about the bank and the overall economic and financial cultural context also matter for the organization's remembering and use of history and thus decision-making and risk-taking. Organizations that are aware of the dominant cultural context and actively use or have embedded history as a strategic and organizational resource are most likely not to repeat past mistakes.

From a theoretical perspective, then, a banker's decision-making under uncertainty is based on historical narratives, imaginaries, and a priori assumptions about how the world works in a given context. From an empirical perspective, the challenge is how to use this framework to examine if Danske Bank's management remembered the crisis of the 1920s, how it shaped their worldview, practices, and cultural blueprint and how it changed over time as the institutional and cultural context was transformed.

It is difficult to trace if and how the bank directly used history, but I search for statements by the bank's management to understand if they were aware of and familiar with the history of the failure in the 1920s and how it affected them. I also look for stories in the media on the bank's actions and practices to see whether its history was used and embedded in the organization, thus contributing to shaping its worldview and cultural blueprint.

'Landmandsbanken's tradition'

In 1896 when the Landmandsbanken celebrated its 25th anniversary, it had outgrown the competition to become the nation's largest bank.[15] The media had already shaped a narrative about 'Landmandsbanken's tradition' pointing to 'the diligence, the persistence, and the work for the benefit of all that have characterized the bank's activities in the past years'.[16]

A few years later, at the turn of the century, another newspaper added to the tradition-narrative noting that Landmandsbanken's business 'falls in line with the bank's rather established tradition: consolidation and stable dividends'.[17] As the bank distanced itself from its closest competitors it was recognized for its conservative and careful management under the leadership of Isak Glückstadt.

Another sign of the strength of the bank's tradition came during the banking crisis of 1908, when Isak Glückstadt and his bank emerged victoriously. When Isak Glückstadt passed away in 1910, his son Emil took over as the bank's new CEO on the back of a powerful dominant narrative about Landmandsbanken as the undisputed leader of financial Denmark.

[15] For general information about Danske Bank's history, the article draws on Hansen, *Danske Bank*.
[16] Anonymous, 'Den Danske Landmandsbank- Hypothek- og Vexelbank'. See also Hansen, *Danske Bank*. All translations from Danish into English are by the author.
[17] E.L., 'Penge og papirer. Landmandsbanken'.

The bank expanded dramatically during Emil Glückstadt's reign. He initiated domestic takeovers of local banks, and with a Swedish and a Norwegian bank he established sister banks in Paris and London. Despite emerging criticism of the bank's size and power, it seemed as if Emil was en route to surpass his father's success and take the bank to new heights.

The outbreak of war in late July 1914 changed the institutional and cultural context and radically increased uncertainty about the future. As a banker, Emil had only seen success and expansion, so he did what he did best and expanded the bank's balance sheet further and intensified Landmandsbanken's role in the founding of public companies and acquisitions, imagining a future with unlimited opportunities.

As 1921 and the 50th anniversary approached there seemed to be reason for celebration for the bank, now the largest in Scandinavia, it commissioned a festschrift from the economist Julius Schovelin, who wrote a hagiographic piece but also ended on a cautionary note, 'a large bank has first and foremost a societal purpose—it must be a servant, not a master. If this is understood, a bank such as Landmandsbanken will undoubtedly enter a new era.'[18]

From there, it went downhill. Fast. In the spring of 1922 the Bank Inspector's Office, established by the first Danish Bank Act of 1919, made the fateful decision to examine Landmandsbanken's books. In July he reported that the bank had lost most of its capital of DKK 150 million.[19]

What followed was a deeply traumatic experience for the bank, the financial and political system, and society at large. The failure resulted in a reconstruction with new capital paid in by the state, the central bank, and some private companies in September 1922. In response, management was fired, and Parliament appointed a Banking Commission to examine the failure.

The Banking Commission's report from January 1924 blamed the bank's management for all wrongdoings. The failure was 'first and foremost caused by the credit and financing policy, which the bank's management conducted before the business cycle downturn in 1920'. The report also blamed the system of interlocking directorates and the bank's practice of speculating for privileged customers and the bank's management.[20]

It was a serious lesson in how wrong things can go with a strong CEO, a weak board and a radically transformed context in which to do business. When the Commission's report was published, the Social Democrat, a left leaning newspaper cleared the frontpage with the headline 'The Report about Capitalism's Horrific Crimes against the Danish People'.[21]

[18] Schovelin, *Den Danske Landmandsbank*, 432–433.
[19] Mørch, *Det store bankkrak*.
[20] Bankkommissionen, *Beretning om forholdene*.
[21] n/a, 'Beretningen om Kapitalismens'.

In 1928, after several years of lingering and further massive losses, the state unenthusiastically took over the bank and installed the shipping magnate A.P. Møller as chairman of a new board. Oluf Nielsen, a long-time employee of the bank and a member of the executive board since the ousting of Glückstadt in 1922 became CEO and Poul Ingholt, also a veteran employee, was appointed his co-director. Both had experienced the expansion and implosion of the bank firsthand.[22]

Landmandsbanken's failure was just one among many, but it was the largest and most dramatic. The bank's total losses amounted to about DKK 450 million, similar to an average annual state fiscal budget in the 1920s, with DKK 176 million covered by the state.[23]

The costly, devastating, and humiliating crisis of the 1920s fostered a generation of risk-averse bankers.[24] For young ambitious bankers the 1920s and 1930s was one long walk in the wilderness. They certainly noticed the economic, cultural, and human costs of being too optimistic, powerful, and risk seeking. For several decades, the history of the crash contributed to shaping the worldview and practices of Landmandsbanken's top management and its staff throughout the organization.

In addition to new organizational practices, the experiences from the banking crisis also made the public distrustful of banks and led to a new bank act of 1930, which increased capital and liquidity requirements, reduced exposure to individual borrowers, and all but prohibited interlocking directorships. The cultural and institutional consequences of the Danish banking crisis put a stop to finance capitalism and the banker as master epoch.[25]

A new kind of banker with a different worldview, different practices, and less autocratic power was born out of the interwar years and the Great Depression.[26] The new generation of bankers came to work under a completely different institutional and cultural frameworks with more regulation and different business models. They were the generation of depression babies.

Oluf Nielsen had been with the bank for years when he took over after Emil Glückstadt in 1922 and moved into the CEO's office where he stayed until Poul Ingholt took over in 1954. He too had been in the bank during Emil Glückstadt's time, and he was instrumental in sorting out the bank's situation after 1922. Oluf Nielsen and Poul Ingholt were tasked with rebuilding their bank's business and reputation. They never forgot the traumatic failure they had experienced first-hand.

22 Hansen, *På glidebanen*; Hansen, 'Making sense'.
23 Hansen, *På glidebanen*.
24 Nyboe Andersen, *Laanerenten*, 210–211.
25 Hansen, 'Bank regulation'.
26 Chernow, *The Death of the Banker*.

In 1932, as Oluf Nielsen celebrated 25 years in the bank, Børsen, a Danish business newspaper, wrote, as the 'CEO he is now the connection between the good past, which lies before the dark events, and the present'.[27] A.P. Møller stayed on as chairman of the board until 1952 when the state sold its last shares in the bank. In 1946 Møller coined his firm's motto 'no loss should hit us which can be avoided with constant care'. That might as well have been Landmandsbanken's motto. To this day, A.P. Møller Mærsk is a major shareholder in Danske Bank.

Hidden reserves and new ownership, the 1930s to 1980

The burden of history weighed heavily on the bank. In the 1940s the Bank Inspection repeatedly criticized the bank's new practice of accumulating hidden capital reserves for deceiving shareholders and the tax authorities. Oluf Nielsen and Møller strongly defended the practice and stressed the need for the bank's 'accounts to be conservative and we consider ourselves obligated to take into consideration the experiences from the previous war and post-war period. It is our firm conviction that our general reputation requires that we do not repeat the mistakes made by the earlier management, but that we exercise the utmost care in preparing our accounts'.[28]

The new management's worldview and cultural blueprint was shaped by the memory of the failure in the 1920s. It led to a narrative that amounted to a return to 'Landmandsbanken's tradition', though the bank was not keen to discuss the history of the failure in public. The traumatic crisis years were also silenced when in a retirement interview in 1954 Oluf Nielsen saw no reason to discuss 'the difficult years'. They belonged to the past and many 'do not even remember them'. To secure the bank's future success he advised his successors to be diligent.[29]

Poul Ingholt took over as CEO after Nielsen and when, in 1958, he was asked about banks' reluctance to lend to business, he did not dodge remembering. Avoiding specific references to Landmandsbanken, he replied that banks should 'not take on too many risks. And when one such as I have worked in banking for nearly 50 years and has experienced the banks' difficult years around World War One and again in the twenties one understands that it is in the interest of all that banks are responsible in their lending'.[30]

Landmandsbanken's failure had become embedded in the organization's worldview and practices and managers used the history of the crisis to legitimize their conservative banking and credit policies. With direct firsthand experience from

[27] '25 aar i Landmandsbanken'.

[28] Danish National Archives, The Bank Inspection's Archive, Undersøgelsessager, B18, File: Report on Examination in 1943 and 1947.

[29] Anonymous, 'En bankmand ser tilbage'.

[30] Anonymous, 'Bankerne husker erfaringerne og de daarlige minder fra tyverne'.

the crisis of the 1920s Nielsen and Ingholt had been deeply involved in getting the bank back on the track of tradition. Their personal history was interwoven with that of the bank's breakdown and was embedded in the organization's banking principles as well.

When Ingholt retired in 1964 he became chairman of the bank. In 1967 Svend O. Sørensen was appointed new CEO. He had started in the bank in 1930 shortly after it was taken over by the state, and he too had personal experience with the consequences of failure.

When employees walked the corridors of the bank's headquarters, they could see busts of Isak Glückstadt, Oluf Nielsen, and Poul Ingholt. In the executive suite there were paintings of Isak Glückstadt and A.P. Møller among others. In the CEO's office, the fireplace with a clock and mantles on top of it was an important symbolic material marker of the bank's history, tradition and continuity. Every CEO of the bank since 1875 have led the bank from that office with the fireplace. Day in and day out, such 'lieux de memoire' served as reminders for the CEOs and their guests about the bank's tradition and troubled history.[31]

In 1971 the bank turned 100 years but there was no reference to the 1920s in the 20-page internal staff magazine that celebrated the anniversary. While the bank's management remembered the failure and the resulting worldview and cultural blueprint was embedded in the organization, the dominant approach to using history was one of silencing; don't mention the failure.

Tage Andersen, Knud Sørensen, and the financial crisis of the 1990s

In a recognition that the times they were a'changing, Landmandsbanken changed its name to Den Danske Bank in 1976. It was in the midst of the worst economic crisis since the interwar period and it would lead to a great transformation of societies as old ideas about politics and economics re-emerged.

Still in its infancy, the influence only became visible with time. When S.O. Sørensen stepped down as CEO in 1980 the firsthand link back to the interwar period was broken. As Tage Andersen took over, he was the first CEO secondhand generation without live experience from the failure. Andersen joined a provincial bank in 1943 at the age of 16 and came to Landmandsbanken in 1951. Still, there were plenty of links back to the 1920s as he started climbing the ladder. Oluf Nielsen, Poul Ingholt, and S.O. Sørensen's conservative and cautious approach to banking permeated the organization and its culture at the time.

Tage Andersen was CEO from 1980 to 1990 when Knud Sørensen took over. Like Andersen, Knud Sørensen had joined the bank in 1951 when Oluf Nielsen was CEO and A.P. Møller was chairman of the board. Den Danske Bank's failure

[31] Nora, 'General introduction'.

in the 1920s was not part of their own experience, but a secondhand story experienced and handed over as part of the bank's narrative, worldview and cultural blueprint, including the conservative and credit focused approach.

To some, Andersen and Sørensen were the essence of 'Landmandsbanken's tradition'. Their appearance and tone were conservative and serious with a stiff upper lip, and their nicknames Cold Tage and Black Knud were not coincidental. Tage Andersen and Knud Sørensen came to symbolize Danske Bank's conservative, diligent, and centralized approach to banking with a strong focus on credit policy inherited from their predecessors. If there ever was a 'Landmandsbanken's tradition' they were its representatives. They did not spend much if any time talking about the 1920s, but their actions, decisions, and practices bore the trademark of conservative banking borne out of history.

First and foremost, internally and externally, Den Danske Bank's narrative under Tage Andersen and Knud Sørensen was about a conservative bank with a careful credit policy, integrity and constant care. They were credit-people, and proud of it. Credit assessment and credit policy constituted the very core of the bank's approach to business. After all, Tage Andersen said in 1980, 'it is not our own money we lend. They belong to our depositors and shareholders, and it is our clear duty to protect the means they have entrusted with us.'[32]

Banking became less regulated and less boring during Andersen's and Sørensen's time as CEOs. Executives were increasingly represented as superstars while Hollywood began showcasing the exciting and alluring world of finance, leveraged buyouts and the market for corporate control.[33] This narrative construction of CEOs and Wall Street traders as masters of the universe and heroes of society had been rather limited in the post-war social state, where political leaders were considered more important than business leaders in realizing Denmark's potential. Now, things were turned around. Business leaders became the new heroes who should grow the pie, while politicians were supposed to provide the best possible institutional framework for finance to deliver value to shareholders. That meant deregulation of finance and a new culture of efficient markets and shareholder value.

In 1971 S.O. Sørensen had argued 'it is important to constantly look after all four groups, customers, employees, shareholders and society in general. And I want to emphasize that ... there is a close relation between the four'.[34] As the 1970s turned into the 1980s, that view became a voice from the past. Along with other large banks, from the 1980s and 1990s Den Danske Bank adopted more aggressive and expansionary strategies and business models that to some extent replaced

[32] Hansen et al., *Den Danske Bank*, 489.

[33] On superstar CEOs, see Malmendier and Tate, 'Superstar CEOs'. On Hollywood and Wall Street, see Hansen and Magnussen, 'Making sense'.

[34] Sørensen, 'Vi lever i forandringernes tidsalder', 11.

the risk averse, conservative bank's earlier business model. The trigger of this great transformation was the crisis of the 1970s.

The Keynesian social state came to an end and the Bretton Woods system fell apart as stagflation and industrial crisis hit the Western economies. Old economic ideas re-emerged in the shape of monetarism, and shareholder value and efficient markets entered the vocabulary as dominant economic theory shifted from market failure to public choice, agency theory, and government failure.[35]

Politics also changed dramatically. In his inaugural speech on 20 January 1981, Ronald Reagan proclaimed 'Government is not the solution to our problem, Government is the problem', and in 1986 Margaret Thatcher followed up claiming 'there's no such thing as society. There are individual men and women and there is family.' The repercussions completely changed the social structures in which finance was embedded.[36]

As historian Youssef Cassis notes, with time finance came to be seen as the alternative to 'a declining industrial sector and the main engine of growth in post-industrial societies. The rise of finance has been concomitant with the globalisation of the world economy, the deregulation of financial activities and the triumph of the market.'[37]

Tage Andersen and Knud Sørensen were relatively unimpressed with the new era and get rich quick culture, but the rise of shareholder capitalism nevertheless left its imprint as time went by. S.O. Sørensen's stakeholder views could not stand. In 1986, Tage Andersen said: 'The most important thing is that we can deliver a satisfactory return on equity', reflecting the shift in the role of banks and business in society.[38]

Still, this statement did not yet represent an all-out focus on short-term shareholder value. Also in 1986, a business magazine put the executive board on the cover with the headline 'The Victors'. Tage Andersen told the magazine: 'we are somewhat old fashioned. We have heavy demands on quality, are very direct and we have certain demands on style', on discipline, hard work and team spirit. The bank did not speculate for its own account and did not engage in tax dodging.

The bank prided itself of not having lost large amounts of money on individual loans for more than decade. It did not accept 'odious business engagements' and 'we want to be absolutely spotless', Knud Sørensen said and continued 'we do not like quick speculative transactions ... highly leveraged speculative transactions are not part of our business'.[39]

[35] Fama, 'Efficient capital markets'; Jensen and Meckling, 'Theory of the firm'; Moss, 'Reversing the null'.

[36] Beckert, 'How do fields change?'. See also Polanyi, *The Great Transformation*; Blyth, *Great Transformations*.

[37] Cassis, 'Banking and finance in Europe since 1945', 47. See also Brine and Poovey, *Finance in America*; Balling and Gnan, 'The development of financial markets'; Llewellyn, 'Fifty years'; and for a longer term perspective, Hansen, 'From finance'.

[38] Hansen et al., *Den Danske Bank*, 512; Lazonick and O'Sullivan, 'Maximizing shareholder value'.

[39] Lund et al., 'Disciplin og korpsånd'.

Andersen's crowning achievement and confirmation that the bank's conservative business model had paid off was reached by the end of 1989 just as he retired. Den Danske Bank acquired two large competitors as a step towards realizing a vision of a 'broad-based financial services business'.

It was a sign that Danske's conservative approach had prevailed, and it soon became clear that this culture would also dominate the new organization.[40] Knud Sørensen was appointed CEO in 1990 at the age of 55. A Danske Bank veteran who had been in the bank since 1951, he was tasked with refocusing and integrating the new and much larger bank at a time of re-emerging financial instability, deregulation, and increased competition at home and abroad.

The spirit of 1928

As Sørensen settled into the CEO's office with the fireplace, the clock and the mantles, the sense of continuity and tradition must have been clear to him. But one thing was new to him. For the first time since the Great Depression, financial instability was back.

The Nordic financial crisis of the early 1990s ravaged Finland, Norway, and Sweden and to a lesser extent Denmark. Indeed, Danske Bank sailed through, but there were tough decisions to be made anyway. The bank had not laid off employees since the 1920s, but in the new competitive environment Sørensen announced a massive layoff of 3,000 people. It was a break with the bank's self-perception and the idea of lifetime employment.[41]

The reduction of staff and other reputational issues led to negative press for the bank, but for some reason it never really seemed to harm Knud Sørensen's image. People believed him when he stressed old virtues such as 'accuracy, precision and orderliness' and said that one has to 'dutifully carry out one's work and be polite and honest'.

This approach in the midst of get rich quick schemes underlined the conservative focus on credit policy and risk assessment and gave the bank a somewhat old-fashioned reputation. Few were surprised when Danske Bank was untouched by the Nordic Feather company's bankruptcy in 1991. Like Isak Glückstadt before them, Andersen and Sørensen would rather let a business opportunity pass than deal with people or companies who did not live up their conservative principles. There was 'too much noise about the financial statements and reporting principles', Sørensen told reporters.[42]

This conservative culture led to Den Danske Bank being cast as the saviour of the financial sector during the financial crisis of the early 1990s. 'Finance Denmark

[40] Hansen et al., *Den Danske Bank*, 527–533.
[41] Hansen and Jensen, *Vi kan når vi skal. Finansforbundets historie*, 134–136.
[42] Hansen et al., *Den Danske Bank*, 555–556, 559.

in Panic' the business newspaper Børsen's cover announced on 22 March 1993, while the next day, the same paper's editorial carried the reassuring heading 'Den Danske Bank or Chaos'. An influential weekly argued 'without Den Danske Bank's intervention, state measures for billions of kroner would have been unavoidable'.[43]

Den Danske Bank was seen as a solid rock in an unruly sea of financial instability. The head of the Financial Supervision Authority went as far as to call the bank infallible and the minister for business agreed that the bank 'is relatively infallible meaning that it is well managed and orderly bank with a very high hedging of risk and conscientiousness. It conducts a very conservative lending policy, and it is careful.'[44]

A newspaper explained the bank's solid standing with 'the spirit of 1928'. The 'discipline and military-like orderliness that rules in the bank can be traced directly back to 1928', a former executive told the newspaper. That was when A.P. Møller, Oluf Nielsen, and Poul Ingholt decided that 'in the future the bank should always be run conservatively and safely. The bank must never again take part in speculation and should always be careful and avoid mistakes at any cost—it would rather miss out on a profitable business opportunity.'[45]

This narrative reinforced the perception of Den Danske Bank as the most orderly and conservative bank, where the 'second generation' after 1928, Knud Sørensen and his predecessor Tage Andersen, had learned the bank's values at an early age.[46]

Therefore, it came as a surprise when, in early 1996, Den Danske Bank and Knud Sørensen received unwanted attention for its role in 1992 in the crisis of Hafnia, the country's largest insurer. To save Hafnia a capital issue of DKK 1.9 billion was injected into Hafnia during the summer of 1992. Den Danske Bank participated in underwriting the issue and prepare the prospectus, so it was unfortunate that the money disappeared in a black hole in the course of a few weeks and left Hafnia insolvent again.

There was a whole lot of speculation about Den Danske Bank's role in the affair, but it was only in February 1996 when an insider leaked board minutes from the summer of 1992 that criticism turned into a scandal with massive media coverage. The leaked material strongly suggested that the prospectus had withheld information, and that Hafnia should have set aside another DKK 600 to 800 million of provisions. But, as the chairman of the board had remarked, the bank's position would not be worse if the issue was carried through. After all, it would reduce Den Danske Bank's potential losses.

Together with another case related to the bank's ownership of a bank in the Faroes, the Hafnia case questioned whether Den Danske Bank was still the

43 Hansen et al., 564.
44 Politiken, 'Forsvar for storbank'.
45 Gustafson, 'Guldflippernes modstykke'.
46 Gustafson.

conservative bank it used to be. The bank's reputation took a hit, but three months later, Knud Sørensen was nevertheless picked as the nation's best business leader by his peers.[47] Whether correct or not, consensus seemed to coalesce around the idea that Peter Straarup, Sørensen's right-hand man and later successor as CEO, had been the man behind the problematic decisions.[48]

Eight months later, on 5 October 1996, the bank turned 125 years. Surely an occasion for celebration. And celebrated it was, though not by engaging with its history like Deutsche Bank had done the year before.[49] Instead the bank sponsored an exhibition of 125 years of Danish sculpture and funded three professorships in finance and economics. It also published a richly illustrated booklet about its corporate headquarters building in Holmens Kanal.

Internally, the bank's internal staff magazine celebrated the anniversary by presenting a brief historical overview of the bank. As a first, it even mentioned the crisis in the 1920s and its influence on the present. 'It caused great societal shock when, following the post-war crisis and economic chaos, in 1922 the bank ... experienced so big problems that it had to be reconstructed with the assistance of the state.... Den Danske Landmandsbank recovered relatively quickly after the reconstruction. It was still Denmark's largest bank, but now with a reputation—taught by experience—as a somewhat conservative bank. It is a reputation that still sticks to some extent, even though it is both correct and not.'[50]

The text skipped over the bail-out and socialization of the bank in 1928 and seemed to struggle with how to present the conservative business model that grew out of the bank's failure. For present purposes it might not be a good thing to describe the bank as too conservative, so it ended up being both true and not true.

Knud Sørensen, too, has argued on several occasions that the bank had learned from and remembered its history without being explicit about it. 'Vestigia terrent', he said in 1997, indicating that memories of the crisis of the 1920s were still alive and at work in the bank.[51] Sørensen insisted on a long-term view of business. Den Danske Bank would never present quarterly reports, he said, and he warned against 'fads in management theories ... the latest is shareholder value'.[52]

In retrospect, the failure in the 1920s 'was clearly a part of our worldview', Knud Sørensen told me in 2020. 'Never a 1922–1924 again and the bank must never become dependent on the state again.... In a way it was our mantra ... caution, caution, consolidation, consolidation, consolidation'.[53] In a note, he wrote: 'The memory of the 20s and the 30s never left us. Naturally it has not been as present

[47] Hansen, *Danske Bank*, 182–184.
[48] Mikkelsen, *Straarup: Et portræt*, 59–74.
[49] Gall et al., *The Deutsche Bank*.
[50] Danske Bank, 'Den Danske Bank'.
[51] The author's interview with Knud Sørensen, 21 July 1997.
[52] Hansen, *Danske Bank*, 185.
[53] The author's interview with Knud Sørensen, 20 January 2020.

for younger colleagues as for older ones, but it was never forgotten'.[54] As Knud Sørensen stepped down in early 1998 after 47 years in the Bank it was time for a younger colleague to take over.

Peter Straarup and the financial crisis of 2008

In 1968, a 17-year-old Peter Straarup entered Landmandsbanken's Fredericia branch to begin his career as a banker. His talent was spotted early on, and after being transferred to Copenhagen, he had longer stays in London, Los Angeles, and Dallas. In 1983, Straarup was appointed head of Danske Bank's branch in Singapore and two years later he returned to the USA to start up the bank's new branch in New York City. Only 35 years old, he was called back to Copenhagen in 1986 to become member of the executive board.

Both Knud Sørensen and Tage Andersen had international experience, but not like Straarup who spent several years in Singapore and the United States and acquired an international outlook in an increasingly de-regulated financial world. When he assumed the role of CEO in 1998, globalization and shareholder capitalism were firmly established in the worldview and cultural blueprint of international finance.[55] Born in 1951, Straarup was third generation of leaders since the failure of the 1920s, and any memory would have had to come to him through the bank's organizational culture, conversations with older colleagues, books, reports and articles, and material artefacts.

Straarup was, in fact, aware that the bank had failed and become state owned in the 1920s, but its history was not used directly in the bank. In retrospect, he reflected: 'We did not sit down physically and said now we are going to think about the history and use it for our decisions. That's not how it works, but we were aware of Danske Bank's history.... Credit policy somehow became the cornerstone in the way the bank was managed.... The bank had a shock that led to conservative banking and since then it has trickled down through the bank from the board, Mr. Møller, Ingholt.'[56]

Like in Emil Glückstadt's time, the world of finance underwent dramatic institutional and cultural shifts as Straarup took over the bank from Knud Sørensen. Financialization was at the doorstep with 'the increasing role of financial motives, financial markets, financial actors and financial institutions in the operation of the domestic and international economies'.[57]

As this process played out, Larry Summers, then assistant secretary of treasury in the Clinton administration stressed his imaginary in 1997 that 'financial

[54] Handwritten notes by Knud Sørensen handed over to the author on 20 January 2020.
[55] See Ho, *Liquidated*; Ho, 'Disciplining'.
[56] The author's interview with Peter Straarup, 29 January 2020.
[57] Epstein, 'Introduction', 3; Dore, 'Financialization'; Hansen, 'From finance'.

markets don't just oil the wheels of economic growth—they are the wheels'.[58] As the interwar banking crises and the Great Depression faded into oblivion and efficient markets ideology came to prevail, bankers became at the same time 'masters of the universe, but slaves of the market'.[59]

Straarup's international outlook and the new spirit of globalization, shareholder value, and optimism led Danske Bank into adopting a strategy of expansion at home and abroad. In 1997 Straarup led the bank's acquisition of Swedish Östgöta Enskilda bank and two years later the Norwegian Focus bank became part of Danske Bank. From there things accelerated, but at the same time Straarup demonstrated his awareness of the bank's troubled history.

In 1999 he explained the bank's strong credit culture by referring to the 'events in the 1920's. That's when the bank got this very strong culture with respect to order. The bank had been down and seen what may happen if you don't have very, very orderly formal structures. If you walk through this company today, you will see some very formal structures with respect to decisions and credits.'

Straarup and his executive board colleague, Jacob Brogaard—with the nickname the 'credit ruffian'—met daily to go through the credits. 'And we are punctual. There's a man who keeps a register over all decisions, and there's a hierarchy, that makes sure that everything is in order and communicated. It seems incredibly formal, but it is very efficient, because we know that each decision about a credit is documented.'[60]

While formal credit structures are important, there are other ways of losing money. Formal structures cannot stand alone in securing a solid long-term business model—and a conservative worldview and blueprint—particularly in the face of a strong ideological shift and shareholder value focus on stock price. The bank's strategy focused on growth by acquisition, another parallel with the time before 1922.

In 2000 the bank changed its name to Danske Bank, and in 2001 it acquired Realkredit Danmark, the country's largest mortgage lender, and the large BG bank, completing the financial supermarket vision of offering both banking, insurance, pension, and mortgage services. Next up was the acquisition in 2005 of National Irish bank and Northern bank in Northern Ireland. In 2006 Finnish Sampo bank became part of the business bringing in branches in Estonia, Latvia, and Lithuania as well. Danske Bank was big again, the world of finance was free again, and financial economics went all in. New era optimism and confidence was prevalent. The future looked great, why care about the past?

In 2006, the FSA convened a conference on financial crises. As chairman of Finance Denmark, the Danish financial interests' lobby organization, Peter

[58] Murray, 'New economic models'; Davis, 'Politics and financial markets', 44.
[59] Bell and Hindmoor, 'Masters of the universe'.
[60] Thomsen and Bjerge, 'Fra agtværdig til aggressiv'.

Straarup gave a talk pointing to a significant change in his and banks' understanding of risk and neglect of uncertainty. In Tage Andersen and Knud Sørensen's time risk was handled through careful and well-established practices about how to assess creditworthiness and credit policy.

With the 'advances' of financial economics, complex financial risk models increasingly took over the work of credit people.[61] This approach, while perhaps useful in general, disregarded uncertainty and blind spots and gave an illusion of control in an analytical monoculture that relied heavily on risk-based calculative technologies.[62] It also neglected the risk of overconfidence through new era progress narratives. At the conference, Straarup argued that:

> The rating of the loan portfolio's quality that most financial institutions use today, means that we get much earlier warnings about debtors' inability to service their debts.... We are becoming still better to profit from mediating risk rather than just taking risks. The explanation is advancement in both technology and financial theory. There are a lot of signs that financial derivatives have actually contributed to financial stability.[63]

The development within financial economics and banking practices emphasized by Straarup was generally seen as a sign of progress in finance. Straarup also addressed the issue of historical memory.

> And then there are the less tangible—but no less important—consequences of the crisis [of the 1990s]. Hopefully the event has left a lasting impression ... on the generation of bankers who experienced the crisis.... I am convinced that the most important lesson is still there in the minds of the generation of bankers who are at the helm of banks and savings banks.... It is absolutely crucial that one has a sound credit policy. That is at the core of sound banking. We already have a generation of competent bankers who have not themselves experienced the 1990s financial crisis. It is therefore important that they acquire the understanding and significance of a highly developed 'credit culture'.[64]

Despite this upbeat sentiment and remembering the financial crisis of the 1990s, Danske Bank and many other banks got into serious trouble in the financial crisis of 2008. Danske's problems were not related to CDOs but to aggressive lending in the recently acquired banks in Ireland and Northern Ireland, and aggressive liquidity and capital management. Rather than holding liquidity, Danske Bank and many other international banks saw liquidity as something they could always

[61] Douglas, 'Planning profitable futures; Commission, 'The financial crisis inquiry report'.
[62] Beckert and Bronk, 'Uncertain futures', 11.
[63] Straarup, 'Finansielle kriser'.
[64] Straarup.

borrow in the interbank market rather than something they should hold. Lehman's failure made a fool of that theory. Also, like other large international banks, Danske's leverage was beyond what any of the old credit ruffians or conservative bankers would have accepted. Danske Bank's capital to total assets ratio went below 3%.[65]

Another symbolic event, given 'Landmandsbanken's tradition', was the failure in 2008 of IT Factory, which proved to be a Ponzi scheme and to cost the bank DKK 350 million. In the spring of 2008, Danske Bank analysts had valued the business at DKK 8 billion and the bank's engagement with the company came as a complete surprise of the public—and the bank. Both, it seemed, still subscribed to the historical narrative of the bank as conservative and careful. Suddenly, that narrative was out of step with reality.

It seemed that, despite remembering, Danske Bank was fallible, after all.

Conclusion

In their article quoted above, Bouwman and Malmendier, speculated about the processes by which experience 'propagate into the future and generate some form of institutional memory'. Their quantitative approach does not allow them to explain how such propagation and institutionalization of memory take place in organizations.

In this chapter, I have substituted remembering and uses of history for memory and embeddedness for institutionalization. I have developed a conceptual framework and an analytical strategy that allows for examining how an organization's remembering, and use of history contribute to shape its worldview and cultural blueprint.

By focusing on narratives, I have argued that Landmandsbanken's fatal crash and take over by the state in the 1920s influenced the worldview and cultural blueprint of three generations of executives and embedded conservative banking practices in the organization's culture. They were aware of the crash, though they rarely discussed it or referred to it. While there are few smoking guns, there is some evidence that the crisis was remembered and contributed to shape the bank's worldview and cultural blueprint. This took the shape of a conservative and credit-policy focused business model as the bank's shifting CEOs navigated uncertain futures.

There were, however, subtle differences in the way the crisis was remembered and used depending on whether it was a firsthand experience or further removed in time from the events of the 1920s. While the bank apparently did not actively employ and use history as a strategic resource, the historical experience of the crisis

[65] Rangvid, 'The financial crisis in Denmark'.

took the shape of a conservative tradition. That tradition came under pressure as the institutional and cultural context changed and financial globalization paved the way for dramatic changes in the world of finance.

The apparent silencing of direct and explicit references to the interwar period may well have contributed to Danske Bank and Peter Straarup, a third generation CEO with no direct reference to the events of the 1920s, assuming that the bank was still adhering to the narrative and conservative blueprint of its executive predecessors. In the meantime, blind spots allowed risks to be built up in other areas of the bank's business through acquisitions and increased reliance on financial models in managing liquidity and capital, and most likely through increased governance issues related to managing a transnational bank. All of this happened in a radical new context of shareholder capitalism that put pressure on conservative banking and earlier business models.

It also seems to be the case that in his 2006 talk Peter Straarup shifted the historical reference from the 1920s to the financial crisis of the 1990s, in which Danske Bank emerged as the winner, like after the banking crisis of 1908. It was not only the head of the FSA and the minister of business that saw the bank as infallible. Media coverage of Danske Bank could also easily lead to the idea that the bank was, indeed, infallible.

Both Emil Glückstadt and Peter Straarup were highly competent bankers of their times, but their times were a'changing. Their experiences were about success and growth, which was not conducive to remembering and using the history of bad times. Even if Straarup remembered the crisis of the 1920s and even if the experience was embedded in the organization's culture and blueprint, there are hardly any eternal and directly applicable lessons to be learned from history. Within banks, experiences hardly transcend dramatic shifts in institutional and cultural contexts that calls for different business practices.

Perhaps the best we can hope for is that regulators avoid cultural capture and actively work to remember what banks often forget and have blind spots. On 3 September 2018, Jesper Berg, then CEO of the Danish FSA gave a talk in which he noted that it is important to learn from history. 'We must be Denmark's financial memory' he said of his office.[66]

References

Anonymous (1896). 'Den Danske Landmandsbank- Hypothek- og Vexelbank'. *Nationaltidende*, 5 October.

Anonymous (1958). 'Bankerne husker erfaringerne og de daarlige minder fra tyverne'. *Information*, 4 May.

Anonymous (1954). 'En bankmand ser tilbage'. *Børsen*, 30 December.

[66] Berg, 'FinansDanmark-Direktørkonference'.

Balling, M. and Ernest, G. (2013). 'The development of financial markets and financial theory—50 years of interaction.' In M. Balling and G. Ernest (eds), *50 Years of Money and Finance—Lessons and Challenges*. SUERF—The European Money and Finance Forum, 157–194.

Bankkommissionen (1924). *Beretning om forholdene i Den Danske Landmandsbank, Hypothek- og Vekselbank m.m. Afgivet af den ved Kgl. ordre af 21. September 1922 nedsatte kommission*. København: G.E.C. Gad.

Beckert, J. (2010). 'How do fields change? The interrelations of institutions, networks, and cognition in the dynamics of markets'. *Organization Studies* 31, 5: 605–627.

Beckert, J. and Bronk, R. (eds) (2018). *Uncertain Futures: Imaginaries, Narratives, and Calculation in the Economy*. Oxford: Oxford University Press.

Beckert, J. and Bronk, R. (2019). 'Uncertain futures: Imaginaries, narratives, and calculative technologies'. *MPIfG Discussion Paper* (19/10).

Bell, S. and Hindmoor, A. (2015). 'Masters of the universe but slaves of the market: Bankers and the great financial meltdown'. *The British Journal of Politics and International Relations* 17, 1: 1–22.

Berg, J. (2018). 'FinansDanmark-Direktørkonference'. *København*, September 3.

Blyth, M. (2002) *Great Transformations: Economic Ideas and Institutional Change in the Twentieth Century*. New York: Cambridge University Press.

Bouwman, C.H.S. and Malmendier, U. (2015). 'Does a Bank's History Affect Its Risk-Taking?'. *American Economic Review* 105, 5: 321–325.

Brine, K.R. and Poovey, M. (2017). *Finance in America: An Unfinished Story*. Chicago: The University of Chicago Press.

Bruun & Hjejle (2018). 'Report on the non-resident portfolio at Danske Bank's Estonian branch'.

Cassis, Y. (2014). 'Banking and finance in Europe since 1945'. In Hesse et al. (eds) *Perspectives on European Economic and Social History*. Baden-Baden: Nomos Verlagsgesellschaft, 47–71.

Cassis, Y. and Schenk, C.R. (2021). *Remembering and Learning from Financial Crises*. Oxford: Oxford University Press.

Chernow, R. (1997). *The Death of the Banker: the Decline and Fall of the Great Financial Dynasties and the Triumph of the Small Investor*. New York: Random House.

Commission, Financial Crisis Inquiry (2011). 'The Financial Crisis Inquiry Report, Authorized Edition: Final Report of the National Commission on the Causes of the Financial and Economic Crisis in the United States'.

Danske Bank (1996). 'Den Danske Bank—Ung bank med lang historie'. *Danske Bank Nyt*, September.

Davis, G. F. (2012). 'Politics and financial markets'. In K. Knorr Cetina and A. Preda (eds), *The Oxford Handbook of the Sociology of Finance*. Oxford: Oxford University Press, 33–51.

Donaldson, G. (1990). 'Voluntary restructuring. The case of General Mills'. *Journal of Financial Economics* 27, 1: 117–141.

Dore, R. (2008). 'Financialization of the global economy'. *Industrial and Corporate Change* 17, 6: 1097–1112.

Douglas, J. (2018). 'Planning profitable futures: The introduction of statistical planning techniques in American banks'. *Management & Organizational History* 13, 2: 140–159.

Eichengreen, B. (2012). 'Economic history and economic policy'. *The Journal of Economic History* 72, 2: 289–307.

Eichengreen, B. (2015). *Hall of Mirrors: The Great Depression, the Great Recession, and the Uses-and Misuses-of History*. New York: Oxford University Press.

E.L. (1900). 'Penge og papirer. Landmandsbanken'. *Politiken*, 30 March.

Epstein, G. A. (2005). 'Introduction: Financialization and the World Economy'. In G.A. Epstein (ed.), *Financialization and the World Economy*. Cheltenham: Edward Elgar, 3–16.

Fama, E.F. (1970). 'Efficient capital markets: A review of theory and empirical work'. *Journal of Finance* 25(2): 383–417.

Fisher, I. (1933). 'The debt-deflation theory of great depressions'. *Econometrica* 1: 337–357.

Franklin, J. and Masters, B. (2022). "'I did have a big ego': John Mack reflects on a life spent on Wall Street". *Financial Times.Com*, 23 November. https://www.ft.com/content/7896b7b6-95b8-4ca1-8445-f5cfec478e65.

Gall, L. et al. (eds) (1995). *The Deutsche Bank: 1870–1995*. London: Weidenfeld & Nicolson.

Gustafson, Peter. 'Guldflippernes modstykke'. *Det Fri Aktuelt*, 17 December 1992.

Hansen, P.H. (2001). 'Bank regulation in Denmark from 1880 to World War Two: Public interests and private interests'. *Business History*, 43, 1: 43–68.

Hansen, P.H. (2007). 'Organizational culture and organizational change: The transformation of savings banks in Denmark, 1965–1990'. *Enterprise and Society* 8, 4: 920–953.

Hansen, P.H. (2012a). 'Business history: A cultural and narrative approach'. *Business History Review* 86, 4: 693–717.

Hansen, P.H. (2012b). 'Making sense of financial crisis and scandal: A Danish bank failure in the first era of finance capitalism'. *Enterprise and Society* 13, 3: 672–706.

Hansen, P.H. (2014). 'From finance capitalism to financialization: A cultural and narrative perspective on 150 years of financial history'. *Enterprise and Society* 15, 4: 605–642.

Hansen, P.H. (2024). *Danske Bank: A History of the Bank through 150 Years*. Denmark: Strandberg Publishing.

Hansen, P.H. and Jensen, K. (2013). *Vi kan når vi skal. Finansforbundets historie*. Odense: University Press of Southern Denmark.

Hansen, P.H. and Magnussen, A. (2018). 'Making sense of business and community in Hollywood films, 1928–2016'. *Business History Review* 92, 2: 307–337.

Hansen, P.H., and Mørch. (1997). *Den Danske Bank*. Viby: Forlaget Centrum.

Ho, K. (2009a). 'Disciplining investment bankers, Disciplining the economy: Wall Street's institutional culture of crisis and the downsizing of "Corporate America"'. *American Anthropologist* 111, 2: 177–189.

Ho, K. (2009b). *Liquidated: An Ethnography of Wall Street*. Durham: Duke University Press.

James, H. (2012). *The Creation and Destruction of Value: the Globalization Cycle*. Cambridge, MA: Harvard University Press.

Jensen, M.C. and Meckling, W.H. (1976). 'Theory of the firm: Managerial behavior, agency costs and ownership structure'. *Journal of Financial Economics* 3, 4: 305–360.

Kay, J.A. and King, M.A. (2020). *Radical uncertainty: Decision-Making beyond the Numbers*. New York: W.W. Norton & Company.

Keynes, J.M. (1936). *The General Theory of Employment, Interest and Money*. London: Macmillan.

Kindleberger, C.P. and Aliber, R.Z. (2011). *Manias, Panics and Crashes. A History of Financial Crises*. New York: Palgrave Macmillan.

Krugman, P. (2009). 'How did economists get it so wrong?'. *New York Times Magazine*, 2 September.

Koselleck, R. (2004). *Futures Past: on the Semantics of Historical time*. New York: Columbia University Press.

Lazonick, W. and O'Sullivan, M. (2000). 'Maximizing shareholder value: A new ideology for corporate governance'. *Economy and Society* 29, 1: 13–35.

Lemieux, C. (2014). 'Bank strategies in the new year: Trends and examples'. *Community Banking Connections*, First Quarter, 1: 8–11.

Linde, C. (2009). *Working the Past: Narrative and Institutional Memory*. New York: Oxford University Press.

Llewellyn, D.T. (2013). 'Fifty years in the evolution of bank business models'. In M. Balling and G. Ernest (eds), *50 Years of Money and Finance—Lessons and Challenges*. SUERF—The European Money and Finance Forum, 319–354.

Lubinski, C. (2018). 'From "history as told" to "history as experienced": Contextualizing the uses of the past'. *Organization Studies* 39, 12: 1785–1809.

Lund, K., Reckweg, K., and Alhøj, E. (1986) 'Disciplin og korpsånd'. *Børsens Nyhedsmagasin*, October.

Malmendier, U. and Nagel, S. (2011). 'Depression babies: Do Macroeconomic Experiences Affect Risk Taking?'. *Quarterly Journal of Economics* 126, 1: 373–416.

Malmendier, U. and Tate, G. (2009). 'Superstar CEOs'. *Quarterly Journal of Economics* 124, 4: 1593–1638.

Malmendier, U., Tate, G., and Yan, J. (2011). 'Overconfidence and early-life experiences: The effect of managerial traits on corporate financial policies'. *The Journal of Finance* 66, 5: 1687–1733.

Malmendier, U. and Wachter, J.A. (2022). 'Memory of past experiences and economic decisions'. In M. J. Kahana and A. D. Wagner (eds), The Oxford Handbook of Human Memory, Two Volume Pack: Foundations and Applications, Oxford: Oxford University Press, 2228–2266.

Mikkelsen, O. (2007). *Straarup: et portræt*. Kbh: Gyldendal.

Minsky, H. (2017). 'A theory of systemic fragility'. In E. Altman and A.W. Sametz (eds), *Financial Crises: Institutions and Markets in a Fragile Environment*. New York: Wiley, 138–152.

Mørch, S. (1986). *Det store bankkrak*. København: Gyldendal.

Mordhorst, M. and Schwarzkopf, S. (2017). 'Theorising narrative in business history'. *Business History* 59, 8: 1155–1175.

Moss, D.A. (2010). 'Reversing the null: Regulation, deregulation, and the power of ideas'. In G. Rosenfeld, J.W. Lorsch, and R. Khurana (eds), *Challenges to Business in the Twenty-First Century*. Cambridge, MA: American Academy of Arts and Sciences, 35–49.

Murray, A. (1997). 'New economic models are failing while America Inc. keeps rolling'. *The Wall Street Journal*, 12 December.

n/a. (1924) 'Beretningen om kapitalismens forfærdende forbrydelser mod det danske folk'. *Social-Demokraten*.

Noonan, L. and Armstrong, R. (2020) 'Brian Moynihan: Focused on remembering the financial crisis'. *Ft.Com*, 19 January.

Nora, P. (1996). 'General introduction: Between memory and history'. In P. Nora (ed.), *Realms of Memory: Rethinking the French Past*. New York: Columbia University Press, 1–20.

Nyboe Andersen, P. (1947). *Laanerenten: En teoretisk og historisk undersøgelse med særligt henblik paa renteudviklingen i Danmark*. København.

Plough, A.L. (2020). 'The power of shifting narratives, expectations, and consciousness: Discussion and case studies from Bellagio'. In A.L. Plough (ed.), *Well-Being: Expanding the Definition of Progress. Insights from Practitioners, Researchers, and Innovators from around the Globe*. New York: Oxford Academic, 83–98.

Polanyi, K. (1971). *The Great Transformation*. Boston: Beacon.
Politiken (1996). 'Forsvar for storbank'. *Politiken*, 23 February.
Popp, A. (2013). 'Making choices in time'. *Enterprise and Society* 14, 3: 467–474.
Rangvid, J. (2013). 'The financial crisis in Denmark—causes, consequences and lessons'. Copenhagen: Ministry of Business and Growth. Denmark.
Revell, J.R.S. and Heremans, D. (1981). 'The complementary nature of competition and regulation in the financial sector'. In E.P.M. Gardener (ed.), *UK Banking Supervision. Evolution, Practice and Issues*. London: Allen & Unwin, 161–181.
Rowlinson, M. et al. (2010). 'Social remembering and organizational memory'. *Organization Studies* 31, 1: 69–87.
Rowlinson, M. et al. (2014). 'Narratives and memory in organizations'. *Organization* 21, 4: 441–446.
Schönhärl, K. (ed.) (2017). *Decision Taking, Confidence and Risk Management in Banks from Early Modernity to the 20th Century*. Cham: Springer International Publishing.
Schovelin, J. (1921). *Den Danske Landmandsbank, Hypothek- og Vekselbank, 1871–1921*. København.
Sørensen, S.O. (1971). 'Vi lever i forandringernes tidsalder', *Advis. Landmandsbankens Personaleblad*, October.
Straarup, P. (2006). 'Finansielle kriser. Hvad har den finansielle sektor lært af 90'erne'? In *Indlæg Ved Finanstilsynets konference om 'Finansielle kriser—Hvordan opstår de—hvordan kan de bekæmpes'*. Finanstilsynet.
Straumann, T. (2010). 'The UBS crisis in historical perspective. Expert Opinion prepared for delivery to UBS AG, 28 September 2010.' Zürich: University of Zürich.
Suddaby, R., Foster, W.M., and Quinn Trank, C. (2010). 'Rhetorical history as a source of competitive advantage'. In J.A.C. Baum and J. Lampel (eds), *The Globalization of Strategy Research. Advances in Strategic Management*, 27. Bingley: Emerald, 147–173.
Thomsen, J. and Bjerge, P. (1999). 'Fra agtværdig Til aggressiv'. *Børsens Nyhedsmagasin*, 30 August.
US Department of Justice (2022) 'United States v. Danske Bank A/S. Plea Agreement'. US Department of Justice.
Wadhwani, R.D. et al. (2018). 'History as organizing: Uses of the past in organization studies'. *Organization Studies* 39(12): 1663–1683.
Weick, K.E. (2010). *Sensemaking in Organizations*. Thousand Oaks, CA: Sage.
Yu, G. (2025). 'Do bank CEOs learn from banking crises?'. *Journal of Financial Economics* 166: 1–21.

11

The Global Financial Crisis of 2008

Memory, history, legacy

Youssef Cassis

The return of financial crises that marked the post-Bretton Woods era culminated with the Global Financial Crisis of 2008.[1] This was indeed a shock of unprecedented magnitude, usually considered as the most severe crisis since the Great Depression, but arguably the worst financial panic in modern history. Nearly 20 years after the crisis, the moment is appropriate to reflect on what is left of the Global Financial Crisis, and how this crisis relates to previous financial shocks. This will be done at three levels: memory, history, and legacy. Their interconnectedness can help to better understand the extent and limits of learning from the past.

There have been many debates on the relationships between memory and history since the 'memory boom' of the 1980s.[2] Considered for a long time as a lower form of recounting the past, guided by subjectivity rather than 'objective' academic methods, memory has been rehabilitated, and oral history, in particular, recognized as a perfectly respectable methodology.[3] Recent historiographical trends have tended to play down the differences, whatever the allegedly more dynamic nature of memory, centred on the identity and perception of agents as objects of study, and the more static, codified nature of history.[4] In any case, memory and history are both subject to changes over time, though not necessarily at the same rhythm and in the same way. The distinction is less clear for the very recent past, to which the Global Financial Crisis of 2008 still belongs, where direct memory plays a major role—if only because much of the 'history' of the crisis has been written

[1] The project leading to this application has received funding from the European Research Council (ERC) under the European Union's Horizon 2020 research and innovation programme (grant agreement No. 884910). The content of this document represents only the views of the MERCATOR team and is its sole responsibility. The European Commission does not accept any responsibility for use that may be made of the information it contains.

[2] Winter, 'Notes on the memory boom'.

[3] Portelli, 'On the peculiarities of oral history'; Thomson, 'Four paradigms transformation in oral history'.

[4] Nora, 'Between memory and history'.

Youssef Cassis, *The Global Financial Crisis of 2008*. In: *History, Memory, and the Return of Financial Crises After Bretton Woods*. Edited by: Youssef Cassis and Giuseppe Telesca, Oxford University Press.
DOI: 10.1093/9780198950158.003.0011

by witnesses of, and even participants to the events. Paradoxically, this makes it even more necessary to discuss separately the two approaches.

A legacy can be defined as something that is transmitted from one person, generation, or period to another. In a similar way, it can be seen as the lasting impact of particular events, or actions that took place in the past. The idea of what is left from the past clearly refers to memory and history, including the lessons drawn from the past. But the notion of legacy also has a dynamic dimension: the nature of what has been left from the past, whether it is an asset or a liability; and its transformative character, what can be done, and what has been done with this inheritance.

Memory

It is usually assumed that financial markets have a short memory. John Kenneth Galbraith, the author of a classic history of the Wall Street Crash, observed that 'financial memory from one period of sophisticated stupidity to the next is about 10 to 15 years'.[5] Does this rule apply to the global financial crisis? Has its memory already faded? Possibly, though there have been attempts to keep it alive, not least by Ben Bernanke, Timothy Geithner, and Henry Paulson Jr in their collective memoir, *Firefighting*, published on the 10th anniversary of the crisis, where they lament that: 'Financial crises recur in part because memories fade'.[6] Soon after, however, an article in the *FT Weekend* reflecting on the Covid pandemic, noted that: 'Recent history has somewhat dwarfed the 2007–2008 financial panic. But prior to 2020, it had been considered the most severe global financial disaster since the Great Depression'—without further elaborating on the reasons for this fading of memory.[7]

Fifteen years is the right time to assess if financial markets do indeed have a short memory. Two measures can be taken. First, the personal memories of financial actors taken at one point in time. This has been done through a survey of 150 senior executives in the financial industry conducted in October 2023.[8] Second, the collective memory of financial actors as mediated by the financial press, namely the *Financial Times* and the *Wall Street Journal*, focusing on the articles published around the 15th anniversary. The former is a snapshot, the latter a flux.

[5] Appleyard, 'The seer who saw it coming'.

[6] Bernanke et al., *Firefighting*.

[7] *FT Weekend Magazine*, 18–19 September 2021.

[8] A survey has been conducted, in collaboration with YouGov, among senior individuals working in financial services in October 2023, that is, 15 years after the collapse of Lehman Bothers. The sample includes 150 business leaders from the US (77), the UK (36), Germany (25), and France (12). They were all leading large companies with more than 1,000 employees, across all financial services: banking (50%), including commercial banking, investment banking, and private banking; insurance (23%); accounting (13%); asset management (9%); and others (5%, including brokerage, hedge funds, and private equity).

Personal memory and collective memory are related. As Maurice Halbwachs argued a century ago, individuals' memory is actually dependent on socialization;[9] while the memory represented by media and institutions must ultimately be actualized by individuals.[10] However, despite these interactions, the two memories are not identical and, especially, proceed in different ways.

The survey of senior executives shows that 15 years after the collapse of Lehman Brothers, the Global Financial Crisis had not been forgotten, even if its precise memory might have been starting to fade away; its significance had been fully understood; and its impact was still strongly felt.

These memories manifested most commonly in changes to firms' approaches to risk management (half the respondents), but also in changes to firms' business models (one in three) and exit from certain markets (one in four)—still a sizeable number in 2023. The persistence of these memories could also be seen in discussions at board level, internal documents, and, to a lesser extent, lectures by guest speakers. It is equally significant that for seven out of ten senior executives in financial services, 2008 was the worst financial crisis in the previous 20 years—though for one dissenter from the UK, 'Brexit is harming this country more than all the financial crises combined'; and that 75% regarded the Global Financial Crisis as a 'traumatic event', thus with lasting after effects.

There were some signs that memories of the crisis had been obscured by the Covid pandemic (two-thirds of respondents thought so) or had simply faded away (just over half). But only to a certain extent: four in ten discussed it within their organization during the Covid crisis. And its memory was reactivated a couple years later, with more than half discussing it during the financial turbulence of early 2023, marked by the collapse of Silicon Valley Bank (SVB), First Republic Bank, and Signature Bank, as well as the takeover of the failed Credit Suisse by UBS—a more significant moment for senior people in financial services as it concerned the risks of bank failures, whereas banks were no longer the problem during the Covid crisis.

As will be discussed later in the chapter, an essential legacy of the Global Financial Crisis has been the regulatory measures introduced in its wake. Interestingly, most respondents (83%) thought that these measures had worked as an effective or very effective reminder of the ill-advised risks that were taken by the sector before the music stopped in 2008. 'Markets', as one participant observed, 'have short memories and new generations reinvent old practices'. And half of them (53%) considered that these measures prevented the memory of the crisis from fading.

This probably explains why 70% of respondents or more viewed such measures as higher standards for risk reporting, stronger supervision, more explicit

[9] Halbwachs, *Les cadres sociaux de la mémoire*.
[10] Erll, 'Cultural memory studies'.

resolution and recovery frameworks, and stricter capital and liquidity requirements as having a positive or very positive effect; stress-testing (67%) and bail-in-mechanisms (59%) were also approved, though a little less enthusiastically. Even more strikingly, four in five thought these measures should either be maintained or tightened.

Fifteen years after the shock, senior executives in financial services were thus still aware of the persisting risks to financial stability. This could help prevent, at least for a while, the recurrence of a systemic crisis on the scale of the Global Financial Crisis. There are, however, reasons to question the persistence of this memory over the longer term. Nearly two-thirds (64%) of the young business leaders in the survey (under 35), and nearly three-quarters (72%) of those who had recently started working in the financial sector (less than five years) agreed or strongly agreed that the memory of the Global Financial Crisis had largely faded away. In other words, the crisis had been largely forgotten by the younger generation, who would soon entirely replace the older one at the helm of the banking industry.

Turning to collective memory, the *Financial Times* and the *Wall Street Journal* are the most commonly used sources of information in the financial world. The former was read most often by 53% of the respondents to the survey, the latter by 47%, well ahead of other titles such as *The New York Times* or *The Economist* (both at 39%). Equally significant, 70% of respondents considered that the financial news and comments from newspapers were very influential or quite influential in terms of informing their own views on financial matters.

The memory of the Global Financial Crisis as mediated by these two financial newspapers can be assessed in both metrics and narratives.[11] The numbers point towards a fading of memory. Whereas the two newspapers devoted 83 articles to the crisis in September 2009, that is, on the crisis's first anniversary, the number dropped to 50 on its 10th anniversary, in September 2018, and to 40 in September 2023 on an admittedly less meaningful 15th anniversary.[12] In the same way, one can observe a decreasing engagement with the memory of the event: in 2009, 27 articles out of 83 either *invited* or *necessitated* the memory of the Global Financial Crisis, a proportion that was maintained in 2018 (17 articles out of 50). In 2023 all but two articles *indulged* the memory of the Global Financial Crisis.[13]

In fact, the *Financial Times* and the *Wall Street Journal* engaged less and less with the Global Financial Crisis as an event per se, and rather considered 2008

[11] I am grateful to Giuseppe Telesca for his contribution to this part of the chapter.

[12] While the number of anniversary and non-anniversary pieces are roughly equally divided in 2009 and 2018, the ratio is 0 to 40 in 2023.

[13] Articles *necessitating* memory engage with the past and are characteristic of commemorative and anniversary journalism, with the article written for this specific occasion. Articles *inviting* memory have a foot in the present and essentially consist in historical analogies, comparisons between present and past, and so on. Articles *indulging* history address the past so as to better treat an event in the present, the past is brought into a news story as an aside or an afterthought. See Zelizer, 'Why memory's work on journalism'.

as a watershed from a period of optimism and confidence in the markets, to one of pessimism and polycrisis. As Martin Wolf, of the *Financial Times*, put it: 'The financial crisis of 2008–09 and the resulting recession were a historical watershed. The pre-crisis world was one of globalisation, belief in the markets and confident democracies. Today's a mirror image.'[14]

The story, however, is more complicated than a simple remembering versus forgetting dichotomy. The *Financial Times* and the *Wall Street Journal* might have only published, together, 40 articles in September 2023, but they had published 89 articles in March and April 2023, in other words during the SVB crisis.[15] As observed for the memory of the Great Depression over several decades, financial crises rather than anniversaries provided the trigger for its remembrance in the financial press.[16] The difference is not only quantitative. As also observed for the Great Depression, its memory is changing, depending on prevailing narratives and economic consensus. The memory of the Global Financial Crisis of 2008 was revived in 2023 as an event from which lessons should be—and had been—drawn. But it also addressed a new danger, the return of inflation, whose memory implied a different set of lessons.

In some quarters, especially the *Wall Street Journal*, the memory of 2008 was evoked to attribute the SVB Crisis to bad monetary policy, the inability of central banks, the Fed in particular, to rein in the post-2008 monetary expansion; and to bad regulation: 'Efforts to make the U.S. banking system less risky have had the opposite effect';[17] while bailing out SVB and Signature Bank was seen as an error encouraging moral hazard: 'Capitalism without failure is like religion without hell', wrote Jason Zweig in the *Wall Street Journal*.[18] Others, more likely to be found in the *Financial Times*, took a different view, seeing the SVB crisis a failure rooted in (premature) deregulation: 'I think if we didn't rollback Dodd-Frank in 2018, it would have been less likely that SVB's problems went unnoticed.'[19]

[14] Wolf, FT, 2018.

[15] The Silicon Valley Bank (SVB) failed on 10 March 2023 after depositors attempted to withdraw $42bn. A high proportion of its assets (55%) was in fixed-income securities, mainly Treasury bonds, whose yields increased but value decreased with higher interest rates from early 2022. Deposits withdrawals forced SVB to liquidate assets at conspicuous losses, leading to a run on the bank as the news spread on social media. The US government guaranteed all SVB deposits, including those above the FDI $250,000 limit.

[16] Cassis and Knaps, 'The memory of financial crises'; Telesca and Cassis, 'Battles of narratives, battles of memory'.

[17] M. Faulkender and T. Goodspeed, *WSJ*, 21 March 2023. They went on to write that 'the stress testing mandated by the Dodd-Frank Act led banks to diversify in the same way, which elevated systemic risk even as individual banks became less risky. The collapse of Silicon Valley Bank is a case in point.'

[18] *WSJ*, 18 March 2023.

[19] Prof. Saule Omarova, Cornell University, interviewed in Yuk, Whiffin and Franklin, *FT*, 31 March 2023. The Dodd-Frank Act of 2010 had extended the Basel III requirements—regarding capital requirements, stress tests etc.—to all American banks with at least US$50 billion assets. In 2018 the US government decided to limit these special Basel III requirements only to banks with total assets exceeding US$250 billion.

Fifteen years after Lehman, the personal memory and the collective memory of the Global Financial Crisis differed from one another, especially as far as the object of memory is concerned—the crisis itself for the former, its broader significance for the latter. As a lived experience, personal memory was more stubborn, while collective memory was more changing, more dependent on events and prevailing narratives. But they were not contradicting one another. The Global Financial Crisis had not been forgotten, its impact was still felt, and, interestingly, it started to emerge as the new reference in times of financial crises, replacing the hitherto unmovable Great Depression, as evidenced by SVB crisis.

History

Nearly 20 years after its outbreak, the Global Financial Crisis cannot yet be considered as an object of historical study. Most archives are not accessible, and the temporal distance remains too short to put the event in a proper perspective. However, there have been a number of instant histories, mostly written by journalists, and relying on oral history, as well as the wide coverage of the crisis by the media. Andrew Ross Sorkin's *Too Big to Fail* is one the best examples of such works.[20] Professional historians have kept their distance, with the exception of Adam Tooze, whose book, *Crashed*, published on the 10th anniversary of the crisis, provided an impressive synthesis putting a 'decade of financial crises' (2007–2017) in a broad geopolitical context.[21]

The unprecedented number of books published on the Global Financial Crisis in a fairly short period—more than 600, in English only, between 2009 and 2018 according to a survey by the EUI library[22]—have been written by a vast array of authors, including economists probably the greatest number, most of them financial economists; other social scientists; journalists, above all financial journalists, many of them turning into books their daily coverage of the crisis; financial analysts and consultants; executives and former executives in various banking and financial companies; and in a different genre, some of the major protagonists of the crisis, above all central bankers and politicians, who wrote their memoirs.[23]

This is not the place to review a non-historical literature, even if some publications tell the story of the crisis. Such a quantity of publications is inevitably of uneven quality. Some are polemical, denouncing bankers, greed, or capitalism;

[20] Sorkin, *Too Big to Fail.*

[21] Tooze, *Crashed.*

[22] European University Institute Library, 'Bibliography of the Global Financial/Economic Crisis', 38th edition, May 2018. Compiled by Thomas Bourke. This was closed after 10 years, as the literature also evolves in a different way.

[23] The most prominent among them include Bernanke, *The Courage to Act*; Geithner, *Stress Test*; Paulson, *On the Brink*; Brown, *Beyond the Crash*; King, *The End of Alchemy.*

others, mainly by journalists, recount the events leading to, and happening during the crisis; those written by academics analyse the crisis from various standpoints: global imbalances, central banks and monetary policy, regulation, market failure, risk management, governance, taxation, and so on, ascribing responsibility, prescribing remedies, envisioning future developments; a number of books are about financial crises in general, from a theoretical and/or comparative perspective.

In the first, early post crisis period, the task of economic and financial historians has mainly consisted in putting the Global Financial Crisis in a long-term historical perspective, by establishing parallels and making comparisons with previous financial crises, and trying to make sense of the event. And here, the Global Financial Crisis has unquestionably been read through the lenses of the Great Depression. There has been an obsession with the Great Depression—and not only by historians, in fact mainly by non-historians. How many times has one heard or read in the press, without much further elaboration, that the Global Financial Crisis was the most severe since the Great Depression? The question of the 'Great Depression analogy' was addressed from the start by Michael Bordo and Harold James with regard, in particular, to monetary policy failures, microeconomic issues such as regulation, and global imbalances.[24]

Such comparisons make sense given the magnitude the two shocks, even if the Great Recession never reached the depths of the Great Depression. The reasons for this difference were one of the first issues to be investigated by historians, not least by Barry Eichengreen and Kevin O'Rourke in their hugely successful column in *VoxEU* first published in April 2009 and updated afterwards.[25] And policy-makers made some use of historians' interpretations of the past, above all the Great Depression, in their response to the crisis in 2008–2009.[26] The uses, but also the misuses of history are discussed in the major historical comparison between the two crises, Barry Eichengreen's *Hall of Mirrors*.[27] For the author, lessons from the 1930s were learned, some mistakes not repeated, but despite different conditions and inevitable political constraints, policy-makers could have done better in 2008–2009 and avoid a mistaken early return to fiscal austerity that prolonged economic stagnation.

But is the Great Depression the most appropriate crisis with which to compare the Global Financial Crisis? The answer depends on what one wants to analyse and better understand through a historical comparison. There are two interrelated sides of the Global Financial Crisis: its causes and its consequences. Its causes are multiple. In a book published soon after the collapse of Lehman

[24] Bordo and James. 'The Great Depression analogy'.

[25] Eichengreen and O'Rourke, 'A tale of two depressions'. An initially strong stimulus enabled industrial production and world trade to recover much more quickly after the Global Financial Crisis, even though they had initially declined more sharply than during the early stage of the Great Depression.

[26] Schenk, 'The Global Financial Crisis ten years on'.

[27] Eichengreen, *Halls of Mirrors*.

Brothers, Howard Davies identified 39 factors to answer the question of who was to blame.[28] Explanations range from global imbalances and rising inequalities to highly complex and opaque financial products and the greed of bankers and financiers through the failure of regulation and the periodical outbreak of financial crises in capitalist economies. There are some parallels with the Great Depression, but fundamentally, the differences far outweigh the similarities.

Of course, Galbraith's account of the excesses of the 1920s remains a classic.[29] But they are related to the stock market crash of 1929, which was originally contained, rather than the banking crises of the 1930s. And at no point in the 1930s did most of the world's leading banks find themselves, at almost exactly the same moment, requiring state intervention to save them from failing—as was the case in 2008. It happened in Germany in July 1931, but not in other countries. It did not happen in the United States, despite the severity of the banking crisis, and the banking system virtually coming to a standstill in March 1933. The thousands of bank failures involved small and medium-sized banks, not big systemic banks. And it did not happen in either Great Britain or France, where the banking crises were less severe. In many respects, the banking crises of the 1930s were a consequence of the slump rather than the recklessness of the bankers. Bank failures did not make things easier and in turn contributed to the slide into the Great Depression.[30] In 2008, by contrast, the financial crisis was clearly the cause of the Great Recession that followed; the near collapse of the international banking system was, in part, the result of the banks' irresponsible behaviour, not of an economic downturn.[31]

On the other hand, the comparison with the Great Depression is entirely relevant if one wants to understand how a financial crisis can lead not only to a recession, but to a deep depression. It tells us little about how the behaviour of commercial and investment bankers can lead to a massive financial panic, but very much about how the responses of central bankers and policy-makers to a massive financial crisis can lead to—or prevent—a disaster. There has been more emphasis on the latter in the historical parallels between the Great Recession—rather than the Global Financial Crisis per se—and the Great Depression. The much talked about 'lessons of the Great Depression' are about what the authorities should do, or should not do, to avoid a depression, not a financial crisis.

There are clearer parallels if one wants to put the outbreak of the Global Financial Crisis in historical perspective. The most relevant is the International Debt Crisis of 1982, when Mexico unilaterally declared a three-month moratorium on payment of its debt principal. The crisis is discussed in Chapters 3 and 4 of this book. To recall: most major banks, primarily American but also European, were

[28] Davies, *The Financial Crisis.*
[29] Galbraith, *The Great Crash.*
[30] Bernanke, 'Nonmonetary effects'.
[31] Cassis, *Crises and Opportunities.*

seriously exposed and risked failure in case of defaults—by Mexico and other Latin American countries, especially Argentina and Brazil. Reckless lending and herd behaviour by the world's leading banks in search of inordinate profits, had led, alongside irresponsible borrowing by Latin American countries, to a situation threatening the international financial system with paralysis or even collapse. A major banking crisis was averted when agreement was reached between the banks and the Latin American countries.[32]

The similarities with September 2008 are striking as far as the role of the big banks is concerned. The risk that the financial system would implode was very real, even though the financial crisis turned out to be more potential than real and was not followed by an economic crisis in advanced economies.[33] This is probably why—though it remains surprising—the International Debt Crisis of 1982 has been largely forgotten in connection with the Global Financial Crisis.

Another parallel is with crisis of July–August 1914, at the outbreak of the First World War, when the entire financial system, both in the countries fighting in the war and in the neutral countries, threatened to collapse. And when only exceptional measures requiring state intervention saved the day.[34] The panic in August 1914 had similar symptoms to the panic in September 2008. But it had different causes: the outbreak of a world war, not an unbridled financial boom. And it was followed not by an economic crisis, but by all-out war. The crisis is more meaningful with respect to governments' response than bankers' behaviour.

By the early to mid-2020s, the role of the historian was no longer to establish meaningful historical parallels with the Global Financial Crisis, which had been amply debated and made sense of, though within divergent frameworks of analysis. But writing the history of the crisis still seemed premature. Historians, including economic and financial historians, looked unlikely to put the Global Financial Crisis on top of their agenda. There had been a glut of publication in the decade following the crisis, and interest would reemerge in different conditions, both practical—the opening of archives—and epistemological—new questions emerging in a changed economic and political climate.

Research in the history of financial crises, stimulated by the shock of the Global Financial Crisis, should not necessarily abate, but might well focus on one or several other crises. The Global Financial Crisis had already started to be integrated into longer-term historical perspectives, whether added to existing theoretical

[32] The banks rescheduled the debt and agreed to new loans; the Latin American countries accepted the International Monetary Fund's restructuring programmes; and the US monetary authorities acted as mediator and offered the banks guarantees.

[33] The International Debt Crisis heavily penalized the Latin American countries, whose standard of living took a decade to return to pre-crisis levels.

[34] See Roberts, *Saving the City*.

frameworks,[35] or as part of a broad reflection on financial crises.[36] Writing the history of the Global Financial Crisis would have to rely not only on newly opened archival material, but also on studies of specific aspects of the crisis, for example controversial decisions, such as the decision not to rescue Lehman Brothers;[37] or neglected areas of the crisis, in particular bankers' decision-making before and during the crisis,[38] and their changing definition of risk in the couple of decades preceding the crisis.[39]

A grand narrative looked unlikely to be produced on the Global Financial Crisis's 20th anniversary, but very likely to be discussed in connection with the centenary of the Wall Street crash of 1929 and the Great Depression.

Legacy

At the time of writing, in late 2024–early 2025, while the memory of the Global Financial Crisis had started to fade away, and its history had not yet taken off, we were left with a legacy of the crisis, which should be distinguished from its consequences. Banks' failures or near failures were a consequence of the financial crisis, as were their rescues. The legacy of the crisis relates to the state of the banking system after the crisis, as well as the mechanisms set in place to cope with future crises, such as bank resolution to manage bank failures or monetary and fiscal policies to mitigate their macroeconomic effects. But a legacy can also be of a social, cultural, and political nature, and thus less easily perceptible—for example changes in professional behaviour, or the emergence of a new economic paradigm. The problem is to disentangle what should be attributed to the crisis, and what should be attributed partly or entirely to other factors.

In a recent book on the topic I argued, with my co-author Jean-Jacques van Helten, that the legacy of the Global Financial Crisis had primarily consisted in the financial regulations enacted after the crisis.[40] The crisis, and especially the regulatory measures taken in its aftermath have had a profound impact on the banking industry, in terms of regulation, supervision, risk management, compliance, governance, as well as culture.

The changes were most pronounced in risk management with, among others, stress testing emerging as a major supervisory tool, in parallel with detailed bank

[35] See the updated reeditions of Kindleberger's *Manias, Panics and Crashes*, first published in 1978, with Robert Aliber in 2011, and Robert Aliber and Robert N. McCauley in 2023.

[36] See for example James, *Seven Crashes*, for a broad long-term historical perspective; and Yueh, *The Great Crashes*, for a narrower business perspective.

[37] See for example Ball, *The Fed and Lehman Brothers*.

[38] Some preliminary answers can be found in the chapters of bank monographs devoted to the financial crisis, see in particular Roberts and Kynaston, *The Lion Wakes*; Augar, *The Bank that Lived a Little*; Plumpe et al., *Deutsche Bank*.

[39] See for example Bautzer, 'The state and the transformation'.

[40] Cassis and van Helten. 'Introduction'.

risk-appetite statements, internal capital adequacy assessments, liquidity adequacy assessments, and more generally a strengthening of the risk-culture. The changes in risk culture were expressed in the enhanced role of the Chief Risk Officer (CRO) in banks' governance, and, more subtly, in codes of conduct and ethics guiding bankers' behaviour, from junior staff to top executives, introduced in many banks.[41]

This was in large part the result of the regulatory measures introduced in the wake of the crisis. In particular, regulators imposed increased capital requirements; new liquidity and leverage requirements; and increased requirement in terms of loss absorbing capacity of major banks. Regulators also introduced bail-in mechanisms, thus reducing tax-payer liability in support of insolvent banks via governments bailouts. At the same time, in an effort to further limit excessive risk taking, regulators deferred components of managers' compensation and introduced clawback clauses. Interestingly, these regulations have been more intrusive and required far more compliance officers than those inherited from the Great Depression, leading to an early backlash against what some considered as a regulatory overkill—some talked of a regulatory tsunami.

However, this new regulatory framework did not amount to a complete overhaul of the financial system. The culture had only partly changed. The incentives to take risks with other people's money had not been entirely eradicated, including top bankers' packages, especially in the United States. Banks might have been tamed, but not to the same extent as their forerunners during the Great Depression. At the same time, other players had risen to new prominence and started to overshadow the banks, in the first place assets managers. They were part of an ever-growing shadow banking system, the Non-Bank Financial Institutions (NBFI), controlling about 50% of the world's financial assets while remaining unregulated, with the risks, possibly systemic, that this entails.

This reflects the limits of the wider legacy of the global financial crisis, especially in the social and political spheres. Take the rise of inequalities in advanced economies. Should they be considered as a legacy of the crisis (with quantitative easing leading to returns for some, and austerity policies penalising others) or as an existing trend that was accelerated by the crisis? The same question can be asked about populism, whose rise has been fuelled by the socio-economic impact of the crisis, though very unevenly depending on countries; one of its main causes, immigration, predated the crisis, though the crisis might have reinforced negative attitudes towards immigration.[42] These are clear cases where other factors than the financial crisis have been at play.

The Global Financial Crisis did not have a dramatic impact on the international financial order. The weight of East Asia in world finance had been steadily growing

[41] Beyssade, 'From sets of rules to codes of conduct'.
[42] Isaksen, 'The impact of the financial crisis'.

since the beginning of the new century (with China) and earlier (with Japan, Hong Kong, and Singapore). But 15 years after the Global Financial Crisis, New York and London remained at the top of the hierarchy of international financial centres.[43] Here again, we have a long-term trend somewhat accelerated by the crisis rather than a legacy.

Beyond financial regulations, the Global Financial Crisis clearly left its mark on Europe. The crisis, above all the Eurocrisis, itself a sequel of the Global Financial Crisis, was an extremely violent shock, which tested to the limit the strengths and weaknesses of Europe's monetary union, and ultimately of the European Union itself. But while the immediate effects were negative, the legacy was on balance more positive, with a series of institutional improvements in the fields of macro and micro supervision and regulation, economic governance, and the role of the European Central Bank. Was Brexit a legacy of the Global Financial Crisis? The question has been debated, but the answer has to be no, whatever the role of the protest vote in the leave victory: the decision to call a referendum was a political decision which had much more to do with divisions within the Conservative party than with the Global Financial Crisis.

Ultimately, when considering the legacy of the Global Financial Crisis, the question has to be: what has really changed after the crisis? What difference, if any, did it make?

Here, comparisons with the Great Depression are difficult to avoid. One point is clear: the Great Depression was an epoch changing moment in history in a way that the Global Financial Crisis, and the Great Recession, cannot claim to be. In terms of economic policy, the Great Depression marked a break with the nineteenth century predominantly laissez-faire attitude, which continued throughout the 1920s. The break is particularly visible in the far higher level of state intervention in the economy, including widespread nationalizations in a number of countries; Keynesian contra-cyclical economic policies aiming at ensuring full-employment; a steep deglobalization, with the introduction of exchange controls and the collapse of international capital flows; a much more tightly controlled financial sector, sometimes described as 'financial repression'; and a new monetary order established in 1944 at Bretton Woods. Beyond these specific measures, the legacy of the Great Depression can be seen as the emergence of a new *Zeitgeist* favouring state intervention and financial stability, which was to last for nearly half a century.[44]

The Global Financial Crisis has left no such legacy. The massive state intervention that followed the collapse of Lehman Brothers, including the quasi nationalizations of banks in several countries, was destined to prevent the collapse of

[43] *The Global Financial Centres Index*. 2023. Published by Z/Yen since 2007.

[44] There is a huge literature dealing with the transformations brought about by the 'Thirty Years War' of the twentieth century. Here are four very different books: Van der Wee, *Prosperity and Upheaval*; Hobsbawm, *Age of Extremes*; Crafts and Toniolo, *Economic Growth in Europe*; Judt, *Postwar*.

the international financial system, not as a break with the neo-liberal order of the preceding 30 years or so.[45] The state retreated once this risk had been avoided.

The other compelling comparison is with the financial instability of the early 1970s, marked by the return of financial crises, the end of Bretton Woods, the oil shock, the first recession since the Second World War, and a period of 'stagflation'. The crisis of the 1970s marked another epochal change, with the beginning of the undoing of the legacy of the Great Depression; the mounting challenge on Keynesianism by monetarism; a wave of financial liberalization starting in the 1980s and culminating in the repeal of the Glass-Steagall Act in 1999. And, more generally the advent of a neo-liberal view of the economy and of society advocating a smaller state and the strengthening of market mechanisms.[46]

This strong legacy has not been matched by that of the Global Financial Crisis. There have been contestations but no undoing of the main tenets of the neo-liberal order. Globalization has been dented but has not ended and, as we have seen, the financial system has remained fundamentally unchanged. This might be a good thing or a bad thing, but in terms of legacy, it is in sharp contrast with previous global financial shocks.

How to explain these differences? Essentially by the conditions within which these three crises took place. Regarding the Great Depression, there is obviously the sheer magnitude of the economic downturn and its social consequences. But the Great Depression was part of a deeply troubled period, which included two world wars—the 'Thirty Years War' of the twentieth century. The financial instability and recessions of the mid-1970s and early 1980s were not on the same scale as the Great Depression. But the period, starting in the late 1960s, was a time of profound uncertainties and transformation, not only at economic level, but also at social, cultural, political, and international levels, with unprecedented challenges.

The Global Financial Crisis broke out in less troubled times. But it was followed, without necessarily being their cause, by a series of crises and setbacks, especially the Covid-19 pandemic just over a decade later, but with the problems raised by the financial crisis not entirely solved; and new tensions arising soon after, with the war in Ukraine, the war in Gaza, and the second Trump presidency. These new uncertain times have been described in various terms: the notion of 'polycrisis' has reappeared in the vocabulary, while 'permacrisis' has been voted the Collins Dictionary's word of the year 2022. What will be the legacy of the crises of the 2020s? The answer was unclear at the time of writing, especially its transformative character. In any case, the Global Financial Crisis of 2008 would likely be seen as one of the factors leading to what might be an epochal change.

[45] Crouch, *The Strange Non-Death of Neo-Liberalism*.

[46] In addition to the books dealing with post 1945 Europe quoted above, see more specifically on the 1970s, Ferguson et al., *The Shock of the Global*.

As such financial crises leave a legacy of a predominantly financial nature, concerned with the shaping of the financial system and its regulatory framework. While not entirely ephemeral, a legacy is not immutable. The history of the previous major crises shows that regulation cannot prevent the fading away of the memory of the crisis; it outlives it but only for a while: financial regulation has to adapt to changing conditions resulting from competition, innovation, and successful attempts to circumvent existing regulation. However, in the absence of memory, deregulation, and re-regulation risk moving in the wrong direction; while history, where lessons from the crisis can be found, tends to be ignored by the protagonists. There is little chance that this pattern should change in the future.

References

Appleyard, B. (1987). 'The seer who saw it coming'. *The Times*, 26 October.

Augar, P. (2018). *The Bank that Lived a Little: Barclays in the Age of the Very Free Market.* London: Allen Lane.

Ball, L. (2018). *The Fed and Lehman Brothers: Setting the Record Straight on a Financial Disaster.* Cambridge: Cambridge University Press.

Bautzer, A.R. (2024). 'The State and the Transformation of British and American Commercial Banking, 1945–2008'. PhD dissertation, University of Cambridge.

Bernanke, B. (1983). 'Nonmonetary effects of the financial crisis on the propagation of the Great Depression'. *American Economic Review* 73, 3: 257–276.

Bernanke, B. (2015). *The Courage to Act. A Memoir of a Crisis and Its Aftermath.* New York and London: W.W. Norton & Company.

Bernanke, B., Geithner, T.F., and Paulsen, H. (2018). *Firefighting. The Financial Crisis and its Lessons.* New York: Penguin Books.

Beyssade, J. (2021). 'From sets of rules to codes of conduct'. In Y. Cassis and J-J. van Helten (eds), *The Legacy of the Global Financial Crisis.* London: I.B. Tauris, 191–200.

Bordo, M. and James, H. (2010). 'The Great Depression analogy'. *Financial History Review* 17, 2: 127–144.

Brown, G. (2010). *Beyond the Crash. Overcoming the First Crisis of Globalisation.* London: Simon & Schuster.

Cassis, Y. (2011). *Crises and Opportunities. The Shaping of Modern Finance.* Oxford: Oxford University Press.

Cassis, Y. and Knaps, A. (2021). 'The memory of financial crises: the Great Depression and the Global Financial Crisis of 2008'. In Y. Cassis and C. Schenk, *Remembering and Learning from Financial Crises.* Oxford: Oxford University Press, 18–38.

Cassis, Y. and van Helten, J-J. (2021). 'Introduction'. In Y. Cassis and J-J. van Helten (eds), *The Legacy of the Global Financial Crisis.* London: I.B. Tauris, 1–18.

Crafts, N. and Toniolo, G. (eds) (1996). *Economic Growth in Europe since 1945.* Cambridge: Cambridge University Press.

Crouch, C. (2011). *The Strange Non-Death of Neo-Liberalism.* Cambridge: Polity Press.

Davies, H. (2010). *The Financial Crisis: Who Is to Blame?.* Cambridge: Polity Press.

Eichengreen, B. (2015). *Hall of Mirrors. The Great Depression, the Great Recession, and the Uses—and Misuses—of History.* Oxford: Oxford University Press.

Eichengreen, B. and O'Rourke, K. (2009). 'A tale of two depressions'. *VoxEU*, 6 June.

Erll, A. (2010). 'Cultural memory studies: An introduction'. In A. Erll and A. Nünning, *A Companion to Cultural Memory Studies*. Berlin/New York: de Gruyter, 1–15.
Ferguson, N., Maier, C.S., Manela, E., and Sargent, D.J. (eds) (2011). *The Shock of the Global. The 1970s in Perspective*. Cambridge: Cambridge University Press.
Galbraith, J.K. (1954). *The Great Crash, 1929*. Boston: Houghton Mifflin Co.
Geithner, T. (2014). *Stress Test. Reflections on Financial Crises*. New York: Random House Business.
Halbwachs, M. (1925). *Les cadres sociaux de la mémoire*. Paris: Presses universitaires de France.
Hobsbawm, E.J. (1994). *Age of Extremes. The Short Twentieth Century 1914–1991*. London: Michael Joseph.
Isaksen, J.V. (2019). 'The impact of the financial crisis on European attitudes toward immigration'. *Comparative Migration Studies* 7, 24. https://doi.org/10.1186/s40878-019-0127-5.
James, H. (2023). *Seven Crashes: the Economic Crises that Shaped Globalization*. New Haven and London: Yale University Press.
Judt, T. (2005). *Postwar. A History of Europe since 1945*. London: William Heinemann.
Kindleberger, C. (1978). *Manias, Panics and Crashes. A History of Financial Crises*. London: Macmillan.
King, M. (2016). *The End of Alchemy. Money. Banking and the Future of the Global Economy*. London: Little, Brown.
Nora, P. (1989). 'Between memory and history. Les Lieux de Mémoire'. *Representations* 26: 7–24.
Paulson, H. (2010). *On the Brink: Inside the Race to Stop the Collapse of the Global Financial System*. New York: Business Plus.
Plumpe, W., Nützenadel, A., and Schenk, C. (2020). *Deutsche Bank: The Global Hausbank, 1870–2020*. London: Bloomsbury.
Portelli, A. (1981). 'On the peculiarities of oral history', *History Workshop Journal* 12: 96–107.
Roberts, R. (2013). *Saving the City. The Great Financial Crisis of 1914*. Oxford: Oxford University Press.
Roberts, R. and Kynaston, D. (2015). *The Lion Wakes: A Modern History of HSBC*. London: Profile Books.
Schenk, C. (2021). 'The Global Financial Crisis ten years on: Using and forgetting the past?'. In Y. Cassis and J-J van Helten (eds), *The Legacy of the Global Financial Crisis*. London: I.B. Tauris, 39–58.
Sorkin, A.R. (2010). *Too Big to Fail. The Inside Story of How Wall Street and Washington Fought to Save the Financial System—and Themselves*. New York: Viking Press.
Telesca, G. and Cassis, Y. (forthcoming 2026). 'Battles of narratives, battles of memory. Making sense of the ebbs and flows of the memory of the Great Depression'. In S. Berger and T. Fetzer (eds), *Collective Memory of Economic Crises and Transformations*. Basingstoke: Palgrave Macmillan.
Thomson, A. (2007). 'Four paradigms transformation in oral history'. *The Oral History Review* 34 (1): 49–70.
Tooze, A. (2018). *Crashed. How a Decade of Financial Crises Changed the World*. London: Allen Lane.
Van der Wee, H. (1986). *Prosperity and Upheaval. The World Economy 1945–1980*. New York: Viking.

Winter, J. (2006). 'Notes on the memory boom. War, remembrance and the uses of the past'. In D. Bell (ed.), *Memory, Trauma and World Politics. Reflections on the Relationship between Past and Present.* Basingstoke and New York: Palgrave Macmillan, 54–73.

Yueh, L. (2023). *The Great Crashes. Lessons from Global Meltdowns and How to Prevent Them.* London: Penguin Business.

Zelizer, B. (2008). 'Why memory's work on journalism does not reflect journalism work on memory', *Memory Studies* 1, 1: 79–87.

Index

For the benefit of digital users, indexed terms that span two pages (e.g., 52–53) may, on occasion, appear on only one of those pages.

Tables and Figures are indicated by *t* or *f* following the page number.